MURDER
At Green Springs

THE TRUE STORY OF THE HALL CASE,
FIRESTORM OF PREJUDICES

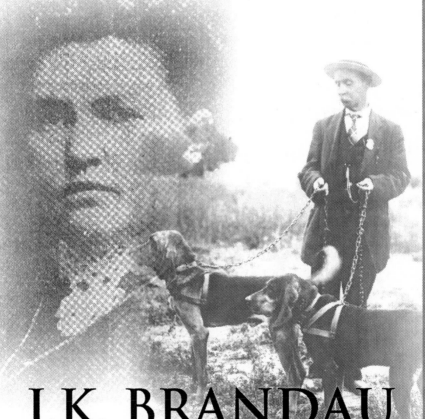

J.K. BRANDAU

New York

MURDER AT GREEN SPRINGS

By J.K. Brandau

ISBN: 978-1-60037-288-9 (Paperback)
ISBN: 978-1-60037-290-2 (Hardcover)

Published by:

MORGAN · JAMES
THE ENTREPRENEURIAL PUBLISHER
www.morganjamespublishing.com

Morgan James Publishing, LLC
1225 Franklin Ave. Suite 325
Garden City, NY 11530-1693
800.485.4943
www.MorganJamesPublishing.com

Habitat
for Humanity®
Peninsula
Building Partner

Cover & Interior Design by:

Megan Johnson
Johnson2Design
www.Johnson2Design.com
megan@Johnson2Design.com

Cover Photos Courtesy of:

The Library of Virginia &
The Louisa County Historical Society

To Evelyn, Mary Ann and my beloved Sharon, three ladies who dared to want the truth.

TABLE OF CONTENTS

ACKNOWLEDGMENTS

Gathering information on the Hall Case would have been impossible without the cooperation of many individuals. The author is greatly indebted to each, for there were no insignificant contributions.

The author gratefully acknowledges the invaluable interviews granted by children of principals: R. Lindsay Gordon, III; Frances Anne Atkins, daughter of Elsie Wood; Eugenia Bumpass, daughter of George W. Trainham; Charles C. "C.C." Dunkum, son of William R. "Buck" Dunkum; and Albert G. "Sambo" Johnson, son of Jimmy Johnson.

Wayne G. Dunn supplied specifics on the Dunkum and Marks families. Edward J. Westlow, grandson of Channing Boston, provided information on the Boston family. Likewise, Alice S. Murphey provided substantial insights into the Yancey family, and Kathryn D. Bubb supplied facts on the Dowdy family.

Clerk of Court Susan Hopkins and her staff at the Louisa County Courthouse were most helpful as were the many archivists at the Library of Virginia and the University of Virginia Library. The author thanks Dr. G. C. Waldrep, III and Dee Randall for their guidance and shared research which illuminated many relationships in Green Springs. Cathy Collins, managing editor at the *Central Virginian*, and her staff always helped when able. Research assistance by Stephen Gawtry at the Virginia State Climatology Office, Deborah Pugh of the Randolph-Macon College Library and Tom Dixon of the Chesapeake and Ohio Historical Society were invaluable. Pattie Cooke graciously mined facts whenever asked. The author recommends her book *Louisa and Louisa County* as a companion volume. Pattie's prolific writings were vital resources as were the many relevant monographs from other contributing members of the Louisa County Historical Society. Much appreciation goes to David L. Hancock and his staff at Morgan James Publishing for recognizing the importance of this project and ushering it into print.

The author acknowledges fellow chemists Lennie F. Routten, Walter I. Fortenberry, and G. Randall Ware for their expert organoleptic analyses and lab technician Jerry E. Butler for assistance in ballistic field experiments. Their cooperation validated key forensic issues.

History owes a debt of thanks to the late Edward McAuley, the last of a generation and son-in-law to Mrs. Hall, who inadvertently revealed the existence of her past to his daughter the late Evelyn McAuley-Winston-Harris. Evelyn pursued the matter with her first cousin Mary Ann Williams-Haske. They shared discoveries about their grandmother with Sharon Winston-Brandau. Sharon's interest provoked the attention of the greatest skeptic of all, her husband. This book is the result.

The author thanks his father-in-law Joseph M. Winston, Jr. who married into Mrs. Hall's family early enough to know Mrs. Hall and her daughters personally. As an attorney, Joe interacted professionally with lawyer Tom Williams, a stenographer at the Hall trial, and socialized with others involved on the periphery of the case. Ironically, all of these died over a decade before Joe knew anything about Mrs. Hall's past; thus, her story came as great of a shock to him as to any one else: a true testimony to the principals' remarkable determination to guard their secret. The many hours of sharing discoveries with Joe and tapping into his legal insights are experiences the author treasures always.

Ultimately, all thanks go to the Author and Finisher of our faith, the Revealer of all secrets; to Him be all glory, honor and praise forever!

MURDER AT GREEN SPRINGS

INTRODUCTION

*B*ehold a hushed sensation!

The decade before the First World War was unique. Horses and buggies shared dirt roads with automobiles. Telephones coexisted with telegraphs. Railroads and steamships were the major carriers. Gas lights and electric bulbs illuminated cities, but most homes used oil lamps. A minority had indoor plumbing.

Socially connected white men ruled stratified society; money was the upper crust; and women had few rights at any level. People feared smallpox and other deadly diseases. Life was brutal for those in humble situations.

Reading and conversation were chief entertainments. Newspapers prospered. Yellow journalism flourished. Government agencies relied on Pinkerton and Baldwin-Felts detectives as special police, and their presence was common in great newspaper sensations.

The murder trials of Samuel McCue, Henry Beattie, Floyd Allen, and Elizabeth Hall grabbed headlines across Virginia and beyond. Books chronicled each of the three men and their crimes; strangely, no work ever recounted the woman who was front page news for seven months. Why?

The Hall murder was the last in a series of great, regional sensations. Hysteria gripped a community with all the intensity and irrationality of the Salem witch hunts. But this was not Massachusetts 1692. It was twentieth-century Virginia!

A firestorm of prejudices supplanted reason and trampled the legal system in a media circus. The aftermath of the Hall Case so profoundly embarrassed the state, the newspapers, the detectives and everyone involved that all shunned remembrance of the singular affair. The courthouse even discarded the trial transcript contrary to law. The principals resumed their lives as if the event never happened and died leaving only fragmented lore and disassociated records dispersed piecemeal throughout Virginia and elsewhere in public and private caches ranging literally from government archives to dresser drawers.

The twenty-five year history of the little store at Green Springs Depot prior to the Hall murder had been the repeated focus of headlines statewide. These earlier tragedies energized the Hall phenomenon. Their ultimate contribution to the Hall verdict proved so troubling that all preceding events at Green Springs Depot were virtually obliterated from recollection.

The author first learned of the Hall trial by chance and assumed it just a curious skeleton in an in-law's closet. Eighteen years later, the author found himself providentially placed at the very center of relational convergences, each a strange, different, and shocking route back to *that store* at Green Springs Depot. These unique avenues of discovery yielded facts like dried bones scattered across a landscape. The full skeleton came together over a period of five years. The astounding, true story of Green Springs Depot then fleshed itself out and returned to life as the key witness ignored at trial.

Understanding the Hall Case in context required not just one murder investigation, but at least six. It is not the record of an isolated event, but a phenomenon, a synergy of convoluted social and political situations peculiar to a region transitioning from Post-Reconstruction into Prohibition.

The author relied on techniques acquired over thirty-five years as an analytical chemist and material failure investigator to research, organize and present the story of the Hall murder as accurately as possible with a goal to provide both reliable historical record and starting points for derivative research. Other than a few compelling exceptions, quotations are the actual words of the principals as recorded in primary sources. The author offers this historical narrative as the best fit of all data available at this writing.

For the first time in nearly a century, one may now consider a story of stories withheld by a generation, the disturbing, but truly remarkable, episode in Virginia history that was the Hall Case.

MURDER AT GREEN SPRINGS

Elizabeth Ann Dunkum, nee Dowdy [later Mrs. Hall], with first husband David Asa
Dunkum about the time of their marriage in 1894. (Photo from author's collection)

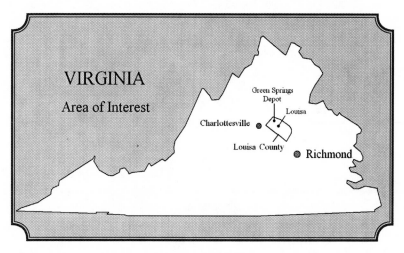

Map by J. K. Brandau

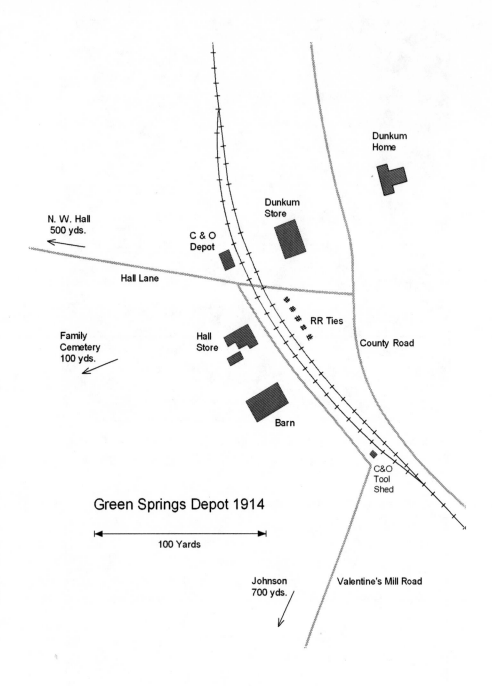

Dunkum
Home

N. W. Hall
500 yds.

Dunkum
Store

C & O
Depot

Hall Lane

RR Ties

County Road

Family
Cemetery
100 yds.

Hall
Store

Barn

C&O
Tool
Shed

Green Springs Depot 1914

100 Yards

Johnson
700 yds.

Valentine's Mill Road

Map by J. K. Brandau

MURDER AT GREEN SPRINGS

CHAPTER
One

SOMEONE SHOT VICTOR!

MURDER AT GREEN SPRINGS

*T*he spring of 1914 was very dry in Louisa County until the evening of April 14th when a northeast wind brought rain in wind driven sheets. Wealthy planters in the Green Springs District welcomed the water. Their relief was rivaled by that of the poor subsistence farmers and sharecroppers living just to the north in the vicinity of Green Springs Depot. Folks there depended on a successful growing season for their very existence. Most of these went to bed that night thanking God for the rain and fell asleep to the narcotic sound of water running off their shake roofs. By midnight nearly an inch had fallen. This was good for the wells and fields. The rain slackened and became intermittent. The wind remained gusty, causing even stout frames to creak with strain. Thick clouds blocked all light from the Easter moon and completed the cliché that it was a dark and stormy night.[1]

Fifty-six year old Jennie Hall lived with her brother Nicholas Hall and his wife Ellen in their two-story weatherboard, tin roofed house at Green Springs Depot. Jennie slept soundly, snug beneath the multiple blankets and quilts typical for unheated quarters. Not so typical was her preference to sleep on the davenport in the dining room. Her custom seemed eccentric to some, but sleeping in the dining room distanced her from the snoring upstairs.

Shortly after midnight Jennie transitioned from a deep sleep and became conscious of the gusting wind. The pelting rain had stopped. A sudden awareness of light jolted her awake. The window shade glowed with a flickering yellow with light from outside. Fire!

Up and to the window in an instant, Jennie raised the shade and saw the blaze beyond their apple orchard, about six hundred yards away.

Flames licked above the trees. She could not tell exactly what was burning, but there was fire at the railway. Jennie hurried to the steps and shouted up to her brother's bedroom.

Nicholas Hall awoke and sprang to his window. He had a direct line of sight to the blaze. He hollered back to Jennie that Buck Dunkum's store was on fire. Nicholas assured wife Ellen while he quickly pulled on his pants and shoes, tucked in his nightshirt, shouldered his suspenders and rushed downstairs. He grabbed his hat and coat on his way out.

The lean, sixty year old farmer hurried between the ruts in the watery lane to the depot. As flames leaped skyward from the rear half of the store, the firelight reflected from the low clouds and illuminated the area to the extent that Nicholas gave no thought to a lantern.

Nicholas was first on the scene. Even if a bucket brigade mustered, the store was lost. There was nothing to do but alert Buck and warn son Victor Hall to protect his own store. Nicholas began shouting, "Fire!" He crossed the railroad tracks and hurried toward Dunkum's home.

One hundred yards past the burning store, Nicholas reached Buck's house. He pounded on the front door yelling for Buck to wake up. His store was on fire!

Mary Dunkum heard the alarm. She shook and shouted her husband awake. Buck opened his eyes to firelight. He sprang out of bed and told his wife to get up and get the children. He thought their house was burning again. However, once on his feet, he could see his store ablaze through the window. Buck appealed to heaven as he threw on his clothes, jumped in his shoes, and rushed downstairs. He fumbled with the latch and opened the door.

Buck was aware of the situation; Nicholas hurried off to tell Victor and retraced his route over the tracks. Buck rushed toward his flaming store hoping to somehow save his account ledger and cash drawer. The intense heat stopped him short of the porch steps. Buck retreated to a tolerable distance and watched in disbelief as his entire store and stock burned.

      MURDER AT GREEN SPRINGS

The other general merchandise store run by Victor Hall was diagonally across the rail crossing from Dunkum's business. Nicholas hurried through the front gate to the residence, strode onto the wood porch, and banged on the door shouting for Victor. No one in his son's household was yet aware of the danger. Nicholas yelled and banged on the door.

Victor had not felt well for days. He had gone to bed sick about seven that evening, gotten up briefly for a cold supper about nine, and returned to bed. His family and boarders gathered around him until ten; the women were all anxious about a Negro who had just escaped from a chain gang. He calmed their fears, then slept, such as his congested head allowed, until his father's alarm. Victor got out of bed and went to the door. Light streamed into the hallway through the sidelights. He could see Dunkum's store ablaze. Upon opening the door, his father urged him to make sure everyone in the house was awake in case the fire spread.

Lizzie heard the men talking but could not make out what was said. Recent ear infections had left her nearly deaf on her left side. She raised herself on one arm and turned her head to listen. Still unable to understand, she got up, joined Victor and saw Buck's store ablaze. Nicholas left to help Buck. Lizzie asked Victor if he was going out to the fire.

"I feel so badly I don't think I shall. Nothing can be done. It's going as fast as it can." answered Victor.[2]

Lizzie felt like she ought to go check on Mary and her family. She went to the bedroom, put on her shoes and pulled a black dress over top of her white nightgown. Being thrice bereaved, she owned mostly black dresses. Sounds overhead let her know that others in the household were awake. She put on her hooded cloak and left the house.

Lizzie crossed the railroad tracks and continued on to Dunkum's house. Mary met her at the door anxious to know if Lizzie had seen Buck. Mary feared that Buck might have gone inside the store and become trapped. Mary left her babies asleep in the house to find Buck. The women hurried toward the fire. Mary called frantically for her husband.

SOMEONE SHOT VICTOR!   5

Buck and Nicholas stepped into sight from the opposite side of the fire and waved. Relieved, the two women turned back toward the house and met Jennie and Ellen Hall arriving on the scene. Ellen, bent by her sixty-four years, ignored her aches and pains aggravated by the cold and damp to aid her friends. The four women went inside. Mary checked on the children. The three neighbors assured Mary that everything was going to be all right. Mary was afraid. This was their third fire within a year. She had no doubts now that it was arson at the hand of an enemy.

Victor Hall changed his mind. He threw on some clothes and went out to the blaze. He stopped at the railroad tracks, stood in the drizzle and watched the flames lick at the low clouds. The store was fully engulfed. Wind gusts blew the flames almost horizontally hurling showers of sparks and hot air towards him. Each blast accelerated the fire and intensified the heat on his face and hands.

After a few minutes, Victor had had enough. His adrenal rush ebbed. His head was so congested that he could only breathe through his mouth. Feverishness returned, and he shook from chills. Victor thought of Lizzie's first husband's death from pneumonia and felt as if he might die in like manner. Satisfied that his own store was in little danger, Victor went back inside.

In the rooms above Hall's store, Elsie Wood and Mamie Rosson, two young school teachers who boarded there, gathered at the window with sixteen year old Essie Dunkum, Lizzie's oldest daughter from her first marriage. Miss Wood had awakened to old Mr. Hall's alarm. The first light she saw shocked her into thinking their building was on fire. She woke up the other two women and then realized that Dunkum's store was burning.

All three women had head colds in varying degrees and dared not venture out into the cold damp. In fact, Essie went back to her room to get her coat in order to stay warm enough to view the fire from the window. They watched neighbors gather. They could see old Mr. Hall beside Uncle Buck who was talking to Burnley Harris, a colored neighbor who occasionally worked for him. Buck gestured toward the rear of the store

MURDER AT GREEN SPRINGS

where the fire apparently started. Two other forms carrying a lantern approached from the county road and stepped into the firelight. These were Nannie Harris and her twelve year old son Aubrey.[3] They were white Harrises, no kin to Burnley. Nevertheless, distinctions between white and colored in the neighborhood were often vague.

All of a sudden, the girls heard noises downstairs. It sounded like someone in the hallway. The startled young women looked at one another. Each assumed the downstairs empty and the rest of the household at the fire.

Elsie and Essie both recalled that Mamie Rosson mentioned early in the evening that she thought she heard someone prowling around outside. Those convinced at the time it was just the wind were no longer sure. The big, old, frame house and store with its dark history was a scary place at times, especially then with the mysterious fire and an escaped convict on the loose. Imaginations churned unaware that it was only Victor back in his bedroom knocking around rekindling the fire in his fireplace.

The concerned neighbors stayed with Mary Dunkum about twenty minutes. Lizzie went back home while Jennie and Ellen Hall joined Nicholas on the depot platform with Buck and everyone else drawn to the fire. The burning store collapsed in on itself. Debris toppled and plunged. Showers of sparks flew skyward into the mist. Soon there would be little to see.

Once inside, Lizzie went to her bedroom and found Victor back in bed and a fire roaring in the hearth. She stopped for a moment to warm herself and asked Victor how he was feeling. Victor had taken sick two days before on Easter Monday. Lizzie was away that day visiting family in Richmond while Victor minded the store. She returned home that evening to find Victor sick as a dog. Victor now said he felt bad enough to do himself in and be done with it. Lizzie told him to hush that kind of talk.

Lizzie's dress was wet at the bottom as was her nightgown underneath. It was her last clean nightgown. Lizzie had been busy minding the store that day and unable to gather laundry for the washwoman. There was not

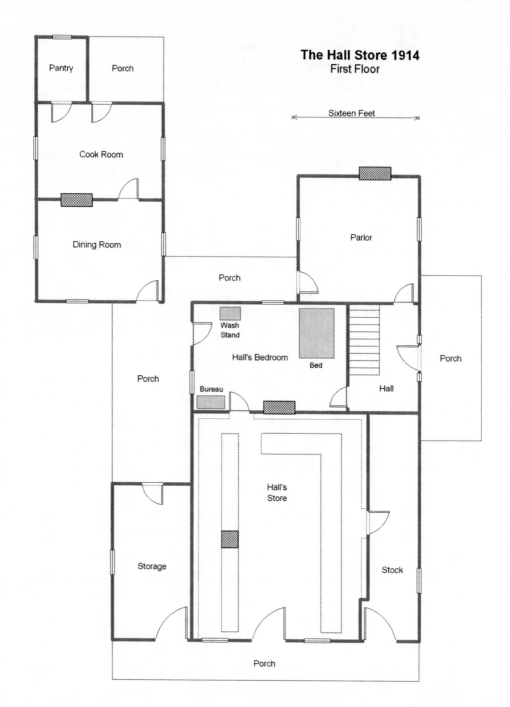

The Hall Store 1914
First Floor

Sixteen Feet

Pantry

Porch

Cook Room

Dining Room

Parlor

Porch

Wash Stand

Hall's Bedroom

Bed

Porch

Hall

Porch

Bureau

Hall's Store

Storage

Stock

Porch

Drawing by J. K. Brandau

MURDER AT GREEN SPRINGS

The Hall Store 1914
Second Floor

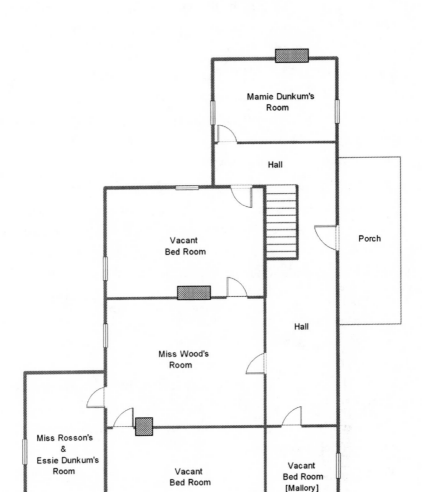

Drawing by J. K. Brandau

SOMEONE SHOT VICTOR!

much clean around the house. Even their bolster had to do without a slip. She looked for something dry to wear.

Lizzie remembered her black, silk robe in the bottom bureau drawer. It was not as comfortable, but it was clean and dry. Lizzie changed clothes in front of the fire and put on the kimono-like garment. After hanging up her wet clothes on the wall pegs and satisfied that Victor was comfortable, Lizzie went upstairs to check on her daughters.

Twelve year old Mamie Dunkum had awakened to join her sister Essie and the school teachers. They finished watching the spectacle from the several upstairs windows. By then all that remained of Dunkum's store was twisted metal roofing heaped upon glowing coals. They sat and talked about poor Aunt Mary and Uncle Buck.

At 1:15 A.M. westbound No. 33 rumbled down the tracks and through the cloud of smoke and steam blowing across the railway from the burning ruins.[4] Shivering neighbors started to leave. With wind gusts blowing sparks around, the ever cautious Nicholas Hall figured it best to keep an eye on the fire a while longer. He asked Jennie to go have Victor open up the store room. They could watch from inside and out of the drizzle.

Jennie assumed correctly that Victor was in bed. She walked around through the side gate to the bedroom window. The shade was down. She knocked on the window and called for Victor to open the store for Nicholas. She retraced her path around front in time to see Victor let his father inside. Jennie rejoined Ellen, and the two went home. Nicholas continued to observe from the behind store window. He was still cold, but at least out of the wind.

Buck Dunkum stood at the depot staring at his burned business dumbfounded at his loss. His store was only nine months old. In fact, Buck built the store right after he finished rebuilding their home after it had mysteriously burned to the ground last spring. A week before that Buck's broom factory burned. That structure had stood beside the county road on a plot adjacent to the burning store. Thankfully, no one had been injured in any of the fires. Buck would rebuild this time too. But this was his third fire within a year. Buck Dunkum knew he either had the most incredible bad luck or an enemy intent upon burning him out. Which? He did not know. Buck needed to go home and write down as many accounts as he and Mary could remember. The last spectators also went home when Buck left. The show was over.

Meanwhile, Lizzie urged Essie and Mamie to go to bed and give their boarders some peace. She then said good night and went downstairs. She started for the laundry basket to retrieve a used, dry, nightgown to sleep in, but Victor urged her to hurry up and get in bed, so his father could come in the room and warm himself. Lizzie decided that the robe was adequate and slipped between the covers. Victor called his father in from the store. Nicholas pulled a chair in front of the fire and sat down. They talked about Buck's latest misfortune.

They spoke over the sounds of movement and talking upstairs as the girls settled down. They heard Essie say it was time to go to sleep. Someone answered that they doubted if anyone could go to sleep anyway. Little Mamie was too upset to go back to her room alone and climbed into bed with Elsie Wood.[5]

Nicholas was warm again and stood up to leave. He repeated his caution to Victor and Lizzie that they keep an eye out for sparks that could set their house on fire. Victor escorted his father to the door and, lamp in hand, lighted their way through the dark store. Victor asked his father to please check the stable and make sure there were no live embers there. Nicholas assured Victor he would and told him to lock the door behind him as he left. Victor keyed the latch and plodded back to bed.

Lizzie lay in bed with her lamp out. Once Victor was in bed again, he leaned over and turned his lamp down. He felt most miserable and collapsed with a heavy sigh. Victor asked Lizzie what they should do about Buck. Perhaps they should take him in again as a partner until his store was rebuilt.

SOMEONE SHOT VICTOR!   *11*

After a pregnant pause Lizzie reminded Victor of the problems encountered when Victor first married into the original Dunkum Bros. partnership and later when the Dunkums lived with them while their house was being rebuilt.

"No, we are getting on all right, and I think we better remain apart," Lizzie said.[6] Buck had insurance and would recover soon. She was sure he would be fine.

Victor supposed so. With a deep sigh, Victor managed a faint, "Good night."

A knocking came at their outside bedroom door followed by the voice of Nicholas Hall. He told Victor not to get up. He just wanted Victor to know that he had checked the stable and everything was all right. The ailing son thanked his father, turned over and went to sleep.

Lizzie lay on her side in the dark listening with her good ear. Things quieted upstairs. The mantel clock struck two. She closed her eyes and slept.

There was no sensation of time from the moment Lizzie fell asleep until she sensed a disturbance. Someone knocked at the front of the store. Victor sat up with his legs hanging off the bed. The maneuver raised the covers like a bellows sucking in chilly air and purging out warmth.

"There's Papa at the door," said Victor.

Lizzie was barely conscious of Victor sitting on the side of the bed, turning up his nickel lamp and thinking aloud.

"I reckon Mama's sent him back again."

Victor got up, carried the light with him into the store and shut the bedroom door behind him. The mantel clock struck four.

Lizzie thought it odd for Victor's father to return so early and come to the storefront rather than the residence. The bed warmed again. Lizzie slumbered and lost track of time. Seconds or minutes passed.

MURDER AT GREEN SPRINGS

Victor cried, "Oh! Lord! Have mercy!"

Bang!

Jolted awake, Lizzie threw the covers off and sat up on the side of the bed. Her inner ear imbalance made her head swim. She sat in the dark disoriented and confused. Her equilibrium returned. It seemed like a hundred competing thoughts filled her mind at once. A gunshot! Victor! She had to do something. But what?

Lizzie looked around the dark room stunned and scared. It was a dark night. Victor had taken his lamp into the store. The faintest, yellow light shown beneath the door; otherwise, the room was pitch black. There was not even enough light outside to discern the window. She groped for the matchbox on her nightstand. She found it, fumbled for a match, struck it, removed the chimney with her free hand and kindled the wick. All the while her mind frantically sorted her confusion for a rational action. She blew out the match, adjusted the wick with one hand and fumbled with the glass chimney with the other. It seemed to take forever to get it back on the lamp.

Lizzie glanced toward the store door beyond which the shot had occurred. Inexplicably, out of the corner of her eye, the outside door caught her attention. The outside door! The impression clicked into place like the last tumbler in a combination lock and released the thought: Becky!

There had been no thought of Becky Coates since the household first retired that evening. No one gave a thought to the little, twelve-year-old, colored servant throughout the excitement of the fire. Little Becky, quartered way out in the pantry, simply slept through it all. Yet now, Lizzie's reaction was to contact the nearest human being. Becky!

Lizzie hurried to the outside door of the bedroom, tossing the spent match into the fireplace as she passed. She unlatched the two bolts, opened it, stepped onto the porch and hollered in the direction of the outbuilding.

"Becky! Becky!"

SOMEONE SHOT VICTOR!   *13*

Oh! What to do? Lizzie's mind struggled. Buck! She thought. Yes! She must call Buck! She rushed back through the bedroom while shunning the unknown situation behind the store door. Reaching the hallway on the opposite side of the house, she unlocked the front door and stepped out onto the porch. She hollered toward Dunkum's house.

"Buck! Oh! Buck!" The call was futile at that distance.

Oh! What to do? Lizzie went back inside and stopped briefly in the hallway to yell up the stairs for her eldest daughter.

"Essie! Essie!"

Mamie Rosson answered. Lizzie knew it was Miss Rosson, but did not make out what she said. At least she knew someone else was awake. The shot had awakened the two young teachers and Essie.

"Come quick! Someone shot Victor!" shouted Lizzie.

The exchange woke up little Mamie who had slept through the gunshot.

Lizzie hurried back into the dimly lit bedroom. She stood for a moment with her hands pressed to her face. The door! Dare she even open the door to the store? Victor was on the other side, probably hurt. Was the gunman there also? She heard Victor groan. In spite of her fears, she went to the door, turned the knob and opened it. There before her lay Victor crumpled up on the floor. He lay curled up on his side between the counters with his head away from her and his feet near the doorway.

Lizzie carefully stepped into the store and over Victor. She knelt down and shook Victor's shoulder.

"Victor? Victor? Are you all right? Oh, Victor! Say something! Victor, who shot you?" There was no response.

From the light of Victor's lamp on the distant counter, she saw his eyes closed as if sleep. Blood was on his face and running out of his mouth. Again she asked Victor if he was all right and again no response. Obviously, Victor was not all right.

Lizzie's heart pounded, and her mind raced. Oh! What to do? Where was everyone? Becky? Where was Becky? Lizzie got up and hurried to the bedroom where she grabbed her lamp and went outside to the outbuilding. She entered the dining room and went through to the rear of the kitchen where she found Becky still asleep in the pantry.

"Becky! Get up! Quick!"

The little form beneath the covers sat up on the floor pallet confused at the happening. Mrs. Hall needed her to rally. She reached down and grabbed Becky by the arm and pulled her to her feet while pleading for her to wake up, get dressed and come inside.

Satisfied that Becky was awake, Lizzie returned to the bedroom. The commotion overhead indicated others were up and stirring. Surely someone would be down shortly to help. Lizzie placed the lamp on the bureau and went to the doorway. Victor still lay crumpled up as she found him.

Lizzie hurried to the bed and grabbed the bolster and the red quilt. She gathered them up in her arms and rushed back into the store, stepped over Victor, dropped the bedding and knelt down at his head. She reached down and tenderly lifted Victor's head with her hands. The back of Victor's head was wet. Cradling his head with her right hand, her left hand positioned the bolster underneath. She then eased his head down onto the soft support.

Blood! There was blood! Her hands were covered with it and her black robe felt wet. Lizzie bent down for a closer look and saw the wound. Victor had been shot in the back of the head! Carefully, Lizzie grabbed Victor's shoulder and rolled him onto his back. She crawled over to straighten his legs, and then returned to fold the ends of the bolster underneath his head for added support. She reached for the quilt, stood up, and covered Victor and his cold, bare legs. Lizzie was not sure this did any good, but at least, Victor looked more comfortable.

Lizzie fretted anxiously over what to do next. She stood and shook her bloody hands. Buck? Where was Buck?

SOMEONE SHOT VICTOR!

Footsteps sounded down the stairs and through the bedroom. Elsie Wood appeared lamp in hand at the bedroom door. Her eyes widened at the sight of Mrs. Hall with bloody hands and a blood speckled face standing over her husband.

"Oh! Mrs. Hall, are you all right? What happened?"

"Somebody shot Victor" replied Lizzie choking on the words. "Victor knows who shot him. He knows. Someone came to the door. He thought it was his Papa, and he shot him."

"Did he say who shot him?"

"No. He can't talk. But he knows. Oh, where's Buck?" wondered Lizzie. She went to the front of the store. Finding the door unlocked, she opened it and hurried out to the edge of the porch.

"Buck! Oh! Buck!" she cried. Several more times, "Buck! Oh! Buck!" There was no response.

Meanwhile, Elsie Wood stooped down, placed her hand on the wounded man's shoulder and nudged him.

"Mr. Hall? Are you all right?"

There was no response. Elsie stood and started to the front of the store as Mrs. Hall returned from calling Buck. Lizzie locked the door behind her. Elsie suggested that they call a doctor. Lizzie agreed and asked Elsie to ring Dr. Porter.[7]

Elsie lit another lamp and carried it over to the counter near the telephone. Lizzie knelt again beside her husband as daughter Essie entered and stopped aghast at the sight of her bloodied mother.

"Mama! Are you all right?" cried Essie.

Lizzie assured Essie that she was fine, but Victor was hurt awful bad and Miss Wood was trying to get Dr. Porter. Little Mamie came to the doorway just ahead of Mamie Rosson. Rosson was the last one downstairs having been delayed looking for her shoes. Both beheld the scene and re-

coiled hysterically into the bedroom. The screaming Mamies only added to the confusion.

Essie, mature beyond her years, went into the bedroom and pulled down the remaining covers. She coaxed the Mamies into the bed and covered them up to help calm them down.[8] Meanwhile, Elsie Wood had difficulty reaching the operator. She repeatedly cranked the telephone and hollered into the mouthpiece.

Lizzie called for Essie to get the medicinal whiskey out of the washstand. Essie looked inside. There was none. Neither was there brandy nor wine. Victor must have used it all.

Elsie stopped cranking the telephone. It was no use. The line was dead.

Lizzie grieved that Buck was not there yet. He must not have heard her. She returned to the bedroom, grabbed her shoes, and sat on the edge of the bed to put them on.

Becky finally came in from outside with her dress partly buttoned. Lizzie looked up while wrestling with her shoes and told Becky to run to Mr. Hall's as fast as she could, and tell him that Victor was shot.

"Shot?" asked Becky, "Where at?"

"In the back of the head," blurted Lizzie and told Becky again to hurry up and go get Mr. Hall. Lizzie, now shod, rushed out the bedroom, slowed to step over Victor, and hurried out the front of the store to call Buck again. Becky finished buttoning up her dress and left barefoot down the cold, muddy lane to fetch Victor's father.

Fearing that the assailant might be lurking to finish the job, perhaps kill them all, Elsie Wood stepped to the bureau, opened the top drawer, and grabbed Victor Hall's .38 Smith & Wesson revolver. It was right where he normally kept it. Elsie borrowed it occasionally for protection. Gun in hand, Elsie declared, "I'll shoot the first man who comes in here!"[9]

With that she went back into the store. Essie followed. Elsie placed the pistol on the counter in easy reach and then lit several more lamps.

SOMEONE SHOT VICTOR!

Essie tried the telephone, still nothing.

Outside, Lizzie reached the rail crossing and stood at the tracks hollering, "Buck! Oh! Buck!" The wind lulled just enough for her voice to carry.

Buck Dunkum threw up his window sash and shouted back, "Yeah! Lizzie! What in the world is the matter?"

"Come quick! Someone shot Victor!"

"What? Hold on! I'm coming!"

Lizzie, somewhat relieved at the prospect of help, returned to the store and announced that Buck was on his way. Essie locked the door behind her mother as Lizzie went to Victor's side. Kneeling down she could hear gurgling. Victor was strangling on his own blood. Lizzie sent Essie to get some cloths from the washstand and asked if Becky had gone to get Mr. Hall yet. Elsie reported that she had.

Lizzie took a cloth and wiped the blood out of Victor's mouth. He was having trouble breathing. His clogged sinuses did not help. Elsie brought over a bottle of camphor and offered it to Mrs. Hall. Lizzie took the bottle and opened it. She scooped some of the salve with her fingers and smeared it under Victor's nose hoping it would help him breathe.

"Forget that. It don't do no good," concluded Lizzie and handed the salve back.

Elsie took the bottle and placed it on the counter. Lizzie asked Elsie to help her roll Victor over to place the quilt under him to cushion him from the bare wood floor and called for Essie to bring more covers. By the time they repositioned Victor, Essie returned with the slumber robe.[10] A knock on the door startled everyone. Essie answered the door while her mother and Elsie covered Victor. After verifying it was Uncle Buck, Essie unlocked the door. Buck Dunkum entered the store excitedly with exerted breath and walked over to the group standing around Victor.

Buck asked what happened. Lizzie explained that Victor got up thinking his papa was at the door and someone shot him.

"What on earth is going to happen here next?" reacted Buck and began pacing back and forth anxiously in the middle of the store grasping for ideas. He asked if anyone had called for the doctor. Lizzie explained that they tried, but the phone was dead. Buck went over to the telephone and tried it for himself. Indeed, the line was dead. Buck said that he was going outside to find out what was wrong with it.

The gun on the counter caught Buck's attention. He asked about the pistol. Miss Wood explained that she got Mr. Hall's gun in case the robber came back. Buck hated guns, but decided to take the pistol with him in case he ran into the assailant. He promised to return shortly, stuck the gun his coat pocket and strode out of the store.

Lizzie started to cry. Elsie Wood put her arm around her and told her not to cry for the girl's sake. They were already to pieces. Elsie was right. Lizzie had to remain strong. She took a couple of deep breaths and got a hold on herself. She went over and knelt beside Victor again.

Nicholas Hall arrived. He hurried to the back where everyone was gathered, knelt down, and examined his son. Seeing that his son was badly wounded, but still alive, he asked if the doctor had been called. Lizzie explained that they had tried to call Dr. Porter, but the phone was dead. She finished telling the father how his son was shot just as Buck Dunkum returned, this time, with his wife and children. Mary had their youngest in arm and their toddler by the hand. She explained to Buck that she just could not stay at home by herself with all that was happening.

"The telephone line is cut," declared Buck and added that he was going to Johnson's for help. With that, he turned and left again. Essie locked the door behind him. Mary left the children with Essie in front of the store and approached Nicholas and Lizzie kneeling beside Victor.

"Oh! Lizzie," gasped Mary. "What are we to do?"

SOMEONE SHOT VICTOR!   *19*

Lizzie replied, "I don't know. Your trouble is nothing to mine. Look at Victor lying here shot. Victor knows who shot him." She repeated, "Victor knows who shot him."[11]

Nicholas suggested that they move Victor to his bed. Essie shooed the two Mamies out from under the covers and cleared a place for Victor. Lizzie and Elsie Wood got on one side with Nicholas on the other. Essie stood at his feet. Each took hold of the quilt and carefully lifted Victor up with Mary supporting the bolster under his head. Essie lead the way as the others squeezed through the door carrying Victor into the bedroom. They placed him in his bed as gently as they could and covered him up. Lizzie grabbed a rag and sat on the side of the bed and wiped blood from Victor's mouth.

Essie answered knocking at the front door. She let in Ellen and Jennie with Becky and led them back to the pitiful scene. The family was at a loss as to what to do. Nicholas pulled a chair beside the bed for Ellen who became unsteady at the sight of her son. Victor groaned and moved as if trying to roll over on his side. It was the first real effort to move they had seen him make. As Lizzie and Jennie helped him turn, they sensed a resistance to the change and eased Victor onto his back again.

Thinking a fresh pillow would make him more comfortable, Lizzie and Ellen lifted his head while Jennie removed the blood-soaked bolster and replaced it with his regular pillow and pressed a folded towel against the wound before easing his head back down.

The school teachers went upstairs to change out of their night clothes. Lizzie suggested that Essie and Mamie do the same.

Buck left the store on foot and splashed across the soggy pasture. He climbed over the fence and hurried along the muddy road toward the

MURDER AT GREEN SPRINGS

Johnson farm. John Sims Johnson, a good friend and neighbor, had two, spry, young sons still living with him. If anyone was able to fetch help quickly, they could.

Days start early on working farms. Everyone in the Johnson household was already awake and dressed when they heard Buck coming down their lane.

"Victor Hall's been shot! Victor Hall's been shot by a highway robber."[12]

By the time Dunkum reached their house, the Johnson men, uniformed in overalls, were standing outside on the porch. While struggling to catch his breath, Buck explained that Victor was shot and needed a doctor right away. The telephone line was cut. Someone needed to go for help.

Quickly, they decided that youngest son Jimmy would ride to Dr. May's house.[13] It was doubtful that the retired physician could help directly, but his was the nearest other telephone. In the hopes that the telegraph at Green Springs Depot still worked, the elder Johnson and Dunkum would take the buggy to fetch Robert Woody, the local telegraph operator. Son Johnny would ride back to Hall's store to see what help he could offer.

Johnny and Jimmy wasted no time. They rushed inside to grab their hats and coats and donned them as they ran to the stable. Jimmy finished saddling his horse first and mounted. Hooves threw mud in the air as he galloped off into the cold and rain to get help. Dr. May lived a couple of miles up the road toward Melton's store. The nineteen year old passed Hall's store and crossed the tracks at the depot. Jimmy reined his horse left onto the county road at the smoldering ruins of Dunkum's store. Fear struck him that the gunman lurked in the woods along the way ready to shoot him too. Nevertheless, Jimmy rode on.[14]

As the elder Johnson and Dunkum hitched up the buggy, Johnny finished saddling his horse and galloped off down the lane to help his friend. Johnny was twenty-seven, the same age as Victor. They had grown up together.

SOMEONE SHOT VICTOR!

It was five o'clock. The faint gray light of the overcast dawn illuminated the surroundings as Johnny arrived at the store. An hour had passed since the shooting. Johnny tied his horse to the wrought iron fence and strode toward the house. There he met Mrs. Hall on the porch. She had dressed and stepped outside for a breath of fresh air, though wafts of the smoldering store provided little refreshment.

"What happened?" asked Johnny stepping onto the porch?

"The Dunkum store burned, and Victor is lying on the bed shot," Lizzie replied.[15]

Johnny went inside. Those at Victor's bedside related the events of the past hour. Johnny took a cloth and wiped Victor's face. He turned Victor's head to see the bullet wound.

"Has anyone called a doctor?" Johnny asked.

"We tried to call a doctor; but, the phone line is cut," said Mamie Rosson now present and somewhat composed.

Johnny wanted to check the telephone for himself and went into the store. Mamie followed and told him that Buck Dunkum had left to get help. Johnson said that Buck had just been at his place, and Jimmy was riding for help.

The elder Johnson in his buggy dropped Dunkum off at the store. Dunkum intended to find the problem with the telephone line while Johnson fetched Woody. If the line was cut, a simple splice would restore service. However, in the early light it was clear that the downed telephone line was not cut, but burned by the fire.

Dunkum went into the store to report that he could not fix the telephone. He stepped to the counter, removed the pistol from his pocket and laid it down. Johnny Johnson, standing nearby, recognized it as being like the one Victor bought eight years before when he became the station master and express agent. Dunkum affirmed it was Victor's pistol and that he had borrowed it from Miss Wood.

Johnson picked up the familiar piece and broke it open. The gun was loaded, except for one position; the cartridge over the barrel had been fired. Johnson showed it to Dunkum. Keeping an empty shell under the firing pin was a good idea in case the gun was accidentally dropped. Safety was a concern with so many women folk around. Johnson closed the action and brought the gun to his nose. There was no powder smell. He put it back on the counter.

Mary Dunkum appeared and urged Buck to take her home so she could tend to the children. Dunkum rejoined the Hall family briefly to let Lizzie know that he could not fix the telephone. Then he and Mary took their babies home.

In light of the situation, Johnson suggested that he ride to Louisa to get Dr. Porter, the Hall's family doctor. It was a good seven mile ride, but Nicholas agreed that it was the best the thing to do and thanked him for his help. Ellen and Lizzie both urged him to please hurry. Johnson bounded out of the house, mounted up, and galloped away.

The family agonized over what to do next. Perhaps a little medicinal whiskey would help? But there was none. Jennie suggested that "Nick" go over to Dunkum's to get some.

The idea was abhorrent to the ardent Prohibitionist. Nevertheless, Nicholas agreed to the task. But the last thing Nicholas Hall needed was for some rabble to see him carrying a liquor bottle under any circumstances. He found Becky and took her with him. She would carry the bottle: maybe wrap it in a rag or hide it under her dress.[16]

Meanwhile, Jimmy Johnson reached Dr. May's house. Son-in-law Charles Danne[17] awoke to the knocking and received the excited, wet youth into the house. The obese, sixty-eight year old Dr. May waddled into the room to investigate. The recently retired physician was neither prepared nor physically able to meet the demand himself. Danne hurried to the telephone and asked the operator to summon a doctor.[18] Within a few minutes, young Dr. Thomas M. Taylor rushed to his automobile and left Louisa.

At a quarter to six, the Johnson's buggy pulled up to Green Springs Depot. A disheveled Robert Woody got out and went inside with the elder Johnson to summon help by telegraph. The line was up. Woody keyed a message. Gordonsville acknowledged receipt. Louisa copied. Neither telegrapher could leave his post. They were unable to send for help until their respective station agents arrived to open the depot. Shortly after seven o'clock, Gordonsville telegraphed Woody to expect Dr. F. M. Banks on the 8:00 A.M. train.

In similar fashion, the Louisa telegrapher acted on Woody's request, but by that time, help was already on the way. Nevertheless, he sent a runner to Sheriff Wash's home with news of the shooting. As it happened, Sheriff Wash was already away on a posse hunting the escaped convict from Culpeper.

Charles Chisholm, Mrs. Hall's colored man, arrived as the day dawned to fodder the livestock just as he did every day. When he found Dunkum's store burned and sensed unusual activity at the Hall's store, Chisholm knocked at the kitchen door. Normally he did this after chores to get breakfast and find out what else to do that the day. Becky told Chisholm that Mr. Victor was shot in the back of the head.

"Lawd hab' mercy!"

First, Mr. Acey Dunkum took sick and died. Now Mr. Victor was shot, and Mr. Buck Dunkum had had another fire. Clearly shaken, Chisholm tearfully set about his routine. The animals still needed tending despite the turmoil. Obviously, there would be no gainful employment that day, but Chisholm remained handy to fetch fuel, draw water and do whatever other chores needed to be done. He reckoned being useful while praying and rebuking the Devil was the best way to help the family.[19]

Dr. Taylor drove as fast as conditions allowed. The road was in good shape considering the rain. It had been so dry beforehand. There were many puddles, but not the miry mess that usually characterized the rutty roads after a spring rain. Just past Trevilians Depot, Dr. Taylor encountered Johnny Johnson on horseback racing toward Louisa. At the sight of the approaching car, Johnson reined the horse to a stop on the side of the road. Given the urgency of the matter, Taylor hesitated to stop, but did so to confirm that Johnson sought help for Hall and not some added emergency. Upon confirmation, Taylor's car proceeded to splash down the road. Johnson continued on to Louisa at a moderated pace to notify Dr. Porter and the authorities.

Upon reaching the depot, Dr. Taylor turned left at the smoldering ruins of Dunkum's store. The automobile crossed the railway and stopped in front of Hall's store at six o'clock. Dr. Taylor, black leather grip in hand, stepped from his mud splattered vehicle, dodged several sizeable puddles, and stopped briefly on the porch to wipe his feet on the planking. Essie opened the door and led the doctor back to the bedroom where everyone made way for him to examine Victor.

Dr. Taylor checked the man's pulse and dilated pupils. He asked how long it had been since Mr. Hall had been wounded. Lizzie explained that someone shot Victor about four o'clock in the morning. They moved him to the bed a little while later and had done what they could to comfort him since then.

Victor's head rested on the dark red stained towel, his face ashen from blood loss. Dr. Taylor called for clean rags to replace the compress. While examining the wound, Dr. Taylor asked if the patient had said anything. Had he been conscious since the shooting?

The women explained that Victor sometimes moaned and once tried to turn himself. They had given Victor a little whiskey, but he could not swallow and choked on it. Dr. Taylor reached into his medical bag and removed a syringe, hypodermic needle and a vial of cocaine solution. After filling it and displacing the air he swabbed a site on Victor's arm and injected the dose into a vein. Upon withdrawal, he wiped the puncture, removed his watch from his vest pocket by its chain, and noted the time.

Minutes passed without any observed reaction to the drug. Dr. Taylor suggested that he and Mrs. Hall repair to the sitting room alone to discuss her husband's condition. Nicholas and Ellen Hall remained at their son's bedside.

Once seated in the parlor, Dr. Taylor explained that Victor had sustained massive injury to his brain. He had given Victor a strong stimulant with no observable effect. The physician confirmed everyone's fears; Victor's wound was mortal. Dr. Taylor asked Mrs. Hall to explain more fully how the incident happened. Lizzie related the events beginning with Nicholas Hall's alarm and the store fire. She told her story simply while controlling her distress.

Meanwhile, Becky carried out instructions and stoked the kitchen stove and set pots of water on to boil. The girls and school teachers had all finished their toilets and dressed for the day. Nicholas suggested that Essie and the schoolteachers examine the store for missing items. The survey was quick. They noticed nothing out of the ordinary. No goods appeared missing or disturbed. The money was still in the cash drawer and the five-dollar bill was in the post office's leather pouch. Everything in the store was the same as it had been at the close of business the previous day.

By a quarter to seven, the family maintained a deathwatch. Lizzie and Ellen took turns attending Victor, wiping his brow, mopping the blood from his mouth and doing whatever they could to assure his comfort. Nicholas mostly stood to the side, his head often bowed in prayer. Occasionally he stepped away for brief periods just to move around. Dr. Taylor remained at hand monitoring Victor's condition. In the kitchen, Essie boiled coffee and organized breakfast. This was as much for diversion as to service any want, for none were disposed to eat.

The train arrived from Gordonsville at 8:00 A.M. Dr. Banks stepped from the coach and hurried to the Hall Store. He found Victor in the bedroom surrounded by family and already attended by a physician. Dr. Taylor greeted Dr. Banks and encouraged his own examination. Dr. Banks concurred; the man was dying. There was very little to do other than provide comfort.

Dr. Banks asked Mrs. Hall for a word alone. In the parlor, she rehearsed the entire story as with Dr. Taylor. Dr. Banks listened intently. However, Mrs. Hall's rural speech left much to interpretation. The facts were clear in her own mind, but her mouth spoke generalities. Dr. Banks stopped Mrs. Hall often to clarify actions and expand descriptions. Sometimes this confused the good doctor even more.

The bad news traveled fast. Neighbors hurried over to the depot. Some came to offer assistance, but most just wanted to be part of the excitement and see the smoldering ruins of Dunkum's store. By nine o'clock, the little station swarmed with people. Rail foreman Wiley Woody, father of the telegrapher, resigned himself to playing host. Those inside the depot warmed themselves and talked excitedly about the events.

Who shot Victor Hall? Who burned Dunkum's store? Emotions ran high! Most agreed; "It'uz'at dam' nig'ah wut dun 'scayp't f'um up'n Culpepah!" They swore to hang him first chance they got!

It was April 15th. Some remembered it as two years since the *Titanic* sank.[20] Was the date coincidence or omen? An old timer said he thought it was also the day Lincoln died, but most folks there considered that a good thing and not something to be reckoned in their superstition.

Undoubtedly, the most conspicuous visitor at the store was William J. Roberts. "Bill" Roberts was a county constable and had managed the waterworks in the town of Louisa for several years. Bill was forty-two years old, raised in the county and known as one of the kindest men around. Like so many others, he came as soon as he learned of the shooting. Bill generally appeared whenever a neighbor needed a helping hand. The cruel irony was that this was all the man had: one hand, and then, only part of one!

Years earlier, an accident took Bill's left arm at the elbow. Later, another mishap took three fingers and part of the forth from his remaining hand.[21] The simplest daily activities presented challenges; in addition, he had a son to raise. Bill considered himself a widower, but everyone knew that his wife had been unable to cope after his second mutilation and divorced him.[22] She had since died.[23]

Bill and his fourteen year old lived with his sister Lennie and their youngest brother Eddie. Aunt Lennie assumed a maternal role for the boy's sake. This was good, for there was no foreseeable possibility of remarriage to replace his mother's love.

Bill depended heavily on his siblings.[24] He managed to earn a little something being local constable, supervising repairs at the waterworks, doing odd jobs, and running errands with his brother Walton's car.

Yes! Bill drove! It was an astounding sight to behold. He steered and shifted gears skillfully and with reasonable safety. The chief hazard to Bill, of course, was starting the car. A kickback when cranking the engine could easily break his only arm.

Indeed Bill took his alterations in stride. He was not one to feel sorry for himself, at least not openly. Consequently, people in the community viewed their friend more as a curiosity than a pity case, though he was certainly that too. Despite his winning ways, it was difficult to feel at ease around a man so badly pruned. Bill's uniqueness always attracted attention. So it was no wonder that from the very moment he drove up, everyone noted Bill's involvement.

At 9:30 A.M., the store shook with the approach of the train. Dr. Banks saw no further need of his services and excused himself to catch the rail coach back to Gordonsville.

Westbound No. 19 rang its bell as it pulled to a stop at Green Springs Depot. It was unusual for a train to stop at the tiny rural station just to let off passengers. Because of the shooting, a most notable group from Louisa stepped from the train including Commonwealth's Attorney William C. Bibb; Louisa County Treasurer J. Reid Wills, a former county sheriff; Clerk of Court Philip P. Porter; his brother Dr. Harry W. Porter; and county auctioneer J. Frank Bickers, a former deputy sheriff. Accompanying them was Lee Rosson, Mamie Rosson's father and a member of the Louisa County Board of Supervisors. He had boarded the train at Trevilians.

The new arrivals constituted a powerful contingent of the county's *courthouse clique*. Collectively, their presence magnified the significance of the tragedy in the minds of the onlookers. However, lost upon the gawking country folk was the fact that of these prominent men, only Bibb was there in any official capacity.

The anxious Lee Rosson jumped to the platform as the train rolled to a stop and dashed over to the store to check on his daughter. The others stepped down and tarried briefly while Dr. Banks spoke with Dr. Porter.[25] The conductor shouted, "All'board!" Dr. Banks doffed his hat, grabbed the handhold and mounted the car. The train whistle blew, the bell rang, the couplings bumped and the engine thrust off belching smoke and steam.

Dr. Porter led the way over to and inside the store; whereupon, the doctor went straight back into the bedroom where Victor Hall lay surrounded by his family. The county officials waited respectfully in the store. At the moment, there was little else they could do and maintain decorum.

Dr. Taylor briefed his colleague about Victor's condition. Dr. Porter confirmed with his own evaluation. Victor's weak, rapid pulse and labored breathing indicated death neared.

At ten minutes after ten o'clock, Dr. Taylor pronounced Victor Hall dead. The school teachers wept. The girls cried aloud. Lizzie sat numbed in disbelief. Victor's mother Ellen Hall, gray and bent with age, buried

SOMEONE SHOT VICTOR!

her face in her hands and sobbed uncontrollably while comforted by husband Nicholas at their murdered son's bedside.[26]

The piteous scenes at the store that day greatly affected everyone.
No one acquainted with Victor Hall could imagine the friendly, earnest,
young man ever having an enemy. The senselessness and ruthlessness of
his killing intensified contempt for the crime.

Victor Hall in the *Richmond Virginian*,
May 14, 1914. (Photo Courtesy of The
Library of Virginia)

CHAPTER
Two

FAMILY MATTERS

*F*or the third time in as many hours Lizzie sat on the chesterfield in the parlor recounting the details of the fire and shooting to a physician. Dr. Porter listened intently. He had known the family a long time, and being the family's doctor, viewed Mrs. Hall more as his patient than simply the wife of the victim. He had attended Mrs. Hall's first husband during his fatal illness three years before and those of her infants lost prior to that. Recently, Dr. Porter had treated Mrs. Hall for stubborn ear infections.

At the end of her account, Lizzie asked Dr. Porter if he thought an autopsy would help catch the murderer. Dr. Porter agreed that there may be benefit in, at least, recovering the bullet. He consulted Dr. Taylor. Together they recruited bystanders to prepare a place in the store for the autopsy.

On that gray morning, the store's white interior reflected the diffuse daylight to provide marginally adequate illumination. Helpers moved display cases to the back counter and cleared a work area on a front counter where the windows provided best light. The doctors ordered white cloths tacked half-way up the windows to screen their work from outside view.

The county officials adjourned to the residence. The Hester family was also among those recently off the train. Magistrate James E. Hester offered his assistance. The young man carried a torch for Essie and paid her special mind at every opportunity. Older brother Charles and his wife Emma[1] were long-time friends of Mrs. Hall. Emma assumed management of household matters. She found the kitchen in good hands. Neighbor Nannie Harris had already sent her colored cook Anna to fix dinner.

Lee Rosson was relieved to find his dear Mamie safe, but insisted that she pack her things and be ready to leave whenever he did. Rosson had never liked his daughter living there no matter how nice the Hall family seemed. He knew the neighborhood. He had helped investigate the shooting at that same store nine years earlier and was mad at himself for having unnecessarily exposed his daughter to danger by permitting her to stay there.

The physicians directed transfer of Victor's body from his bed to the counter top in the store. By eleven o'clock, a basin of warm water, some rags, and a clean slop jar completed preparations. The doctors undressed the body. The victim was about average height and thin: about one hundred and thirty pounds. The only visible injuries were to the head. There was a gunshot wound about one and a half inches above the bony protuberance, no powder burns and no exit wound. There was considerable bruising and swelling around the left eye consistent with a blow or a fall.

Dr. Porter cut the scalp from ear to ear across the top of the head, and then pulled the skin back exposing the skull. The doctors worked together to saw the top of the cranium free and exposed the bloody mess inside. They traced the bullet's path from its entrance through the brain and found the projectile lodged just above the left eye socket. Dr. Porter carefully extracted the deformed slug. After rinsing it, he inscribed a mark on it for later identification and noted a waxy, yellow substance in the grease grooves assumed to be lubricant.

There was no reason to proceed further. The doctors replaced the skull's cap, stitched the incision closed and cleaned up as best they could. After covering the body, they notified Magistrate Hester that their job was done.

While the autopsy was underway, N. W. Hall stepped over to the depot to send a telegram to his elder son Sterling in North Carolina to inform him of his brother's death and to summon him home. Rev. C. T. Thrift arrived by buggy from Louisa to minister to the family.[2] Meanwhile, Magistrate Hester assigned former deputy sheriff J. Frank Bickers the task of assembling the coroner's jury. The county officials offered condolences to the family and delicately questioned them about the shooting. The men from Louisa knew Sheriff Wash and his deputies were busy just a few miles away capturing the escaped convict. Most everyone privileged to that matter already attributed the arson and murder to the fugitive.

Culpeper was twenty-five miles away as the crow flies. The very night before the tragedy at Green Springs, every able bodied man in Culpeper fought a devastating fire in the heart of that town.[3] A prisoner left unguarded during the confusion broke free and fled south. Sheriff Wash had been leading a posse hunting the fugitive since being notified that the man was headed their way.

Shortly before boarding the train, Commonwealth's Attorney Bibb received word that the escapee was asleep in a colored woman's house at McGehee's store near Trevilians.[4] Deputy Sheriff Robert Trice detrained at Trevilians Depot to verify the rumor and take the fugitive into custody. Officials hoped the sheriff and posse arrived there in time, for once word got around about Victor Hall, the convict might well face a lynch mob.

Frank Bickers assembled the panel of neighbors in the store. Magistrate Hester then convened the coroner's jury over the shrouded body of Victor Hall. The jurors included Charles Hester, Grover N. Kennon [5], Charles B. Vest [6], Fritz P. Wills, J. Maury Hill, and Lee Rosson. [7] Other county officials sat in on the inquest.

Commonwealth's Attorney Bibb examined Victor Hall's pistol. He carefully eyed the piece and broke it open. He temporarily removed the cartridges as a precaution noting especially the one discharged round. He looked closely and sniffed. Bibb detected no residual odor and was satisfied that the gun had not been recently fired. He passed it along to the members of the coroner's jury. Each juror in turn smelled the weapon, looked down the barrel, broke the piece open, and handled the empty cartridge. Some produced pen knives and scraped powdery residue from the barrel and verdigris from the spent round. Only C. B. Vest declined to examine the gun in detail. Everyone concluded that the pistol had not been fired recently, some guessed not for a month; therefore, the gun merited no official attention at the inquest.

Miss Elsie Wood was sworn in as a witness and asked to tell the jury all she knew about the matter.

"Well the first I heard of it was Mr. Nicholas Hall knocked at the front door of the dwelling. He said fire! I got up and looked out the back window. I could see a light. I thought if it was this building. It was around front at the store. I went in the other girl's room and I could see it was Mr. Buck Dunkum's store on fire. We all looked out that window. We went in all the rooms up stairs and looked out all of the windows. We stayed up until the fire was practically out and went back to bed at two o'clock.

First one I saw at the fire was Mr. Buck Dunkum and Mr. N. W. Hall: also Mrs. Harris and her little son came down and Mrs. Hall and Miss Jennie Hall and Victor Hall and his wife. Mr. Victor Hall was sick and did not go at first.

The first thing I heard after returning was the shot which aroused me, and when I came down stairs it was ten minutes after four. Before the shot I thought some one spoke. It was about half a minute after hearing the shot I came down. My room is over the store, but in coming down, I passed through the room occupied by Mr. Victor Hall and his wife in order to reach the store room. When I reached the store room I found Mr. Victor Hall lying on the floor of the store room and Mrs. Hall, his wife, standing by. I went to Mr. Victor Hall and caught hold of him, then I went and got the pistol from the middle bureau drawer, then I got a bottle of camphor. Mrs. Hall and myself tried to put a quilt under him and then Mr. Buck Dunkum came in. Mrs. Hall called Mr. Dunkum before I came down stairs and also called him after I came down. She called him several times. I supposed it was about fifteen minutes after Mr. Hall was shot before Mr. Dunkum reached the store. Immediately after the shot I heard two or three hurried foot steps on porch at store.

Mrs. Dunkum also called Mr. N. W. Hall before he came. This is all I know of the main details of the shooting except when I came down there was a lamp in the store room. I understand Mr. Hall carried it in. Mr. Hall died 10:10 A.M. this morning as result of the shooting. I do not know who did the shooting, nor have any suspicion. My home is at Poindexter, Va. and at present am teaching school at Forest Hill."[8]

In like manner, Mrs. Hall was sworn in. Commonwealth's Attorney W. C. Bibb asked, "After the burning of Mr. Dunkum's store what occurred from that time to time of shooting?"

Mrs. Hall answered:

"After the fire my husband and my self retired in our room back at the store and adjacent thereto. Mr. N. W. Hall after the fire sat in our room some time after my husband and myself retired then he left and cautioned us to look out again and see about the fire and when about two hours afterwards that Mr. Hall left my husband heard the knocking at the door of the store he said there is Papa. I reckon Mama has sent him back again.

My husband got up took the lamp turned it up and went into the store. The next thing I heard was him Oh! Lord, then in a second or so I heard the shot. I called Rebecca and went in the store and called for the girls. Mamie Rosson answered. I found my husband lying between the two counters with his head towards the front door at the store. The lamp was burning on the counter. The next thing I did was to put a pillow under his head. Then I called Mr. Dunkum from the door at the store. I think I called him two or three times though was excited and don't remember. Miss Elsie was the first one to come down after I had gotten in store, then the others came down. Then I laid a quilt over him and put my shoes on and went out on railroad and called Mr. Dunkum several times again, and then he came with his wife and children. Mr.

Dunkum was very much excited and do not know exactly what he said. It seemed to be hard for him to realize that Victor was shot. I remember his saying what will happen here next. Mr. N. W. Hall helped me and girls to take Victor up and put him in bed. Then Mrs. N. W. Hall and Miss Jennie came. This is all I know of main details of shooting."[9]

Dr. H. W. Porter was the third sworn witness. He testified as to the cause of death.

"The Ball penetrated the skull and entered the brain about one and one half inches above bony promince [sic] at back of head, it having entirely passed through brain and lodged over the socket at left eye, no evidence of powder burns and death resulted from the wound at 10:10 A.M. of the 15th of April 1914. The ball was removed and shown to the jury."[10]

Dr. Taylor's testimony concurred with Dr. Porters.

Shortly after 1 p.m. the coroner's jury concluded with their official statement:

"We the jury having heard the testimony of the witnesses find that Victor Hall came to his death from the effect of a pistol bullet fired by some unknown person on the morning of the 15th of April 1914."[11]

As soon as the coroner's business concluded, Emma Hester informed Lizzie that the cook had dinner on the table. There was plenty of food. Mrs. Hall invited the officials and jurors to stay and eat. Southern hospitality prevailed even under these most awkward circumstances. Nearly everyone was hungry and accepted the offer. However as the clock approached half past one, the county officials excused themselves to the depot to catch the train back to Louisa. Lee Rosson left with his daughter to take her back to their home in Trevilians.

Elsie Wood also needed to leave. Her father Ollie Wood, a friend of the Halls, ran the store and post office at Poindexter.[12] He had been at Hall's store since midmorning. Once Elsie finished packing, her father loaded her things in their buggy. The two assured Mrs. Hall and her family of their sympathies and support, and then drove home.

Drs. Porter and Taylor recruited men to move Victor Hall's body back to his bed where Lizzie and Ellen would later clean and dress it for burial. Nicholas took it upon himself to purchase a casket and make arrangements. The family agreed to have the funeral on the following day as was customary.[13] Nicholas joined the others boarding the train for Louisa.

Many people left the store. Others waited to go in. The telephone lineman needed to verify his repair having replaced the burned wire. A Richmond newspaperman seized the opportunity and approached the workman with a proposal to earn extra money. The telephone company employee accepted the offer and verified that the telephone was working again by telephoning the reporter's story to the newspaper.[14]

Someone put Becky Coates to work scrubbing blood from the floor and counter top. Magistrate Hester passed along a bundle of bloody clothes and rags to Constable Bill Roberts who had taken charge of the crime scene. Roberts told the Hall's colored man to take the things away. Chisholm reverently carried the bundle out beyond the pasture buried it.

Funeral director A. B. Woodward received Nicholas Hall warmly. He had anticipated the family's request and agreed to handle arrangements.[15] Hall scheduled Victor's burial for the next morning. Woodward promised delivery of the casket that afternoon. After concluding business, Nicholas walked back to Louisa Station. An hour remained before the return train. Hall sat quietly in the corner of the empty waiting room, withdrew a pencil and notepad and drafted Victor's obituary.

Nicholas Hall returned to Green Springs Depot at 4:25 P.M. The depot was still crowded. Men always hung around the depot on weekdays seeking incidental work like loading lumber or pulpwood onto flatcars; some were idlers. Never were there so many and never so late in the day. Some sat on the bench, crates and kegs on the platform. Others leaned against the wall. All eyes turned toward "old man Hall" as he stepped off the train.

Some removed their hats as he passed. Each hoped that the no-good who shot Victor Hall would be caught and hanged like he deserved. Some voiced sympathies. Nicholas acknowledged them with a simple touch to his brim while he proceeded to the store. He saw more men in the oak grove beside the station. Some used boards for benches. Others leaned against trees or against the fence.

Those at the depot spent the better part of the afternoon watching the extraordinary comings and goings and discussing every detail. The excitement replaced checker games and other common amusements. Cheeks full of tobacco ruminated over the crimes until dark. Some whittled sticks while listening to others shave rough edges off outlandish theories. Weeks later when an arrest was finally made, some proudly referred back to that afternoon as when "I told'em so!"[16]

Nicholas Hall entered the store. The floors and counter tops were clean. In the bedroom, Victor lay covered on the bed. Nicholas needed not to lift the sheet to know that Lizzie and Ellen had already washed Victor and dressed him in his Sunday best.[17] He found the women in the outbuilding comforted by neighbors. Most had brought food. A number of friends and neighbors spent the day at the residence helping the family in one way or another. Some planned to stay overnight through the wake.

As Nicholas reported the success of his errand, the black, horse drawn hearse pulled up outside the residence. After paying respects to the widow, A. B. Woodward and his assistant unloaded the casket and brought it into the house. In minutes, they had Victor positioned in it and set on trusses in the parlor. Under the circumstances, the family insisted that the lid be closed.

This done, the family gathered with Mr. Woodward and discussed burial details. Others excused themselves to the outbuilding to congregate with friends already in the dining and cooking areas. The family wanted a simple funeral in keeping with rural custom. They would recruit pallbearers from friends attending the wake. A ten o'clock service was good.

Funeral arrangements were settled. There was much food in the dinning room. Everyone was invited to stay and sup with the family. Lizzie did not feel like eating, but encouraged guests to do so. Eventually she ate a little something.

Lizzie was exhausted. She went upstairs to lie down. She managed a little rest. By sundown the traditional black crepe was draped over the entrances. A black embellished evergreen wreath fashioned by a neighbor hung on the door to the home. All the mirrors were draped in black and the mantle clocks stopped. At evening, the gray skies darkened and the gloom became exceedingly oppressive.

Lizzie donned her widow's weeds. It had been just three years since beginning deep mourning for her first husband and even that had been thrust upon her before completing mourning for their baby son. Now she found herself renewing the ritual.

Lizzie returned downstairs and sat with the Halls and others in the parlor. Lamps and candles illuminated the room but did little to dispel the dark spirit. More friends and neighbors arrived throughout the evening with more food and consolation. The love expressed by words and actions made the unthinkable events of the day bearable. Even so, this was only by the grace of God.

Shortly after ten o'clock, Nicholas and Ellen excused themselves. It was time to meet Sterling's train.

SOMEONE SHOT VICTOR!

A telegram only bode evil. When Sterling Hall received it at his Southern Railway office, he feared something terrible had happened to Mama, Papa or Aunt Jennie. The news was worse than feared: "VICTOR SHOT – DIED TODAY." Sterling sent reply to expect him on train No. 6 that evening. He hurried home, packed, kissed his wife and baby good-bye, and taxied to the station to catch the first northbound train.

Sterling could not believe Victor was dead. The trip to Charlottesville gave him time to reflect, but the fact was hard to accept. It was not until he walked from the Southern Railway station to catch his connection at the C & O terminal that Sterling began to grasp that he was back in Virginia. Train No. 6 arrived promptly at 9:25 P.M. and left with Sterling on board at 9:30 P.M. Green Springs was forty-five minutes away.

Sterling and Victor had been close. They were the only children in their family and only twenty months apart. Both were blond, blue-eyed and similarly featured. The boys might have been mistaken for twins growing up were Victor not so sickly. Even as an adult, Victor was prone to tonsillitis and other ailments to which Sterling seemed immune. Be-cause of Victor's many bouts with this or that he reached adulthood as a shorter, skinnier, less robust version of his older brother. However, when Victor was well, his industry masked his frailties.

Sterling had always been healthy, energetic, and ambitious. His self-assuredness as a young man often surprised his family. He broke tradi-tion in 1901 when he joined nearby Wills Memorial Church. His father had no bias against Presbyterians, but the fact that Sterling did not hold membership with the rest of the family at Lasley Methodist Church upset his mother.

Sterling, then sixteen, began clerking for the Yancey brothers who then managed the store at Green Springs. Working there gave him real business experience.

Sterling regretted living so far away from his family. Prospects for young men in Louisa County were slim, but at Green Springs Depot they were dismal. This had been obvious to Sterling even as a boy when he determined that he needed to leave the county for any chance of success in life. Had there been the slightest hesitation to follow through, the smallpox outbreak at the depot the winter of 1902-03 erased all doubt. After being quarantined in the store ninety days, Sterling never really cared if he ever saw the place again. Green Springs was cursed.

Upon turning eighteen in June '03, Sterling left home for Charlottesville and secured a job with Southern Railway. Sterling advanced rapidly. He accepted a position as freight clerk. This required his moving to Charlotte, North Carolina where he now lived. Sterling eventually met and married wife Alice, a nice North Carolina girl. Together they had a one year old daughter Margaret. Yes. Leaving Green Springs proved the right thing to do.

Sterling thought of his parents. Victor was their chief joy. They lived on adjoining property and saw each other daily. Now Victor was gone. What would they do without him? Sterling didn't know. He now lived out of state caring for his own family. His parents were not alone. Aunt Jennie still lived with them, and they had many friends.

Sterling felt both grief and anger. That damned store! In all his memory, there had been nothing but death and misery associated with it: killings and smallpox. Victor might still be alive had it not been for that infernal place. And then, there was that woman Victor married: Lizzie Dunkum. Sterling never accepted their union. Lordy'bove! Why did Victor marry that cow?

True, Sterling had had little acquaintance with the Dunkum family personally. Most of what he knew about them was strictly what his parents and Victor told him. Sterling had been gone two years when the Dunkums bought the store and the acreage surrounding the depot. The Dunkums viewed it as a golden opportunity. The store had all the conveniences afforded by the railway with telephone and telegraph. Sterling never envied the Dunkums. The place was a hellhole.

The good people of the neighborhood were relieved to learn that the Dunkums were God fearing folk. They would not turn the store into a *blind tiger* typical of so many other county stores. Victor was eighteen at the time and worked as the depot's telegrapher. Victor earned a meager living even after his promotion to station agent, an opportunity which, Sterling shuddered to recall, resulted from a shooting at the depot. Victor later accepted an offer to clerk for the Dunkum brothers. His life became an enviable lot by local standards. If only "Acey" Dunkum had not died.

A year after Dunkum's death, being a respectful mourning period, Victor courted the widow Dunkum. Sterling knew his little brother. Despite all Sterling heard to the contrary, he believed that Victor interested himself in the widow Dunkum chiefly with an eye on partnership in the store. What other reason could there have been for him to pursue an *old bag* with two half-grown daughters? Sterling could not believe otherwise. Victor was twenty-five and she thirty-eight. Sterling thought the arrangement absurd. Victor was closer in age to the eldest daughter than he was to his wife.

Even though Victor convinced himself that he loved the woman, she should have had better sense. Their age difference was scandalous! How could she have so willingly exposed herself and her entire family to neighborhood gossip? Talk was inevitable and predictably vicious.

Sterling snickered to himself as he fancied Victor and Lizzie's marriage as a *fifty-fifty* proposition; indeed, she was fifty percent older and fifty pounds heavier. His derisive amusement ended with the thought of the couple together as man and wife. What a revolting image that conjured!

If only Victor had been willing to leave Mama and Papa. Victor could have easily advanced within the railroad just as he had. But then again, Victor had health issues. Anyway, Victor would probably still be alive. What if . . .? For much of the trip, Sterling troubled himself with a legion of *what-ifs*. The reality was irreversible. Victor was dead.

Shot? How was Victor shot? A robbery? An accident? Sterling wondered. Hopefully, the sheriff already had the killer. If Sterling identified any positive aspect to the tragedy, it was that Victor was a railroad employee. The Chesapeake and Ohio Railway would assign their detectives to investigate. The resources of the railroad were far greater than those of the county. They would catch the culprit if anyone could.

Nicholas and Ellen stood on the platform in the moonlight. They heard the train's whistle blow for the Forest Hill crossing. A shaft of light preceded the locomotive beyond the trees. The train's bell tolled Sterling's arrival as it slowed to stop. The couple saw their son through the windows of the lighted passenger car as he moved toward the exit. Sterling stepped from the train and greeted his mother and father solemnly.

The train chugged away and revealed the ruins of the Dunkum store illuminated by the moon. Sterling focused on his parents, his eyes unaccustomed to the dark. The sight escaped Sterling's notice until his mother pointed out that Dunkum's store had burned. This was the first he had heard of the fire. It happened just before Victor was killed? The coincidence was too weird.

The three walked over to his brother's residence. Sterling dropped his bag in the hallway. They proceeded into the parlor where family and friends were gathered around Lizzie on the chesterfield. The evergreen covered casket against the adjacent wall was the room's most prominent feature. For Sterling, it no more projected the presence of his brother than any other stick of furniture. The closed lid indicated that his brother had been disfigured. He was not prepared for that.

Neighbors were glad to see Sterling. He greeted Lizzie and spoke briefly with her. The exchange was sterile. He presented himself politely without betraying the fact that he loathed everything about the situation: the closed casket, the pudgy widow, his *step-nieces*, and especially, the haunting memories of that damned house.

After the expected pleasantries, Sterling and his parents excused themselves and walked home in the cold moonlight. The Hall's needed time with Sterling to acquaint him with the situation and allow him to unpack.

Sterling sat and talked with his parents in their warm kitchen. Nicholas shared his version of Victor's death beginning with the store fire. The events begged connection.

Nicholas showed Sterling the obituary he had written that day. There was plenty of time to refine it because the *Central Virginian*[18], the county newspaper, was a weekly journal and not due out again until next Thursday. Nicholas had his own printing press in a shed out back and published his own newspaper. *The Pen* was a single, eight and a half by eleven inch sheet folded in half to form four pages of personal editorial, religious exhortation and moral commentary. *The Pen* would eventually carry Victor's death notice, but not before it appeared in the county paper.

Who killed Victor? His father had no idea who could have done such a thing. He had few answers to Sterling's questions. Dunkum's fire was just as big a mystery.

The family was glad to have Sterling home. Lizzie needed his help to settle the estate.

By the time the Halls returned to the wake, Lizzie had excused herself again upstairs to rest. She listened as those gathered in the parlor sang hymns to accompaniment of the pump organ. Lizzie doubted it was Essie at the keyboard, likely a neighbor.

MURDER AT GREEN SPRINGS

She drifted off for brief periods, but rest evaded her troubled mind. She thought of Easter Sunday. Was it just three days ago? It was such a pleasant day. Life had become good and enjoyable again. But now it seemed so long ago. Victor was dead and horribly so. She had faced loses before, but nothing like this. Murder! Who shot Victor? Would the killer come back for her or her daughters? Uncertainties nagged relentlessly.

Lizzie got up at first light and freshened herself at the washstand. She then went downstairs. Most neighbors had returned home by dawn to ready themselves for the funeral, but a few friends were still there. Nicholas, Ellen, and Jennie were awake and sitting on the chesterfield. Sterling sat in the armchair. They asked how she felt and encouraged her to eat something. Ellen accompanied her outside to the dining room. The cold, fresh air struck Lizzie. The sky was as gray as it had been the day before.

Essie was already up and in the kitchen. She greeted her mother with a cup of coffee and something to eat. Lizzie accepted the coffee, but declined food.

Lizzie noticed activity outside. Neighborhood men were digging Victor's grave. Many country folk believed it unlucky to leave a grave open overnight, so Mr. Woodward arranged to have it dug early in the morning.

Lizzie had asked Buck to be a pallbearer. During the night she had had second thoughts. Buck might be more comfortable standing with the family. Lizzie would ask Sterling to find another pallbearer to replace Buck.

The Halls returned home to dress. Essie went upstairs to do the same. Lizzie asked her to let Mamie sleep as long as possible. Essie could help Mamie get ready after she took care of herself. Friends and neighbors arrived throughout the morning.

The day had begun with another chilly, overcast dawn. The same full cloud cover that added so much gloom to the tragic day before persisted until midmorning then partially cleared. Idle men, mostly farmers, gathered at the depot station since they were deprived their normal congregating places at the Dunkum and Hall stores. The little potbelly stove heated the cramped quarters for those wishing to warm themselves.

The depot was a typical, rural station. It was a little, rectangular shed about twenty by thirty foot and sat next to the rail siding. The unpainted, weatherboard structure had a metal sheathed, "A" roof. Facing the lane was a single entrance flanked by two small windows.[19] On the west side there was a holding pen for livestock. The trackside had an open freight platform, a bench and little else, other than a narrow, white sign fixed top center on the wall. Black block letters identified the stop as "Green Springs."

The seasonally cool air was fresh and invigorating, but the fields were too wet to work. Even had conditions been perfect for plowing, there was too much excitement to be had in gathering to discuss the recent goings on. Those outside ignored the gusty spring breeze blowing down the tracks. An occasional shift in the wind brought wafts of nearby hog pens.

Discussion of the fire and murder deferred conversations about weather, planting or even the seasonal greening of the landscape, which otherwise would have been much appreciated and commented upon. The first new leaves emerged on the hardwoods giving their gray extremities a greenish cast. White and purple blossoms on full blooming dogwoods and redbuds dotted the base of distant tree lines bordering meadows and fields. The oaks surrounding the buildings at the depot were still bare. Those were always the last trees to sport new growth.

Songbirds warbled loudly. Their spring songs impinged on every ear and lightened spirits weighted by the more somber sounds of horses, carriages, and people arriving for the funeral. All this was overpowered occasionally by the scheduled discord of a steam locomotive.

Preceded by its whistle, the black engine and coal tender of the train No. 19 came into view as it chugged around the slight curve at milepost 154. Its bell clanged as it slowed to a stop to deliver passengers at Green

MURDER AT GREEN SPRINGS

Springs Depot for a second consecutive day. Relief valves loudly vented clouds of steam on both sides of the engine. The cadmium yellow passenger cars glowed especially bright in the burst of sunlight through parting clouds. The cheerful sight befitting a circus train was consistent with the carnival atmosphere of excited, morbidly curious travelers opening windows and straining to wonder at the burned ruins of Dunkum's store and alternately crossing the aisle to view the sites of the fire and murder just the day before.

A station hand received freight from the express car: several wooden boxes addressed, ironically, to Dunkum's store. The conductor assisted persons stepping from the train then checked his watch. It was 9:40 A.M. Trains stopped at Green Springs only when flagged. The number of passengers for this destination rivaled the novelty of the stop.

Most people arrived specifically for the funeral. Three men in particular stopped on the platform to survey the area. These watched the other arrivals cross the road to the Hall residence. After the train gained distance, the songbirds became audible again, but the mood at the depot had changed.

The locals hanging around outside the depot sat on benches or leaned against the building and eyed the strangers who appeared intent on the burned store. They rightly guessed that the three men were investigators of some kind. They also had better sense than to get friendly on their own accord with strangers sent there to snoop around. One never knew what might slip out while talking with authorities. An unguarded answer to some question might arouse suspicion in an unrelated matter: maybe betray somebody's moonshine still.

Eventually, the funeral procession left the residence. Reverend Thrift and Mr. Woodward led the way followed by the casket. Each pallbearer wore a black armband on a coat sleeve. Some of the men's clothes were obviously homemade, perhaps sown from cloth sold by the deceased. The family came next. All the women wore black. The widow and the mother of the victim both wore veils. Lizzie walked with Essie and Mamie at her side. Nicholas and Ellen Hall were behind them; next Sterling Hall escorted Aunt Jennie ahead of the Dunkums; friends and neighbors followed. Lastly, the three inquisitive looking strangers left the depot and fell in behind the last guests.

In less than ten minutes the entire procession walked the two hundred yards down the lane to the family plot. Reverend Thrift took his place at the head of the open grave. The pallbearers stopped and eased the casket down beside it. When everyone had gathered around, the men lifted the casket on ropes and lowered it into place. They removed the ropes and found places in the crowd.

Lizzie stood in that cemetery for the fourth time to bury a husband or infant. The widow remained silent and the victim's mother sobbed profoundly. Veils hid their faces. The stepdaughters stood expressionless as Reverend Thrift began the commitment service.

The preacher spoke of righteous Able, the first man slain. Cain killed Able. But the question on everyone's mind was "Who killed Victor Hall?" So far as anyone knew, Victor Hall did not have an enemy in the world.

Nicholas, Lizzie, and Essie listened and maintained their composure throughout the service. Each was diverted at times to comfort Ellen and Mamie, who were both emotional wrecks as was Mary Dunkum.

Buck Dunkum, normally a tall, well postured man, slouched with his arm around his wife. He was visibly troubled. In a short span of time, Buck had lost his brother and business partner, a child, and suffered three major fires on his property. Always wanting to believe the best of people, Buck had dismissed the possibility that someone was intentionally trying to burn him out. Perhaps he now acknowledged the fact too late. He feared that this time his mysterious enemy had framed him for murder. The culprit must have hated Victor also. But who was it? Buck glanced around occasionally and caught probing looks from others. How many thought he did it?

  MURDER AT GREEN SPRINGS

Reverend Thrift eulogized young Victor and proclaimed Jesus Christ the sure and certain hope of resurrection. Two men stepped forward with shovels. Those with hymnals opened them. People sang somberly as the men filled the grave.

"Now the laborer's task is o'er;
Now the battle day is past;
Now upon the farther shore
Lands the voyager at last.
Father, in Thy gracious keeping
Leave we now Thy servant sleeping."

"There the teas of earth are dried;
There its hidden things are clear;
There the work of life is tried
By a juster Judge than here.
Father, in Thy gracious keeping
Leave we now Thy servant sleeping. . . ."[20]

Buck mouthed the hymn, but worry muted his voice. Certainly, whoever torched his store killed Victor. So far as he knew, the authorities still assumed the escaped convict guilty. Buck knew it was only a matter of time before the law looked for another suspect, and he was keenly aware of the many circumstances pointing to him. His stomach knotted with dark anxiety. He had slept very little.

As workmen dressed the last dirt into a tidy mound, the gathering sang *Rock of Ages*. Victor liked that hymn. When the singing stopped, Reverend Thrift lifted his arms for the benediction. Heads bowed and eyes closed as if mechanically actuated by the preacher's motion and held firmly until disengaged by the "Amen."

Victor Hall was dead and buried. Who would have ever thought it possible just two days earlier? Friends consoled the family graveside. Neighbors mingled hubble-bubble. It was a large gathering with as many drawn by curiosity as out of respect.

Understandably, Ellen Hall grieved hardest. In contrast, Lizzie, twice widowed at age forty, was sad, not devastated. She loved Victor, but her loss could not compare with the bereavements of her first husband and their two infants. Now, they all lay buried there together with an empty plot reserved for herself between her husbands.

Lizzie believed God worked all things for good. Experience had taught her that bad times did not last forever. Happier times lay ahead. Life cycled that way.

Lizzie viewed herself as blessed. She knew that she and her daughters would not end up charity cases like so many other widows she knew. Lizzie owned their home, the store, and assets from her first marriage. Victor had some insurance. They were not alone. Victor's parents lived on adjoining land and Buck's family was just across the tracks. Lizzie had eight siblings and their families for support as well as many local friends and church family. There was also Victor's brother Sterling.

Only one thought plagued Lizzie. Would her husband's killer return to harm her or her daughters? The uncertainly frightened her. She could not openly express this fear. She had to be strong for the girls' sake.

The crowd dispersed. Buck and Mary excused themselves and went straight home. Others begged pardon to attend pressing chores, but most friends and associates followed the family back to the house for the traditional post-funeral feed and fellowship. Meanwhile, standing to the side watching and waiting for a convenient moment to speak with the widow were three detectives.

MURDER AT GREEN SPRINGS

CHAPTER *Three*

DETECTIVES PUT ON THE CASE

MURDER AT GREEN SPRINGS

n Richmond, chief claims agent for the Chesapeake and Ohio Railway Luther L. Scherer ordered the company's investigation of Victor Hall's shooting within hours of the event. Scherer was the most well known detective in Virginia next to William G. Baldwin.[1] Scherer's chief duty was that of managing security operations for the large railroad. His reputation was such that state governors relied on his abilities. The national publicity surrounding Scherer's investigation of the Beattie murder three years before had made his name a household word.

Victor Hall had served as stationmaster and express agent at Green Springs Depot for nine years. Hall was now the second C & O station employee murdered in less than a year. Someone killed a telegrapher in Scottsville eight months earlier. Scottsville and Green Springs were about the same distance west of Richmond, but on separate tracks. Both hard-working, upright young men were railroad employees. Both were shot to death in the wee hours of the morning with the same caliber weapon. There were no witnesses to the crimes. Neither victim was robbed. It had rained both mornings. Similarities suggested a relationship.

Scherer assigned Special Agents Myer S. Angle[2] and Joseph E. Mallory to the Hall Case. Angle was senior detective for the division, intimately familiar with the Piedmont routes and had served as lead investigator for the Scottsville killing.

Railroad detectives were hired specifically to protect the interests of the railway. For this reason, they concerned themselves chiefly with matters associated with railroad property. They generally investigated trespassing, theft, vandalism, or an occasional threat or assault against a railway employee. An accidental death on the tracks was common. Murder was rare.

DETECTIVES PUT ON THE CASE

In 1904, the Commonwealth of Virginia vested railroad detectives with full police authority.[3] Thus, they commanded particular regard. Despite the lofty title the C & O Railway applied to their detectives, *Special Agents* employed an unsophisticated approach to anyone on railroad property. The work was clear cut. If one was not conducting official business, then one was trespassing. This intimidating, presumptive approach effective in routine railroad work was dubious, even reckless, in a murder investigation. Nevertheless, Myer S. Angle was a seasoned railway detective and had recently become one of the very few experienced—such as he was—in murder investigation.

On August 24, 1913, twenty-five year old Richard Wheat Harrison went on duty at the Scottsville station at midnight. At 2:30 A.M. the young telegrapher copied orders for a westbound freight train. When the train stopped for orders at 3:00 A.M., the conductor found Harrison on the floor of his office shot dead.

Luther Scherer dispatched Special Agents Myer S. Angle and John W. Light to the scene. Scherer reacted as he had in the Beattie murder and ordered bloodhounds sent from the state farm in Goochland. By the time the detectives and bloodhounds arrived, excited townsfolk had trampled the scene and obliterated any tracks and scents which, though highly unlikely, might have survived the thunderstorm.

The shooting made front pages of the Richmond and Charlottesville newspapers. There was no evidence other than the obvious fact that Harrison was dead beside his desk with two bullets in his body. An autopsy revealed one .38 caliber slug penetrated his liver; a second pierced his aorta and killed him immediately. There was no apparent motive. The previous morning had been payday, so there was little or no money left in the safe to provoke robbery. The victim had no known enemy and had not been robbed. Nevertheless, Special Agent Angle had a lead. A depot employee reported that Harrison had twice chased away a loitering hobo named Louis Jackson.

Local outrage over the senseless killing drew Scherer to Scottsville. He toured the crime scene with Mayor Beal. The two men discussed the progress of the investigation. Beal mentioned that the town had placed its own detective on the case. The mayor related a telephone call he received from a young man confident that if the town needed a detective to find the killer, "he was the man."[4] Desperate to ease public pressure to catch the killer, Beal accepted the man's offer.

When Beal named his new employee, Scherer realized that the town's novice sleuth was none other than twenty-five year old Louis Jackson, the drifter already under investigation. Scherer relayed Jackson's curious ambition to Angle. Angle, in turn, assumed a defined mission.

Angle found Jackson loitering around Warren Depot just six miles up the tracks toward Charlottesville. Angle ferreted out witnesses there who admitted that on the morning of the shooting, they first heard about the killing from Jackson. Considering the time and distance from the scene, Angle concluded that Jackson reported information privileged only to the killer. On the fifth day after the crime, Angle arrested Jackson for suspicion of murder. Thereafter, Angle's name frequently appeared on front pages of newspapers as the case developed.

Harrison had been a popular young man and prominent in local fraternal orders.[5] His death so shocked and enraged local citizenry that lynching appeared imminent. Jackson was transferred to the Richmond jail for his own protection. Newspapers used the regional story to hold readers' interest as the sensational trial of Leo Frank concluded.[6]

Angle never doubted Jackson's guilt. Proving it was difficult. Angle established that Jackson was a drifter from Oklahoma. He used a number of aliases, but had no distinguished criminal record. Jackson had a .32 caliber pistol on his person. It was the wrong caliber to have killed Harrison. Angle learned that local authorities had given Jackson the gun.[7]

On September 19th, Angle escorted Jackson back to Scottsville for a preliminary hearing before the mayor and the commonwealth's attorney.[8] Miss Grace Carroll testified that a thunderstorm woke her on the morning in question.[9] When she looked out her window between midnight and four o'clock, lightning flashed, and she saw Jackson sleeping on the Warren Depot platform.[10] Nevertheless, the magistrate felt evidence was strong enough to hold Jackson. With sentiment against Jackson still high, authorities returned him to Richmond. The grand jury indicted Jackson for murder.

On October 14th, Jackson was taken to Charlottesville and arraigned in Albemarle County Court. Judge John W. Fishburne appointed an attorney from Scottsville to defend the indigent man. Jackson pleaded not guilty. Commonwealth's Attorney Duke asked for a continuance because key prosecution witnesses failed to appear. The judge continued the case until December and remanded Jackson to the county jail to await trial.[11]

On December 18th, Duke renewed his request for continuance because "very important and necessary witnesses were absent."[12] Greatly irritated, Judge Fishburne continued the case again. He fined one witness for not appearing and ordered all of them not to leave the area. The judge also required these to post bonds guaranteeing their appearance on the next trial date.[13]

Jackson was finally tried February 4, 1914. It was the second case on the docket. This time all witnesses were present; however, when the case was called, only eleven of the sixteen *venire facias* qualified. Judge Fishburne ordered the sheriff to provide eight more names immediately. The sheriff scrambled, but only mustered six. Five of these qualified and completed the required number. The prisoner then struck four of the names, and the court empanelled the twelve jurors necessary for the trial to proceed.[14]

Richard Harrison, a fine young man, had been brutally murdered.[15] The community demanded justice. The prosecution vowed to deliver it. Dr. Luther R. Stinson testified to the gruesome nature of the victim's

MURDER AT GREEN SPRINGS

wounds. Key prosecution witnesses Lou Mack, a colored laundress, and her sons Ed Harris [22] and Bill Harris [13] each took the stand. Together they totaled half of the Commonwealth's witnesses.

Lou's husband Charles Mack was a section laborer for the C & O Railway.[16] Angle had produced the poor, black laborer's family as witnesses. Angle was Mack's employer's own policeman. Intimidation was unavoidable and produced selective remembrances. Testimonies rang hollow. Besides, black witnesses carried little weight against a white man.

Angle's remaining witnesses testified to statements by the accused placing Jackson in both Columbia and Howardsville at the time of the murder: towns in opposite directions from Scottsville and further removed than Warren. The prosecution asserted that these inconsistencies proved Jackson had something to hide.

The defense produced only three witnesses. Telegrapher Herbert Faulconer testified that just months before Harrison was killed, someone shot at Faulconer while on duty at the Scottsville station. The bullet missed his head by a mere inch.[17] The prosecution objected to Faulconer's tale claiming it provided added interest, but had no relevance to Harrison's death. The court agreed. Nevertheless, Miss Bell Shaw and Miss Grace Carroll testified to seeing Jackson illuminated by lightning while he slept on the Warren Depot platform about the time of the shooting.

The prosecution's case rested solely on Angle's work and his assumption that the Jackson could not have delivered facts about the shooting as early as he did unless he killed Harrison. But what time was that? Neither the hobo nor the indigent witnesses owned timepieces. Could any of them even read a clock face? These were moot points. The two white women provided a solid alibi.

Even after a very late start, the jury heard the evidence, the arguments, and the judge's instructions, deliberated, and decided the case in a single day. Foreman W. B. Bibb read the verdict, "We the jury find the prisoner L. L. Jackson not guilty."[18] Jackson was then freed and wisely left the area.[19]

The prosecution's case was so weak that the public accepted the verdict without a whimper.[20] After six month's newspaper publicity, Special Agent Angle's investigation had been, essentially, laughed out of court. The real killer remained at large. Angle was mortified.

The aggravation and humiliation of Jackson's acquittal diminished little after two months. Now Special Agent Angle prepared to investigate another murder. Scherer had provided few facts. Not much was known other than there had been a fire at Green Springs Depot and one of their railway agents shot dead. Angle and Mallory left the C & O's office at Ninth and Main. Each went home, packed their bags and met at Main Street Station to catch the afternoon train.

They arrived in Louisa at 4:03 P.M. Angle and Mallory sensed the excitement about the shooting when they stepped from the train. They walked directly to the sheriff's office beside the courthouse. They found the jail under unusually heavy guard. Sheriff Andrew M. Wash sat behind his desk talking with friends who had stopped by to inquire about the arson and murder. It had been a long couple of days for Wash. He was due for some rest.

Wash expected the C & O to send their detectives. He knew Angle from previous assignments, but was not acquainted with Mallory who had only recently become a detective having transferred from freight inspection. After introductions, Wash informed the agents that Deputy Bob Trice had captured and jailed a fugitive that afternoon. Most agreed this was fortunate for the man. With local feelings running high, summary justice was expected for any real suspect.[21] If Mr. Bibb had not sent Trice to investigate the escapee's rumored location, the convict might have fallen into the hands of a lynch mob.

The Negro denied having been anywhere near Green Springs. Upon learning of the murder, the captive's calm demeanor turned to panic, and he begged not to be taken near the crime scene.[22] Judging from his behavior, the time of escape and the route taken, the miserable wretch had to be telling the truth.

There was little action the sheriff could take that day other than sending out posses. Deputy James C. Trice, brother of Bob Trice, was county jailor and keeper of the county's two bloodhounds. Normally Wash would have employed the bloodhounds at the crime scene, but because of the heavy rain the night of the murder, the dogs were useless.[23] Wash expected to get out to Green Springs the following afternoon. He saw no need to trouble the families until after the funeral. Wash felt relief knowing that the two detectives had arrived to begin the railroad's investigation. The Chesapeake and Ohio Railway took the deaths of their employees seriously.

Wash asked Angle about the Harrison case. Like many folks in the county, Wash had followed the newspaper reports of the Scottsville shooting and the trial. Angle believed the hobo had gotten away with murder, and the verdict was still a sore spot. The outcome had reflected badly on his efforts and spoiled his notoriety.

Was there any connection between the Harrison and Hall killings? Angle doubted it. The sheriff wished him better luck with this new case and suggested that he and Mallory check back with him in the morning.

Angle and Mallory left. They stopped at the corner barbershop for shaves. Until they could get to Green Springs, there were few better places to start an investigation than the local barbershop, especially one next to the courthouse in the small county seat. The barbershop society had already formed opinions. Leaks from the courthouse lifted suspicion from the recaptured convict, though many remained skeptical.

Angle and Mallory took turns in the chair. They learned that most considered the Dunkums and Halls good people living in the roughest section of the county and that whoever torched Dunkum's store must have shot Hall. That seemed reasonable.

The two freshly shaven detectives crossed Main Street at the nearest mud boards and walked down the block to the Louisa Hotel. One seldom had trouble finding accommodations there, except perhaps on court day. Many residences in Louisa offered rooms and board, but the Louisa Hotel was the only proper hotel in town. Two dollars per day was more expensive than other lodgings, but it suited Angle's needs best when on assignment in the area.[24] Besides, he and Mallory lodged together at the railroad's expense.

Proprietor S. S. Griffith welcomed the detectives and showed them to their room. The murder of young Hall was big news around the supper table and afterwards in the lobby. Such excitement was rare in the county. Guests eagerly shared whatever they had heard. Angle and Mallory each noted the emphasis everyone placed on the couple's ages. The victim was only twenty-seven while his wife was forty. The age difference was extraordinary, though not necessarily improper as some inferred.

Angle and Mallory awoke at dawn. They dressed and readied themselves for the day. There was no need to hurry; the sheriff's office did not open until eight o'clock. The detectives went down to the dining room and accepted the hospitality of several already seated for breakfast. All were enthusiastically engaged in the first newspaper reports about the murder.

The editions published the previous afternoon reached Louisa early that morning. The headlines of Charlottesville's *Daily Progress* read "TRAGEDY AT GREEN SPRINGS: Burglary, Arson and Murder Reported: STATION AGENT SHOT." The front page of Richmond's *News Leader* was even more dramatic: "MANY MEN SEEK MURDEROUS FIEND." The subheading continued about posses, firebugs and murder. Angle noted that the publicity was far more intense than any given the Harrison case.

Angle and Mallory ate breakfast and listened to locals recount several other murders in Louisa County. Some remembered an arson-murder in Yanceyville in 1879. But the Hall store was especially notorious. Two other murders had already occurred there; the second in 1905 made headlines in the big city papers. The detectives absorbed the amazing facts. They downed their last swallows of coffee and headed over to the sheriff's office.

The men learned that Sheriff Wash was sending Deputy Bob Trice back to Trevilians to look for a pistol just in case their prisoner discarded one before recapture.[25] Nevertheless, the search for Hall's killer had shifted to Green Springs. Wash allowed the detectives to read the coroner's report, the only written record available. Wash relayed instructions for them to report their findings to Commonwealth's Attorney Bibb. Angle and Mallory left the jailhouse, walked to the depot and waited for the westbound train due at 9:10 A.M.

The train left Main Street Station in Richmond at 7:00 A.M. By the time it reached Hanover at 7:41 A.M., passengers talked excitedly about the newspaper reports of the arson-murder and anticipated viewing the scene as they passed through Green Springs.

Detective George W. Scott of the Virginia State Insurance Bureau sat austere and aloof while attentive to every mention of the subject. Scott, a man in his early sixties, wore a dark brown, vested, wool suit which fit his heavy-set frame well. A cane and leather portfolio accented his distinguished appearance. A dark bowler surmounted his head of thick, neatly trimmed, gray-white hair. White, mutton-chop sideburns covered the jowls of his aging, ruddy, round face. These connected to the full, white moustache hanging over pouting lips. His bulbous nose and bushy set of white eyebrows completed the impression that someone's loveable, old "Uncle George" was going somewhere for a visit. But as the trip progressed, Scott's countenance grew rather bulldog-like.[26]

The Virginia Fire and Marine Insurance Company had already paid claims twice to W. R. Dunkum for fires at Green Springs. Though arson was suspected in both instances, the company could prove nothing. The store fire was the third such occurrence within a year. This eliminated any notions of coincidence. The fires were arsons. The insurance company demanded action. The Virginia State Insurance Bureau opened Case No. 188 and assigned Scott to investigate.[27]

Scott had been an investigator with the bureau since its founding in 1902. He feared that unless the matter was clear cut, identifying an arsonist in the small, clannish, rural community was virtually impossible. To complicate matters further, the arson-murder was statewide news. No case had ever received higher visibility. Negative attention in this limelight was unthinkable. Failure meant public embarrassment to the bureau. Scott was but a few years from qualifying for his pension. He was too old to risk starting over. The investigator earnestly hoped for the simplest solution: namely, Dunkum discovered that the arsonist was his chief business competitor and killed Hall in retaliation.

Special Agents Angle and Mallory boarded the train at Louisa and took the first open seats. The train accelerated then slowed to stop at Trevilians. After a brief freight delivery, it chugged on to Green Springs.

Most passengers expected only a brief glimpse of Green Springs Depot in passing, but as the train slowed again, they realized it was flagged to stop there. The coaches pulled to the platform. The brashest passengers sprang into the aisle for a better look. This encouraged those more reserved to follow suit. Seated passengers winced at the buffeting as rude bodies bumped and pushed against them straining for views and catching their balance as the cars lurched to a stop. Despite apologies, curiosity overcame courtesy, and the behavior continued. About half the travelers were out of their seats alternately looking out one side then the other.

MURDER AT GREEN SPRINGS

Debarking passengers pressed their way awkwardly through the confusion and exited the cars. Ladies stepped down assisted by their companions and the conductor. The detectives exited and positioned themselves to survey the other arrivals. Scott's eyes met those of Angle's in mutual recognition, and then both redirected their attentions back to the other passengers.

Except for the detectives, everyone stepping from the train had come for Hall's funeral. These walked from the depot across the dirt lane to the large gray weatherboard structure. The Hall store and residence was not much by city standards, but it was a significant structure in a neighborhood of little log houses.

"'Board!" shouted the conductor signaling the end of the train's brief business and its departure. The whistle blew a short blast, the bell clanged and the engine thrust off on its way. Scott nodded good morning to the gawkers giving him the eye, some sat on a bench, others leaned against the depot, but all watched the three detectives intently.

Angle and Scott already knew each other. Angle bore a similar, serious countenance to Scott, but in contrast to Scott's bulldog-like image, Angle looked weasel-like. He was average height, thin, wiry looking and in his mid-forties. Angle had on a well-worn, wrinkled suit jacket, narrow necktie, and a battered, pork pie hat. Angle was the stereotypical *Railroad Dick*.[28] Mallory was a little older and heavier than Angle. He was similarly dressed, but being new in the position had not yet attained a detective's bearing.

The number of buggies and wagons already parked around the store and a few arriving in the manner of latecomers indicated that the funeral was about to begin. The detectives would not be able to interview the Hall and Dunkum families until afterwards. Scott decided to look around. He stepped from the platform and walked to the road with Angle and Mallory following. They crossed the tracks and approached the blackened foundation of Dunkum's store. Scott walked the perimeter intently observing details and pondering impressions.

DETECTIVES PUT ON THE CASE

The detectives turned their attention to the funeral procession and joined in behind the last mourners. After the interment, they followed the family back to the residence. It was an indelicate time to interview the widow and her family, but the investigation needed to proceed. The men minimized their intrusion by interviewing Mrs. Hall together.

The dwelling was full of family, friends and neighbors staying for the traditional post-burial meal and fellowship. The detectives introduced themselves to the widow Hall. Each displayed a gold badge bearing the seal of the Commonwealth of Virginia. The men offered their condolences and asked to hear her story.

The widow told what happened. She showed the detectives the bedroom, the store and the site of the shooting. Scott inquired about William R. Dunkum. Lizzie answered questions about Buck and their unique family and business relationships. The men also wanted to talk to Dunkum, but Lizzie explained that Buck and his family had gone home. Scott begged leave and excused himself to find Dunkum. Angle and Mallory remained to speak with other family members.

Lizzie received a large number of guests including good friends Elsie Yancey and her husband Lewis. Elsie and her mother served together with Lizzie in their church's ladies aid society. Lewis had known Lizzie for over a decade, since when she and her family lived in Fluvanna County. Lewis had also managed the store before Lizzie and her first husband bought it.

Lizzie shared details of her ordeal with the Yanceys and other friends. She was tired, weary of the tale, and tended toward brevity. Consequently, when recalling conversations days later, what Lizzie intended and what guests remembered varied somewhat in context.

Most visitors had gone by mid afternoon. Even though Lizzie expected two of her sisters to be with her before evening, she and her daughters were afraid to stay at the store overnight. They planned to sleep at the Halls. Lizzie told friend Lennie Roberts that she worried about leaving the store unoccupied. Upon hearing this, Bill Roberts offered his *helping hand.* Roberts suggested that he stay overnight, watch the store, and to do whatever else he could to help. Lizzie was not sure what to do. She appreciated Bill's offer and believed him sincere, but she did not know Lennie's brother well. Lizzie preferred to decline; however, she knew she would rest easier with someone guarding the store. She accepted his offer.

Lizzie's sisters Carrie Dowdy and Katie Wooten arrived at 4:20 P.M. Nicholas Hall met their train with Charles Chisholm and walked the ladies over to the residence. Lizzie greeted them at her door. The three women kissed and embraced. Chisholm stood behind them with their bags. Lizzie broke into tears and sobbed. This was the first emotional release she had allowed herself since the shooting.[29]

The women tarried a few minutes in the parlor until Carrie's and Katie's attentions were diverted by the vibration and sounds of another arriving train. Lizzie, accustomed to living beside the tracks, never paid much attention to the trains much. It was the 5:00 P.M. train flagged to shuttle the three detectives back to Louisa.

Sheriff Wash visited Mrs. Hall early that evening. Green Springs resident George Trainham drove the sheriff there in his car. Trainham, a prospering lumberman, volunteered to assist the sheriff during the sudden flood of work and was duly deputized.

The mannerly Wash had delayed approaching Mrs. Hall. He was still recovering from the taxing manhunt of the past two days. Hat in one hand, Wash pushed his sparse gray hair back over his balding, round head with the other, and then knocked on the door. Essie answered and welcomed the men inside. She showed them into the parlor and summoned her mother who was busy with her sisters visiting and tidying up together in the kitchen.

Wash and Trainham paid their respects and apologized for having to pursue duty at such a sad time. They asked Mrs. Hall to tell her story of what happened the night Victor was killed beginning with the fire. This she did. With Essie accompanying her, Mrs. Hall walked the men through the bedroom and store recounting the events as she had done so many times already. Trainham produced a notebook and pencil from his coat pocket and began writing.

"Victor got out of bed saying, 'Papa has come back. Guess Mama sent him.' In a few moments, I heard him holler 'Oh! Lordy! Help me!' or a 'Mercy!' and almost immediately I heard a shot. I think [I] got up and run [sic] out and called the little colored girl. I thought I would never wake her. I then came back and went into the store and found Victor crumpled up between the counters.

"I called to him, but he did not answer me. I then run [sic] out in front of [the] store and called Buck – I don't know how many times I called him – I then came back and got a pillow and put it under Victor's head. When I raised his head to put the pillow under it, the blood got all onto my hands and spurted up in my face."

Essie injected, "Oh! Mama was so bloody; I thought . . . I really thought Mama was shot."

Mrs. Hall continued, "Then the girls came down. . . ."

Sheriff Wash stopped her to ask, "Was the door [to the front of the store] open?"

"I was so excited," Mrs. Hall apologized, "I am not sure whether it was or no[t]. I think it was closed, but not caught to – as that door does not catch when left open, but goes nearly shut, but does not catch togather [sic]."[30]

When Mrs. Hall finished, Wash probed Buck Dunkum's personal and business dealings with Victor and Buck's actions at the crime scene. Lizzie told everything she knew, but assured the sheriff that Buck could not have done it. Satisfied with Mrs. Hall's answers, Wash and Trainham thanked her and Essie for their time. They again expressed sympathy for their loss and left.

Lizzie, her daughters, and sisters finished straightening up. They left the store in the capable *hand* of Bill Roberts and walked to N. W. Hall's to spend the night. The interviews that day became chief topic for the rest of the evening. Everyone was upset over suspicions about Buck. Sheriff Wash only hinted at his misgivings, but Angle and Scott clearly suspected that Buck killed Victor for setting fire to his store. The idea was ridiculous, and Nicholas Hall had let the detectives know it when he spoke with them.

Sterling Hall was incensed over the detectives' crass notion that Victor burned Dunkum's store. This not only threatened to ruin his late brother's good name, but jeopardized his estate. Sterling voiced concerns and proposed that they hire their own private detective to find the killer and protect their interests. Lizzie knew little of such matters and deferred to Sterling's judgment. Nevertheless, Lizzie suggested that Sterling ask their insurance company which detectives they used. Sterling nodded as if considering Lizzie's suggestion, but he had already decided to hire a Pinkerton man.

Upon returning to Louisa at 5:12 P.M., Scott, Angle and Mallory met with Commonwealth's Attorney Bibb in his office beside the courthouse.[31] The detectives now had multiple suspects, but favored one in particular. The murder was not as clear cut as Bibb had hoped. He needed to interview Mrs. Hall personally.

The detectives lodged at the Louisa Hotel that night and dined together. Scott was acquainted with "Monte" Angle, as friends knew him, and his family. Scott was, perhaps, most familiar with Special Agent Angle's uncle James B. Angle. "Jimmy" had retired several years before as a solicitor for the Virginia Fire and Marine Insurance Company. This followed an earlier career on the Richmond police force. Jimmy Angle held the rank of police captain for many years until forced to resign in 1902 to avoid prosecution in a gambling and prostitution scandal.[32] Jimmy then secured a position with the respected insurance company through his social connections and veneration as a Confederate veteran. Scott found it ironic that he and Jimmy's nephew were now investigating the same case.

The detectives compared notes on the arson and murder. Collectively, their information agreed, and the day's research cast considerable doubt on Buck Dunkum's involvement. If Hall burned his store, it clearly gave Dunkum motive to retaliate. But opportunity was tenuous since Dunkum's wife provided him a strong alibi. Unless her complicity could be proved, Dunkum's guilt was unlikely. Who else had reason to kill Hall? Their investigation had not progressed that far, but the detectives were determined to unmask the culprit.

Scott was leery of the whole Dunkum clan. Their valuable property embraced a full mile of railroad track and main county road. The family managed the post office and rail depot, at one time a broom factory, owned the only two general stores for miles, and all located right smack dab in the middle of their own farmland. They essentially controlled their own fiefdom. Green Springs Depot might as well have been called *Dunkumville*. It was hard for Scott to imagine people with such control not wanting to press advantages.

Did the success of those *come here's* from Buckingham County provoke some disgruntled native to jealous rage? Was there a power struggle within the family? Common sense narrowed the choice to one or the other.

What about that gun? Bibb's revelation that afternoon about examining the victim's .38 revolver with a spent round was a surprise. What chance was there that that was coincidence? Angle and Scott thought it very odd for such a detail to be omitted by the coroner's jury. Why was it that no one involved at the scene mentioned this to them? Surely a business man in that neck of the woods kept his pistol fully loaded.

As best as they could tell, the position of the body coupled with the description of the wound suggested that the victim was shot as he lay and then dragged from the bedroom. If so, the killer was someone within the family. Who was it? Was there an accomplice?

Friday morning Angle, Mallory and Scott checked out of the Louisa Hotel at eight o'clock and consulted Sheriff Wash at the jailhouse. There were no new developments other than Mrs. Hall had told Wash the same story she had told them.

The detectives went to the Louisa Station and waited for train No. 19 to Green Springs. They sat and read the latest newspapers. Angle fumed over the *Daily Progress's* report. It identified "L. H. Jackson" as the escaped convict caught and jailed.[33] The front page story not only confused the prisoner with Angle's suspect in the Harrison Case, but wrongly presented half a dozen other facts. The doctors, the wound, and the general situation had all been misstated.

While Mallory listened to his partner rant, Scott's solemn countenance broke into a rare smile. Angle was clearly the newspaper's source. Facts were not the real issue. Angle was disgusted that the newspaper had made no mention of Angle.

Upon arrival at Green Springs, the detectives stored their bags at the depot for the day. Scott agreed to rendezvous back there in the afternoon and parted company with the Special Agents.

At the Hall store, the entire family, including visiting sisters, pitched in to clean the residence and store and set things in order. Sterling Hall attended to estate matters. He telephoned the New York Mutual Life Insurance Company about Victor's two life insurance policies. He also called the district office of the Pinkerton National Detective Agency in Richmond. Hall spoke with Superintendent J. W. Erb and arranged for a private detective. Erb quoted the standard nationwide agency rate of eight dollars per day plus expenses.

The estate was due $2,000 from policies. Considering risks in light of the investigations already under way, hiring a Pinkerton man was cheap protection. Sterling accepted the terms and scheduled a meeting with Detective Robert MacKay in Louisa the next afternoon.

Sterling briefed Lizzie and his father on matters. The insurance claims were in order, but because of the events surrounding Victor's death, the redemptions were best handled through an attorney. Sterling also informed them that he had hired a Pinkerton detective.

Eight dollars a day! That seemed so expensive. Lizzie felt overwhelmed by matters anyway. She looked to Nicholas. Sterling's father balked at the notion of spending so much money for a private detective, but ultimately agreed that Sterling was doing the right thing.

Sterling suggested calling his friend Mr. Bibb, the commonwealth's attorney to handle the insurance claims. Lizzie normally used attorney R. Lindsay Gordon, Jr. Since Bill Roberts had his brother's automobile, Lizzie asked Roberts to go to Louisa and deliver the policies to Mr. Gordon. Roberts, always eager to lend his hand, drove the papers to Louisa.

Roberts and Gordon had been on friendly terms since the settlement of his son's custody the previous year. After divorcing Bill, wife Pattie contracted tuberculosis.[34] On account of Bill's disabilities, the dying woman asked Lindsay Gordon to take care of raising her son Henry.[35] Gordon agreed to the request. The kind hearted Gordon and his wife took young Henry in to live with them upon Pattie's death.

MURDER AT GREEN SPRINGS

Bill believed his son belonged with his father and filed for custody. Bill convinced Gordon that he and his siblings were able to care for Henry, who was then nearly fourteen and wanted to live with his papa. Gordon allowed Henry to do so without contest. Roberts and his family were very grateful for Gordon's understanding.

Upon sending Roberts on his errand, Lizzie returned to domestic matters. While dusting in the downstairs bedroom, Essie called her mother's attention to the spent pistol cartridge on the mantel. Lizzie had no idea why it was there and paid it no mind. Essie stored it in matchbox rather than discard it.

Earlier in the day, Commonwealth's Attorney Bibb called upon his uncle J. Frank Bickers to drive him to Green Springs Depot to interview Mrs. Hall. Unable to reach Mrs. Hall on her busy phone, Bibb and Bickers arrived unannounced in the late morning to find the family hard at work trying to order their lives sufficiently to reopen the store. By then, Elsie Wood had also come to help. Sterling greeted Bibb and Bickers, and then brought Mrs. Hall out to her callers.

Bibb questioned her at length about her story and concentrated on her immediate actions after hearing the shot and the strange position of Victor's body. Bibb sought fine detail. Mrs. Hall framed simple answers. Bibb often rephrased his questions hoping to elicit more precise responses. Mrs. Hall heard only the same questions and gave the same answers. The interview taxed the patience of both.

Mrs. Hall invited Bibb to stay for dinner. As was normally the case from noon time until about two, the dining room was crowded with family, railroad hands, and others taking meals there. After eating, Bibb asked to speak with Elsie Wood alone. The two went into the store for a while and then walked around outside for nearly an hour.

Bibb asked her what she knew about Victor Hall's pistol. Miss Wood had grown up on a farm and liked to ride and shoot. Many wild animals in the area had hydrophobia, and ranging mad dogs were common. Also, she and Miss Rosson frequently encountered hobos along the road beside the railroad tracks on their way to the school. Carrying a gun made her feel safe. She sometimes borrowed Victor Hall's pistol after both of hers broke.

Mr. Hall's revolver was a type known as a *lemon squeezer* because the grip safety must be squeezed when firing.[36] Miss Wood explained that she fired Hall's gun once at a railroad milepost on the way home from teaching school.[37] It was late February or early March as best she recalled. She had never fired a pistol like that before and was curious how it worked. Her story made sense.

While Bibb and Woods walked and talked, Ernest Marks stopped by to visit Mrs. Hall. Ernest, one of Mary Dunkum's brothers and a long time friend of Lizzie and her family, had arrived that morning on the train from Richmond to spend the day. He paid his respects and found Lizzie fretting about Mr. Bibb's inquiries. She anxiously rattled on about the murder.

Ernest became uncomfortable and excused himself. As he left, Lizzie urged Ernest to warn Buck to be careful about what he said because the detectives suspected that Buck killed Victor.

Bibb concluded his business. He and Bickers thanked Mrs. Hall for her hospitality. They apologized for any inconvenience and left. Lizzie wondered why Bibb asked so many questions and why he spent so much time with Miss Wood. She nervously asked Elsie about her conversation and wanted to know all that was said.

Sterling Hall sat at a desk studying papers within earshot of the women. Mrs. Hall seemed particularly overwrought about Bibb's visit. Sterling grasped that the issue was more than mere concern over Buck. When Elsie Wood left the room, Mrs. Hall turned to Sterling and said that she reckoned she would go to the electric chair if it were not for the two school teachers.[38] The remark troubled Sterling Hall deeply.

Bibb and Bickers discussed their visit on their way back to Louisa. Bibb was satisfied with both women's answers. Still, he had problems with the position of the body. The more Bibb considered his interview with Mrs. Hall, the more he wondered whether or not her responses were characteristically simplistic or intentionally evasive. The thought occurred to him that if Victor Hall was shot in his bed, as detectives suggested, the bed clothes must certainly evidence the fact. Bibb regretted that he had not thought to see them. He would have someone check on those later and make sure they were preserved for examination.

About an hour after Bibb left, Elsie Wood said goodbye and returned home. Detective Scott then arrived with Special Agents Angle and Mallory. Their day's work prompted more *bulldog* and *weasel* questions about Buck Dunkum and his relationships with Victor and herself. Mrs. Hall answered as best she could. She declared flatly that there was absolutely no way Buck could have been involved in Victor's death.

The detectives switched topics. They anticipated a long investigation and arranged room and board with Mrs. Hall. The men were taking the train back to Richmond that evening. Scott and Mallory planned to return to Sunday night. Angle had leads to pursue in Richmond. Until his return, Mallory would be his eyes and ears in Green Springs.

Mallory requested the corner room overlooking the depot with a view of Dunkum's property: the room best for surveillance. Mrs. Hall did not currently have a bed in that room, but promised to have one there by Sunday. Scott voiced no preference.

Mrs. Hall explained that she charged a dollar a day room and board. She served a hot dinner at noon each day with supper and breakfast scheduled to best suit them. Satisfied with the terms, the detectives left for the weekend. The three hour train ride together gave the detectives time to talk and theorize.

Despite the many interruptions throughout the day, order slowly replaced chaos. The family had dismantled Victor's bed and moved it to the storage room. Now they needed it again. Other than this, everything was straight by evening. Yes. They would reopen the store Saturday morning. The girls would go back to school Monday. Lizzie knew that renewing their daily routines was good medicine. Fears and uncertainties would subside and hurts heal in time. They always did. Lizzie looked forward to their lives returning to normal.

CHAPTER
Four

HER VERY OWN
PINKERTON MAN

MURDER AT GREEN SPRINGS

*S*aturdays were always the busiest days for rural merchants. The fire and murder forced neighbors who normally bought from Dunkum and Hall to travel to Melton's or Danne's store for necessities. Lizzie was determined to reopen her store on Saturday for the sake of her customers and her livelihood. Lizzie's sisters left after breakfast on the 8:00 A.M. train. She expected their brother Hubert to arrive by evening. Essie, Mamie and Becky busied themselves with household chores while Lizzie reopened the store.

The Hall store was typical for the time. It was a *jot'em down* store. Customers told the counter clerk what they wanted. The clerk jotted down requests on slips of paper, collected the goods from the various shelves along the walls and brought the items to the front of the store for the customer's approval and purchase by cash or charge against their account.

Nicholas and Ellen Hall swept floors, stocked shelves and manned the counters while Lizzie sorted mail and put the post office in order. Charles Chisholm, who had been on the job since sun up tending livestock, as he did every day, transferred accumulated freight deliveries from the depot to the stock room and unpacked crates. Bill Roberts, who had stayed overnight at the store since Thursday, hung around long enough to make sure everything was under control before leaving to return his brother's car.

People trickled into the store to check mail. A few bought necessities. Friends stopped in to see how Lizzie and the girls fared, but sales were light compared with a normal Saturday. Lizzie expected business to pick up again once word got around that her store had reopened. In fact, she expected business to spike until Buck rebuilt his store, but she soon realized things had changed.

Murder made folks skittish. Everyone knew Lizzie and her daughters were afraid to stay there. Superstitious minds believed the ghost of Victor Hall joined those of two other murdered men, smallpox victims and Mrs. Hall's first husband. They all died at *that store!* Many considered the place "*hainted!*"

Lizzie accepted the shunning as temporary and made best use of the slow morning to organize paperwork. She wrestled over whether or not to stay at the store overnight. Sleeping there would draw customers back sooner. This was not an option with just her and the girls there alone, but her brother would be with them by night fall and the detectives after that.

Sheriff Wash arrived in his surrey with Deputy Sheriff Robert Trice. Commonwealth's Attorney Bibb had asked Wash to examine all clothing, furnishings, bedding, and other materials related to the crime and make sure that they were preserved. There had been a fire the previous night at Oakland seven miles away.[1] Wash needed to return to investigate the fire in the daylight. The Sheriff delegated the job of examining the articles to Deputy Bob Trice.

Trice entered the store and identified himself to Mrs. Hall stating that he was there to examine the scene and various items involved. Lizzie welcomed the officer and proceeded to show Trice the spot where she found Victor. The deputy interested himself in the blood stains and squatted for a better look at the floor. He then stood and walked around the counter. Nicholas Hall followed. Trice halted at the bloodstained floor beside where the autopsy was performed. Nicholas pulled a bundle from underneath the counter. The square yard of oil cloth contained sundry bloodied rags from the autopsy.[2] Trice looked through the pile then moved along. Hall rewrapped and returned the bundle to its place.

Nicholas stayed in the store while Lizzie ushered the deputy into the bedroom. Ellen Hall went with them. The bed was gone. Lizzie explained that they had moved the bed to the storage room since nobody wanted to sleep on it anymore. Trice asked about the clothing and bed linens. Lizzie

said that they buried Victor's bloody nightshirt after the autopsy, but she still had her bloodstained nightgown. The bloody bedclothes and bolster were taken off the bed after Victor's death. She had those too. Trice wanted to see the items for himself.

Lizzie fetched the key and led Trice outside to the storage room. She unlocked the door and both went inside. The room was intended as a stock room when the store was built. It had once been used as a bedroom. Victor had tried it briefly as an office; writing materials were still kept there. The family mostly considered the space a junk room and moved Victor's death bed there to get it out of sight.

As they entered the room, the blood soaked bolster was in plain sight on top of some junk against the wall. A nominal putrescence from the blood matted feathers inside the bolster tainted the musty air. Lizzie opened the window. She got her black nightgown and the bed linens from off top a trunk in the corner. Lizzie draped her nightgown open over a chair and unfurled the bed sheets and held them up for inspection. Trice examined the brown stains on the black garment and the spotted linens. He picked up the pillow, looked it over and set it down. Trice did the same with the disgustingly bloodied bolster and handled it just enough to determine that the blood soaked through the feathers and not just covered the outside. Trice advised Mrs. Hall that she needed to retain everything until the investigation was completed.

Lizzie agreed, but added that she needed to furnish rooms for the detectives and asked if she could move Victor's furniture upstairs.[3] Trice said that only Sheriff Wash had authority to approve such use.

Meanwhile, Sterling Hall took the 1:30 P.M. train to Louisa to meet with Pinkerton Detective Robert Mackay at the Louisa Hotel. Sterling found Mackay waiting for him in the dining room. Mackay's shock of red hair immediately caught Sterling's attention. After introductions, Mackay briefed Sterling on the company's procedures.

When Alan Pinkerton first founded the Pinkerton National Detective Agency, he established guidelines to prevent his detectives from working at cross purposes with legal authorities and to avoid representing criminals. Company procedure always required clients to contract work directly through the district superintendent. This isolated detectives from business entanglements.

Detective Mackay needed to meet with his client to sign the work agreement and gather background information. Once accomplished, Mackay would check with local authorities for permission to proceed with the investigation. This last step was particularly important in criminal matters.

The Pinkerton National Detective Agency normally serviced large firms and wealthy clients. Experience had taught the agency to be leery of ordinary citizens employing their services. It was common for a person with something to hide to hire a detective in order to appear innocent. With so much publicity and so many people involved already, Victor Hall's murder was already *red flagged.*

As arranged through Superintendent Erb, Mackay's assignment was to investigate the murder of Victor Hall on behalf of his estate. Per company procedure, Mackay would report daily to the Richmond office. The clerical staff would prepare formal reports. Once approved by Superintendent Erb, these would be mailed to the person or persons contracting the work. In this case, Erb recognized North Carolina resident Sterling Hall as the client.

Sterling explained that Mrs. Hall was administratrix of his brother's estate and, therefore, the proper person to sign the payment agreement. Though Sterling was anxious to get the investigation under way, Mackay still had to clear his mission with local authorities. Mackay had already spoken briefly with Sheriff Wash. Wash, in turn, directed Mackay to speak with Commonwealth's Attorney Bibb before proceeding. Wash called Bibb's home for Mackay, but was unable to reach him. Mackay hoped to meet with Bibb on the morrow. That day being Sunday, Mackay had to wait and see.

Sterling offered Mackay accommodations at the Hall store during his investigation. Mackay agreed that the store would make the best base of operations and minimize expenses. Still, he had to remain in Louisa until Bibb permitted him to proceed.

Sterling returned on the afternoon train with news that Mrs. Hall now had her very own Pinkerton man. Lizzie had already anticipated her detective staying there. Sheriff Wash had granted Mrs. Hall permission to use Victor's bed, so there was ample sleeping space. The big advantage to the policemen rooming there at the store was that Lizzie and the girls could safely move back home.

In the process of shifting items around the junk room earlier, Becky Coates knocked over a large bottle of India ink. Over a pint spilled. Ellen Hall saw the hopeless mess and got after Becky. The blackest black ink stained a trunk, the floor, ruined some clothes and other items including the bloody bolster. They set the messy bolster aside to dry since they had been told to preserve it.

Lizzie's brother Hubert Dowdy arrived by buggy. The family went out back to welcome him at the watering trough where he tended his horse after the long trip from Cumberland County.[4] Lizzie was delighted to see her brother who had driven so far, but disappointed to hear that he only planned to stay one night. Essie and Mamie went with "Uncle Hugh" as he walked his rig into the barn to unhitch, feed, and groom his traveler.

Lizzie felt safe with Hugh there. But no one was happy about sleeping at the store.

The many God fearing people of Louisa observed Sunday as a day of rest. Nevertheless, Commonwealth's Attorney Bibb met with Mackay before church. Both men regarded the employment of a private detective by an individual as extraordinary. Bibb granted the detective permission to proceed under the expected stipulation that Mackay keep him informed and provide copies of all reports. Thus, having complied with company policy, Mackay left for Green Springs.

The weather was seasonably mild. Those loitering outside the depot hushed when Sterling Hall approached to meet the 4:18 P.M. train. Mackay stepped from the passenger car bag in hand. Sterling greeted Mackay and walked him over to the store.

After introductions, Lizzie took Mackay upstairs and showed him to his room. They then went back downstairs to the parlor where Mackay reviewed procedures with her as he had with Sterling. He stated that he would interview each family member separately. Individual statements would then be typed and presented for signature. Once signed, the statements would be returned to the Richmond office as part of the case record. Mackay explained that at no time was he at liberty to discuss his findings outside of official reports.

Everything sounded good to Lizzie. She dipped her pen in ink and signed the payment agreement. Sterling signed as witness. Mackay went to work.

Lizzie told her story as she had done so many times already. She spoke mechanically and few with gestures. Her tone was flat and her narrative simple. She said that the first thing she did after hearing the shot was go wake the little colored girl. She walked Mackay back and forth through the bedroom and the store. Mackay jotted notes as the widow Hall identified positions related to the crime. Mackay asked questions and rehearsed events in his mind. When Mackay asked for clarifications, Mrs. Hall qualified most answers with an "I think" or "I don't know exactly."

They went out onto the front porch of the store where Lizzie told how she called for Buck. She told how Elsie Wood fetched Victor's gun because she was scared that the burglar might come back. Mackay asked to see the weapon. Lizzie went back inside and got the pistol out of the bedroom dresser where it was normally kept. She returned and handed the pistol to Mackay. He flipped the thumb latch and broke the pistol open. There were four live rounds and an empty cylinder position where the detective expected to find the spent cartridge.

Mackay wanted to know what happened to the empty shell. Lizzie did not know. She remembered Essie finding one on the mantel the other day, but she did not know what Essie had done with it. Mackay emphasized the importance of finding that shell.

Mackay asked if there were any more guns in the house. Victor owned a .22 caliber rifle. Mackay passed over that. Mrs. Hall said that there were two more pistols and led the detective upstairs to Elsie Wood's room. Lizzie opened a dresser drawer and explained that both guns belonged to Miss Wood. Mackay examined each and determined that the .32 caliber pistol had a broken spring and the .38 caliber Bulldog revolver was rusted tight; the cylinder would not turn at all. Neither pistol could be fired.

The initial interview ended as Ellen Hall announced supper on the table. Mackay met the rest of the family. Afterwards, Sterling, Nicholas, and Mackay talked in the parlor while the women cleaned up.

At 8:30 P.M. Scott and Mallory arrived on train No. 1. Mrs. Hall introduced the detectives to Mackay and then showed Scott and Mallory to their respective rooms. The Halls left soon afterwards. Sterling promised to be back early in the morning with his father's buggy to take Mackay around the neighborhood. The women retired after making sure their guests were comfortable. Lizzie and her daughters slept sound and secure in the presence of so many armed protectors.

The detectives rose early Monday. The men finished their toilets and met in the dining room for breakfast. The smell of freshly ground coffee was distinct and complemented the other savory aromas. Detectives Scott and Mallory ate and then went on their way.

Sterling Hall arrived to pick up Mackay. They were about to leave when Mrs. Hall called them into the parlor. The widow produced a matchbox and opened it. She reached in with her fingers and picked up a spent cartridge from inside. Handing it to Mackay she explained how Essie had found the shell on the mantel Friday and put it in the matchbox for safekeeping.

Mackay examined the shell inside and out. The .38 caliber U.M.C. cartridge bore markings identical to the live rounds in Victor Hall's pistol. After placing it to his nose, Mackay passed it to Sterling who repeated his actions and handed the shell back. Each looked the other in the eye as if sharing a mutual discovery. Mackay replaced the shell in the matchbox, pocketed it for safekeeping, and thanked Mrs. Hall for finding it. This done, Sterling and Mackay left. Once outside, the two men discussed the cartridge's timely reappearance. And both agreed. It smelled like coffee.

For the first time since the shooting, Essie and Mamie left the house on their two mile trek to Mr. Blackwell's school.[5] Lizzie opened the store. For the moment, her greatest concern was for her business. There was none. She was not particularly surprised that sales were slow when they first reopened, but Monday was essentially dead. There was considerable activity across the road at the depot. Lizzie paid that little mind until Charles Chisholm returned after checking for deliveries and reported that Buck was selling his wares at the train station. Not only had the Chesapeake and Ohio Railway made Dunkum temporarily station master on Friday, but they had also granted him special permission to operate his grocery business out of the depot shed until his store could be rebuilt.

Lizzie spent much time that morning calling her few friends with telephones. She wanted to know what they had heard and their opinions

MURDER AT GREEN SPRINGS

on whether or not her business would ever return. Lizzie spoke freely of developments as she knew them and shared with everyone that she now had her own detective on the case. The employment of the Pinkerton man made her feel secure.

With no customers and little else to do in the store, Ellen Hall cleaned and straightened the shelves. She called Lizzie's attention to the bundle of bloodstained rags wrapped in the oil cloth under the counter. Recalling Deputy Trice's disinterest in them, Lizzie told her to throw them away. Ellen gave them to Chisholm to bury.

When Sterling Hall and Mackay returned at midday for dinner, they pulled up beside the barn and noticed Chisholm, shovel in hand, coming back from across the pasture. When questioned, Chisholm told them that he had just buried some bloody rags like he had done before.

The action struck both Sterling and Mackay as suspicious. Hall told Chisholm to go dig up everything and bring it all to the stable. Sterling Hall, Mackay and Scott gathered after dinner to examine each dirty, bloodstained article. They found nothing remarkable. Sterling told Chisholm to go rebury everything. The men tarried and discussed their perceptions of Mrs. Hall.

On Tuesday morning detective Scott finished his breakfast and informed Mrs. Hall, much to her surprise, that it was time to settle his account. He explained that since he was there to investigate the arson, he thought it best to lodge with the Dunkums instead.[6] Scott paid his bill and left with his things.

Sterling Hall had stayed at Green Springs as long as he dared and needed to return to his job in Charlotte. Before catching the morning train, he stopped at the store briefly for a word with Mackay and learned of

Scott's relocation. Special Agent Mallory still roomed there, as far as Mackay knew, but he had not seen Mallory that morning. He had apparently gotten up with the chickens and was already out in the neighborhood.

Lizzie opened the store. A few close friends came by and purchased items, but it was obvious that people preferred to buy from Dunkum. Special Agent Mallory returned with Angle for dinner at midday. After eating, Mallory asked to settle his account. Mallory was the last of her paying guests.

Lizzie was troubled about finances, but now, even with the loss of her last boarder, income became a secondary concern. The detectives' coolness and their abrupt departures made Lizzie feel uneasy. Everything seemed wrong. Her apprehension swelled throughout the day like a fermenting yeast cake.

Wednesday marked the passing of one full week since the murder. Detective Scott roomed with the Dunkum's. Detective Mackay still worked in the neighborhood on behalf the estate. Special Agents Angle and Mallory had become scarce. Customers avoided Mrs. Hall's store. In contrast, Buck Dunkum's had continuous traffic.

Mamie Rosson telephoned midmorning to ask if she could stop by that evening to collect the rest of her belongings. Lizzie welcomed her visit. She needed to talk to people.

Lizzie telephoned Maggie Smith, her friend in Louisa. Maggie was about to call her. The dentist's wife said that the latest rumor from the courthouse was that Lizzie was suspected of killing Victor. Lizzie's heart sank. How could that be?

There was more. Some people thought she killed Victor in order "to get" Bill Roberts.[7] Lizzie could not believe her ears. Some were also saying that she poisoned her first husband.

Lizzie telephoned Roberts' sister Lennie to ask her about the gossip. Lennie had already heard some of the tales, but not the one about Lizzie and her brother. Lennie promised to do what she could to counter the lies before they spread further. Lizzie spoke freely. Neither Lizzie nor her friends considered that someone might be listening in on her party line.

That afternoon, Lizzie had Nicholas walk her over to the Dunkum's house. She needed to talk to Mary but was too uncomfortable to go alone past staring eyes at the depot. Lizzie felt helpless and confided her fears to Mary. Detective Scott was away, so Lizzie spoke her mind. Mary sympathized with due ambivalence, for suspicion of Lizzie, meant suspicion diverted from Buck.

The latest rumor about killing Victor to get Bill Roberts shocked Mary. Land sakes! She had never heard such hogwash!

Despite everything, Lizzie clung to the fact she had witnesses. She told Mary what she had already told Elsie Yancey and a number of others that "If it were not for the two school teachers, I probably would go to the electric chair."[8] It felt good to air her feelings. However, these details also interested Scott when he returned.

That evening Mamie Rosson came to the store to gather her remaining possessions. Like so many other friends that day Miss Rosson lent a sympathetic ear to Mrs. Hall, who again vented her concerns without a thought to how her words might sound when repeated.

On Thursday, the obituary Nicholas Hall wrote for his son appeared in the *Central Virginian*:

Victor Kelso Hall, youngest son of N. W. and Ellen F. Hall, was born February 6th, 1887, and was killed at Green Spring Depot by an unknown murderer, April 15, 1914, aged 27 years, 2 months and 8 days cut down in the bloom of life without a moment's warning or a chance to say farewell.

Victor had many good qualities. He was kind and tender-hearted in his family relations. He was brave, honorable, and scorned tattling and back-biting. He had great confidence in people, and his uniform courtesy and kindness made him many friends. Everybody liked him, and nobody thought he had an enemy. He hated anything that was mean and contemptible, and despised the sham and the hypocrite. He held membership with the Methodist church and we have reasons to hope that he had laid hold on eternal life.

Victor was quick of mind and hand, and when he took hold of anything something was going to be done. He was indeed a busy man when called from his labor. Besides attending to all the offices at Green Springs he had lately started out in the mercantile business for himself, and was making rapid progress. He leaves father and mother, one brother, and wife and two step-daughters to mourn their sad loss. Surely such a noble soul, real strong mind and determined will, have survived the shock of death.[9]

The announcement published a week after the fact made the tragic death of the youthful merchant all the more distressing. When the family submitted the obituary, the hunt for Victor Hall's murderer had scarcely begun. By the time it was printed, many folks in Louisa County had heard the stories about the widow and believed they knew who the killer was. The tribute fomented outrage. The public pictured Mrs. Hall as being as dangerous and as ruthless as any old black widow spider who preyed upon her mates.

Shrew! Poisoner! Arsonist! Murderess! Hussy!

On Friday April 24th, Mackay presented Mrs. Hall her typed statement for signature. She obliged and seized the opportunity to ask Mackay about his findings. Mackay reminded her that he was not allowed to discuss the case with anyone. He explained that he submitted daily reports to the Richmond office and that he expected the agency to issue its reports soon.

Mackay inquired further into Mr. and Mrs. Hall's relationship with each other. Mrs. Hall produced several love letters Victor had written during their courtship. Victor expressed high admiration and affection for Lizzie in each. While Mackay read the letters, Mrs. Hall rattled, "I know they are suspecting me."

The widow vented to *her detective* that she worried about gossip making more and more people think that she killed Victor. She and Victor had always gotten along well. Where did people get such notions? The widow said her relationship with Victor differed somewhat from that with her first husband. Acey, she said, was of such a nervous and excitable temperament that "If it had been my first husband that was shot, I would have gone to jail right away without any question."[10]

Mackay looked up at Mrs. Hall and probed her expression. Under the circumstances, the statement was a remarkable thing for her to say.

Mrs. Hall spoke her mind. Many statements begged elaboration. She knew what she meant; however, charitable interpretations eluded Mackay. When Mrs. Hall finished, Mackay excused himself to pursue other signatures.

Shortly afterwards, detective Scott appeared at her door. The array of suspicious quotes and rumors prompted Scott to interview Mrs. Hall again. She answered his questions as best she knew how. She felt she had nothing to hide and informed Mr. Scott of other gossip and related all the tales she had heard.

Scott was not familiar with some of the stories and was surprised at her, of all people, calling attention to them. Concluding the interview,

Scott candidly asked Mrs. Hall if she killed her husband. His bulldog-like demeanor conveyed to Lizzie that he believed she did.

"What motive would I have for killing Victor?"[11] challenged Mrs. Hall.

Scott said nothing but looked hard at Mrs. Hall while trying to read her face. Why did she respond with that question? Why did she not deny the killing? Lacking any hint of indignation, her response seemed evasive. Scott offered a mannerly, though superficial, apology for the question and left.

On Sunday Mackay completed a full week's investigation in Green Springs and prepared to return to Richmond for a couple of days. Mackay planned to take Victor's revolver and the bullets back to his office for examination. Mrs. Hall agreed to his request. She gave them to him and vented more anxiety about suspicions against her and the recent conversation with Scott. She told Mackay that Scott accused her of killing Victor. Again she asked, "What motive would I have for killing Victor?"

Mackay politely reminded Mrs. Hall again that it was inappropriate for him to discuss the case. His job was to gather facts and file reports, not render opinions to the parties involved. Mackay then went to catch the train to Richmond.

With Mackay gone, Lizzie and her daughters had no protection at night. They resumed sleeping at Nicholas Hall's.

Early in the week, Attorney Lindsay Gordon contacted Mrs. Hall concerning one of the insurance policies. In light of the many rumors about the widow, Gordon realized how bad it appeared for her to receive all monies due the estate. He suggested that she best settle one claim by declaring Victor's father heir.

On Wednesday, April 29th, Lizzie and Nicholas Hall took his buggy to Louisa. Two weeks had passed since the shooting. Lizzie had spent the most recent week combating viscous rumors. From the moment they reached town, heads turned their way. People stopped to stare. Lizzie tried to ignore them.

Lizzie appeared before Clerk of Court Philip Porter and certified N. W. Hall as Victor's legal heir.[12] All seemed routine within the clerk's office. Lizzie and Nicholas Hall conducted their business and departed. They only noted the same curious attention upon leaving town as when they entered. Victor Hall's father and widow left unaware that even while they were in the courthouse, legal action was being set in motion against her.

The growing uncertainties gnawed at Lizzie and robbed her peace. The stares and finger pointing in Louisa was all she could bear. On the way home Lizzie wondered, where was Mackay? Her detective had spent the last three full days in Richmond. What was he doing there? Why was he not in Louisa solving the case and clearing her name?

Lizzie had not received a single report from her Pinkerton man, yet she still accrued a charge of eight dollars a day! Lizzie concluded that it was a waste of money to employ her expensive detective any longer.

Arriving back at the store just before the afternoon mail train, Lizzie scribbled a note, stuffed it in an envelope, cancelled the stamp and shoved it in the outgoing mail. Chisholm then carried the sack to the depot for pick up. The letter arrived next day at the Pinkerton's Richmond office. Stamped on receipt April 30th, the abrupt, hasty scrawl requested an end to the investigation:

Pinkertons National Detective Agency,

Richmond, Va.

Dear Sir:

Mr. Mackay has been working for 11 days in which I am more than willing to pay for havent as yet gotten in to any thing & I cant imploy any more from the fact I feel like its more than I am able to bear hope to hear from you all soon.

Yours truly,

Mrs. V. K. Hall

Please send bill[13]

While Mrs. Hall's letter was being read in Richmond, Mackay was back in Louisa delivering carbon copies of his reports to the commonwealth's attorney. Mackay discussed his inconclusive weight comparisons between the bullets from Victor Hall's gun and the fatal round. He also surrendered Victor Hall's pistol to Mr. Bibb.

As soon as Mackay left Bibb's office, he boarded the train to Green Springs to see Mrs. Hall one more time. Mackay needed to confirm one last detail for conscience sake. The widow greeted him coolly being aggravated that she had still not received any reports from the Pinkerton agency. What was going on? She demanded to know.

Mackay had no answer other than clients receive official reports directly from the Richmond office. Mrs. Hall asserted that it was ridiculous for her to be charged eight dollars a day for nothing. She informed Mackay that she had already notified the agency to stop the investigation.

Mackay tactfully pushed the issue aside and asked Mrs. Hall if she thought that there was any way Victor could have killed himself. Mrs. Hall collected herself and explained that Victor had been sick. He was so sick, in fact, that Victor told her that he did not think that he would live much longer. Yes. She would have thought it possible for Victor to have shot himself except for the fact that Miss Wood said that she took Victor's gun from the bureau after the shooting.[14]

MURDER AT GREEN SPRINGS

The answer satisfied Mackay. He politely thanked Mrs. Hall for her hospitality during his stay and said goodbye. But Mrs. Hall's request to terminate the investigation did not end Mackay's involvement. The Pinkerton man remained available to the commonwealth's attorney. It was agency policy.

A new rumor spread like wildfire throughout Louisa County that Mrs. Hall had fired *her own detective* after he provided evidence against her. All suspicions pointed to the widow like so many weathervanes aligned with the wind. Local sentiments charged to an explosive level.

MURDER AT GREEN SPRINGS

CHAPTER *Five*

BUT I'M INNOCENT!

MURDER AT GREEN SPRINGS

William Chew Bibb, the commonwealth's attorney for Louisa County was born in the town of Louisa in 1882. He grew up enjoying every advantage afforded by a prominent and established family. Educated in local schools, he graduated from Randolph-Macon College and then earned his Bachelor of Law degree from the University of Virginia Law School in 1905.

His father William Emmett Bibb, also an LL.B. alumnus of the same school, was a prosperous lawyer who had already served as local commonwealth's attorney and Virginia state senator.[1] Father and son formed their law partnership together shortly after "Willie" received his law degree.

The young attorney soon proved himself when representing Lewis F. Yancey's bankrupt business. Bibb won compensation in circuit court from the Louisa County Board of Supervisors for commandeering the man's store for use as a smallpox hospital during the 1902 outbreak at Green Springs Depot. [That very same store later became Hall's!] Bibb successfully fought the county's successive appeals and eventually argued the case before the Virginia Supreme Court of Appeals. However in 1909, the high court reversed the lower court's decision. The able advocate lost the protracted battle to his local rival R. Lindsay Gordon, Jr., then Louisa County's commonwealth's attorney.

One of the most sophisticated men in Louisa County with social and political connections, Willie Bibb tended to be pragmatic and rigid. Tall with thinning blond hair and handsome features, his deportment and athletic build generated a presence people perceived as either confidence or arrogance depending from which side of an issue one viewed him. He was a principled man of serious demeanor and devoted to his family and community.

BUT I'M INNOCENT!   99

His father W. E. Bibb both preceded and succeeded Lindsay Gordon as commonwealth's attorney. Reelected to the post in 1907, W. E. Bibb served until appointed assistant attorney general of Virginia in 1910.[2] Young Willie was then appointed to the senior Bibb's unexpired term as county prosecutor. The advancement in his father's footsteps was bitter sweet in that nine months later, his father fell down the steps of his Richmond residence and died from injuries on December 10th.

Willie won election to office proper in November 1911.[3] Many viewed this as simply the coronation of the heir apparent. Indeed, a son succeeding a father in office was all too common in Louisa County. The situation masked the fact that Willie retained office on his own merits.

In April 1914, Willie Bibb found himself in the political hotbed surrounding the Hall case. He answered clamoring citizens and newspapermen alike stating firmly that the murder was under investigation and that he intended to bring the guilty party to justice. But Bibb's assurances failed to satisfy the majority. The killing was yet another incident at the most notorious site in the county. People wanted the *murderess* arrested. Public sentiment against Mrs. Hall grew daily. The Louisa County Board of Supervisors and influential citizens pressed for action before civil unrest grew out of hand.

Bibb generally agreed with the detectives' findings. Few ignored the fact that Mrs. Hall was thirteen years older than her young husband. Neighbors alleged strife between the Dunkum and Hall families over her marriage. Some declared that bad blood between Buck Dunkum and Mrs. Hall was evident in the dissolution of their partnership and subsequent business rivalry. Others said it was healthy competition.

The series of unexplained fires at Dunkum's began within months of Mrs. Hall's remarriage. When Dunkum's house burned, the Dunkum family lodged Mrs. Hall until they rebuilt. Some said this charity originated with her husband. The cozy living arrangement would have only aggravated any existing tensions between Buck Dunkum and Mrs. Hall.[4]

MURDER AT GREEN SPRINGS

Much was hearsay, but there were particulars of substance like the victim's pistol with the fired cartridge. Bibb personally examined the gun the day of the murder. At the time, he did not think it had been recently fired. Now he doubted his judgment. How much was he influenced by the detectives and others? He thought hard about that.

On a dark and stormy night, a man with no known enemies was shot dead in his own home shortly after a mysterious arson destroyed his competitor's store. When McCue and Beattie killed their wives, both blamed the murders on mysterious strangers. Mrs. Hall's tale sounded suspiciously similar. If a burglar shot her husband, as the widow Hall claimed, then why was nothing taken or disturbed?

Typically, whenever a spouse kills a spouse, there are no witnesses, only circumstantial evidence. Circumstantial evidence fingered McCue and Beattie and established guilt to which each confessed before their executions. This case was less clear. Mrs. Hall had opportunity, but no motive; unless, she was the arsonist and killed her husband to hide her crime.

The position of the body seemed inconsistent with the widow's story. If Victor Hall was shot fleeing an intruder, the victim should have fallen headfirst toward the bedroom. But Hall lay contrary to expectation with his feet at the door. The detectives thought this very strange. They concluded from the description of the wound that the victim was either shot from above while standing or shot while lying down.[5] The policemen all asserted that this and the position of the body suggested that Hall was shot in bed and then dragged into the store. Bibb agreed. These facts incriminated Mrs. Hall.

Mrs. Hall hired her own detective. This bothered Bibb. The action surprised even her Pinkerton man. Was this a ploy to appear innocent?

The few telephones around Green Springs Depot were all on the same party line. When someone received a call, everyone's bell rang. One never knew how many eavesdroppers listened. The detectives recruited a *public spirited* neighbor to monitor Mrs. Hall's phone conversations and report them directly to Bibb.[6]

The widow's conversations became more frequent. Mrs. Hall seemed preoccupied with rumors and perceptions. She talked a lot about the detectives, their questions, what others were saying about her first husband's death and her relationship with Bill Roberts. Her behavior suggested a guilty conscience.

One week after the shooting, the community churned over the rumored romance between Mrs. Hall and Bill Roberts. Bibb did not take that story seriously. But then, what about this case was ordinary?

Accusing the widow of murder and securing conviction were two different matters altogether. Bibb dreaded trying a case on tenuous evidence. He would avoid trial if at all possible.

People demanded action, and it was common for Virginians to take matters into their own hands when their judicial system wavered.[7] The last thing Bibb or any other responsible person in the county wanted was to see a woman harmed. This left Bibb no choice but to quickly put the matter before a grand jury.

At Bibb's request, Judge George S. Shackelford issued the vacation order on April 29th to summon the special grand jury.[8] On May 1st, newspapers across the state focused on the escalated investigation into Victor Hall's death scheduled to convene May 11th. The newspapers avoided direct mention of the suspect, but they all inferred it was Mrs. Hall.

News of the action shocked the Hall family. The morning Lizzie learned of the development, a reporter from the *Daily Progress* showed up to interview her. She, Essie, and visiting sister Jenny Leistra were minding the store at the time. Lizzie indulged the reporter. She showed the newspaperman around the store and pointed out each feature of the crime scene.

Mrs. Hall spoke in a matter of fact tone. She was weary of the whole affair and struggled to suppress her emotions. The reporter took notes and politely asked questions. The interview flowed smoothly. There were no interruptions from customers.

Mrs. Hall admitted knowing about the various rumors. Her voice quivered pathetically.

"Yes. I know they are talking. I know they are talking about me. God knows I have nothing to conceal, but what can I do?"[9]

The situation was beyond Mrs. Hall's control and growing grimmer by the day. The reporter listened sympathetically. He thanked the widow Hall for her time then left to speak with Victor Hall's parents. The resulting article was very favorable to Mrs. Hall. It was her last interview before being told to avoid the press.

Since Mackay left, Lizzie was scared to stay in the store even during the day. Neighbors no longer kept company there. Near neighbor Johnny Johnson refused her requests for help to look after the place. He was afraid to stay there.[10] Folks stopped by only long enough to check their mail. They shunned her store and bought groceries from Dunkum.

Beyond the hurt she felt, Mrs. Hall knew she could not survive without the viability of her business. Suspicions, slanders, and legal jeopardy all threatened financial ruin. Overwhelmed by it all, she sat down and penned the following letter to J. F. Bickers to auction off her property:

Green Springs, Va.

Mr. Frank Biggers [sic]
    Louisa Va.

Dear Mr. Biggers [sic]

I would like to get you to help me to advertise my stock of goods consisting of dry goods shoes & notions groceries can goods hard ware etc., I will send you a list of every thing more fully have 10 beds (white mans) good springs & mattress lot of beding [sic] & the like kitchen dinning room furniture farming implements two wagons good ones 2 buggies lot of other things at barns 2 horses 3 cows 4 hogs chickens

I am afraid to stay here in the day with out some protection & that's hard to get. I would also like for you to auction off same have parlor furniture & organ desk all my furniture is in good condition no shoty [sic] stuff let me hear from you in regard to same & oblige

    Mrs. V. K. Hall[11]

On Monday, Deputy Robert Trice served Mrs. Hall her summons. The paper was real, but idea of having to testify before a special grand jury was surreal.

Lizzie's conscience was clear. She had nothing to hide. What hurt her most was that so many people took stock in the rumors. How could they think and say such things about her?

Lizzie looked forward to telling her story under oath. Surely, the grand jury would clear her of all suspicion and, perhaps, end the shunning of her and her business.

Hope waned as Lizzie realized the gravity of the summons. Lizzie called friends on the telephone. She then learned the unsettling rumor that Elsie Wood planned to change her story and say that it took ten minutes for her to reach the scene after the shooting.

Lizzie panicked. She had often repeated that she depended on the schoolteachers' testimonies to keep her out of the electric chair, especially Elsie Wood's. If Elsie changed her sworn statement, a considerable length of time was accounted for by Lizzie's word alone.[12] She had to get in touch with Elsie Wood fast. The Woods had no telephone.

Millard Filmore Peers, a relative of Elsie Wood, lived about three miles down the road. The West family was Peers' nearest neighbors with a telephone. Lizzie called *Westlands* and asked someone to please relay a message to M. F. Peers to contact her right away. Peers came to the store that afternoon. Lizzie asked him to urge Elsie to tell the same story. Peers said he knew that Henry Flannagan, another relative of the Woods, was going to see them soon. He would get Henry to deliver the message.

Nicholas Hall had encouraged Lizzie to consult her lawyer a number of times. She balked at the notion until the summons appeared. The stories about her were untrue. The rumors were bound to go away, so she thought. However, malicious talk only became popular *truth*. Now Lizzie urgently needed legal counsel. N. W. Hall hitched up the buggy and drove the veiled widow into Louisa to meet with her attorney.

Reuben Lindsay Gordon, Jr. was born in Albemarle County January 21, 1855. He attended private school taught by his grandfather William F. Gordon and finished his last two years in public school. He then moved to Louisa and read the law for one year under his uncle James L. Gordon. Lindsay Gordon was admitted to the bar in May 1878 and practiced in Louisa.

The following year he was assigned to defend William Talley, one of three Negroes accused of killing Charles K. Walton,[13] a Yanceyville merchant whose home was torched after he had been robbed and murdered. Gordon successfully defended Talley against prosecutor William E. Bibb. The victory was accentuated by the fact that codefendant Albert Mitchell was tried separately, convicted and hanged.[14] Thus, Gordon founded his reputation as both a skillful lawyer and champion of the weak and less fortunate.[15]

Gordon became commonwealth's attorney for Louisa County in 1892 and held that office for sixteen years. He served as delegate to the Virginia Constitutional Convention in 1901-1902.[16] In 1907, he stepped down as commonwealth's attorney to run for the vacated Eighth District's U.S. Congressional seat. Unsuccessful in this bid, he ran again in 1912, but failed to unseat the incumbent.

However, Gordon's popularity within Louisa County assured his election to the Virginia House of Delegates in 1913. The attorney had completed his first session in the Virginia legislature just weeks before the Hall shooting. Lindsay Gordon was already a very busy man when Victor Hall was murdered.

As a past commonwealth's attorney, Gordon had experience prosecuting criminal cases. In fact, when two previous murders occurred at the Hall store, Gordon prosecuted both cases. Those miscreants easily fit polite society's definition of *poor white trash*. The trials did much to soil the image of Green Springs Depot. In the latter case, Gordon summoned Mrs. Hall, then Mrs. D. A. Dunkum, and her husband as witnesses for the prosecution.

MURDER AT GREEN SPRINGS

Lindsay Gordon was very familiar with Mrs. Hall, her family, and their legal and financial matters. He knew Mrs. Hall to be a virtuous woman. From the onset of suspicions against her, Gordon knew Mrs. Hall's predicament to be a mere misunderstanding based largely on associations with the depot's past and complicated by misguided outsiders acting on misinformation. There was every reason to believe the whole matter could be resolved in a forum of rational people.

Without a doubt, R. Lindsay Gordon, Jr. was the best attorney in Louisa County to represent Mrs. Hall. Nevertheless, the fair minded, big hearted, busy, country lawyer possessed only nominal experience in actually defending a criminal matter.

A kind and generous man, Lindsay Gordon helped pay for his brother's education. Upon receiving his law degree Alexander Tazewell Gordon, known to folks as "Sandy," left Virginia for Texas to seek his fortune. He married and settled there briefly, but returned to Virginia to practice law with his brother.

Lindsay and Sandy shared an office on the second floor of the Gates building.[17] Each brother honed a particular talent. Lindsay was the orator. Sandy was the legal mind and normally found at his desk with his head buried in bound volumes and papers while puffing on his clay pipe. In this respect, the day of Mrs. Hall's first consultation was no different from any other.

Moments before the Hall's arrival, the polite and gracious Lindsay Gordon redressed his brother again, as he often did, for his foul language. Lindsay was not one prone to profanity and tired of Sandy's strings of invectives at every frustration. Some combinations exhibited astounding creativity.

"I see no reason, Sandy, why any man should use such language. It isn't becoming," admonished Lindsay.[18] Sandy responded with an oath. To Sandy's way of thinking, *salt and pepper* words only seasoned expressions to taste.

Lindsay dropped the subject short of an argument having said what needed saying. However, it was not unusual for this frequent topic to result in a heated argument where the elder brother, being the more gifted at projection, ended the conversation by drowning out Sandy with stronger, more profane language.[19]

Nicholas Hall parked the buggy and escorted Lizzie upstairs to the law office of Gordon & Gordon. At the top of the landing, they entered the dingy room. The open windows vented stale tobacco and coal odors accumulated over winter. The mess around the little sheet-iron heater betrayed the fact that spring cleaning had not yet begun.

Lindsay Gordon received the Halls cordially. He had followed developments from their onset, and agreed to represent Mrs. Hall without reservation. His only caution was to refrain from discussing the case, especially with newspaper reporters. In the meantime, Gordon would interview witnesses and keep her abreast of findings. He assured her that everything was going to be all right, for she had the full protection of law.

On May 11th, Nicholas Hall was up with the dawn as was his custom. He tended his livestock while Ellen and Jennie busied themselves with kitchen chores. The day promised to be warm and clear. Nick harnessed the horse and hitched up the carriage. Helpful Bill Roberts arrived for breakfast. He had come from the store where he had spent the night. The family believed it best not to leave the store unoccupied with so many of the Halls and Dunkums away in Louisa at one time. Roberts agreed to watch over things while those summoned appeared before the grand jury, at least until Lizzie's brother returned.

After breakfast, Nicholas Hall and Lizzie left for the courthouse. The sun was above the horizon, but hidden by the grove of tall oaks in full

foliage surrounding the store. The buggy caught full sun as it crossed the tracks to the courthouse road. The direct sunlight made the black widow's weeds uncomfortably warm for Lizzie, who was already perspiring over her situation.

William G. Owens, a reporter for the *News Leader*, had posted himself at the courthouse about sunrise and interviewed people as they arrived. Commonwealth's Attorney Bibb told him that he expected to send Mrs. Hall before the grand jury sometime in the afternoon. She would likely be the fifth or sixth witness. About forty witnesses had been summoned. Bibb expected the proceedings to last three days. The Commonwealth intended to first call witnesses of the crime scene to familiarize the jury. The detectives would not be called until tomorrow.

Bibb stated that every probable solution to the tragedy was being considered, but admitted that no information had yet been received that would result in a conviction. The Commonwealth hoped to show that the burning of Dunkum's store created a motive for murder, but there was no real evidence as to who set the fire.

Owens asked Bibb about the most recent gossip circulating about the courthouse concerning officers withholding information hoping that a reward would be offered for the arrest of Victor Hall's killer. Bibb countered that officers of the court were ineligible for such rewards then proceeded inside the courthouse leaving the reporter to speculate on the intent of the private investigator.

The early bird reporter also obtained a statement from Judge Shackelford who said the case had shocked the entire community. He was determined to give the matter a thorough investigation, and there would be no hurry in taking evidence. Shackelford asserted that the grand jury was composed of splendid men who would probe to the very heart of the terrible murder.[20]

Nicholas Hall and Lizzie pulled up before a growing crowd. Nicholas tethered the carriage near the public well and escorted Lizzie by the arm.

A group of reporters anxious for statements met them before the steps. Nicholas Hall firmly excused himself and the veiled widow past the men.

The grand jury was sworn in at 11 o'clock.[21] Familiar faces filled the witness room: some friendly, some not at all. Coroner James E. Hester was called first, next Dr. Porter who attended Victor Hall and performed the autopsy, and then J. F. Bickers, the special deputy who assembled the coroner's jury.

At half past noon, Judge Shackelford adjourned for lunch with instructions to reconvene at two o'clock. Lizzie did not feel like eating nor did she feel like facing the hundreds gathered outside. She preferred to remain inside. Nicholas took the opportunity to get some fresh air, tend his horse, and fetch lunch from the carriage. Reporter Owens approached Hall, introduced himself and requested a statement.

Did he think Victor committed suicide? Did he think Mrs. Hall killed his son? The questions begged answers. Nicholas Hall wanted to make the truth known.

"The theory of suicide is out of the question. He could not have shot himself without a pistol," quipped Hall. "The theory that his wife might have killed him is preposterous. She could have had no motive. They knew each other well before marriage, lived happily together, and she could not have gotten along without him. She well knew that no one in the community could have carried on the business as he did. And the fact that her home and business are ruined and she is afraid to live at the place and afraid to stay there at night without protection, should be sufficient to silence all untimely, unjust and cruel suspicion, and should make those hang their heads in shame who have without looking in any other direction, been so ready to heap suspicion upon an innocent and grief-stricken widow. And as to his life insurance, what was that to be compared with a thriving and growing business such as was carried on under Victor's management?

"The theory that a burglar was concealed inside the store and shot Victor is not unreasonable. If Mr. Dunkum's store was burned in order to draw everybody away from Victor's store while Victor was out someone might have slipped in from a side way and hid himself in the storeroom when he heard Victor coming in so quickly from the fire, for Victor was sick and the weather inclement, and he only stayed out a very short time.

"Being then caught in the store he had to wait there until he could get out unnoticed; but as day was near at hand at the time Victor was shot and the man must have made one move and a noise which Victor thought was some one at the front door. If the man did not have time to escape without being identified, he possibly shot Victor and escaped. The front door had been locked and the key left inside by Victor himself at the time his father went home from the fire.

"The theory that Victor went to the front door and opened it is, to my mind, a very strong one. It was his intention when he left the bedroom. As the wind and rain were blowing in at the door, and Victor was in his night clothes and barefooted, he would not have thrust himself into the door, but would more likely have opened it at arm's length. And as he was very quick naturally in his movements, the man facing him at the door with a drawn pistol would likely have had to follow him as he quickly turned and retreated toward the bedroom, the lighted lamp which Victor had put upon the counter enabling his assailant to take deadly aim.

"The theory that Victor had no enemies is a surface one. The un-called for suspicion, the wild and senseless rumors, the slanders and cruel insinuations which have found expression far and near, and the seem-ing determination to ruin Victor's family seem to show that both he and his family had enemies, not enemies perhaps through spite, but through envy, prejudice, or sordid self interest."[22]

The commonwealth's attorney focused on foundational testimonies. After dinner, Bibb examined coroner jury members Charles Vest and Fritz

Wills. Mary and Buck Dunkum were the last of seven witnesses examined that day. Being the initial suspect, Buck's testimony was of particular interest. Dunkum spent nearly two and a half hours delivering statements generally favorable to Mrs. Hall.

Buck Dunkum had hoped his testimony satisfied his obligation to the grand jury, but was told to return as long as the jury remained in session. Dunkum's inquisition coupled with his fears that suspicion might be cast his way again left him exhausted.

Buck went home physically and emotionally drained. He went to bed shortly after sundown. Buck fell asleep immediately, but later awoke to knocking at the front door. He got out of bed, went over to the window and called down asking who was there. Buck heard no response. He asked several more times, again without reply.

He could not see who it was, but guessed it was a man. There was moonlight, but his view of the doorway was blocked by the porch roof. He decided to go to the door.

Aroused by the commotion, father-in-law Jesse Marks was already downstairs. Jesse hollered up that he had the door. Buck returned to his room and looked out the window again hoping to catch a glimpse of the visitor.

Buck loathed firearms and did not own one. Jesse, however, always kept a loaded revolver handy. He went to the front door and demanded to know who was outside. There was still no answer. He carefully stepped to the door's side light and pushed the curtain away just enough to peep out. He saw nothing, but thought he heard a man grumble.

"I'll get my pistol and make you answer," said Marks loudly hoping to evoke a response.[23]

The visitor walked off the porch and left the premises. The full moon was just above the trees. Dunkum saw a figure leave. He thought it was a man. Frightened from that point on, members of the Dunkum family lived in fear for their lives and dared not leave their house after dark.[24]

A crowd had already gathered at the courthouse that morning when Dunkum arrived visibly upset. Folks watched him rush to the sheriff's office and guessed there was a problem. Dunkum reported the threatening visit. He suspected retaliation for his testimony. Dunkum then went next door to attend the next grand jury session.

News of the trouble at Dunkum's house spread like wildfire and drew even more curiosity seekers. The previous day's turnout was one of the largest crowds ever assembled there. The present group grew bigger and more intense.

What man would threaten Buck Dunkum? Folks wondered and speculated. Some even proposed that it was Mrs. Hall dressed like a man![25]

The grand jury began its second day promptly at nine o'clock and called Elsie Wood. Meanwhile, the number of spectators outside swelled. Judge Shackelford became concerned. He could see and hear the excitement from his window and asked Deputy Sheriff Bob Trice to investigate while testimony proceeded.

Miss Wood's story remained consistent with her statement before the coroner's jury. The grand jury felt that the young school teacher was withholding information. This was no surprise. Rumors abounded that Miss Wood was not telling everything. To support this notion, the commonwealth's attorney next called Wood's friend Miss Ruby Chewning to whom, according to one detective, she had confided certain details shortly after the murder.

But Chewning was absent from the courthouse. Miss Wood had spent the night with Miss Chewning at her home in Richmond and explained that Miss Chewning declined to come. Judge Shackelford ordered Sheriff Wash to go to Richmond and bring the young lady before the grand jury.

Bob Trice returned from his survey of the crowd and reported that it seemed that most of the people outside were there to see Mrs. Hall's trial.[26] Judge Shackelford issued an announcement that only a grand jury investigation was being conducted. There was no trial or any other public proceedings underway. There was nothing for anyone to see. The crowd reluctantly dispersed; many lingered.

The jury examined Dr. Taylor and then Mamie Rosson. When called to the jury room Miss Rosson stood and gave the worried widow a reassuring glance. Mrs. Hall stopped her as she passed. To fulfill a need to say something, Mrs. Hall urged Mamie, "Don't say anything that would put it on me."[27] Mamie nodded reassuringly. Unfortunately, Mrs. Hall's words impinged upon other ears.

County Supervisor Lee Rosson, Mamie's father testified next followed by little Becky Coates. When finished, the jury knew the essentials. Bibb intended to call Mrs. Hall next, but because of the convenient hour, Judge Shackleford adjourned for lunch.

Lindsay Gordon believed the situation had changed materially. The charged atmosphere now made it unlikely Mrs. Hall could say anything to prevent an indictment against her. The jury had his client's sworn statement before the coroner's jury. She had nothing more to add. When the session reconvened, Lindsay Gordon informed Judge Shackleford that he advised Mrs. Hall not to testify.[28]

The refusal to testify excited everyone in and around the courthouse. Many interpreted the unusual twist an admission of guilt and an indication that the grand jury would soon deliver a true bill against her.

Bibb fumed. Mrs. Hall's unavailability killed any chance Bibb thought he had to defuse the situation. Gordon's maneuver virtually guaranteed Bibb the unenviable task of prosecuting a high visibility murder case on flimsy evidence. Delegate R. Lindsay Gordon, Jr. stood to gain substantial publicity and political clout from a successful defense of the widow. Bibb, on the other hand, faced yet another humiliation heaped upon his previous defeat by Gordon before the Virginia Supreme Court. While acting in good faith on behalf of his client, Lindsay Gordon had, in effect, incited war.

In the unsettled atmosphere, the afternoon session featured testimony by merchant Morris J. Maddox,[29] Special Deputy George Trainham, and Pinkerton Detective Robert Mackay. Many observed that Mrs. Hall was more subdued than the previous day. A reporter from the *News Leader* spoke with her afterwards. She asserted that her husband was killed on account of jealousy over his business successes, but she had no idea who could have done such a thing.

Mrs. Hall concluded, "I know the people around here are saying I killed Victor, but I did not do it. Victor did not have an enemy in the world, but I have plenty of them. That is being proved right now, when so many persons are accusing me of killing him. I did not do it. He was shot by someone while he was in the store. I found him there and put a pillow under his head."[30]

The day had taken its toll on Lizzie. She concealed her haggard looking face behind her black veil. Lizzie and Nicholas ignored the stares and made their way through the crowd across the courthouse green to their carriage. There seemed no end to the humiliation.

Lizzie still needed to fulfill her daily responsibilities as acting postmaster to pick up and sort the mail. When they arrived at Green Springs Depot, Nicholas parked the buggy and went inside with Lizzie.

Robert Woody ran the depot and Dunkum's makeshift store while Buck attended the grand jury. Buck had arrived a little before the Halls and worked to catch up on business. As Woody passed Lizzie the mail sack, Buck called Lizzie's attention to her accumulated freight. He politely asked her to have it removed that day because it took up so much space in the building. Although it was already late in the day, Lizzie agreed. The timing was inconvenient and aggravating.

The carriage pulled up to the barn just as Charles Chisholm finished his chores for the day. He had just unhitched the wagon and put the horse in the stall. Mrs. Hall told Chisholm he needed to hitch up the wagon again and fetch her freight. Chisholm did as he was told, and by sundown, Mrs. Hall's freight was gone from the depot.

Hubert Dowdy waited for Lizzie at N. W. Hall's home. He had just arrived from his home in Cumberland County. Hugh's presence lifted Lizzie's spirits as nothing else could. Accommodating her brother with the Halls was more awkward than when her sisters visited. Lizzie felt safe with her brother around and suggested that she and her family spend the night at the store. They had not done so since the detectives left.

After dinner, Lizzie, her brother, and daughters returned to their residence and settled in for the night. Everyone slept upstairs. Lizzie, Essie, and Mamie slept over the junk room. The girls were in one bed, Lizzie in another. Brother Hugh slept in the next room over top of the store with his door half open.[31] Hugh interposed himself between them and outside threats. Lizzie and the girls felt secure. Still, no one was happy about sleeping at the store.

Lizzie lay in bed exhausted from the two days of grand jury proceedings. She worried about the result and its effects on Essie and Mamie. She wondered what she would do when it was all over. She considered how thankful she was for her family, but realized the store could never be home again.

Lizzie drifted in and out of sleep until an unremarkable dream flashed images of fire. Fire? Lizzie's eyes popped open. A man was yelling, "Fire!"

Hubert Dowdy heard the alarm outside and jumped into his trousers. He rushed to the front room for a look outside then went to the ladies' bedroom and shouted them up. The depot was on fire!

Lizzie and Essie sprang from their beds. Mamie sat upright in her bed scared and began crying. The familiar yellow light through the window struck them with horror. Lizzie rushed to the front window, threw up the sash and stuck her head out to verify that it was not their house. The station shed was ablaze. Jesse Marks stood alone on the dirt road illuminated by the flames.

Lizzie called for her brother, but his name was scarcely out of her mouth when she saw him join Marks. The fire was fully developed. There was nothing anyone could do.

Nicholas Hall arrived. The scene was all too painfully reminiscent of the month before.

The family went downstairs to the hallway. Ellen and Jenny Hall arrived. The Halls came inside, and together, the family watched the depot burn to coals.

Lizzie and her daughters sat on the stairway embracing each other. Unlike the night of the store fire, no one went back to sleep. The weather had been too warm for the stove in the depot. The fire had been deliberately set. Nicholas prayed for divine presence in the situation. This brought some comfort; nevertheless, their faces were portraits of gloom.

Shortly before four o'clock, Nicholas rose to leave. He had to get back to the house. He had chores to do before getting ready for another day at the grand jury. Ellen and Jenny left too. Hubert went upstairs to prepare for the day before tending his horse and hitching up the buggy. Lizzie asked the girls to go make up the beds and get dressed. Lizzie went to light the stove for coffee and breakfast.

As soon as Lizzie entered the dining room, she smelled kerosene and smoke. She hurried into the kitchen. There was a faint glow under the pantry door. She opened it to find a small fire in the middle of the floor. She quickly grabbed the nearby water bucket and put the fire out. Minutes later Nicholas Hall hurried into the kitchen. Ellen and Jenny soon followed. They had gotten halfway home when Nicholas looked back and noticed the flare in the pantry window and hurried back. The arsonist had struck the Hall store!

Lizzie went immediately to the telephone and rang the operator for Sheriff Wash. Wash called the Louisa Hotel and had Griffith wake up Angle and Scott. These in turn woke up newspaper reporter Owens, who was also staying there. Wash sent word to Deputy J. C. Trice to bring the county bloodhounds to Green Springs Depot, and then picked up the detectives and Owens in his carriage.

About six o'clock, Sheriff Wash and his party arrived at Green Springs. The sun had been up an hour. The little country depot looked more like a war zone than a rural community. Mrs. Hall, N. W. Hall, Buck Dunkum, Jesse Marks, Robert Woody, and Charles Chisholm were gathered outside the store when the officials arrived.

Mrs. Hall took them around back to show them the pantry. There was not much damage other than a blackened area with burnt debris in the middle the floor. There was a strong odor of kerosene and bits of excelsior scattered between the charred floor boards and the window. Mrs. Hall explained that when she found the fire, it had almost burned out.

The one window in the room had a broken pane, and its left shutter lay on the ground. Mrs. Hall said she thought someone must have broken the glass and tossed the lighted material inside. Meanwhile, the others examined the window and were unable to conclude whether the window had been intentionally broken or shattered by heat of the fire. Nevertheless, the wire screen was missing.[32]

Angle used the telephone to notify C & O headquarters of the incident and that he was on the job. Wash, Angle and Scott began interviewing those present. J. C. Trice arrived and put the bloodhounds to work, but the dogs failed to pick up a trail. This did not surprise Trice considering the foot traffic in and around the site.

While speaking with Chisholm in the yard, detectives Angle and Scott thought it odd to hear that Mrs. Hall removed her freight from the depot just hours before the fire. The detectives then went inside the store seeking an explanation from Mrs. Hall. Angle's pointed questions insinuated that she removed her goods from the depot because she intended to burn Dunkum's business again.

How dare he talk to her so!

Stressed from the weeks of personal and business losses, suspicion, the grand jury ordeal, and robbed of yet another night's sleep, Mrs. Hall lashed out like a cornered animal. She moved the freight because Buck Dunkum told her to move it! In Angle's face she demanded, "I would like to know from you, as a representative of the Chesapeake and Ohio Railway, what right Buck Dunkum has got to use the depot as a store. I have to provide my own store, yet he is allowed to use the depot as a store and light and all and compete with me in the same line of business. It was not right that he be allowed to do this."[33]

Her exploding indignation terrified her daughters standing nearby. They had never seen their mother so upset. Essie stepped forward, grasped her mother's arm and pleaded with her to calm down. Eyes flashing, lips quivering, Lizzie told the men to get out and leave her alone.

Scott and Angle retreated outside into view of heads turned in the direction of the redress. The detectives had no more questions. Mrs. Hall's outburst satisfied them. Anyway, it was time for their party to return to Louisa in time for the next grand jury session. Angle stayed at the depot with Trice and the bloodhounds.

Back in Louisa, Judge Shackelford ordered Hall's store placed under guard around the clock to prevent any further attempts to burn it. George Trainham and other special deputies went to the scene. By midmorning, Luther Scherer of the C & O Railway dispatched Special Agent Mallory to assist Angle, and Pinkerton Superintendent Erb sent Captain A. G. Smith to support Mackay until his grand jury obligations ended.

Reporter Owens went by the Farmers and Merchants Bank and arranged for clerk David B. Harris to return with him to Green Springs to take photographs for the newspaper. Owens had met the amateur photographer days before and arranged for Kent's Drug Store to provide Harris a Kodak camera in exchange for free advertising.[34] Harris eagerly agreed to join Owens after work.

Several freshly assigned deputies caught the 9:30 A.M. train to Green Springs as the grand jury began their third day. The courthouse was again crowded with curiosity seekers. Newsmen estimated three to four hundred that day. In light of developments, Detective George W. Scott was the first witness of the day.

Scott presented his findings and his preliminary assessment of the depot and pantry fires. In his opinion, the pantry fire could not have been set from outside.

The jury asked if they might view the scene. Judge Shackelford agreed to the request. Shackelford asked Clerk of Court Philip Porter to telephone Mrs. Hall and announce their intentions. The judge issued an order for the 4:00 P.M. mail train to take the jury to Green Springs.

The grand jury next heard testimony from Miss Ruby Chewning. Now present after having been brought from Richmond under bailiff's escort, Miss Chewning's dramatic arrival that morning at Louisa's station was yet another eye catching event drawing special attention that day.

The jury asked Chewning to comment on certain statements made to a detective as to what Elsie Wood confided regarding a bottle of camphor and the extent of Wood's knowledge.[35] One reporter said that Chewning said that Wood said that Mrs. Hall said that she gave Victor something "to make him forget what just happened."[36] The reporter also said that Chewning said that Wood said that she had not told all she knew about the matter. Despite the fact that the jury totally discounted Miss Chewning's dubious evidence, newspapers presented the multilayered hearsay as fact and stoked imaginations already hotly fired against Mrs. Hall.[37]

The grand jury recalled Elsie Wood. Noticeably apprehensive about her reexamination, she gradually relaxed. Miss Wood remained on the stand until time came to adjourn the jury to Green Springs.

Elsie Wood emerged from the grand jury room with regained poise. She and her father Ollie stopped briefly on their way out of court to speak with a reporter. Miss Wood said that so far as she knew, the grand jury had finished with her. She stood by the same story as originally sworn to before coroner's jury and as presented the previous day before the grand jury.

She said, "They told me that they believed I had not told them before all that I knew about the case, and I replied that I had told everything, and that I had nothing to hide and nothing to add. I told them everything I knew about the case and the conditions in the store as I saw them on the morning of the murder."[38]

For the third day, Nicholas Hall returned home without being called. Because Mrs. Hall declined to testify, it appeared to many that "those witnesses who are known to agree with the widow in her version and opinion of the murder will not go before the grand jury."[39]

The grand jury members and officials walked across the crowded courthouse green and down the street to Louisa Station. The train departed on time at 4:03 P.M. Judge Shackleford, Commonwealth's Attorney Bibb, and detectives Mackay, Scott, and Mallory accompanied the grand jury. Reporter Owens and photographer Harris were also onboard.

At 4:18 P.M. the grand jury detrained at Green Springs on the scorched platform beside the ruined C & O depot. Each felt the heat radiating from the hot, smoldering plot where the depot once stood. About a hundred spectators milled around the area. All were excited over this latest sensation.

Special Agent Angle and the county deputies posted to guard Hall's store watched the jury step from the train along with Judge Shackleford,

Commonwealth's Attorney Bibb, and detectives Mallory, Mackay and Scott. The group crossed the road and gathered at the front of the store.

The jury stopped briefly on the narrow porch and turned to gain perspective on the area's layout. After the train chugged off, they took in the scene of the smoldering depot, the blackened Dunkum Store site, and Dunkum's house all located within a couple of stone throws from where they stood. Local gawkers kept their distance from the guarded sites and watched with keen interest.

Angle approached Mallory, Mackay and Scott. He said the bloodhounds found nothing. Some neighbors reported seeing a couple of strangers whom they thought might have had something to do with the fires. They saw two men on the railroad tracks just before sundown the previous evening a mile south of the depot. Two men fitting the same description were spotted again that morning two miles north of the depot. Angle believed his eyes and ears were best employed in the immediate area and did not pursue the men.[40]

Hubert Dowdy was the only family member inside the store. Once the group entered, Dowdy excused himself to the residence where Mrs. Hall and her daughters had removed themselves to avoid interaction with the grand jury.

Commonwealth's Attorney Bibb pointed out key features of the crime scene with the detectives present and available for commentary as needed. Jury members pressed together at the back of the little store. They strained to see around each other as Bibb indicated the spot where Victor Hall fell and described the position of the body. Meanwhile, reporter William Owens cleared bystanders from various camera angles and directed his photographer in recording depot images.

The visit was brief. The group was outside again with time to kill before the return train. Some took occasion to more closely inspect the two scorched sites. Harris' camera captured others waiting in front of the Hall store.[41] The jury and officials saw all there was to see in thirty minutes and caught the 4:50 P.M. train back to Louisa.

The next morning the special grand jury reconvened at the courthouse and spent the first several hours re-examining witnesses Detective Robert Mackay and Special Deputy George Trainham. After their testimonies, the body began deliberating all the statements and evidence presented.

At Green Springs Depot, the oak grove shaded a half dozen or so deputies and agents charged with guarding the Hall store from further mischief. They talked among themselves and with sundry curiosity seekers. Except for neighbors checking mail, those outside Mrs. Hall's immediate family or employ were ordered to stay clear of the store.

Lizzie and her family had been at the store since about the time Charles Chisholm finished foddering their livestock. The detectives watched as Chisholm spoke with Mrs. Hall. He then hitched up a wagon, pulled it around to the front of the store and loaded various wares. Chisholm worked throughout the day and carried away four full wagon loads of goods.

Hall's store and C & O Depot circa 1910. Pulp wood awaits loading beside railroad turnout. The depot shed that burned appears at far right. In foreground is rail tie stack area. The *Richmond Virginian*, May 14, 1914. (Photo Courtesy of The Library of Virginia)

Hall's store during visit of special grand jury. The *News Leader*, May 15, 1914.
(Photo from author's collection)

Hall's store prior to demolition in 1939. (Photo Courtesy of Charles C. Dunkum)

MURDER AT GREEN SPRINGS

Deputy Sheriff James C. Trice with county bloodhounds "Gay Boy" and "Gypsy Girl." Photograph likely taken at Green Springs Depot by D. B. Harris on the day of the depot fire investigation. (Photo Courtesy of the Louisa County Historical Society)

Mrs. Hall's Pantry – Snapshot by D. B. Harris taken after first fire and published on the front page of the *News Leader*, May 15, 1914. (Photo from author's collection)

BUT I'M INNOCENT!

Lizzie expected cancellation of her fire insurance, and she had no idea how long the property would remain under watch. Fearing destruction of her inventory, she had some of it moved to N. W. Hall's barn. She and her daughters would never live at the store again, so they moved their personal effects to the Hall's home.

The men guarding the premises wondered about the wagon loads. Onlookers sprang to conclusions. Word spread that the *crazy woman* was going to try to burn the place again!

About nine o'clock that morning, U.S. Post Office Inspector W. J. Carr arrived in a rented buggy. Since the Hall store was an official U.S. Post Office, the fire required investigation by the federal officer.

Essie and Ellen Hall directed Chisholm's work while Mr. Carr interviewed Mrs. Hall until noon. Mrs. Hall offered him dinner and apologized that they were cleaning out the kitchen and only having cold food. Carr declined the invitation and departed satisfied that no mail had been involved in the fire. After eating, the family worked all afternoon.

Special Agent Mallory arrived by train at 4:25 P.M. to relieve Angle. Angle immediately ordered Mallory back to Louisa on the 4:50 P.M. train to inform officials that Mrs. Hall spent the day moving things out of the store and that another incendiary attempt was expected.

Minutes after the train left, George Trainham drove up in his automobile with Johnny Johnson and parked beside the blackened Dunkum store plot. They had just returned from the grand jury in Louisa. Buck Dunkum and Robert Woody came over to the car and talked to them about the day's activities.

Across the tracks near the front of the Hall store a group of men unloaded lumber from a wagon. They were among the few people legitimately employed at the depot that day. About ten minutes after Trainham arrived, the Hall family left the store for the day.

Ellen, Essie, Mamie, left together with little Becky Coates. Scores of people watched them walk down the lane toward N. W. Hall's. Each

MURDER AT GREEN SPRINGS

carried a bundle except for Becky Coates who pushed a squeaky wheelbarrow with a number of items in it including a ham boiler which rattled loudly and clanged each time the rusty, metal tire hit a bump. This made considerable racket.

Mrs. Hall was the last to leave the store. She followed about one hundred feet behind the others and carried an armload of books.[42] All eyes watched the women walk away and stared after them until after the harsh noises of the squeaking wheel and clattering ham boiler faded, and Mrs. Hall disappeared beyond the apple orchard.

The crowd relaxed and resumed efforts to attach meaning to everything observed that day. Trainham and Dunkum continued their discussion. Dunkum shared that some folks wanted to gather at the depot that night for a candlelight vigil, a one month's observance of Victor Hall's death.

"Hey! Look! Fire!" shouted nine year old Johnny Graves.

The foursome at the automobile turned toward the little towhead in front of the Hall store. The boy had been helping unload lumber from a wagon and stood beside it pointing to the far side of the store where a plume of black smoke rolled skyward as from a cook stove.

"Fire! Fire!" shouted others as they realized the smoke rolled from the eaves of the outbuilding.

Someone hollered, "Let it burn!"[43]

Dunkum and Woody dashed toward the fire. Trainham and Johnson jumped from the car and followed their friends. Johnson overtook them on the other side of the tracks and led the way around to the back of the store. Once there, they could see the fire was in the rear of the outbuilding. It was the pantry again!

Otto Sherwood found the dining room door locked. Others tried the side windows. All were fastened. Johnson tried the back door. Finding it locked, he leaped from the porch and joined Trainham at the pantry window where George had already knocked aside the washtubs hanging on nails beneath it and now pulled at the shutters. The left shutter had been nailed back in place the previous day. A sharp tug ripped it completely off the window again. The right shutter swung open. Johnson felt heat through the glass and worked frantically to push up the sash.

Dunkum and Woody had grabbed the wash tubs and manned the pump at the kitchen well. Buck worked the handle vigorously. By the time a couple of gallons gushed out, Johnson had the window open. The fire flared with the inrushing air.

Woody swapped tubs beneath the spout and passed the first partially filled tub to Trainham, who then handed it off to Johnson who threw the water in on the fire. Others took places in the brigade.

The pantry wall began to catch. The heat was intense. The splashes of water barely arrested the spread.

King Bibb and other neighbors broke open the kitchen door and re-directed tubs of water in that way. They had caught the fire in the nick of time and extinguished it after a few intense minutes.

The men continued to pump water and throw it on hot spots until satisfied the fire was completely out. The smell of kerosene was strong.

Nicholas Hall came down the county road in his buggy returning from the grand jury in Louisa. Crossing the tracks he encountered people in a commotion over another fire. Hall drove around to the barn. From his perspective, he could see no damage, just people gathered around the rear of the kitchen. He turned around and drove home to his own barn, unhitched his horse, and then went inside to tell Lizzie. The family hurried on foot to see what had happened.

Neighbors crowded as near as they could to the pantry to watch the detectives. Others pressed onto the back porch to stick their heads inside for a look. The detectives ordered folks to stand back while they worked. The men emerged a few minutes later with handfuls of dripping wet rags, some charred. All smelled of coal oil. Detectives held each cloth up in the daylight for examination. The rags looked like women's clothing. There was one particular shirtwaist with a dark stain. It looked like blood.

"Those are the clothes of my little servant," volunteered Lizzie.[44]

Heads turned in surprise to see Mrs. Hall standing there. She asked what had happened. The detectives wanted to know the same from her and began firing pointed questions. Caught off guard, Lizzie offered her first impression; it looked to her like someone had broken in through the pantry window and set the place afire. But those present knew that Johnny Johnson had forced opened the pantry window to fight the fire.

The point became salient over whether or not Johnson had removed the window screen. Obviously, a firebug would never stop to replace a window screen. Johnson was adamant that he tore the screen off in order to open the window. The family asserted the screen had been missing since the first fire.[45] In any event, no one disputed the fact that Mrs. Hall was the last person seen leaving the building before the fire.

At the Louisa courthouse, the special grand jury adjourned at five o'clock to reconvene on the morrow at a half past nine. They had finished hearing testimony and decided to vote in the morning; a true bill against Mrs. Hall was a foregone conclusion.

About half past five o'clock, detective Mallory reported to Shackelford that many people expected another incendiary attempt on the Hall store. The judge listened politely. Such brazen behavior was too outlandish to be taken seriously. Judge Shackelford expressed his appreciation for the report and insisted that Mallory join him and the county officers for dinner across the street at the Louisa Hotel.

At seven o'clock and midway through their meal, George Trainham sped into town trailing a plume of dust "like a meteor" and stopped outside the hotel.

"Green Springs is on fire again!" shouted Trainham from the dust cloud.[46]

Everyone in the dining room sprang at the alarm and hurried outside. Some, still with napkins tucked under their chins, ran outside while struggling not to choke on food. Judge Shackelford moved along with the others as smartly as the dignity of his office allowed and, upon reaching the gathering, nudged his way to Trainham, who was surrounded and blocked in his car by the growing attention.

Trainham's report of another fire at Hall's store left Judge Shackelford no alternative. For the safety of both the community and Mrs. Hall, the judge issued a bench warrant for the widow's immediate arrest. Sheriff Wash called Dr. Porter and pressed him and his vehicle into service. Within minutes Sheriff Wash and Deputy Bob Trice were on their way to arrest Mrs. Hall. Cars full of reporters and sensation seekers chased after them.

At news of another fire, most of the neighborhood flocked to the Hall store. An overcast sky threatened rain and hastened the onset of darkness. In the fading daylight, clusters of people stood under the big oaks and talked excitedly about the latest developments. They strained to discern the activity of that central group assembled at the rear of the outbuilding. Mrs. Hall parried question after pointed question from detectives who believed that the last family member seen leaving the store that afternoon had to have torched the pantry again.

The noise of approaching automobiles grew. Dr. Porter's car led the caravan down the county road. His car with the sheriff and deputy turned onto the lane, bounced across the tracks, and then drove up behind the store. A second vehicle followed with more deputies. Other automobiles full of reporters and curiosity seekers from Louisa parked around the store

　　　　　MURDER AT GREEN SPRINGS

and as close to the scene as they could. The headlamps cast their yellow light onto those gathered behind the residence. Sheriff Wash and Deputy Trice stepped from the car and walked toward the group. Exasperated, Mrs. Hall strode to meet Sheriff Wash. Her family followed her. Mrs. Hall stopped in front of the sheriff.

"You have come here to arrest me," said Lizzie, "but I am innocent of my husband's death, and I had nothing to do with these fires. You haven't any evidence against me. You can't convict me. Why should I want to burn down my own store?"[47]

Shaking his head, unable to consider her arguments, Sheriff Wash raised an open hand gesturing silence then spoke, "Mrs. Hall, I have a warrant for you, charging you with the murder of your husband."[48]

At that dreaded moment, Lizzie looked as if she had been struck. Daughter Essie threw her arms around her mother while younger daughter Mamie shrieked and began crying. White haired and bent with age, Ellen Hall hid her face in her hands. She sobbed and shook pitifully.

To everyone's surprise, Lizzie collected herself as if resigned to the fact and asked Wash if she might first be permitted to go to Mr. Hall's house to change clothes and pack a few things.

"I can't go like this," she said.

Wash hesitated. He was used to arresting men and was caught off guard by the request.

Hubert Dowdy stepped forward and spoke. "I am her brother. I will go with her and bring her back to you."[49]

Dr. Porter also offered to escort Mrs. Hall. Wash agreed to allow Mrs. Hall to change clothes and pack under the supervision of her brother and her doctor. Sheriff Wash and Deputy Trice escorted Mrs. Hall and her brother to Dr. Porter's car. Together the five drove down the lane to N. W. Hall's home where Lizzie went inside with her escorts to refresh herself and gather a change of clothes. This done, all five climbed back into the car with Mrs. Hall seated on the rear seat between the Sheriff and his Deputy.

Rather than return the way they came, Sheriff Wash avoided the crowd. Dr. Porter drove behind N. W. Hall's house. They then skirted the far side of the orchard to reach the depot and the rail crossing. Light rain began to fall. The crowd missed the maneuver until Dr. Porter cut on his headlights after crossing the tracks. The car turned onto the county road and left those waiting for Mrs. Hall standing in the wet sprinkle and momentarily confused. The newspaper reporters scrambled to their rides and hurried to catch up.

"I'm innocent. I'm innocent," Lizzie repeated over and over to Sheriff Wash who ignored her declarations.

The officers reached the courthouse ahead of their pursuers. Lizzie faced yet another crowd outside the courthouse. Dr. Porter parked behind the jail. The sheriff and deputy helped Mrs. Hall out of the car and led the prisoner around to the front of the courthouse, past jeering men and up the steps to the door where her attorney met her.

Lindsay Gordon had rushed there as soon as he received news of the warrant. He assured Mrs. Hall that she had nothing to worry about. Oh! How she wanted to believe that!

Standing before Judge Shackelford, Lizzie declared, "But I'm innocent!"

The judge instructed Gordon to advise his client to keep quiet. Commonwealth's Attorney Bibb recommended that Mrs. Hall be held pending formal indictment by the grand jury on the charge of murder.

Lindsay Gordon responded, "Your Honor, I think this is an outrage. There is absolutely no evidence against this woman. I have no confidence in the action of the grand jury preparing an indictment against her. This woman, Your Honor, is no more guilty than yourself, the commonwealth's attorney, or I. I consider her arrest an outrage," reiterated Gordon. "Your Honor, I ask that she be placed in custody of her father-in-law, N. W. Hall."[50]

Judge Shackelford shook his head in disagreement. He remanded her to Sheriff Wash's custody and ordered her appearance in court the next day at ten o'clock.

Lindsay Gordon requested bail for Mrs. Hall. Judge Shackelford flatly refused. Gordon countered that the Louisa jail was unfit for a woman and requested that she, at least, be held at the Louisa Hotel that night. Judge Shackelford considered the request reasonable and ordered the prisoner so accommodated. The fall of the gavel concluded the proceedings.

Mrs. Hall stepped forward and offered her hand in appreciation. Caught off guard by the gesture, Judge Shackelford accepted her handshake.

"I'm innocent," said Mrs. Hall.

The judge forced a smile in the awkward moment and returned the woman's hand without reply.

Sheriff Wash and Deputy Trice escorted Mrs. Hall out of the court-house to the Louisa Hotel accompanied by her brother Hubert Dowdy. After much ado over shifting guests around, the sheriff secured adjoining rooms in the crowded hotel. The door between the rooms was kept open to maintain surveillance.

Before Lindsay Gordon left the courthouse, a newspaperman approached him for comment. Gordon responded adamantly. "I consider the whole affair an outrage. There is absolutely no evidence against this woman, and I shall prove it. You may say for me that I shall fight this case to the finish. Mrs. Hall is as innocent as you or I, and when the case comes to trial I shall prove it to the satisfaction of the whole county. They had to find a victim, and they settled upon Mrs. Hall. It will all come out in the trial."[51]

BUT I'M INNOCENT!

CHAPTER *Six*

EXILE AND CABAL

*M*rs. Hall spent a fitful night locked in her room while Sheriff Wash and Deputy Trice took turns standing guard in the hallway. When the prisoner arose at daybreak, the alert guard awakened the sleeper. Wash went downstairs to clear a table in the corner of the dining room and warned reporters at the hotel to keep their distance. Trice remained on station outside Mrs. Hall's room while she attended her toilet. Wash returned with word that Mrs. Hall's family was already in the lobby waiting to see her.

Mrs. Hall looked tired, but presented her usual well kempt self. Wash and Trice appeared disheveled, more like vagabonds than county officials. Their alternating watches left both feeling bedraggled with dark circles beneath reddened eyes.

Wash and Trice escorted the black clad widow down to breakfast. Nicholas and Ellen Hall sat at the table with Lizzie's brother Hubert. Nick and Hugh stood as Lizzie entered the room. The family kept her company while she ate. They asked about her treatment and needs. Wash and Trice watched their charge from the next table and took turns eating.

Lizzie ignored her guards and the gawkers. She interested herself only in news of Essie and Mamie. Nicholas reported that Essie bore the situation stoically while Mamie was an emotional wreck. Both girls were back at the Hall's home with Aunt Jennie.

Reporters watched from the hallway and through the windows on the porch. One noted the "bountiful breakfast" Mrs. Hall consumed, as if that in itself carried significance.[1]

EXILE AND CABAL

The family talked until Sheriff Wash announced it was time to go. Lizzie adjusted her black veil and proceeded out the hotel flanked by the two officers with her family close behind.

They crossed Main Street on mud boards to the courthouse grounds. The crowd parted for the officers. Mrs. Hall walked solemnly past onlookers with an air described as "self-possessed" and ascended the courthouse steps with unaltered pace. Onlookers expected more emotion.

They went inside to the second floor where Lindsay Gordon waited in the courtroom. Gordon greeted Mrs. Hall and helped her into the chair beside him. She lifted her veil and smiled at him. She turned an indifferent glance to the staring spectators.

As Lizzie's family found seats near the front of the room outside the rail, Gordon informed her that the hearing was delayed until all the members of the grand jury were present. Time dragged until the last tardy juror arrived.

The grand jury finally assembled about a quarter after ten. Fifteen minutes later, foreman Deane handed the indictment to Philip Porter, the clerk of court. The courthouse bell tolled signaling court was about to open. The remaining spectators made their way from the courthouse green into the courtroom filling it to capacity.

All rose for Judge Shackelford's entrance. Court opened and the judge confirmed that the special grand jury found a true bill against Mrs. Hall in the death of her husband. Judge Shackelford announced that he was ready to hear prayer for bail.

Gordon began with characteristic eloquence, "Your Honor, I am perfectly satisfied that when all the evidence in this case is heard and when all the facts surrounding the mysteries which have made Green Springs notorious are learned, the cloud of suspicion hovering over my client will be blown away, and that she will be proven innocent. It is a pitiful case. This woman is the mother of two young children, one twelve and the other fifteen [sic] years of age. They are dependent upon her, and they are now all that she has. Her store, upon which she had depended for a living, is ruined, and because of this fatal suspicion in the neighborhood, her stock must be sold. The fair reputation which she so lately bore has been poisoned by the foul breath of suspicion, and there is now, Your Honor, none more lonely than she. Her children cry for her, and her own heart bleeds for them. I submit, Your Honor, a motion for bail."

Bibb countered, "Your Honor. The effect of what occurred at Green Springs yesterday is too far-reaching that this woman should be bailed. She should not be allowed to go at large. When this case comes to trial, the Commonwealth will be able to prove that Mrs. Hall is guilty of the crime as charged."

Gordon argued that his client posed no flight risk. She should be allowed bail.

Bibb strongly opposed Mrs. Hall's bail both for the sake of her own personal safety and that of the community. He made it plain that he had no desire for Mrs. Hall to be retained in the Louisa County jail; however, he asserted that the Richmond jail, for instance, had suitable facilities to accommodate the prisoner.[2]

"Your Honor," objected Gordon. "The Richmond jail is worse than the Louisa County jail. It is full of people – and other things.[3] I most respectfully urge, Your Honor, that my client be allowed to go under bond."

Judge Shackelford said that he recognized Mrs. Hall posed minimal flight risk, but the Commonwealth voiced legitimate concerns. Therefore, the court would admit her to bail in the sum of $5,000 provided that she leave and remain outside Louisa County until her trial. The court would permit occasional visits to consult counsel as necessary.

Gordon protested, but the judge offered only two choices: exile or jail. The attorney submitted that Mrs. Hall's needed to remain in Louisa to confer with him and requested that she be allowed to spend the next day at Green Springs putting her affairs in order. The court granted the concession, and Gordon accepted the terms.

The judge called the guarantors to the bench individually. Mrs. Hall was first to sign the bond. Many saw her smile as she returned to her seat. She sat and watched as others assured her appearance at trial. The one-armed, two fingered W. J. Roberts was second to sign followed by Magistrate James E. Hester, Jr., N. W. Hall, Ellen F. Hall, R. L. Gordon, Jr., and dentist Dr. W. O. Smith.[4]

As to trial date, Gordon asserted that he and his client were ready to go to trial immediately. Bibb, on the other hand, argued that the Commonwealth required considerable time to assemble its witnesses. Judge Shackelford scheduled the trial for July 14th, the beginning of the court's next term. The gavel fell, and Mrs. Hall was free to leave.

Gordon suggested to Mrs. Hall that she meet at his home later in the day to clarify matters. She agreed. Lizzie, her family, and Lindsay Gordon stepped from the courthouse into the group of newsmen waiting outside on the stoop ready to fire questions like so much artillery. Hubert Dowdy locked arms with Lizzie, and they pushed their way clear. Gordon acted as rear guard and remained to make a statement.

The reporters volleyed. "Where is Mrs. Hall going?" "Is it true she's going to Richmond?" "What about a guilty plea?" "Will Mrs. Hall plead insanity?" "Will the defense hire additional counsel?" "What about a change of venue?"

In most diplomatic manner, Lindsay Gordon stated simply that Mrs. Hall had relatives in Cumberland County, Buckingham County, and Richmond and that she would probably divide her time between them. He promised that the Commonwealth would find it more than ordinarily difficult to secure a conviction. There was no planned request for change of venue and no need for additional counsel. There would be no trial before a commission, no insanity plea, and no guilty plea.

Gordon concluded emphatically, "There is no ground for this charge against Mrs. Hall. She is innocent. This case will be tried on its merits."[5]

MURDER AT GREEN SPRINGS

At the Louisa Hotel, Lizzie and her party seated themselves in the dining room. They ignored the stares and ate dinner. The family took the day's success as a positive sign. After dinner, Lizzie and her brother stepped to the desk to arrange accommodations for the night. The clerk informed them that the hotel was filled.

Hugh inquired after Lizzie's bag. The clerk produced it from behind the desk and handed it to him. The family left the hotel. Nicholas and Ellen said goodbye and went home. Hugh then drove Lizzie in his buggy from boarding house to boarding house looking for a place to stay.

Hugh had no trouble finding quarters for just himself; however, all lodging in the town was closed to Mrs. Hall.[6] Upon realizing this, they proceeded to meet with Lindsay Gordon at his home. Gordon and his wife extended their hospitality for the night.

That afternoon, Gordon advised Mrs. Hall on a number of points. The attorney cautioned her again not to speak with reporters. Since newsmen expected her in Richmond the following evening, he suggested an alternate plan to avoid being hounded. The consultation renewed Lizzie's confidence that everything was going to be all right.

Hugh needed to go to the train station and send their sister Carrie a telegram to expect Lizzie. Dowdy politely excused himself past the newsmen posted outside Gordon's gate. They hungered for a word from anyone entering or leaving. Their frustrations grew as Mrs. Hall cloistered herself with her attorney.

In the middle of the afternoon, Dr. Porter's automobile came down the street and stopped beside the reporters. He greeted them and extended a special invitation to tour part of the county. The reporters accepted the offer. They piled into his motorcar and rode away.

Everyone assumed the best opportunities for news were right there in Louisa. The departure of the newspapermen *en mass* was a sight to make the world stop and stare. The automobile disappeared in the direction of Green Springs Depot. This fueled fresh rumors. However, the depot was not their destination. Instead, several prominent residents of the county had arranged for the reporters to tour the *real* Green Springs.

The railroad tracks through Green Springs Depot stretched over a watershed ridge. The soil there was poor, and the terrain restrictive to small, subsistence farms. By contrast, large, prosperous plantations dating back to colonial times stretched across the adjacent rolling plain known as the Green Springs Valley.

Eroded volcanic intrusions formed fertile, sandy loam in a five-by-seven mile, saucer-like depression. The long direction stretched from the South Anna River in western Louisa County southwards. In the mid 1700's, successful tobacco planters built large plantations in this region and amassed fortunes. Richard Morris established one such estate about 1772. On his property were natural springs with lush vegetation. This inspired his plantation's name *Green Springs*.

Morris built a resort at the springs. This became a popular retreat for wealthy, health-seeking colonists. Thomas Jefferson commented on the medicinal benefits of the springs.[7] The iron and magnesium rich waters remained popular for many years, but the resort fell into disuse with the development of more popular spas featuring natural, warm, mineral springs elsewhere in Virginia. The Green Springs resort closed in the early 1800's.

Tobacco production rapidly exhausted the once fertile soil and threatened the Green Springs plantations with ruin. While serving as Virginia Commissary during the Revolutionary War, Richard Morris, then Colonel Morris, conceived the idea of growing wheat. The idea proved sound.

Neighbor James Watson at Ionia (ca. 1770) experimented with crop rotation and fertilization with clover and other green manures. This replenished the soil, and within a relatively short period of time, the local plantations became mainly grain producers.

Roads were bad. For planters in Green Springs, the best route to market was by wagon to neighboring Fluvanna County for loading onto bateaux at Palmyra or Columbia. Transport via the Kanawah Canal was cumbersome and expensive, but preferable to shipping overland. By 1840, construction of the Louisa Railroad overcame the county's lack of navigable waters and provided planters a more expedient and economical access to markets. By the 1850's, existing plantations in the Green Springs area thrived and more were established.

Though the wheat fields of Green Springs were productive throughout the Civil War, the plantations remained untargeted and relatively untouched by the conflict. The Battle of Trevilian Station in June 1864 was the only significant engagement in the county and focused on disrupting the Virginia Central Railroad, formerly the Louisa Railroad.

The Civil War ended slavery in the South and drastically changed the lives of most Virginia planters. Those in Green Springs adapted well. "Not only did wealth remain concentrated in Louisa after the war, but most of it remained in the same hands."[8]

Historian Crandall Shifflett documented the transition in Louisa County's economic structure from paternalism to patronism. Planters switched from crops raised by slave labor to grass farming and share cropping. The end result was that poor whites experienced the same poverty after the war as before, and the freed blacks who stayed in the county joined them in subsistence living. "Tenancy ensnared black and white alike wherever it occurred."[9]

Dr. Porter took the road toward Poindexter with its vistas of large grass farms accented by the Blue Ridge Mountains in the distance. The newspapermen were struck by the scenic beauty as they drove into the *real* Green Springs. They rode past *Ionia* and other plantations crowning the hills of the rolling farm land.

At *Sylvania* (ca. 1738), the reporters met owner Frank Morris.[10] As the reporters stood beneath the massive "original oaks" in front of the manor house atop a hill, they beheld his brother George Morris' plantation *Green Springs* and much of the verdant valley that comprised the *real* Green Springs. To their right was *Harkwood* (ca. 1852), where former owner Richard O. Morris constructed its Italian style mansion.[11] Before the Civil War, Morris worked its 2,800 acres with at least 104 personally owned slaves.[12]

Dr. Porter carried the reporters from *Sylvania* to *Bracketts* (ca. 1791), the neighboring estate built by the Watson family and maintained in their possession for one hundred years. Carl H. Nolting, the current owner, entertained the newspapermen and escorted his guests around his realm. Nolting called special attention to his pedigreed livestock: Welsh and Shetland ponies, Hereford cattle and Cheviot sheep. The reporters were greatly impressed by their host, who was arguably the most influential man in Louisa County.

Carl Nolting was born in Richmond July 31, 1874, the son of Emil Otto Nolting, "One of Richmond's most prominent and highly respected businessmen."[13] Carl attended prestigious private schools and graduated from the University of Virginia in 1895. Nolting then worked as a bank teller for five years until inheriting great wealth from his father's estate. His family's connections opened many doors. He served as a director of the Virginia Central Railroad and treasurer of the Virginia Airship Company. In 1903, Nolting bought *Bracketts* and moved to Green Springs. Like his father, Nolting was an ardent Democrat and party supporter. In 1908 and 1910 he was elected from Louisa to the Virginia House of Delegates. That was just the beginning of a life of public service and political aspirations.[14]

MURDER AT GREEN SPRINGS

Over refreshments, Nolting tactfully asserted that the reporters needed to realize that there were actually two Green Springs. The Green Springs District of Louisa County had, obviously, assumed its name from the Green Springs region in which the original *Green Springs* plantation was built. However, as a matter of course, the district's train depot also assumed the name Green Springs. The prestigious plantation owners and the citizenry of the depot environs were, most assuredly, at extreme opposite ends of economic and social spectra.

Morris and Nolting made it clear that those living in the *real* Green Springs regretted the tragic events nearby, but hoped the tour would prevent any further confusion. Residents of Green Springs wanted none of the depot's stigma transferred to them by mistaken association with their community.

The newsmen got the point. Two days later, A. R. W. MacKreth of the *Times-Dispatch* included the following mention in his article that Sunday:

"At the request of people who live in Green Springs district proper, which is several miles southeast of the little wayside station of the name, it should be stated that there is both a difference and a distinction between the two places. Green Springs district lies upon fertile fields and fallow land near the foothills of the Blue Ridge Mountains. Here is one of the richest sections of farming lands in the State, and here are the ancestral seas of families whose names still live in Virginia's history. Dr. Harry W. Porter took several newspaper men on a sight-seeing tour of Green Springs section this afternoon, and they were hospitably received by Carl Nolting, Frank Morris and others living here. The scene of the murder and incendiary fires lies at a small station eight miles west of Louisa Courthouse, which was named after the Green Springs section, and has no social or other connection with the Green Springs district proper."[15]

Though a week passed before publication, a reporter from the *News Leader* also honored the hosts' wishes. Along with the latest innuendo about Mrs. Hall, he dutifully printed his account of the excursion:

> "The Green Spring valley section of Louisa county, one of the prettiest pieces of country in the state of Virginia, is in no way connected with the Green Spring Depot part of the county and the residents of the valley are very much worried over the fact that a crime so terrible could be committed in their neighborhood, although the railroad station by the name is located about ten miles from the real Green Spring."[16]

The two Green Springs were distinctly different, and the confusion was no small matter to the Virginia gentry.[17] Following their intensive, thirty-five mile long tour, reporters of the state's major papers used a new geographic term "Green Springs Station" crafted specifically to designate Mrs. Hall's neighborhood.[18]

Indeed, George H. Browne, Frank C. Morris, George W. Morris, and Carl H. Nolting, the respective owners of *Harkwood*, *Sylvania*, *Green Springs*, and *Bracketts*, represented considerable economic power. The Nolting and the Morris families of Green Springs were vestiges of Virginia's antebellum aristocracy and possessed considerable clout.[19]

In Louisa County, the residents of the *real* Green Springs were as privileged and revered as much as any First Family of Virginia. Assuming the noblest intentions on their part, there remained considerable question as to what extent others might venture to court favor in satisfying either the expressed or perceived desire of an *FFV*. Any accommodation benefiting the rich and powerful ultimately generated a corresponding negative repercussion for Mrs. Hall, even if only by the simplest mechanism that illuminating the *real* Green Springs diverted light and made Mrs. Hall's corner proportionately darker. Nevertheless, very little in

Louisa County lay beyond the reach of a tentacle stretched from the *real* Green Springs.[20]

On the very day that the reporters toured *Sylvania* and *Bracketts*, A. R. W. MacKreth wrote for the *Times-Dispatch* that "Several Louisa County citizens already have begun a movement to employ additional counsel for the Commonwealth, to aid Mr. Bibb. Outside counsel may be employed through private subscriptions, or the citizens who are interesting themselves in the sensational case may ask the county supervisors for an appropriation."[21] The specific citizens "interesting themselves" were not identified; however, the affairs hosted by Morris and Nolting coincided with MacKreth documenting the beginnings of a cabal.

Like warm waters power a tropical storm to hurricane force, the occult interests in the county energized a vortex of visceral virtue swirling around Mrs. Hall. MacKreth's next report was the red sky in the gathering tempest:

"At the request of one of the County Board of Supervisors, Judge Shackelford communicated with Edward Grimsley[22], a well known attorney of Culpeper County, suggesting that he might be employed to assist Commonwealth's Attorney Bibb in the prosecution of the case. Mr. Bibb received a letter from Mr. Grimsley this morning, and immediately replied that he would not take any hand in employing outside counsel to assist in the prosecution, and that the matter, as far as he is concerned, would be left entirely in the hands of the supervisors. The Board of Supervisors meets on June Trades Day, which falls on the second Monday in that month, but it is probable that a special meeting will be called before that date, and that the supervisors will decide to employ additional counsel to assist in the prosecution. Mr. Grimsley will be here on Tuesday to confer with several of the supervisors, and it is now regarded as practically settled that he will be employed."[23]

Ambivalence plagued Willie Bibb. He was the commonwealth's attorney for Louisa; it was his job to prosecute. Pressure had forced Bibb to convene the special grand jury, but prosecution was not his preference. Nevertheless, Bibb believed himself equal to the challenge to pursue conviction. He had faced Gordon one on one in the courtroom before, though never at such disadvantage. Bibb dreaded another high visibility defeat by Gordon. Meddlers shared this concern and demanded that Bibb have *assistance*. The faction's lack of confidence in him troubled the young attorney, but personal concerns were irrelevant. Bibb had lost say in the matter before Mrs. Hall even left the county. The prosecution had acquired a life of its own.

On Saturday morning May 16th, Hubert Dowdy woke Lizzie up at dawn. He hitched his buggy, and they left Mr. Gordon's. Though the sun had risen, few townspeople were out and about at that hour on a Saturday. They left town unnoticed and were back at Green Springs by six o'clock.

The depot presented a depressing sight. Lizzie's store was deserted and lifeless. In front of it on the turnout were the usual flat cars for loading lumber and pulpwood. But now there were also two box cars parked between the burned depot and Dunkum's store. The railroad had provided them to serve temporarily as depot and store until both could be rebuilt.[24]

The Hall home was a happy contrast. Essie and Mamie greeted their mother with hugs and kisses. The family ate breakfast together. This refreshed Lizzie and lifted her spirit.

Lizzie explained to her daughters that she needed to leave for a while, but would write often and, Lord willing, be back with them soon. The girls helped their mother assemble her things. There were no personal items left at the store to retrieve. This made packing quicker and allowed more time for enjoying each other before having to leave.

Sheriff Wash and Bill Roberts came to the door. They needed the store unlocked. Lindsay Gordon had arranged for them to inventory the store preparatory to sale. Also Bill Roberts promised to look after the store while she was away.

Mrs. Hall gave Roberts the key. She refused to go near the building again herself, lest another incident occur.

At half past four, Sheriff Wash returned with Deputy Bob Trice to escort Mrs. Hall to the train. Nicholas Hall had her baggage loaded on the wagon ready to go. He had been to the depot earlier to arrange passage. People had already gathered there to see Mrs. Hall depart.

To avoid problems and as much humiliation a possible, the family waited as long as they dared without missing the train. Fifteen minutes before the train was due, they walked to the depot behind the wagon. Both Lizzie and Ellen were veiled in their widow's weeds. The procession looked very funeral-like.

Sheriff Wash asked folks at the depot to keep their distance. The family stepped to the platform to wait for the train. Deputy Trice and Nicholas Hall unloaded Lizzie's bags and trunk. Wiley Woody and another station hand paid their respects and took charge of the baggage. The whistle sounded the engine's approach.

Woody and his helper loaded the trunk and other luggage into the baggage car. Lizzie held onto one small satchel. She briefly lifted her veil to kiss her daughters goodbye.

Deputy Trice was to ride the train far enough to verify Mrs. Hall's departure to the court's satisfaction. To the onlookers' surprise, Ellen Hall boarded first with Lizzie behind her. Trice followed somewhat puzzled that Mrs. Hall would take her mother-in-law with her to Richmond. Lizzie seated herself at a window with Ellen Hall beside her. Deputy Trice took the closest open seat behind them. Lizzie and Ellen waved to the girls as the wheels thrust the train forward. It gathered speed and left Green Springs behind.

After a brief stop to pick up passengers at Trevilians, the train reached the Louisa Station at 5:22 P.M. There Deputy Trice received another surprise. Lizzie and Ellen got up out of their seats and moved toward the exit.

The unexpected action confused Deputy Trice. Once off the train, he started toward Mrs. Hall as if to take her into custody for defying the court order, but wisely waited. He followed the ladies through the station and out the other side where he saw them meet Lindsay Gordon waiting with his carriage to take them back to his home for the night. There was nothing for Trice to do. Technically, Mrs. Hall was conferring with her attorney.

Gordon's trick worked. Trice's perplexity foreshadowed that of the crowd gathered that evening at Richmond's Main Street Station. The next day's *Richmond Virginian* reported:

"After about a hundred men and women, many of them drawn to the Main Street Station by sheer curiosity had waited for the arrival at 8 o'clock last night of the train from Louisa, and after they had scanned the face of every woman who came though the gates into the station, some one who had been a passenger on the train from a point beyond Green Spring, gave forth the information that Mrs. Hall left the train at Louisa."[25]

Those desiring to catch a glimpse of the reputed arson-murderess now dealt with an uncertain arrival.

Stretching the court's indulgence, Lizzie boarded the Sunday evening train for Richmond. Arriving at 8 P.M., a gentleman from the train offered to carry the widow's suitcase. The impromptu escort delayed her being recognized, but a woman dressed for deep mourning was difficult to ignore. The two exited the staion. Lizzie thought she had evaded reporters.

At the bottom of the steps, the gentleman secured a taxi and opened the door for her. He reached in and placed her suitcase on the seat. Lizzie thanked the man for his kindness. When her escort stepped away, a reporter from the *Richmond Virginian* realized it was Mrs. Hall and rushed the cab.

Mrs. Hall saw the man approach and shouted to the driver loud enough for the reporter to copy. "Please hurry! Take me to 2114 Venable Street!"

The cab pulled away. The newsman jumped on the running board, stuck his head in the window and asked Mrs. Hall for an interview. This brashness frightened Lizzie. She hollered frantically for him to get off and leave her alone. When the taxi slowed at the end of the block to corner, the man jumped off.

The taxi pulled up in front of the home of Nat and Carrie Dowdy. Both Lizzie and the driver were visibly shaken from the experience. Lizzie apologized for the scene. Carrie and husband Nat Dowdy met her at the stoop. Carrie welcomed Lizzie and ushered her inside while Nat settled with the driver and got her bag. Once Lizzie was safely ensconced in her sister's home, reporters gathered outside the house.

Nat Dowdy, a first cousin as well as brother-in-law, worked for the Richmond Locomotive Works. The muscular, former miller presented an imposing figure. Nat strode outside and told reporters that Mrs. Hall would grant no interviews and asked them to leave his premises. The men distanced themselves from his gate, but kept vigil on the house hoping beyond hope that Mrs. Hall might favor them with a few words.

Carrie showed her sister to the guest room where Nat had already stored her preceding baggage. A little later the family supped together. Lizzie savored peace for the first time since April 15th. She had only entered the eye of the storm.

The next week a grand juror commented that "sweet peace" prevailed again in Louisa County.[26] Mrs. Hall's arrest had calmed many people, and the county appeared to have returned to normal. Residents generally maintained that only the conviction of Mrs. Hall would avenge Victor Hall.

On Saturday, May 23rd, the Louisa County Board of Supervisors held a special meeting to decide on hiring additional counsel to assist Commonwealth's Attorney Bibb.

"At a special call meeting of the Board of Supervisors of Louisa, Co. held at Louisa on the 23rd day of May 1914, there were present W. T. Meade, chairman, H. J. Harris, Lee Rosson, and Earl P. Anderson. The question of the employment of additional counsel to assist the Comth's Atty. In the prosecution of the Hall case was taken up and the Board after making consideration decided that additional counsel should be employed and appointed W. T. Meade Chairman, and W. C. Bibb, Comth's Atty, a committee to select such counsel as they Think [sic] best and to arrange with said counsel as to the compensation to be received, W. C. Bibb Comth's Atty, asked the Board to insert in this order the fact that he has not asked for assistance in this case, and that the action of the board in this matter was their individual action and not at his suggestion which is therefore inserted herein.

Ordered that the Board do now adjourn.

W. T. Meade, chairman"[27]

Again Bibb felt humiliated that the Board of Supervisors mistrusted his abilities against Gordon's. Bibb could not escape that it had been just five years since he had fought Gordon before the Virginia Supreme Court

of Appeals and lost. Ironically, Gordon was then the commonwealth's attorney and won on behalf of the same Board of Supervisors.

The board knew from the very beginning what one newspaper later reported: "It is freely stated that if the Commonwealth expects to get a verdict of guilty it must do two things: First. It must prove Mrs. Hall guilty. Then it must overcome the personal influence of Lindsay Gordon."[28] To overcome the latter obstacle, they insisted Bibb have help.

While the *courthouse clique* pondered strategies, Lindsay Gordon worked. He reviewed facts gathered before and during the grand jury investigation. Gordon lacked only the Pinkerton reports. He found no real evidence to incriminate anyone, especially Mrs. Hall. The burden of proof rested with the prosecution. There was no proof.

People acquainted with Mrs. Hall, believed her innocent without reservation. Gordon hired Bill Roberts to chauffer him around Louisa and Fluvanna Counties. The attorney easily gathered an array of respected individuals eager to appear in court to establish Mrs. Hall's character and untarnished reputation.

Mrs. Hall returned to Louisa County on May 27th to confer with Lindsay Gordon. They discussed the list of witnesses. The prosecution would not be able to produce a single witness against her. However, Gordon apprised Mrs. Hall on the troublesome issue of obtaining copies of Detective MacKay's reports. The Pinkerton agency had sent them to Sterling Hall. They had also provided copies to Commonwealth's Attorney Bibb. Both the Pinkerton agency and Sterling Hall repeatedly ignored requests for copies. The commonwealth's attorney flatly refused to share them. Gordon had to know what was in the reports before going to trial.

The following day was particularly painful for Lizzie as she attended the auction of her property. Virtually everything went under the hammer.

J. F. Bickers auctioned off the store's inventory, furniture, livestock and farm implements. Only a few select furnishings remained.

Bill Roberts had occupied the residence since Mrs. Hall's exile. Roberts returned home after the auction having faithfully guarded her property. Lizzie left Louisa County again and stayed with her brother Hubert in Cumberland County.

W. T. Meade and W. C. Bibb narrowed their list of candidates to assist the prosecution. Rumors of Edward Grimsley of Culpeper were superseded by speculation that the famous Richmond attorney Louis O. Wendenburg would spearhead the prosecution. Having successfully prosecuted the infamous Henry Beattie, Wendenburg was a household word. However, Wendenburg was currently running against former Governor Montague for the Democratic nomination for U.S. Senator. The politically astute already knew Wendenburg was preoccupied with his campaign.

Another renowned lawyer rumored for the job was the lead attorney in Beattie's defense Hiram M. Smith, Jr. Just the previous year, Smith had represented Floyd and Claude Allen before the Virginia Supreme Court of Appeals in an unsuccessful attempt to spare their lives.[29]

On June 3rd, the suspense climaxed. Commonwealth's Attorney Bibb took the train to Richmond and reached an agreement with prominent Richmond attorney M. J. Fulton. Bibb reported his success to Judge Shackelford and the Louisa County Board of Supervisors.

Mrs. Hall returned to Louisa on June 12th to confer with her attorney. Lindsay Gordon greeted her at the station with Essie and Mamie. Gordon informed her that Judge Shackelford rescinded the exile order. After Lizzie met with Gordon, she returned to Green Springs to stay with the Halls and her daughters until trial.

The Louisa County Board of Supervisors held its regularly scheduled meeting Sunday, June 14th. Their decision entered the minutes: "The Board of Supervisors after hearing a report from the committee directs the employment of Judge Fulton to assist in the prosecution of the Hall

MURDER AT GREEN SPRINGS

murder case, at the sum of $550.00 provided he will agree to accept employment at this amount."[30]

Securing additional counsel in significant cases was not unusual. Indeed, the McCue and Beattie trials featured legal teams for both prosecution and defense. However, less than two years before hiring Fulton, the Louisa County Board of Supervisors comprised of the same individuals oversaw a "financially embarrassed county" and were ordered to appear before Judge Shackelford "to show cause why they should not install proper heating arrangements in the Court House."[31] In light of Louisa County's recent financial distress, the employment of Fulton by its Board of Supervisors was a curious expenditure.[32] Nevertheless, the body believed the situation justified the extravagance.

On July 1st, W. T. Meade called a special meeting of the Board of Supervisors to issue a warrant in the full amount of $550.00 to pay for M. J. Fulton's services. The announcement of Fulton's hiring appeared in the next day's *News Leader*.

Minitree Jones Fulton was born April 10, 1867 in Grayson County, Virginia. He graduated from Washington and Lee University in June, 1891 with a Bachelor of Law degree. After practicing law sixteen years in Front Royal, he was elected from that region to the State Senate in 1903. M. J. Fulton served with distinction on a number of committees particularly those for Public Roads, Internal Navigation, Schools and Colleges, and Courts of Justice. As state senator he helped create the Department of State Highways and the State Bureau of Insurance.

In 1906, Governor Montague appointed Fulton as one of the directors of the Jamestown Exposition. The following year when his senate term expired, Fulton left his only public office and moved to Richmond to further his law practice. His clientele and reputation grew as he successfully argued many cases before the Virginia Supreme Court of Appeals.

Fulton's first wife died in 1905. Since 1911, he had been married to the former Adelaide Sullivan. Fulton was active in his community and a member of a number of civic organizations. He was a Methodist, a Mason and an Elk.

Fulton, a founder of the Virginia State Bureau of Insurance, was also son-in-law to Lawrence F. Sullivan, comptroller of the Chesapeake and Ohio Railway. Fulton, therefore, entered the Hall Case with a propensity to favor the interests of said agency and railway and likely biased toward the investigations of their respective agents Scott and Angle.

Most importantly, Fulton's impressive credentials did not mask the fact that he was essentially a *hired gun*. His considerable experience and reputation was not sought to enhance fairness or objectivity. Fulton was employed only for one purpose: to convict Mrs. Hall.

Lindsay Gordon became increasingly concerned as the prosecution mustered formidable talent and resources. He realized Mrs. Hall's defense was not as simple as first thought. Gordon knew he must either prevent the prosecution from hiring Fulton or counter with assembling a defense team of similar stature.

Despite the best efforts of Lindsay and Sandy Gordon before Judge Shackelford to block Fulton's employment, there were no legal grounds to prohibit the prosecution from hiring additional counsel. Gordon was forced to concede the point and proceeded to address the bothersome matter of not being able to obtain copies of the Pinkerton reports. The defense asserted that access to the papers was crucial. Judge Shackelford agreed and assured Gordon that he would instruct the commonwealth's attorney to provide them.

Over the next couple of days, Sandy Gordon tried several more times to acquire the Pinkerton reports from Bibb. Bibb repeatedly refused claiming that Mrs. Hall never paid for the investigation.

The Fourth of July was followed by legal fireworks. By Sunday, July 5th, defense counsel had still not been able to get copies of the Pinkerton reports. The trial was just nine days away! Sandy Gordon interrupted Judge Shackelford's *Sabbath* rest with a telephone call. Aggravated with

MURDER AT GREEN SPRINGS

Bibb's obstinacy, if not obstruction, by withholding the information, Judge Shackelford issued the following hand written note:

Orange, Va. July 5th, 1914

Mr. W. C. Bibb:

Atty for Comwlth.

Louisa, Va.

Dear Sir:

I have a phone message from Mr. A. T. Gordon in reference to the Pinkerton reports, in which he says that, Mr. Hall is out of the state and they can not reach him to get his reports. If I understood him right, over the phone, you are willing to give him copies of your reports if he will pay for them the sum of $127.00, the price, I presume, which is due Pinkertons. Mr. Gordon agrees to deposit the money subject to my decision as to liability. It is very hard to get at the point over a phone line, as I have said before, Mrs. Hall is entitled to these reports from somebody and I strongly advise that you let them have copies of yours, if they deposit the money to the credit of the Clerk of the Court, to be paid out on the order of the Court. In a matter involving the life of a human being, the Commonwealth can not be illiberal in its dealings.

Mr. Gordon will hand you this and I have asked him to read it, before delivery.

Yours very truly,

(Signed) Geo. S. Schackelford

I hope you gentlemen will procure the services of a stenographer, between you.[33]

Later that afternoon, Sandy Gordon had the Pinkerton reports in hand and took them to his brother's house. The two men examined the papers, nearly eighty pages. They discovered nothing extraordinary. Mrs. Hall's account appeared consistent. The other statements mirrored information and innuendo already known to the defense. After reading the reports, their chief concerns centered not so much with content but as to how the prosecution might present the information in court.

Lindsay Gordon considered Hill Carter for additional defense counsel. Carter was well known statewide and a familiar figure in the Louisa Court. At the turn of the century, Carter was chief defense counsel in the Pottie Case, a protracted Louisa County law suit disputing rights to certain local pyrite deposits. At the time it was Carter's most important, visible and lucrative case.

Carter battled the Pottie Case for eight years against the Sulphur Mines represented by members of the county's *courthouse clique*. He won reversal of the Louisa court's decision and secured retrial. The prosecution recognized Carter as a formidable opponent.[34]

Gordon and Carter had become well acquainted during the Virginia Constitutional Convention of 1901-02 while representing Louisa and Hanover Counties respectively. Carter had already bested the same adversarial machinery now facing Gordon; it was a match of kindred spirits.

The light-hearted, gracious Hill Carter was in all respects the quintessential southern gentleman. His respect as an accomplished attorney was often surpassed by the honor bestowed by Virginians on their Confederate survivors with distinguished service. He enlisted in the First Virginia Cavalry at age seventeen, and served under legendary generals Fitzhugh Lee and J. E. B. Stuart. He was wounded in the Battle of Spotsylvania Court House and returned to duty to fight in Early's Valley Campaign. Shortly before Appomattox, he was captured and imprisoned at infamous Point Lookout, Maryland.

In contrast to the dashing figure flashing his saber in cavalry charges fifty years before, sixty-eight year old Hill Carter's appearance was, in a word, round. His portly body with round belly was surmounted by a round head with round features. Complementing his round, gray head of hair was a full, gray moustache drooped over his round mouth in a rounded, crescent moon shape. The overall effect was that his bodily presence just seemed to roll in and out of a room.

Like many lawyers, his appearance was more unkempt than that tolerated in other professions and his attire less stylish than general society. He preferred to wear seasonal clothing for the duration of that season with regular cleaning and pressing grossly understating generally accepted frequency. Carter was noted for one particular frayed alpaca jacket worn during fair weather months. He wore that coat for more summers than anyone could remember. "His pants were never pressed, his shoes were never shined, and his hair was never combed."[35]

Carter was well known for his sense of humor. This included a penchant for elaborate practical jokes. Sometimes these extended beyond social and office surroundings finding their way into the courtroom at the expense of some novice attorney.

Three years before the Hall Case, Hill Carter achieved considerable newspaper recognition as a member of the defense counsel for Henry Beattie. Carter delivered the closing argument for Beattie's defense in the nationally publicized case. Beattie was convicted and electrocuted for slaying his wife. The association of Carter with Henry Beattie in everyone's mind was inescapable; nevertheless, Carter was imminently qualified in so many respects that Gordon discounted the potential influence of this recent and most celebrated aspect of Carter's career.

Just weeks before trial, Special Agent Monte Angle delivered a surprise witness to the prosecution. Strangely paralleling his contributions to the Harrison Case, Angle located a man with key information. Charles F. Johnston was a cousin of Elsie Wood and an employee of the Chesapeake and Ohio Railway. The C & O's policeman brought the clerk to Fulton's office in the Mutual Building in Richmond. The man related his story about a visit to the Hall store nine days prior to the murder. The interviewers formulated a damning conclusion from loose assumptions.

Meanwhile, Lindsay Gordon remained as confident in establishing Mrs. Hall's incapacity to kill her husband as he was in the prosecution's inability to prove otherwise. Considering the nature of the evidence, he believed he needed little other than character witnesses. The charge against Mrs. Hall was based solely on rumor and innuendo.

Victor Hall's pistol with the spent cartridge was the only significant piece of evidence. Too many reliable witnesses, including Bibb, dismissed it at the outset as the murder weapon. To support this position, Gordon had Bill Roberts and Samuel H. Flannagan test fire a .38 Smith & Wesson revolver on July 8th using a black powder cartridge. Afterwards, the two appeared at Gordon's office. All three examined the pistol and determined that the burned powder smell of a recently fired weapon was readily apparent.

Lindsay Gordon traveled to Richmond. He met with Hill Carter who agreed to join the defense. Gordon returned to Louisa in time to examine the pistol again with Roberts and Flannagan who had repeated the previous day's test with a smokeless powder cartridge. The results were the same. There was no mistaking a pistol fired after nine hours.[36]

That evening Gordon visited Judge Shackelford and requested a postponement of the trial due to the late addition of Carter to the defense team. The judge agreed and rescheduled the trial for July 28th.

At that same time, Gordon also asked that the list of jurors assembled during the height of hostile feelings against Mrs. Hall be rejected and a new list drafted. Gordon weighed the prosecution's resistance to a change

of venue along with the prospect of facing an imported jury of strangers already exposed to the statewide publicity. Gordon decided early on that it was best to defend his client before the local venire who all knew and respected Gordon, yet the defense preferred a fresh selection. Judge Shackelford rejected Gordon's request to quash the *venire facias*.

On July 14th, Sandy Gordon entered a plea to void the indictment against Mrs. Hall. The plea claimed denial of due process and that the grand jury visited her domicile and mingled with a hostile crowd contrary to law.[37] The court rejected the plea.

Everyone knew that Smith & Wesson manufactured only quality firearms. Gordon supposed that if Victor Hall was shot, as alleged, with his own, premium brand pistol, the bullet would have passed completely through his head contrary to fact. To support his idea, Gordon tasked Roberts and Flannagan to conduct another experiment.[38]

On July 17th, the men fired a number of rounds with a .38 Smith & Wesson pistol into some "old pine boards." Results varied. Some bullets went all the way through. Some did not. The test was inconclusive. Ultimately, it proved evidence only of a slapdash reaction by the defense to late rumors of a surprise witness.

Louisa Courthouse circa 1905-1914 – Beside the courthouse to the left is the jail, to the right the commonwealth's attorney's office. The slab in foreground marks the public well. (Photo Courtesy of the Louisa County Historical Society)

Mrs. Hall as she appeared about the time of her trial and published in the Richmond Virginian, May 14, 1914. (Photo Courtesy of the Library of Virginia)

CHAPTER
Seven

VORTEX OF
VISCERAL VIRTUE

MURDER AT GREEN SPRINGS

n Tuesday, July 28th, there were no vacancies in Louisa. The hotel and houses with rooms to rent were filled with people anxious to attend the trial of the accused murderess. Many homes crowded beds and floor pallets with relatives, friends, and friends of friends. The eastbound train delivered curiosity seekers from Charlottesville; the westbound brought more from Richmond. The dusty, dirt roads were congested with horse-drawn and motorized vehicles of every description. Many came on foot. Only the dedication of the Confederate memorial in front of the courthouse nine years earlier had attracted a greater number, but never such intensity.[1]

The weather was perfect. It was clear and unseasonably cool. People filled the courtroom an hour before the session opened. Ironically, most spectators were women.[2]

Mrs. Hall arrived a half hour early escorted by Hubert Dowdy. Her two daughters and the Halls walked with them. Mrs. Hall met with Lindsay Gordon for some final instructions and encouragement. She then waited with Sandy Gordon while Lindsay led the rest of the family into the courtroom and seated them outside the rail near the defense table. Most of Mrs. Hall's eight brothers and sisters were present.

Prosecutors W. C. Bibb and M. J. Fulton were already at their table. Fulton had arrived the previous evening and conferred with Bibb until late into the night. Both looked fresh, collected, and ready to begin. In contrast, Lindsay Gordon already looked tired.

A man in military uniform seated to the side of the bench caught many eyes. Thomas A. Williams of the Richmond Light Infantry Blues had been summoned from maneuvers to serve as one of two court stenographers. Sterling Hall took a seat in the front of the room away from his parents. He was there to assist the prosecution.

Ca-Clang! Ca-Clang! Ca-Clang!

The courthouse bell rang promptly at ten o'clock signaling the start of court. Sheriff Wash called for everyone to rise. The Honorable George S. Shackelford entered and seated himself at the bench. The judge grasped the gavel and rapped order. The room was packed with every seat taken. Some stood along the walls.

The courtroom was silent when Mrs. Hall entered clad in widow's weeds with veil raised, her pale countenance visible. She ignored the hundreds of stares and went to the defense table. Gordon stood and helped her into the seat beside him.

Lindsay Gordon remained standing to address the court. Spectators focused their attention anticipating the defense's opening volley. Then Gordon spoke. However, the attorney simply begged the court's indulgence to hear a statement regarding settlement of an unrelated estate issue.[3] The court obliged.

The disappointing delay created restlessness in the crowd. They had not come to hear the mundane dribble of a civil matter. After a few, seemingly endless minutes, the gavel fell. Gordon took his seat. Judge Shackelford turned to the prosecution and asked if the Commonwealth was ready with its case.

Bibb replied, "If Your Honor please, the Commonwealth is ready."

In like manner the court asked the defense if it was ready.

"It is," replied Gordon, but in a final attempt to dismiss the charge as groundless added, "If Your Honor please, we wish to enter a demurrer to the indictment."[4] This was an extraordinary motion for a murder charge.

"Denied," replied the judge mechanically. "The clerk will arraign the prisoner."

MURDER AT GREEN SPRINGS

Clerk Philip Porter stepped before the bench and called for Elizabeth Ann Hall to please rise. Lizzie stood and faced the clerk who then read the lengthy indictment. Nicholas Hall leaned forward intent on every word.

The clerk concluded, "What say you? Guilty or Not Guilty?"

"Not guilty," answered Lizzie in a low, distinct voice.

The prisoner seated herself. The clerk read the venire roll. An early survey indicated only about half of the thirty-three men were there. All answered present.

The packed courtroom was already stuffy despite the cool day and the windows wide open. It was only half past ten.

The clerk called the first four veniremen before the bench. Gordon interrupted to declare that his client wished to be tried under the new law giving discretion to the jury to choose either life imprisonment or death for a first degree murder conviction.[5] The court noted the request and resumed the selection. Two of the four men were accepted.

The second four men were called forth and examined. One was selected. Three were refused because they opposed capital punishment.

The courtroom grew warmer. Mrs. Hall and many others sat patiently fanning themselves while the tedious business dragged on. In an hour, nine were chosen. The court approved the required sixteen jurors by noon. All affirmed that they could convict on circumstantial evidence alone. Judge Shackelford charged the men not to discuss the case. Lindsay Gordon requested that the jurors also be instructed not to read newspaper reports. The judge agreed and so ordered.

Prosecutor M. J. Fulton requested that the list of witnesses for the Commonwealth be read. After Clerk Porter read the fifty-five names, Judge Shackelford adjourned court until nine o'clock the following day.

Reporters scrambled to get statements from the principals, especially Mrs. Hall. Shunning the press, Lindsay Gordon escorted Mrs. Hall to the nearby home of his aunt Martha Gordon. Lizzie would stay there during the trial. It was both convenient and safe. Gordon then went to Louisa Station and telegraphed Hill Carter that the jury was impaneled and the defense was ready for him to come.

Newspapers covered the trial's opening and reviewed the events leading up to Mrs. Hall's arrest. They overlooked the irony that it was exactly one year to the day after the start of the Leo Frank trial.[6] *The Daily Progress* noted an encouraging shift in local attitude.

"A rather remarkable change of the sentiment towards Mrs. Hall has taken place in Louisa County. When she was indicted few could be found who believed her innocent. Practically everyone was "absolutely certain," and certain beyond argument, that she was guilty.

Reflection and analysis have changed the minds of a great many people. Even those who believe Mrs. Hall guilty admit that the Commonwealth may experience considerable difficulty in proving it since practically all the evidence will be of the most circumstantial nature, while her defenders – and they are not few – exult in the fact that the Commonwealth faces this difficulty."[7]

The next morning, Detective Robert Mackay and Sterling Hall rose at daybreak. They left the Louisa Hotel together and rode away in a borrowed buggy. They disclosed only that they were going to Green Springs Depot to take measurements.[8] This gave rise to rumors of a sensational development. The action confirmed to doubters that both the victim's brother and *Mrs. Hall's very own* Pinkerton man worked for the prosecution.

The town swarmed with visitors even before the breakfast gong sounded at the Louisa Hotel. At seven o'clock in the morning, Sheriff Wash and Deputy Bob Trice took the jury for a walk around Louisa for exercise before breakfast. The air remained unseasonably cool. The con-

MURDER AT GREEN SPRINGS

tinued relief from the notorious central Virginia heat was appreciated most by those expecting to be in the courtroom all day.

Hill Carter arrived on the eastbound train at 7:50 A.M. Gordon greeted his portly associate on the platform. The pair negotiated the two blocks of congested road on foot, then secluded themselves in the courthouse for a brief conference. Ten minutes before court opened, Mrs. Hall, Lindsay and Sandy Gordon, and Hill Carter seated themselves at the defense table. The rest of the family sat behind them as before.

At nine o'clock, the bell tolled. Twelve minutes later Judge Shackelford ascended the bench before another packed courtroom. Upon opening, the defense struck four names from the list of jurors. The court dismissed those men and swore in the remaining twelve.[9]

Judge Shackelford removed all summoned witnesses from court and sent them to the witness room with exception that Mrs. Hall's daughters and other family members were allowed to remain. Mrs. Hall then stood while Clerk Porter reread the indictment.

An hour into the session, Commonwealth's Attorney Bibb rose to make his opening statement. Clearly, forcefully, Bibb declared that the Commonwealth expected to show that only Mr. and Mrs. Victor Hall occupied the lower floor of the building on the morning of the tragedy; that the accused failed to give immediate alarm; that Victor Hall was killed by a .38 caliber bullet; that a .38 caliber revolver was found in the room with one empty chamber; that nothing was in any way disturbed in the store; that the accused never showed the slightest regret on account of the tragedy; that the accused made many contradictory statements regarding the murder; and that Mrs. Hall was the last person to leave her home before it was discovered on fire. "We will prove the murder," Bibb thundered, "by circumstantial evidence so true and so painted that it will leave no shadow of doubt in your minds as to the guilt of the prisoner."[10]

Bibb returned to his seat. The courtroom was silent after his jolting delivery. No one doubted the man's conviction.

Lindsay Gordon stood and approached the jury. He knew every man. In contrast to Bibb's manner, Gordon spoke to them as to family. The jury responded in kind leaning forward as they "listened to Louisa's best known and best loved citizen with silent attention."[11] The overflow crowd outside the courtroom, which had had no trouble hearing the prosecution's presentation, now strained to catch the defense's opening statement.

Gordon declared that he did not accept any claims made by the prosecution as true. Hill Carter injected agreement from the defense table.

Gordon continued, "The evidence against this woman here is of a purely circumstantial nature, and I wish to say to you, gentlemen, that I have never been prouder of the fact that I am a lawyer and that such an opportunity as is presented to me now in defending this woman. The circumstances in this case will be shown to be not only consistent with Mrs. Hall's innocence, but will, indeed, point to her innocence. The pistol which has been introduced in this case was examined by all the members of the coroner's jury, and they all agreed that it had been fired at least a month before the murder was committed. You will find that though Victor Hall was much younger than his wife, they were happy together, and that he was her chief support, and a hope for her and her two children."[12]

Gordon ended emphatically with firm belief that the jury would find the evidence clear that a man, not a woman, killed Victor Hall. The defense would show to the jury's complete satisfaction that in every calling of his client's life, whether as wife, mother, neighbor or friend, there was not a flaw and that she had every reason to desire to preserve the life of her husband rather than destroy it.[13]

Both opening statements were short and direct. Each effectively spun the jury like a weathervane in one direction and then the other. At twenty minutes to eleven, the prosecution called its first witness. Nicholas W. Hall rose from behind the defense and took the witness stand. Once sworn in, M. J. Fulton began his examination.

N. W. Hall stated he was sixty years old and the father of Victor Hall. The witness recounted his experiences beginning shortly after midnight April 15th. He told about being awakened by his sister Jennie's alarm; hurrying to the Dunkum store fire; waking Buck Dunkum; and then alerting Victor and his family to the danger. After the fire, he lingered with Victor and Lizzie until around two in the morning then left the store. He checked Victor's stable for fire and returned to report everything safe. Finding the door locked, he hollered the news to Victor and returned home. The next time he saw his son, he lay shot on the floor between the counters. Mrs. Hall's servant Becky Coates notified him of the incident shortly after it happened. He and others carried his wounded son to his bed.

Fulton asked Hall if he noticed anyone suspicious loitering around the Hall store while he attended the Dunkum store fire. Hall said no.

Was N. W. Hall certain the store door was locked when he returned from checking the stable? He was.

Did he at anytime that night see anyone other than family inside the store? Hall did not.

The prosecutor inquired as to the locked status of the windows. Hall was not sure about the windows. Fulton pursued the nature and condition of the window locks. The witness answered that he never paid much attention to the window locks because he never had any intention of breaking in.

Some laughed out loud. Judge Shackelford rapped for order in the courtroom.

Fulton inquired whether or not Victor had any enemies. The witness said that he did not know that Victor had any enemies, but thought that there was one man who should have been Victor's enemy.[14] One reporter noted Hall's statement, but it was otherwise ignored.

Gordon cross-examined the witness. Hall affirmed that he would not have been able to see anyone lurking in the shadow of the building during the fire. He remembered seeing a spot of blood on the floor where Victor's head laid. He knew of no unpleasantness between Victor and Mrs. Hall and they appeared happy together. In response to Gordon's question about Mrs. Hall's conduct after the shooting, N. W. Hall said, "She did everything she could for him."

Fulton objected that the witness should state what happened, not his opinion. Judge Shackelford sustained.

Hall described Lizzie's care for Victor and responded to other questions stating that he saw no blood in the bedroom and did not remember seeing blood on Mrs. Hall. Gordon concluded by revisiting the subject of the windows. Hall did not know if they were fastened or not, even though he declared that he must have seen them a "thousand" times.

Fulton re-examined Hall and inquired about the bolster under Victor's head. The witness said that there was so much blood that it soaked completely through. Fulton asked about the bolster slip, but Hall did not remember there being a slip on the bolster. This was not the answer Fulton expected. Shifting topics, the prosecutor asked about the kind of dress Mrs. Hall wore to the fire.

"Objection, Your Honor, leading question," interjected Hill Carter.

"Overruled," responded Shackelford.

Fulton repeated the question. N. W. Hall did not remember what she wore to the fire. Fulton continued by asking what Mrs. Hall wore after the shooting. Again N. W. Hall was not sure. Carter laughingly said he supposed the witness was like himself and at the age where he no longer noticed the dress of women.

Some chuckled. The gavel rapped order again. Judge Shackelford was not amused.

Fulton asked about Hall's business and the two insurance policies. Was it not true that Victor Hall was a clerk in his wife's store stocked by money from her first husband? The witness reckoned that was technically true, but Victor had secured purchase of the store from Mrs. Hall with a note signed by his mother Ellen Hall.

Gordon clarified that $1,000 from one policy went directly to Mrs. Hall. The other $1,000 policy went to Victor Hall's estate from which Mrs. Hall would not receive a cent.

Fulton had no further questions, but requested that both the bolster and Mrs. Hall's dress worn the night of the murder be produced. The defense had anticipated the request and agreed to deliver them that afternoon.

Gordon made a note. Gordon made a long note. In fact, Gordon had been making a lot of very lengthy notes from the time Nicholas Hall took the stand. The attorney meticulously recorded each question and answer long hand. Gordon's action became particularly apparent to all during cross-examination when he paused to write out each question and answer. The tedium grew irksome, especially to Judge Shackelford. The irritated judge dismissed the witness and adjourned for lunch.

Court reconvened at two o'clock. Sterling Hall was back in court having returned from his secretive mission to Green Springs. The victim's brother sat with the prosecution, while his parents sat in firm support of the accused behind the defense table. This fact was lost on no one.

The prosecution called Elsie Wood as next witness. The pretty, young, brown-eyed schoolteacher entered the courtroom wearing a light, tailored suit. A white leghorn hat trimmed with white wings softened her fair complexion contrasted by her black hair. Miss Wood seated herself on the witness stand and took the oath to tell the truth. Her demeanor conveyed unquestionable sincerity.

The witness described the Hall household counting herself and the other boarder a total of six souls. She overlooked the colored servant Becky Coates. She, Miss Rosson, and the two daughters had rooms on the second floor over the store. The evening of the murder, the six sat talking in the Hall's bedroom until about ten o'clock. At that time, she and the other three young ladies went upstairs to bed.

Miss Wood first awoke to N. W. Hall banging on the door and shouting fire. When she saw light flickering into her window she first thought their building was on fire. She ran into Mamie Rosson's room and saw Dunkum's store ablaze. They watched the fire from the upstairs windows. She and the others watched the fire about two hours. Mrs. Hall came upstairs to visit for a few minutes, and then returned to her room. Later, Miss Wood heard Victor Hall ask his father to check the stable for fire, and N. W. Hall left saying it was all right to lock the door. Everyone went back to sleep at two o'clock.

Later Miss Wood became vaguely aware of movement in the store such as she normally associated with the cats jumping down from the counters, and she thought she heard talking. She suddenly awoke to a pistol shot followed immediately by three footfalls on the store porch. Shortly after that she heard a woman's voice and a door slam. Mrs. Hall called, she thought, from outside. "Buck!" Then, "Essie! Someone has shot Victor!"

The witness said that she hurriedly dressed and went downstairs to the Hall's room then the store. Mr. Hall was lying between the counters. She had to step around Mr. Hall's feet to get out of the bedroom. Mr. Hall lay there with a quilt partly over him and his head on a bolster. The ends were bent under his head. Mrs. Hall told her he had been shot. Wood then asked where, and Mrs. Hall told her that he was shot in the head.

Fulton inquired how long it took for her to reach the store after the shot. Wood could not estimate the time. She told how they tried unsuccessfully to telephone the doctor and that Mrs. Hall went back outside to call Mr. Dunkum again.

Did Mrs. Hall have on shoes? She could not remember.

Did she see a pistol that night? Yes. She was afraid that someone might shoot them. After lighting several lamps, she went to the Hall's bedroom and took Mr. Hall's pistol from the top bureau drawer.

"I was scared," she emphasized.[15]

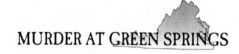

MURDER AT GREEN SPRINGS

She said that when Mr. Dunkum went outside to try to fix the telephone, she gave the pistol to him and added that the chamber under the hammer was empty.

Fulton turned and picked a pistol up from the prosecution table and presented the .38 caliber Smith & Wesson Safety Hammerless revolver to Miss Wood. She identified the blued metal, pearl handled pistol as the one belonging to Victor Hall.

What door slammed after Hall was shot? The outside door to the Hall's bedroom, she thought. She could normally hear when people walked and talked in the store. The witness testified that when they checked the store, money was still in the cash drawer and a five dollar bill was still in the leather post office pouch.

Did Mrs. Hall have blood on her? "Yes," answered Wood, "little specks, scattered over her face."

Fulton asked what Mrs. Hall wore at the time. "She had on a black kimono," said Wood. The witness did not know if Mrs. Hall wore anything else underneath.

In response to Fulton's request, Miss Wood described how the wounded Victor Hall was carried to his bed on the quilt with the bolster held beneath his head.

At twenty minutes to four, Fulton thanked the witness and turned her over to Lindsay Gordon for cross-examination. Gordon began by working the evidence. Were there any other firearms in the house? Elsie Wood reported there were three: a broken .32 caliber pistol and a rusty .38 caliber Bulldog revolver that also didn't work, both belonging to her, and a .22 caliber rifle belonging to Mr. Hall.

Elsie Wood explained that she often carried a pistol in that neighborhood. After both of her pistols broke, she occasionally borrowed Victor Hall's. She carried Mr. Hall's pistol to school one day about six weeks before the shooting. The grip safety was a strange feature to her, so she test fired the pistol at a railroad milepost while walking home from school.

When did this happen? Elsie Wood did not remember the exact date, but could state that it had to be either February 23rd, 24th, or 25th from her teacher's diary.[16]

Elsie explained that on the morning of the shooting, she found the pistol exactly where it was supposed to be. She testified that Commonwealth's Attorney Bibb and the members of the coroner's jury all examined the pistol before noon. No one thought then that the pistol had been recently fired.

Gordon removed his watch from his vest, detached it from the fob and handed it to the witness. He requested her to observe one minute's passing before asking his next question. This done, Gordon asked her how long it took her to reach the scene after hearing the shot. Again she could not estimate the time other than say that it was not very long.

Did she see any blood where Victor Hall's head laid on the floor? Yes, she affirmed seeing two spots about the size of saucers after Mr. Hall was moved.

"What was Mrs. Hall's demeanor?" asked Gordon.

"She did not holler and cry, but the children did. She sat down in a chair and began to cry and I told her not to," answered Wood.

What did Mrs. Hall do after Mr. Hall was moved to his bed? The witness explained that she sat beside him and wiped the blood from his mouth.

Gordon questioned Wood about the atmosphere in the Hall household. She said, "It was as happy a family as I ever saw."[17] Wood declared that she never saw any indications of jealousy and that Mr. and Mrs. Hall always seemed honest and forthright with one another.

At a quarter past four, Gordon completed his cross-examination. Miss Wood stepped down from the stand, and the prosecution recalled N. W. Hall. Fulton asked Hall to identify the blood stained bolster supplied by the defense. Hall identified it as the bolster that was placed beneath his son's head after he was found shot. Fulton inquired about the slip that was on the bolster, but Hall did not remember there being a slip on it.

Fulton displayed the blood stained bolster to the jury. It was apparent that blood had soaked completely through the gruesome object. Areas of blood were eclipsed by two large, black patches. Fulton emphasized the ink stains as much as the blood. The display was too much for Ellen Hall who began to weep pitifully. After the bolster entered evidence, Judge Shackelford adjourned until the following morning.

The defense retired that day concerned over the prosecution's attention to Mrs. Hall's attire and the bolster; nevertheless, they felt they held distinct advantage. The prosecution, on the other hand, ended the day completely satisfied. They had laid their ground work with their two witnesses most favorable to Mrs. Hall.

On Thursday, people filled the courtroom before eight o'clock. Nearly half of the spectators were women, many of them vacationers. Summer tourists stayed in Louisa to escape the seasonal discomforts of the city. Their dresses were distinct from the calico and gingham worn by locals. The trial provided an exciting diversion.

A fair number of people making the daily lark had to stand outside the building. These gleaned whatever was passed along from the lucky ones near enough to the windows to hear what was going on inside.

When court opened, Mrs. Hall's family sat just outside the rail, except for her brother Hubert Dowdy who had been called home on account of his wife's imminent delivery. The prosecution recalled Elsie Wood.

To Fulton's question, Wood affirmed the shot she heard was very loud. The prosecutor asked the witness to describe the bolster as she remembered it. Wood recalled no other discoloration other than blood stains.

Fulton directed the jury's attention again to the two large, black ink stains covering much blood on one side.

Gordon asked Miss Wood about visibility around the store the night of the fire. The witness testified that when Dunkum's store burned, the backyard behind the Hall store remained dark and unlit. Gordon had no further questions.

Miss Mamie Rosson, the other school teacher, was the next witness called. But she had not yet arrived at the courthouse.

The prosecution then called Charles F. Johnston. Johnston was a second cousin once removed to Elsie Wood. Johnston testified that he visited Miss Wood at the Hall home on April 6th just nine days before the murder. The witness said he was certain of the date because he remembered stopping at the store in Lindsay and buying cigarettes on credit just before taking the train to Green Springs.

While visiting Miss Wood, he noticed Victor Hall's pistol on top of the Hall's bureau. Attracted to the handsome, pearl handled piece, he picked it up and carried it outside onto the porch for a closer look. Johnston said that Elsie Wood warned him, "Be careful! That pistol is loaded *all around!*"

What was that? He said the pistol was fully loaded before the murder!

There was a collective gasp as mouths dropped open followed by much hubbub in the courtroom. Judge Shackelford rapped order. Essie Dunkum and her mother looked at each other in disbelief. The defense team was stunned. Prosecuting attorneys exchanged wry looks of satisfaction. The surprise testimony rumored before the trial had, indeed, surprised everyone.

Fulton turned Johnston over to the defense reeling from shock. Hill Carter rose to speak. He bought time while Lindsay Gordon hastily conferred with Mrs. Hall.

Carter managed a calm exterior while desperate for direction. He asked Johnston if he had discussed the pistol with anyone. The witness said he told Sheff Branham about it a week after the shooting. When Carter pursued the question, Johnston added that he frequently spoke with Detective Angle.[18]

Lindsay Gordon rallied and relieved Carter. Gordon confronted Johnston on the subject of his drinking—most of society then considered alcohol an abomination. Mrs. Hall prompted Gordon. The witness admitted to having whiskey on occasion, but not on the day in question. Gordon then tried to shake the witness's story about the pistol.

Johnston remained adamant that Elsie Wood told him that the revolver was loaded *all around.* Johnston said that he turned the cylinder while examining the pistol himself.[19] He said that he knew it to be a fact.

The defense stalled. Lacking resources to pursue Johnston further, Gordon quit the witness. The prosecution next called William R. Dunkum.

Buck Dunkum explained how he, his late brother Acey Dunkum and his wife, now Mrs. Hall, moved to Green Springs from Wilmington in Fluvanna County to run the general merchandise business at the depot. After Acey died, Buck continued to run the store with his brother's widow. She was an equal partner. She soon married their young clerk Victor Hall.

Dunkum said that N. W. Hall woke him around midnight to tell him his store was on fire. He could see a broken pane in the back door and the fire looked like it started in the back near the kerosene tank and the brooms. Nothing could be saved. He said he lost about $3,000 in stock. The store cost $1,800. Dunkum carried $1,000 insurance on each.

Buck lost his ledgers in the fire, so he went back home to try to remember some of the accounts. He gave up about three in the morning and went to bed. Dunkum and his wife could not sleep and lay in bed until they heard Lizzie call a little after four o'clock.

Buck rushed to get his clothes on, but was flustered and fumbled so much that Mary had to help him get dressed.[20] His wife was scared and could not leave the children, but told him to go on, and she would be there shortly. Buck then hurried over to Lizzie's. When he got there, Essie unlocked the door. The family stood over Victor lying between the counters in the back of the store. There was "right much blood" on Mrs. Hall's face and hands. When he came back from checking the telephone line, he saw the pistol on the counter and took it when he left to get help. Later, after he got back to the store, he examined the pistol and found an empty shell under the hammer.

Fulton asked about Mrs. Hall's demeanor. The witness said that she did not appear distressed to him.

Did Victor Hall have any enemies? Dunkum knew of none.

Gordon began cross-examining Dunkum at twenty-five minutes after ten. Dunkum affirmed that it was dark behind the Hall store when his store burned. Dunkum admitted that he was slightly nervous when he arrived at the crime scene.

Dunkum said that he reached the store about five minutes after he first heard Mrs. Hall call him. Was the door locked when he arrived? The witness remembered that Essie let him in.

Yes, but was the door locked? Gordon pressed. Dunkum thought so. "But you don't know that," Gordon followed.

Judge Shackelford interrupted and warned Gordon not to argue with the witness and confine himself to asking questions.

Gordon asked Dunkum about his position on his brother's widow's marriage to Victor Hall. Dunkum said that he was not opposed to the marriage. The defense finished with the witness.

Fulton rose for redirect examination and asked if Dunkum had anything else in the pocket in which he carried the pistol.

Gordon objected to the relevance and was overruled. Dunkum answered saying that he had nothing else in that pocket.

Fulton subtly positioned himself in front of the jury for his last question. Everyone knew Dunkum was the initial suspect in the case. With calculated flare, Fulton suddenly turned to the witness and fired, "Mr. Dunkum. Did you kill Victor Hall?"

Without hesitation Dunkum replied, "No, I did not, and I do not know who did it."[21] Newspapers prized the drama.

The prosecution then called Mamie Rosson, who had finally arrived at the courthouse. Taking time to gather herself from the witness room, the pretty, blue eyed, nineteen year old school teacher entered the courtroom. A black hat surmounted her dark, blond hair and matched the black trim on her shepherd's plaid, silk suit. Rosson took the stand with a lemon in her hand as precautionary refreshment against the hot courtroom.

Responding to questions, Rosson told the jury what she knew about the events on the morning of the murder. In a soft, reserved voice, Rosson described waking up to N. W. Hall's shouts of fire and watching the blaze from her room with Essie Dunkum and the other young ladies. Everyone went back to bed about two o'clock.

The first she heard of the shooting was when Mrs. Hall called for Essie from the front hallway. She dressed and went downstairs. The witness did not get downstairs as fast as Miss Wood because she had trouble finding her shoes. When she got there, she found the family in the bedroom with Becky Coates finishing buttoning up her dress to go to N. W. Hall's. She saw Mr. Hall lying just inside the store. Miss Wood took Mr. Hall's pistol from their bureau and said that she would shoot the first man to come in there.[22]

Fulton pursued Mrs. Hall's attire. The witness said that when she arrived downstairs, Mrs. Hall had on a black kimono, but later changed into a black dress. She did not remember seeing the kimono prior to that morning.

Turning to the grand jury investigation, Fulton asked Miss Rosson what, if anything, Mrs. Hall said to her when the witness was about to appear before that body. She hesitated then reluctantly said that Mrs. Hall told her, "Don't say anything that will put it on me."[23]

The courtroom reacted again as it had to Johnston's revelation. Judge Shackelford gaveled the commotion to order.

Fulton was finished with the witness. Gordon rose for cross-examination.

Mamie Rosson testified that Victor and Mrs. Hall's home seemed happy and their domestic relations agreeable. Upon further questioning about the Dunkum store fire, she remembered hearing a noise downstairs while the fire was in progress. She thought it was someone, but did not know who it was.

"A kimono is sometimes worn as a nightgown, isn't it?" asked Gordon.

"You seem to be an expert in such matters," taunted Fulton.

Many laughed out loud. Judge Shackelford rapped for order. This being insufficient to be heard over the guffaws, Sheriff Wash shouted to be heard. Once order returned, Gordon repeated the question.

"I don't know," answered the witness, blushing bright red. The witness said Mrs. Hall went downstairs in a kimono then corrected herself as wearing an "outing nightgown."

"You did not want to use the word nightgown, did you?" asked a juror.

"No," she agreed, giggling ashamedly and blushing a brighter red.

Establishing usage of "kimono" as synonymous with "nightgown" was about as much positive direction as the defense could manage. Gordon finished with Miss Rosson. The prosecution called Mrs. W. R. Dunkum.

Mary Dunkum took the stand in a neat black dress and modest hat. Her attire, carriage and pleasant, angular features created a business-like presence. In straight forward manner she corroborated her husband's statements about their store's fire, their activities at home afterwards, and their arrival at the Hall store after the shooting. She said that Essie unlocked the door for them to enter, and Mrs. Hall was wearing slippers and a loose dress or kimono. Mrs. Dunkum also admitted seeing blood on Mrs. Hall's face and hands.

"Did it look spattered or smeared?" asked jury foreman Massie.

"Spattered," replied Mrs. Dunkum.

At one o'clock, a half hour into Mrs. Dunkum's testimony, the court recessed for lunch. The room filled with excited discussions of the morning's sensations. Few spectators dared leave in order to keep their places for the afternoon. The judge, jury, and prosecutors exited the courtroom for their midday meal. Mrs. Hall and her family filed out. Food was the last thing on their minds.

The defense team assessed the situation. They needed to dig into Johnston's story fast. Gordon believed he could always combat twisted truth; he had not anticipated outright perjury. There was no time to lose. Lindsay told Sandy to find Sheff Branham and learn exactly what Charles Johnston told him about the pistol. Many folks from Green Springs were at the trial, Branham had to be there somewhere.

Court resumed at two-thirty. Fulton resumed probing into Mary Dunkum's recollections of the murder scene. Regarding the condition of the Hall's bed, the witness said that the covers were pulled back as normal. She did not think that the bolster had a slip on it. Fulton asked Mrs. Dunkum to think back to a year before when she stayed with the Halls while their house was being rebuilt. Mrs. Dunkum remembered that during that time the Hall's bolster usually had a cover slip on it.

The prosecution asked the witness to recall any comment Mrs. Victor Hall or Mrs. Nicholas Hall made any to her. Mrs. Dunkum said only that when she commented that the fires were about as mysterious as the murder, Mrs. N. W. Hall replied, "Yes, but your house burned in the day time."

Fulton pursued the issue. The defense objected. The question was withdrawn.

Fulton asked the witness about Mrs. Hall coming to see her to talk about the store burning and the murder a week after the events. Mrs. Dunkum said that Mrs. Hall never accused her husband of the crime and said that "Buck was the last man to commit such a deed." At the time of their conversation, Mrs. Hall expressed concern that people were then accusing her of killing Victor so she could get Bill Roberts. That was the first time Mrs. Dunkum had heard any rumor associated with Bill Roberts.

During cross-examination, Mrs. Dunkum verified that on the morning of the murder, the Dunkums had their windows closed because it was raining. It was dark when she and her husband went to the Hall store. She did not remember there being any moonlight through the clouds, and that they arrived about an hour before daylight. The witness stated that during the investigation she spoke with two detectives. She signed statements for both Mackay and Scott. Gordon had no further questions.

The prosecution called Johnny Johnson. The twenty-seven year old neighbor testified that he and Victor Hall were the same age and grew up together. They were playmates as boys, and Johnson saw Victor Hall almost everyday of his life. Johnson declared that Victor Hall was a peaceful man and "one of the finest men I ever knew. He never had an enemy that I knew of."[24]

"I heard that Dunkum's store was burned and Victor Hall was shot. I went at once to the place," said Johnson. Upon arrival he asked Mrs. Hall what was the matter. Mrs. Hall told him that "Dunkum's store is burned."

Fulton responded with feigned amazement, "Was that the first thing Mrs. Hall said?"

"Yes," answered Johnson.

"What was Mrs. Hall's demeanor?" asked Fulton.

"As usual, I never saw any change," replied Johnson.

"Did you see Mrs. Hall cry or show any grief?" pursued Fulton.

"I did not," said the witness.[25]

Johnson told about seeing Victor Hall lying in his bed with his parents sitting at his side and how he examined Victor's head and saw the bullet hole for himself. He was told that they tried to call Dr. Porter, but the telephone did not work. Mamie Rosson said that they thought the line had been cut. Johnson told them they had better get a doctor quick because Victor was dying.

Fulton asked about the pistol. Johnson identified the exhibit as Victor Hall's Smith & Wesson. Johnson remembered Victor Hall buying the gun about eight years before. Johnson related how he and Dunkum examined the pistol in the front of the store on the morning of the murder and found the empty cartridge over the barrel.

Before proceeding further with the witness Fulton announced the need to make a statement before the court regarding a line of questioning to which the defense would certainly object. Everyone knew it involved the fires. Judge Shackelford agreed to hear the argument privately with the defense present. Johnson stepped down to be later recalled.

Dr. Thomas M. Taylor was the first physician examined. Dr. Taylor told how he was summoned to Victor Hall's bed side and found the young man in a dying condition. Hall had a gunshot to the back of the head and a severe bruise with swelling over his left eye. Taylor gave Victor Hall a powerful stimulant by hypodermic injection with no effect on his condition. Dr. Taylor attended the victim until he died and pronounced him dead at 10:10 A.M. as recorded on the death certificate.

Dr. Taylor described the autopsy in detail. He said much blood emptied from the skull. The bullet entered the back of the head, passed through the brain, and came to rest against the bone just above the left eye socket. The gunshot wound was the cause of death.

Fulton produced a mashed lead bullet and asked Dr. Taylor to identify it. Taylor affirmed it was the bullet removed from Victor Hall's head. He recognized the mark placed on it by Dr. Porter at the time of the autopsy. The witness also described the groove in the bullet which still held a yellow substance assumed to be lubricant.

On cross-examination, Lindsay Gordon asked Dr. Taylor about the bruise over Victor Hall's left eye. Dr. Taylor concluded that that particular injury must only have come from a blow or a fall. It was not directly associated with the bullet wound.

Gordon asked Dr. Taylor about Mrs. Hall's emotional state at the time. Dr. Taylor testified that he did not see Mrs. Hall cry or weep, but she did have tears in her eyes.

Dr. Harry W. Porter took the stand next carrying a small, black, leather satchel to the stand. Dr. Porter testified that he arrived about nine-thirty at Green Springs Depot and found Victor Hall shot and dying. Hall died only a few minutes after his arrival.

When Fulton asked about Victor Hall's wound, Dr. Porter removed a human skull from the satchel. Ellen Hall broke into tears at the ghastly sight and hid her face in her hands. Mrs. Hall appeared unmoved. Most everyone else in court craned their necks to see the ghoulish curiosity.

Dr. Porter graphically supported Dr. Taylor's testimony indicating the bullet's entry about an inch and a half above the bony protuberance and described its course through the brain and its coming to rest against the frontal bone just above the left eye socket. Meanwhile, jury and spectators alike felt the back of their own heads for the referenced prominence.

Fulton asked Dr. Porter about abrasions to the bruise prior to the autopsy. Dr. Porter confirmed that there were none.

Gordon cross-examined the witness. Dr. Porter described Mrs. Hall as troubled and distressed at the time.

Did he have a conversation with Mrs. Hall? "I did," replied Dr. Porter. "Mrs. Hall sent for me and told me she wanted an autopsy held."[26]

Gordon pursued details about the swelling over the victim's left eye. Dr. Porter affirmed the bruising and discoloration about an inch over the left eye. Dr. Porter testified that the bullet rested against the frontal bone. There was no fracture or other injury to that member. In Porter's opinion,

the bruise likely occurred by either a blow or a fall. Dr. Porter had seen many minor blows result in very black eyes.

As family physician, Dr. Porter described Victor and Lizzie's relationship as "Cordial and pleasant. I never saw anything to the contrary." In fact, he was at the Hall home just one week before the shooting. Victor Hall called Dr. Porter to tend to Mrs. Hall's ear infection. He said that after purging Mrs. Hall's Eustachian tubes, she could hear well enough to hear his watch ticking.

Lindsay Gordon borrowed Dr. Porters pocket watch and allowed each juror to gauge the volume for himself. Dr. Porter continued that Mrs. Hall's hearing problem was not permanent.

Gordon asked Dr. Porter what was the power of a .38 caliber pistol.

Fulton objected.

Judge Shackelford overruled stating the answer was relevant in establishing that the pistol was powerful enough to kill the man shot. However, Dr. Porter said that he did not know much about firearms and was not qualified to comment on a particular firearm's capability.

"Were there any indications that the pistol was placed close to Hall's head?" asked Hill Carter.

"Yes, there were some, but the pistol was far enough to prevent powder burns," responded Dr. Porter.

Dr. Porter was careful to provide complete and precise answers to questions. However, he spoke so rapidly that the court asked the good doctor to pause occasionally in order to allow stenographer Williams to catch up.

On redirect examination, Fulton asked "Was there any burning of the hair?"

"There was not," said Dr. Porter.

In answer to the logical follow up question, Dr. Porter stated that Victor Hall could not have shot himself in the back of the head.

Dr. Porter stepped down from the stand shortly before five o'clock. Judge Shackelford adjourned court until the next morning. The defense retired badly mauled. Their chief worry had only been the fires until Johnston had taken the stand.

On Friday morning, the rare seventy degree weather ended. The uncomfortable central Virginia heat arrived with the sun. There was no breeze, and it would be a humid eighty-six degrees by afternoon.

At nine o'clock, the prosecution and defense attorneys went into chambers with Judge Shackelford to argue the admissibility of evidence concerning the fires at Green Springs. The prosecution outlined a sinister pattern of arsons in which the repeated attacks directed at W. R. Dunkum culminated in the murder of Victor Hall. The subsequent fires, they claimed, were attempts to cover up the crime and throw suspicion off of the accused.

The defense protested adamantly that there was absolutely no evidence whatsoever to connect Mrs. Hall to any of the fires other than rumors and innuendo. The defense astutely argued that the admission of any evidence related to the mysterious and unexplained fires would essentially try Mrs. Hall for crimes for which insufficient evidence existed for an actual charge.

Judge Shackelford agreed and disallowed the three fires preceding the murder. However, the prosecution pressed that the burning of the Chesapeake and Ohio depot and the two attempts to burn down the Hall store were actions by the accused to conceal her guilt. Furthermore, the last attempt on the Hall store and the discovery of a blood stained shirtwaist among the burned rags constituted an attempt to destroy evidence.

The defense countered again that there was nothing but malicious rumor and presupposition associating the accused with those fires. The

crime scene and all the items involved in the fire had all been thoroughly examined by investigators before the fact. Gordon was adamant. There was no evidence to destroy.

The court agreed largely with Gordon's assertions, but not in regard to the attempted destruction of the crime scene. Judge Shackelford decided to ban evidence related to the depot fire and the first pantry fire; however, he considered the second pantry fire germane.

At a quarter after ten, court opened to a warm, restless courtroom. Judge Shackelford ruled to admit evidence related to the second pantry fire. Lindsay Gordon noted an exception. News reporters observed the attorney's pale and haggard appearance. The physical cost to Gordon in combating recent reversals was clearly evident.

As throughout the first three days of the trial, Mrs. Hall sat at the defense table composed and occasionally gave a slight smile to family members. Newspapers commented on her "wonderful nerve." This was maliciously "regarded by some people as indifference and want of feeling."[27]

Dr. Taylor was recalled to clear a discrepancy in the nature of Victor Hall's facial injury. The bruise and swelling around the eye possibly being two injuries was explained by Dr. Taylor to have been the result of the victim's face first striking the counter then hitting the floor. Dr. Taylor also agreed with Dr. Porter's conclusion that the gunshot wound could not have been self-inflicted.

The testimony of Dr. F. M. Banks followed. Dr. Banks affirmed the same facts as the other two physicians, regarding the victim's wound, injury above the left eye, and the effect of the bullet on locomotion. He said of Mrs. Hall's demeanor, "She was more distressed than grieved; more composed than the others."[28] Dr. Banks said that he left before the autopsy.

A juryman asked Dr. Banks if blood would have spurted out of the back of the head. The doctor could not say for certain.

The next witness was Detective Robert C. Mackay. Mackay stated that he had worked for the Pinkerton National Detective Agency since 1910. After being assigned to investigate Victor Hall's murder, he first met with Sterling Hall on April 18th, and then with Commonwealth's Attorney Bibb on April 19th before proceeding to Green Springs that afternoon.

Mackay told the jury Mrs. Hall's story as she related it to him. Mackay explained that he examined the premises and found three pistols in the store building. Two did not work. Victor Hall's pistol was fully functional. The cylinder had four live rounds and one empty chamber. The spent cartridge was missing at the time. Mrs. Hall provided it later.

Fulton asked the witness to read Mrs. Hall's signed affidavit. In it Mrs. Hall stated that after the Dunkum store fire, Victor Hall said to her, "Well, I guess we better take Buck in the store with us." To which she replied, "No, we are getting on all right and I think we better remain apart."[29]

The courtroom was especially attentive to the accused's own words.

"Did Mrs. Hall know your mission on April 19th?" asked Fulton.

"I told her I was investigating the murder and would want a signed statement from every member of the family," replied Mackay.[30]

When asked about later visits, Mackay said that on April 24th, Mrs. Hall showed him several affectionate letters from Victor Hall. While reviewing those letters, Mrs. Hall told him that if she had been accused of the same crime in connection with her first husband, she would have gone to jail without protest as he was of a nervous and excitable temperament.

Fulton handed the witness five pistol cartridges: four live and one empty shell. He asked Mackay if they were the same as taken from Victor Hall's pistol. Mackay affirmed that they were.

The detective explained how he pulled the ball from one of the cartridges taken from Victor Hall's pistol for comparison to the ball removed from the victim's head. Mackay determined the unfired .38 caliber ball weighed 150 grains, and the lethal ball weighed 138 grains. Since a .32

caliber bullet weighed 83 grains, he was confident the fatal bullet was also .38 caliber.

"Was there any lubricant on these balls?" asked Fulton.

"Yes," replied Mackay.

Fulton took the cartridges from Mackay and handed them to the jury to examine. Some spectators stood up in their seats hoping to get a better view of the activity. Judge Shackelford rapped his gavel and ordered the offenders seated and issued a general warning to the courtroom not to repeat the act.

Gordon asked Mackay how he came into possession of Victor Hall's pistol.

"I asked her for it and she brought it out to me on the porch," he said.

Where did he stay while conducting his investigation at Green Springs?

"At the residence of Mrs. Hall," replied Mackay.

Mackay explained that he was there to conduct the investigation on behalf of the agency. He presented Mrs. Hall the written agreement for services at the standard rate of eight dollars per day. She signed the contract on behalf of Victor Hall's estate with Sterling Hall signing as witness. Mackay affirmed that he worked to this contract. Lindsay Gordon then read the document to the jury.

How long did Mackay have the pistol and balls in his possession? He said that he had them from April 19th to April 29th, after which time, he surrendered them to the commonwealth's attorney.

Gordon produced a love letter written from Victor Hall to his wife. Mackay acknowledged that he had examined that letter. Gordon read the affectionate note to the jury and submitted it into evidence.[31]

Throughout the cross-examination, Lindsay Gordon persisted in his tedious practice of taking elaborate notes long hand. The court had had enough. As soon as the witness stepped down, Judge Shackelford demanded that Gordon cease wasting the court's time in this manner. He reminded Gordon that the court employed stenographers to keep records of the proceedings and that counsel was provided copies daily. Thus, soundly rebuked, Gordon apologized for the inconvenience.

The prosecution called Detective George W. Scott of the Virginia State Bureau of Insurance. Scott stated that he interviewed Mrs. Hall on two occasions as part of his investigation of the Dunkum store fire. Mrs. Hall told him the same story about the shooting that she had repeated to everyone. Scott said that Mrs. Hall told him that people suspected her of killing her husband in order to get W. J. Roberts.

Gordon objected to the remark. The court overruled. Gordon noted an exception.

Fulton proceeded to extract that Scott recollected Mrs. Hall seemed intent upon him knowing that there were other rumors concerning her and that some people suspected her of "poisoning her first husband."[32]

"Objection!" shouted Gordon.

"Sustained!" reacted the judge.

The idea was planted nevertheless. Fulton finished with the witness. Gordon had no questions. Witness Scott was dismissed and followed by Millard Filmore Peers.

M. F. Peers identified himself as a farmer and Mrs. Hall's neighbor from three miles down the road, two as the crow flies. Fulton questioned Peers on the purpose of his visit to the Hall store the week before the special grand jury convened. Peers explained that Mrs. Hall summoned him to relay a message to Henry Flannagan to relay to Elsie Wood. Mrs. Hall wanted to tell Elsie Wood to make sure she said the same thing to the grand jury that she said to the coroner's jury.

Peers looked anxious. Clearly, he wanted to say more, but was confined to Fulton's questions.

On cross-examination, Gordon enabled Peers to reveal the reason Mrs. Hall told him she wanted to send the message. Rumors circulated at the time that Miss Wood planned to change her statement.

The process of clarifying the matter evolved into banter between Gordon and the witness. The courtroom burst into laughter. The judge pounded his gavel.

"This is not a funny matter," admonished Shackelford, already impatient with Gordon.

Fulton's re-direct examination of Peers re-emphasized the text of Mrs. Hall's message, but again avoided the purpose of the contact. Peers stepped down. Gordon requested a brief recess to consult a witness. In view of the time, Judge Shackelford adjourned for lunch and ordered court to reconvene at two-thirty.

The first witness that afternoon was Charles L. Marks, a brother of Mrs. Dunkum. Marks said that he went to Green Springs on April 15th just as soon as he heard about the fire and the shooting. He stayed a couple of days to help his sister and Mrs. Hall with whom he was friendly.

Marks told the story of the fire and the murder as Mrs. Hall related it to him on April 16th. He stated that Mrs. Hall told him that she found Victor Hall on the floor all doubled up and went to the front door to call Buck. The door was shut, but she could not remember if it was locked.

Fulton questioned Marks again about Mrs. Hall's statement about the door.

"I am telling as nearly as I can, just what she said to me," said Marks.[33]

Gordon asked to be allowed to compare Marks' testimony with the statement Mrs. Hall made before the coroner's jury. Fulton objected. The court sustained.

Gordon challenged Marks' terminology. Did Mrs. Hall say "all doubled up" or "all crumpled up?" Marks was not positive on the point.

Was the witness sure that Mrs. Hall said that she first went to call Buck before putting the bolster under the victim's head?

Marks replied, "I am pretty sure that is what she told me."[34]

Green Springs resident George Trainham testified to being deputized early in the investigation and accompanied Sheriff Wash to interview Mrs. Hall the evening of Victor Hall's funeral. Trainham repeated Mrs. Hall's story for the jury. Fulton directed attention to the fact that after the victim was shot, Mrs. Hall placed a pillow beneath his head, her hands were very bloody and blood "spurted up in her face."

Trainham said that Essie Dunkum was present during their visit with Mrs. Hall. Essie told them that "Mama was so bloody that I thought at first she was shot." Gordon cross-examined Trainham as to accuracy of his recollections. The witness said that he recorded their interview in his notebook, which Trainham then produced and handed to Gordon. The prosecution then requested that certain pages be entered into evidence.[35] The court so ordered.

Ernest L. Marks, another brother of Mrs. Dunkum, told the jury of his day trip to Green Springs on April 17th and his visit with his friend Mrs. Hall. The witness said that Mrs. Hall wanted to tell him about the shooting, but he was not interested in hearing the details. The widow insisted that there were facts that Marks needed to know. She said that the detectives suspected Victor of doing the burning and Buck doing the shooting. She did not think that Buck had done it, but wanted to make sure that someone warned Buck not to talk too much or he could get himself into a lot of trouble. Gordon was unable to do much with the witness other than establish that he had given his statement to Detective Mackay.

Colored washwoman Lou Pendleton had done laundry for the Halls the previous September through January 1914. After having dismissed her, Mrs. Hall became dissatisfied with the resulting arrangement and rehired her. The witness was at the Hall home on the Saturday before the shooting. She made the Hall's bed with two sheets, a quilt, a counter-

MURDER AT GREEN SPRINGS

pane, a bolster and a pillow with a sham. The bolster had a slip on it then. She said she never saw the bolster otherwise. Pendleton also washed Mrs. Hall's nightgowns. She said that they were all white.

The witness also testified that she was at Green Springs Depot the afternoon of May 14th when the second pantry fire occurred. She said she saw Mrs. Hall come out of the house and put a box on the porch. Then Mamie came out and Mrs. Hall went around and looked in the pantry window. Mrs. Hall then came back, got her box, and left. She left about ten minutes after everyone else. She was the last to leave the house.

On cross-examination, Gordon established that the witness was not currently employed, but at the time of the grand jury, she cooked for W. R. Dunkum. Gordon tried to get Pendleton to admit to seeing the bolster without a slip. She was adamant and insisted that she never saw a bolster in the Hall household without a slip. Hill Carter tried to evoke the desired answer using a different approach, but Pendleton never faltered.

Hoping to demonstrate further the pervasive influence of the detectives, Gordon established that Pendleton spoke with two investigators and gave a signed a statement to the Pinkerton man. Fulton countered by showing that the detectives were not the only people interested in Pendlton's view; the witness admitted that she had also talked to Gordon.

George Trainham was recalled to the stand. Commonwealth's Attorney Bibb rose to question the witness regarding the pantry fire. Trainham testified that he sat in his car talking with several others about the grand jury investigation. He saw Mrs. Nicholas Hall, the two daughters and Becky Coates leave the house together. About five or ten minutes later he saw Mrs. Hall leave. A little after that someone shouted fire. Someone else said, "Let it burn."

The witness said that he ran to the back of the house and pulled at the shutters. The left one broke off. Mrs. Hall had nailed it back in place after the first fire. The window was shut tight. With the help of others, they worked to force it open. The heat was intense. The window was only four feet off the ground. There was a pile of burning rags in the corner. After much effort they extinguished the blaze. There was a strong smell of kerosene, and there was no stove in the pantry.

The courtroom was stifling hot. People had fanned themselves all day to cope. As they listened to Trainham tell of the flames and heat, most had no trouble visualizing the situation.

Trainham was well known and respected in the county. His account carried weight. Gordon had the witness admit that he did not see Lou Pendleton anywhere around the depot at the time. Trainham said that he discussed the case with four or five detectives. The defense pointed to the detectives at every opportunity in hope that the jury would eventually discern their influence.

Trainham was the last witness of the day. Gordon was exhausted and welcomed adjournment. Gordon had successfully blocked introduction of five of the six arson fires. Although admission of the second pantry fire was another setback on top of the previous day's shellacking, the defense was encouraged that all evidence against Mrs. Hall remained shadow and illusion.

The newspapers proclaimed Fulton's strategy "to forge a chain of isolated facts and statements" to establish Mrs. Hall's guilt and avoidance of suspicion.[36] Indeed, Fulton slammed question after clever question into witnesses. But rather than like a symbolic hammer forging steel, it was more like a fist slamming into a hand cupped full of mud. Fulton splattered facts into evidence: tainted facts, like so much Main Street mud mixed with draft animal muck. The prosecution promoted conclusions based on presentation, not analysis.

MURDER AT GREEN SPRINGS

A Crowd Stands Outside Louisa Courthouse During the Hall Trial. (Photo Courtesy of the *Central Virginian*)

MURDER AT GREEN SPRINGS

CHAPTER
Eight

TRIAL BY FIRE

On August 1st, tensions in Europe exploded. Germany declared war on Russia. France mobilized its army. Some feared civilization at risk.[1] Some feared the end of the world at hand. Nevertheless, the Hall trial held Louisa County's attention.

Saturday freed larger numbers of farm folk to attend the trial. Streets were jammed with ox carts and wagons more than in previous days. The courthouse filled early and the overflow situated themselves as best they could beneath open windows hoping to hear the proceedings on the second floor.

The sky was clear. The sun already showed bright on the courthouse dome when court opened at nine o'clock. The courtroom would be hotter than the day before.

The officers of the court were in their places. Mrs. Hall sat at the defense table with Essie at her side. Hubert Dowdy was back from Cumberland County and his wife's false labor. He, two other brothers and four sisters sat just outside the rail in support of their sister. Ever present with the defense throughout the proceedings were the victim's parents; however, N. W. Hall now sat inside the rail at the defense table with the attorneys. After the judge's sharp rebuke the day before, Gordon recruited N. W. Hall to take notes for him to avoid provoking the court any further.

The session opened. The prosecution called Rebecca Coates, Mrs. Hall's twelve year old servant girl. Becky was typical of the many black children in Louisa County who worked outside their homes.[2] One reporter referred to the child simply as the "little pickaninny."[3]

Little Becky entered the courtroom with the timidity of a deer and nervously took the stand. In a nurturing tone, Fulton encouraged Becky to tell her story. The witness spoke in a sad, little voice. Her answers were always succinct, often vague. This forced the prosecution to collect the girl's testimony bit by bit, like picking blackberries.

Becky stated her age. She did not remember when she started working for Mrs. Hall.

"Did Mrs. Hall call you the night of the shooting of Victor?" asked Fulton.

"Yes, sir," said Becky.

"What did she say?" pursued Fulton.

"She said, 'Victor is shot.'"

"Did you ask her where he was shot?"

"Yes. She said he was shot in the head."

"Who else was in the room?"

"Mrs. Hall's daughters and the schoolteachers."[4]

Fulton moved on to the Hall's domestic situation and the child's duties. To the prosecution's chagrin, the one thing Becky was most sure of was that she had never seen Mr. and Mrs. Hall quarrel with each other.

Becky affirmed that she sometimes made the Hall's bed; thereupon, Fulton had her tell how she normally made the bed with emphasis on the bolster and its slip. Becky declared that she never saw the bolster without a slip.

Fulton returned to the morning of the murder.

"Did Mrs. Hall have on a nightgown?"

"Yes, sir."

"What color was it?"

"White – 'twarnt right white."[5]

Wrong answer, obviously, Fulton dropped the subject and shifted to the pantry fire. Fulton asked Becky what she was doing that afternoon.

"Nothing much," she replied.

When asked again, she could not remember.

Fulton worked hard. He extracted that Charles Chisholm moved four wagon loads of goods to N. W. Hall's. Becky said that she locked the doors to the house before they left. The door to the pantry was not locked; it did not have a lock. The kitchen door to the outside was locked. In the pantry were a few shelves with jars, pans, and some of her clothes. There were also towels and a straw hat that got burned up. There was a can of kerosene nearby. It was kept on the hearth in the cook room.

Becky, Mrs. Ellen Hall and the girls left the house after it was locked up. Everyone carried something. Becky pushed a wheelbarrow with a package and a ham boiler in it. Mrs. Hall came later. Becky did not know how long it was after they left until the fire was discovered.

The prosecution produced a pile of charred clothing. Fulton held up the pieces one by one for Becky to identify. They were mostly half-incinerated middy blouses and skirts.

"Dat's mine and dat's mine," she said, "and dat's my skirt."[6]

Fulton asked the witness if she was sure the clothes belonged to her.

"Yas, sir," she said, "I jes' knows dey's mine."[7]

Fulton then turned the witness over to the defense.

Gordon asked Becky about the Dunkum store fire. She did not know anything about the fire. She slept through the whole thing. As always, her testimony consisted exclusively of simple phrases, never a compound sentence.

Becky slept in the pantry. She slept in her dress. She did not sleep there anymore after the shooting. She did not know how long it was after Mrs. Hall called before she sent her to N. W. Hall's. She went barefoot. She could not remember if she walked or ran.

Gordon asked if she had ever seen the bolster in the Hall's bedroom without a slip.

"I don't know, sir," she returned. Becky said that Mrs. Hall had a sham on the bed.

A juror asked, "Did the sham cover the bolster?"

"Yes, sir," said Becky.

Coaxed by the defense, the witness went on to say that on the afternoon of the pantry fire, everyone left the house. They walked to Mr. Hall's. Becky pushed the wheelbarrow with the ham boiler. She left her clothes under the kitchen table. She last saw them there. She cried at the time because Mrs. Hall would not let her take the clothes with her.

In regards to the charred rags, Gordon asked her how she knew they were her clothes.

"'Cause, I know they was mine," she replied.[8]

Becky said that when she left the kitchen, there were two towels hanging on the back porch. Those somehow got burned in the fire. She knew the oil can on the hearth had kerosene in it when she left. She saw no one else in the kitchen. She went to the front porch. She did not remember where Mrs. Hall was then. The witness did not remember from where she got the ham boiler. She found the wheel barrow in front of the house and put the ham boiler in it.

She left through the front gate with Mrs. Ellen Hall, Miss Essie, and Miss Mamie. She did not remember anyone in the yard. Becky did not remember whether she had the key then or not. She remembered Mrs. Hall followed them. She did not know when she saw Mrs. Hall coming down the road. The witness did not remember the time of the pantry fire.

"Was Mrs. Hall the last person to leave the house?" asked Gordon.

"I don't know," answered Becky.

As the cross-examination progressed, the frequency of "I don't know." and "I don't remember." increased. Difficulties mounted in ex-

MURDER AT GREEN SPRINGS

tracting answers predictably; therefore, Becky yielded a string of facts without cohesion.

"Did any detective talk to you?" probed Gordon.

"Yes, sir, Mr. Scott told me I had not told him everything I knew," reported Becky.

"When did Mr. Scott talk to you?"

"Yesterday," replied Becky.[9]

The witness did not remember ever talking to Mackay nor recalled any detective writing down what she said. Gordon's questioning mired completely when the witness did not remember details of earlier conversations with Gordon personally. Exasperated, Gordon quit the witness.

Despite the difficulties, the defense took heart trusting that the jury's overall impression of Becky Coates was, as Elsie Wood later recalled, the testimony of a "half-idiot."[10] However, this perception was not shared by everyone.

The Commonwealth next called William H. Sacre. The witness testified that he carried a load of lumber to Green Springs Depot the afternoon of the pantry fire. He parked his wagon next to the rail siding and east of the Hall store giving him a view of the pantry. Within twenty minutes of his arrival he had unloaded half his stack: about five hundred board feet. His little helper Johnny Graves stood beside the wagon and saw the fire first. At Johnny's alarm, Sacre looked up to see black smoke coming from the house. The witness did not see anyone near the pantry before the fire.

A juror asked, "Did you see anyone leave the house?"

"I did not," replied Sacre.

Under cross-examination, Gordon established that the witness was unfamiliar with the premises. Though Sacre said he had clear view to the pantry, he could not see behind and to the far side of the building. Sacre's line of sight was so restricted that he was unaware of the large vegetable garden directly behind the house and, therefore, unable to detect any activity there.

The next witness was little Johnny Graves. Johnny had been waiting in the witness room bored and restless, squirming like a worm in hot ashes. He sat uncomfortably sandwiched between parents vexed at his inability to sit still in his hot, itchy Sunday best. Glaring adults filled the hot, stuffy room. The youngster lived a boy's worst nightmare. He was confined, uncomfortable, unable to be outside playing baseball with his friends on a Saturday morning, and if that was not misery enough, it was also Johnny's tenth birthday!

The bailiff escorted young Master Graves into the courtroom. Johnny was sworn in and took the stand before the staring crowd. He braced himself in the chair as if about to be executed. Fulton had Johnny state his name and his age. Johnny then affirmed that he was the first to discover the fire and that he did not see anyone near the pantry before the fire occurred.

Gordon declined to cross-examine the boy. The court dismissed the witness, who left greatly relieved.[11]

King Bibb, one of Mrs. Hall's near neighbors, testified that he had been at Green Springs Depot since three o'clock the day of the fire. He stood in front of the Hall store and watched Chisholm carry two wagon loads of goods to N. W. Hall's. When the family left the store, he saw Mrs. Hall follow after them. About fifteen minutes after Mrs. Hall left, the fire broke out in the pantry. The witness ran to the back of the pantry with other neighbors. They found the doors and windows fastened. King Bibb said that he helped break in the kitchen door, and together, he and the other neighbors extinguished the fire.

Gordon asked the witness how he knew it was fifteen minutes from the time they left the house until the fire broke out. King Bibb admitted that he guessed at the time. Pinkerton Captain A. G. Smith was the only detective with whom the witness remembered speaking after the fire.

The prosecution called Charles Chisholm, Mrs. Hall's hired hand. Chisholm testified that on the day of the pantry fire Mrs. Hall asked him to hitch up the horse and haul some things. He began about eight o'clock and carried two loads to N. W. Hall's in the morning and two in the afternoon. The first load was mill feed. The second load was two trunks and some boxes. The third load was bags packed with clothing. The fourth was a bookcase, some sacks of hams, and a hamper basket of things. He took the hams to N. W. Hall's smokehouse and put the rest in the hallway. Chisholm saw Mrs. Hall only while at her house. He finished his work at normal time. The last thing he did was to put up and feed the horse.

Chisholm also testified that he was at the Hall home the day of the shooting. His tone betrayed a bias against Mrs. Hall acquired sometime since May. About three o'clock that afternoon, he buried some bloody clothing. There were rags and two pieces of Mr. Victor's underwear. Mr. Bill Roberts told him to do it. Fulton's questions insinuated an attempt to conceal evidence.

On cross-examination, Chisholm stated that he worked for the Halls from 1910 until the shooting. Since then he worked for Buck Dunkum. The witness testified that the first wagon load was all mill feed. He did not remember how many bags, but the wagon was full. Gordon repeatedly pressed for a more accurate estimate on the number of bags. Judge Shackelford pointed out to Gordon that it was apparent that the witness did not have an exact count.

The attorney shifted focus to the contents of the containers. Chisholm said he could not tell if the trunks were for a man or woman. He did not know exactly what was in the various hampers, buckets, and bags. The containers were all covered. Chisholm said that he loaded several bags of hams and forty pounds of coffee.

Gordon pursued the number of hams in the bags. Chisholm did not know how many were in each bag. Gordon wondered if Chisholm had even looked into the bags.

"How do you know that there wasn't a shoulder in one of the bags?" inquired Gordon.

"Well, hasn't a shoulder as much right in a bag as a ham?" countered Chisholm.[12]

People laughed out loud. Judge Shackelford gaveled order and instructed Gordon to move along.

Gordon asked the witness if he buried anymore clothing besides those items buried the day of the shooting. Chisholm testified that on the following Monday, Mrs. Ellen Hall asked him to bury more blood stained clothing. There was more underwear, two handkerchiefs, and a pair of socks. Chisholm said that the detectives made him dig up everything. After the sleuths inspected the items, they told Chisholm to go bury them all again.

The prosecution examined Robert C. Woody, the depot telegrapher, and Lansey Riley before lunch recess. In the afternoon, W. R. Dunkum and Johnny Johnson were recalled. Isaac Gilmore, Otto Sherwood, and Burnley Harris followed.[13] The prosecution alternated white and black witnesses. A black man's testimony always followed a white man's. Black corroborated white: never the reverse and never two blacks consecutively. The prosecution was particularly careful in this regard. They had to be.

Each of the seven neighbors testified to their participation in fighting the pantry fire. All but Sherwood stated that Mrs. Hall was the last person to leave the building. They all said that they found every point of entry to the outbuilding fastened. Each man witnessed Becky Coates' charred clothes piled in the corner where the fire burned and the strong smell of kerosene. The defense could not refute these facts.

MURDER AT GREEN SPRINGS

In an unusual move to accommodate a defense witness, the court allowed Dr. H. S. Hedges of Charlottesville to take the stand in order that he might return home that afternoon on the train. Dr. Hedges testified that he treated Mrs. Hall for infections in both ears the preceding February and again in March. At first, Mrs. Hall could hardly hear at all. She was virtually deaf in her left ear. By March, her right ear improved to where she could hear a normal conversation. Dr. Hedges last examined Mrs. Hall about a month before the trial and found her hearing maintaining well. The testimony went unchallenged.

Judge Shackelford dismissed the witness. He cautioned the jury not to read any newspapers or discuss the case with outsiders. Court adjourned until ten o'clock Monday morning. All rose and the judge descended the bench.

Nicholas Hall embraced and kissed Mrs. Hall. She exited the enclosure and greeted others of her family. Mrs. Hall walked away with her sisters, but stopped to show newspapermen a picture of Victor.

"That's the best I had. Isn't it good of him?" she asked.

The reporters asked if they might publish it.

"No, you shan't have it until you treat me right in the papers," Mrs. Hall bargained.

One reporter replied, "But you must remember that we have not heard anything but the side of the prosecution, and things will look better for you when your own witnesses take the stand."

Lindsay Gordon collected his notes from N. W. Hall. He looked up and saw Mrs. Hall interacting with the journalists. Aghast, he hurried over to Mrs. Hall just as William Owens thanked her for the photograph and promised its safe return.[14]

"Look here," Gordon said to Mrs. Hall firmly, "These men are fine fellows, but you had better not talk to them. They are worse than detectives."[15]

Heeding her attorney's advice, Mrs. Hall politely excused herself from the reporters. Then she and her family left.

It was barely three forty-five. Court ended earlier than usual that Saturday afternoon to allow weekend travel time for court officers. Judge Shackelford left for his home in neighboring Orange County. M. J. Fulton and Hill Carter left for their respective homes in Richmond and Ashland. Bibb and Gordon stayed in Louisa. Mrs. Hall, two sisters and her daughters were all guests of Martha Gordon. The court kept the jury under the watchful eyes of Sheriff Wash and Deputy Bob Trice.

There was, of course, no court on Sunday. Early on the *Lord's Day*, Sheriff Wash took the jury to worship at the Louisa Methodist church on the corner adjacent to that of the courthouse.[16] Sheriff Wash had spoken with Reverend C. T. Thrift beforehand charging him to avoid all topics related to the trial. The court paid particular attention to this precaution since Reverend Thrift was pastor for the entire Hall family. It was well known that the Reverend attended the trial daily, sometimes with the retired Reverend John Q. Rhodes, Sr.[17]

No one recorded the sermon's topic, but its content satisfied officials. Controversy was highly unlikely on a first Sunday of the month. It was Communion Sunday. Moreover, folks paid as much attention to fanning themselves in the hot, uncomfortable church as they did listening to the preacher.

After dinner, the sheriff and deputy took the jury for a walk in the countryside. Refreshed by the airing, the jurymen then enjoyed a watermelon feast. Afterwards the sheriff again sequestered the men. They spent the rest of Sunday afternoon fighting boredom, isolation, and heat at the courthouse.

MURDER AT GREEN SPRINGS

S. S. Griffith of the Louisa Hotel provided the jury a gramophone with selections of Enrico Caruso and Antonio Scott.[18] Having the Victrola was welcomed diversion, although the men preferred ragtime. Foreman Massie received a note from his wife that one of their children was sick, but soon learned that it was nothing serious.

Sunday was a day of rest. To be sure, Louisa was a *Sabbath* keeping community in which devout folk took the Fourth Commandment seriously. *Sabbath* breakers were subject to arrest. In fact, Lindsay Gordon had once been arrested for cleaning out a ditch at his home on the *Lord's Day*. Gordon appeared before Magistrate G. D. M. Hunter and pleaded guilty to working on Sunday. Gordon paid the fine, but declared before the court that just as he had broken the commandment by not observing the day of rest, others in the room habitually broke the same commandment the other six days of the week by not working.[19]

Since colonial times, Virginia forbade all routine business on Sunday as codified in its *blue laws*. But this was not a typical Sunday. The Hall Case promoted some degree of *Sabbath* breaking among those involved. Reporters, deprived of court proceedings, scoured the village all day for fresh news. Sandy Gordon revealed to one that Mrs. Hall was anxious to take the stand to tell her story, but the defense had not yet decided whether or not this was a good idea. Lindsay Gordon declared to another that the defense could easily refute all of the evidence presented by the Commonwealth. Though visibly worn down by the ordeal, Lindsay Gordon reaffirmed his most sincere belief that truth was on their side; Mrs. Hall would prevail.

The prosecution busied itself that day capitalizing on confusion. Mrs. Hall had already told a number of people that the first thing she did after hearing the shot was to go wake Becky. She signed statements to this effect. A certain man of letters simply pointed to the literal context. Her story, thus condensed, inferred Mrs. Hall told Becky about Victor's wound *before* she checked her husband. The *Times-Dispatch* and the *Daily Prog-*

ress both circulated the contrivance and emphasized the dilemma Mrs. Hall faced in explaining this inconsistency.

Louisa Station, which had seen so much commotion during the week, assumed its usual Sunday activity. Reporters noted several auspicious comings and goings. Local Judge Frederick W. Sims,[20] a man of statewide prominence who had been attending the trial as an observer, left for the Virginia State Bar Convention in Hot Springs. M. J. Fulton returned in time to spend the evening in conference with Commonwealth's Attorney Bibb.

On the same train, the celebrated detective and head of the Chesapeake and Ohio Claims Division Luther Scherer arrived with his wife. Reporters immediately recognized the famous sleuth of the Beattie Case and the Allen Gang[21] investigations. Newspapers reported that there was no significance to Scherer's visit other than, perhaps, to discuss pursuing arson charges against Mrs. Hall. But certainly, Scherer intended to hear his agent Angle's testimony the next day.

As the sun lowered in the sky and cicadas droned from every shade tree, Sheriff Wash escorted the jury back to the Methodist church for the evening service. The crowded church was still hot, but not as uncomfortable as in the morning. Everyone fanned themselves vigorously.

Reverend Thrift had cooperated with the court's request to refrain from any mention of the trial and so cautioned the special guest speakers slated for that evening. Thrift introduced the Rev. William M. Bickers. After expressing his delight in being there, Rev. Bickers began an energized discourse on the topic "The Great Case Before the Virginia Jury."[22]

Upon hearing the title, Sheriff Wash looked up at the speaker as if startled by a gunshot and prepared to usher the jury out of the meeting. Upon realizing that the sermon was about Prohibition and not Mrs. Hall, Wash relaxed, but kept on guard.

Rev. Bickers metaphorically charged the defendant "Liquor License" with countless murders and consignments of souls to an ever-burning hell.

The response was predictable. The congregation received the arguments with enthusiastic nods and shouts "Amen!" Those cheering loudest were the visitors with white temperance ribbons on their lapels.[23]

Rev. Bickers, the acting prosecutor, also spoke for the defense attorney *in absentia*, who was none other than Satan the Devil, the Father of Lies. The verdict was a foregone conclusion. GUILTY! The felon was sentenced in accordance with the severity of his crimes. DEATH! Case closed. No appeal. Justice was served.

The speaker's wife and President of the Richmond-Henrico County Chapter of the Women's Christian Temperance Union spoke for five minutes.[24] The W.C.T.U. and the Anti-Saloon League had recently scored a signal victory. On February 23rd, the Virginia legislature passed the Enablement Act for a September referendum to approve statewide Prohibition. Strong feelings against alcohol prevailed throughout Virginia and particularly Louisa County.

Prohibition and justice, two highly emotional issues, merged that evening. The analogy played on the congregation's fixation with the Hall Case to solidify support for the Prohibition referendum due for vote the very next month.

After the meeting, the speakers made a point to shake hands with the jurors, who were celebrities of sort because of the trial. That evening of notoriety, *kangaroo court* rhetoric, and temperance rally spirit impinged on the minds of the *twelve tried and true*. There was no accounting for effect, but whatever the influence on the jury, widespread Prohibition fervor already guaranteed the prosecution to benefit from any statement associating Mrs. Hall with whiskey.

Hill Carter was the last attorney to return to Louisa. He arrived on the Monday morning train. Everyone was in place when court reconvened at ten o'clock. The temperature was a little cooler, but barely noticeable in the packed courtroom. The courthouse grounds filled as on previous days. Newsmen reported the crowd outside larger than ever. The number was difficult to estimate. Suffice it to say, there were always a lot of people.

Captain A. G. Smith of the Pinkerton National Detective Agency was the first witness of the day. The prosecution continued its line of questioning about the pantry fire. Captain Smith explained that he was put on the case May 14th and arrived early that day. Smith was at Green Springs when the fire broke out and inspected the pantry afterwards.

The prosecution gave Smith a pile of charred clothes to examine. The witness identified the clothes as those retrieved from the pantry after the fire, but commented that a particular shirtwaist was missing.

Gordon and Carter held a brief conference. Carter asked if there was anything on the charred clothes besides scorches. The witness affirmed there was. [No record of specifics known.] The defense seemed satisfied.

Bibb asked Captain Smith if he detected any particular odor in the clothes.

"Kerosene," he replied. The witness stepped down.

Special Agent Myer S. Angle of the C & O Railway was called. He too examined the clothes and confirmed they were the ones taken from the pantry after the fire. Responding to Carter's questions, Angle stated that he thought all the clothing was there which had been retrieved from the pantry.

This was not what the other detective said. The defense recalled Captain Smith to emphasize the discrepancy. Smith was certain that the collection of burned clothes in court lacked a certain shirtwaist which he had seen at the fire. He remembered that the garment had an unfastened safety pin in the back and dark stains resembling blood.

Smith spoke confidently and in detail. Consequently, most listeners trusted Smith's memory more than Angle's. This succeeded in establishing inconsistency between the two prosecution witnesses. However, it reemphasized the fact that the curious, bloody shirtwaist Smith noted was missing and unaccounted for.

Elsie Wood had testified that she heard footfalls on the front porch immediately after the shot. The prosecution sought to cast doubt on the ability of the front porch to so resonate. They recalled Johnny Johnson to establish that the planking was about two inches thick; the porch had no roof and was open to weather. Johnson declared that on the night of the murder the planks were wet and "soggy."

Prosecutors recalled Detective Robert Mackay to establish the size of the porch deck. The defense took the opportunity to question Mackay about his accompanying the grand jury to Green Springs to view the crime scene. Mackay admitted riding the same train as the grand jury, but did not know if he occupied the same coach.

Gordon sought to reveal information about a particular conversation Mackay had with the Commonwealth's Attorney Bibb. After Gordon's several unsatisfactory attempts to extract the desired answers, Fulton objected to the questions as irrelevant. The court sustained.

The prosecution called Mrs. Lewis F. Yancey. Elsie Yancey took the stand with the tormented look of one forced to testify against a friend.[25] Fulton asked the witness to repeat the story of the shooting as Mrs. Hall told it to her that "Victor heard a noise on the front porch and he got up and went to the door. She said she heard a shot and him fall, and then she woke Becky and the others."

Fulton pumped Elsie for more information confided to her by her friend.

Reluctantly, Elsie said that Mrs. Hall told her, "Mr. Buck Dunkum was suspicioned, and they were beginning to suspect her. She said that she reckoned she would go to the electric chair if it weren't for the two school teachers whose evidence would save her."[26]

Lewis F. and Elsie Yancey (Photo Courtesy of Alice S. Murphey)

The prosecution next called Sterling Hall. The victim's brother rose from his seat behind the commonwealth's attorney where he had spent most of the trial. Fulton asked the witness to relate the story of the shooting as told him by the accused. The witness said Mrs. Hall told him that when she heard the shot, she immediately went to the pantry to wake Becky; she told the servant Victor was shot in the head; and then she went into the store to check him.

There it was! That diabolical notion circulated by the newspapers! Was Sterling Hall the originator? No matter, whether author or accomplice, the prosecution had introduced that damnable distortion in court.

Judge Shackelford gaveled to silence the hubbub.

Fulton had the witness tell of Mrs. Hall's asking him to excuse Buck Dunkum as pallbearer. Sterling Hall next gave his version of hiring the Pinkerton detective.

According to Sterling, Mrs. Hall said that Mr. Roberts told her she was being suspected of killing Victor. It was then she suggested employing a private detective to investigate the murder.[27] Sterling spoke confidently as if his version squared with the facts. Listeners became confused.

Mrs. Hall sat horrified. Much of what she heard was what she said, but nothing like what she meant. Everything Sterling said was twisted. It was all wrong!

Sterling continued that when Mackay arrived at Green Springs, he and Mackay examined Victor's pistol. There was an empty chamber, but the spent cartridge was missing. Mrs. Hall later produced the item from a matchbox. Sterling and Mackay examined the shell together. They both thought it "smelled as if it had been boiled in a coffee pot."[28]

"Objection!" shouted the defense.

The court struck the conjecture, but allowed the observation. Once stated before the jury, the alleged, malicious alteration of evidence was as inerasable from their minds as the perceived coffee smell irrefutable.[29] Fulton finished with the witness.

Lindsay Gordon tried to offset the damage by demonstrating Mrs. Hall's cooperation. Sterling Hall admitted that Mrs. Hall produced the pistols on request and without objection. The attorney then turned to the subject of the Pinkerton detective.

"You witnessed the contract with the detective to investigate the case. Was there an understanding that the detective was to report to Mrs. Hall?" asked Gordon.

"There was no understanding to this effect," replied Sterling Hall.[30]

Sterling affirmed that Mrs. Hall was to pay for the detective, but the money was to come from Victor's estate. The witness denied instructing the detective agency not to send the reports to Mrs. Hall. He was simply the only one designated to receive them.

Gordon produced a letter from the Pinkerton detective agency. He asked Sterling Hall to read the letter and state whether or not the witness agreed with the instructions.

Fulton objected. The court sustained.

In regards to same letter, Sterling said that he had requested the detective reports be sent to him at his home in Charlotte, North Carolina because he said he feared the reports might be intercepted if mailed to Green Springs. Sterling admitted that there was a verbal agreement between himself and Pinkerton Superintendent Erb. The terms were ambiguous. Gordon had no more questions.

Fulton stood and delivered his final flourish. He read Mrs. Hall's note to the Pinkerton National Detective Agency. Her halt of the investigation implied pages of sinister motives. The Commonwealth of Virginia rested its case.

The craftsmen had forged their chain of guilt with skill, but of unsound materials. Many saw flaws in the strongest links. At the end of the Commonwealth's evidence, both the *Richmond Virginian* and the *Virginian Pilot-Norfolk Landmark* declared "The general opinion is that not enough testimony has been produced up to the present time to convict the accused."[31]

MURDER AT GREEN SPRINGS

CHAPTER
Nine

TRUTH OR FIDDLESTICKS

When court reconvened in the afternoon, Lindsay Gordon rose confidently and called the first defense witness Miss Elsie Wood. The courtroom sat in anxious anticipation as they waited for Miss Wood to take the stand, but the witness was nowhere to be found. Spectators grew restless.

Gordon concealed his dismay at this awkward start of the defense's evidence and summoned his second witness Mr. Charles Johnston. Gordon reminded the witness of his previous statement given under oath on behalf of the Commonwealth that nine days before the murder, Johnston verified that Victor Hall's pistol was "loaded *all around.*" Was this what he said?

Johnston affirmed. Gordon then launched his attack.

"Mr. Johnston, did you not tell Mr. Ollie Wood in the presence of Miss Elsie Wood that you did not break the pistol, and that you could not know if it was loaded *all around* unless it was first broke?"[1]

"Yes."

"Did you tell him that you did not know if the pistol was loaded or not?"

"I do not remember telling him that."

"Did you tell him the pistol would not revolve unless it was opened?"

"Yes."

"Did you not tell Mr. Flannagan[2] that you did not know if the pistol was loaded *all around* or not?"

"Yes, so many people were asking me what I knew, and I had been instructed not to talk, so I said I didn't know."

"Didn't Miss Wood just say that the pistol was loaded, not that it was loaded *all around?*"

"Yes, sir."

"Did you break the pistol in her presence?"

"No."

"Did you state to Mr. Ollie Wood that you were making the biggest money you ever made and that you were making easy money?"

"No, sir; I did not. I am losing money every day I remain at this trial."

Gordon had no further questions for Johnston.

On cross-examination, Fulton had the witness explain that though he did not break the pistol, it was "slightly broken." Johnston said it was open just enough for the cylinder to rotate, and he saw it was full. The witness affirmed that no one was paying him to appear in the case, and no money was offered him.

Fulton stated for the record that he had interviewed the witness in Richmond and asked him to testify at trial. This prompted the defense to deny that they thought Fulton had made any arrangement to compensate the witness.

Gordon pressed the assault on Johnston's credibility and called A. O. Wood,[3] the father of Elsie Wood. Ollie Wood stated that Charles Johnston was his wife's second cousin. In conversation with himself and other family members present, Johnston told them how he was summoned from his home by a police officer to Fulton's office. Johnston spent the day there talking to lawyers and detectives while they sat around "snapping" the pistol. Johnston said that they wanted him to swear that the pistol was loaded *all around,* but he could not do it because he had not examined it.

Fulton questioned Wood as to what interest he had in the case. Wood said that he contacted the defense because Johnston's testimony was making his daughter look like a liar. The witness said that he had spoken with Johnston Saturday, Sunday, and that morning. He wanted to know why Johnston was telling two tales. Either he lied to him or the jury. Wood reluctantly admitted that he waved his finger in Johnston's face warning him that he had better change his story and tell the truth.

In order to return focus to the point of Wood's testimony, Hill Carter asked the witness, "Did Johnston admit that he made conflicting statements?"[4]

"He did," said Wood.

Wood stepped down and John W. Flannagan[5] followed. Mr. Flannagan testified that he asked Charles Johnston about the pistol. Johnston told him that he didn't know "a damned thing about it."[6] Johnston told him that he could not tell if the gun was loaded or not. The prosecution did not cross-examine the witness.

Having learned of her presence in the building, the defense recalled Elsie Wood. Gordon asked, "What examination did Mr. Johnston make of the Hall pistol?"

In her distinct voice she said, "He picked up the pistol and ran out on the porch, and I said, 'Put it down, it's loaded.' I didn't tell him it was loaded *all around*. He put it back in the bureau drawer, and I did not see him break it."

Miss Wood related Johnston's visit to the Wood's home. She witnessed Johnston's conversation with her father. He said that he was summoned to testify about the pistol, but didn't know anything and that he was making easy money.

When Johnston came to court as a witness, Miss Wood asked Johnston what he knew. "He said he didn't know anything: that he couldn't swear that the pistol was fully loaded. I heard him make that statement twice."[7]

Satisfied that he had destroyed Johnston's credibility, Gordon moved along and called Charles E. Hester, a member of the coroner's jury and brother of Magistrate James Hester. The Louisa confectionary merchant testified that he examined the Hall pistol at the inquest. Probing with his knife blade, he scraped a whitish powder from the barrel and a greenish powder from the cartridge. Both were dry. He remembered some moisture in the cylinder. The pistol had no odor, and it was obvious to him that the pistol had not been fired recently.

Gordon asked if the other members of the coroner's jury shared his conclusion.

Fulton objected. The court sustained.

The prosecution determined that Charles Hester owned a .44 caliber Colt pistol. The witness fired it once or twice a year. He used only black powder cartridges. The witness had never seen smokeless powder used in a .38 caliber pistol. He had never checked the barrel five hours after firing to observe the condition of the gun.

Magistrate James E. Hester followed his elder brother. Gordon handed the Hall pistol to the witness and asked him to examine it. Hester took the pistol in hand, looked it over, snapped the trigger a couple of times, and said the pistol looked in the same condition as when seen at the coroner's inquest. Hester testified that he examined the pistol, the exploded shell and the ball. In his opinion, the gun had not been fired in a month before the shooting. For this reason the coroner's jury excluded it from their verdict.

Hill Carter had the witness state that at the time Commonwealth's Attorney Bibb also did not think the gun had been fired recently.

The prosecution objected. The defense argued that it be entered into the court record. Judge Shackelford disallowed the statement. The defense noted an exception.

Under cross-examination, Hester said that he thought the barrel of a recently fired pistol looked damp. Fulton then had the witness admit that

MURDER AT GREEN SPRINGS

he had never fired a bullet from a pistol specifically to observe the immediate affect on the gun. Hester also had never fired a pistol and examined it a month afterwards.

The defense then called Mrs. Hall's controversial friend William J. Roberts. Always an emotionally affecting sight, the one armed, two fingered, rumored love interest entered the courtroom and made his way to the witness stand. All eyes stared and not a few jaws dropped.

Bill Robert's mutilated presence brought an inescapable, *freak show* distraction to the witness stand. The jurymen, mostly farmers, fancied themselves as knowledgeable about firearms as any other local. The fact that the jurors were all acquainted with this particular *expert* and all knew him to be an especially close *friend* of the accused did not help at all. Robert's testimony was crippled from the start.

Gordon first sought to clarify Robert's relationship to Mrs. Hall. The witness said that he had been acquainted with Mrs. Hall for one to two years prior to Victor Hall's death during which time he had been in her company once when the Hall's visited his home.

Roberts said he was present at the autopsy, but not the inquest. There were a lot of bloody rags and clothes left from the autopsy. He remembered an undershirt, drawers, and an over shirt. Roberts said he told Chisholm to bury the clothes, but he thought the idea was originally "the colored man's."

On cross-examination, Fulton wanted to know when Roberts had last seen Mrs. Hall before her husband's death. He couldn't remember. Roberts admitted occasionally attending the same church as Mrs. Hall. He slept at the store the night after the shooting and again later when the grand jury was in session. He spent about ten days after Mrs. Hall's arrest taking care of the store. Fulton also had the witness state that he signed Mrs. Hall's bail bond and made use of his brother's car available to her. Roberts affirmed that he had done all he could to help Mrs. Hall, but that he would have done the same thing for anybody.

On re-examination by Gordon, Roberts affirmed that Gordon had hired him and his brother's automobile for money to chauffer Gordon while working in Mrs. Hall's behalf. Roberts stated that he had handled firearms all of his life. He told how he examined Hall's pistol the day of the shooting. At the time the barrel was dry. There were remains of burned powder that had turned a dull lead color, and there were some rust particles in the end. He could detect no odor and did not think the pistol had been fired recently. He did not break it open, but laid the pistol back on the counter after looking at it.

Gordon handed the pistol to Roberts. He examined it and stated that there was very little difference in the appearance. There was, perhaps, not as much powder residue, but the rust was still there.

Fulton asked Roberts if he could tell how long it had been since a pistol has been fired. The witness replied that he could not.

The defense parried the thrust and asked Roberts if he could tell if a pistol has been recently fired. The witness stated that he could, indeed, tell whether or not a pistol had been fired within ten hours.

Roberts described testing performed at Gordon's request using a similar Smith & Wesson pistol. He explained that nine hours after firing the pistol, the odor remained distinct and the powder residue had a whitish, greasy appearance. He also fired bullets into old pine boards. Some bullets penetrated. Other bullets just buried themselves into the surface.

"What kind of shell did you make the experiment with?" Fulton wanted to know.

"U.M.C. shells," answered Roberts. It was the same brand as had been removed from the Hall pistol.

"What kind of powder did you use," asked Fulton.

Gordon objected on the grounds that the type powder in Victor Hall's pistol had never been established. Judge Shackelford overruled. The defense noted an exception.

Roberts went on to say that he tested both black powder and smokeless powder cartridges with similar results.

Fulton persisted in wanting to know where the test took place, who was involved and what else they observed.

Roberts said that Sam Flannagan helped him. After firing their pistol, they took it back to Mr. Gordon's office where they all examined it after nine hours. The outside of the cylinder was smoked and the inside of the cylinder was moist.

Quick to exploit the fact, Fulton asked, "So you found moisture in the cylinder and you tell the jury that indicates that the pistol had been recently fired do you?"[8]

"Yes, sir," said Roberts.

Fulton was satisfied and quit the witness.

Gordon asked Roberts to examine the bullet taken from the victim's head and comment on its features. The witness said that he could see lubricant in the groove. This grease groove would have been *outside* the shell on the seated bullet. Roberts said that U.M.C. cartridges, and all other center fire rounds that he was aware of, had their lubricant inside the shell rather than in an outside groove as was the case with the fatal bullet. The bullet that killed Victor Hall was distinctly different from those in the victim's pistol.[9]

Listeners received this *expert* opinion from Mrs. Hall's mutilated friend with due skepticism. Roberts failed to support his conclusion with any specific example of a centerfire cartridge with its bullet lubricant groove *outside* the shell.

After Roberts left the stand, Gordon asked the court to enter a newspaper article into evidence which allegedly showed the power of a Smith & Wesson pistol. The court removed the jury while the defense and prosecution argued their positions. The story concerned a recent suicide with a Smith & Wesson revolver. The article detailed the bullet going completely through the man's head, a plastered wall, and then through the exterior weatherboard. A sworn deposition would have been another matter, but the tabloid report was, of course, hearsay. Judge Shackelford ruled the evidence inadmissible.[10]

Nevertheless, the defense ended their first day confident that they had discredited Johnston's testimony and disqualified Victor Hall's pistol as the murder weapon. Even so, it was painfully obvious to everyone in the courtroom that the prosecution held one powerful advantage. The defense lacked showmanship.

When court reconvened Tuesday morning, Lindsay Gordon called T. Arthur Campbell to the stand. Campbell, a resident of neighboring Fluvanna County, stated that he had been shooting revolvers ever since he was old enough to hold one. He was, after all, the son of that county's sheriff. Gordon sought the witness' *expert* testimony regarding pistol ammunition, but Campbell had left his book outside. He was excused to retrieve it.

Meanwhile, the defense recalled Becky Coates. Gordon asked Becky to explain how the black ink stains got on the bolster. The witness said that she spilled a bottle of ink all over the bolster, a trunk, and some of Mrs. Hall's clothes.

On cross-examination, Becky admitted to Fulton that she did not actually remember spilling the ink on that chief piece of evidence herself. She said that people later told her she spilled ink on the bolster. She remembered only the trauma.

Arthur Campbell returned to the stand with his book. Actually, it was an ammunition catalogue. Fulton objected to testimony related to a non-standard work. The jury was removed while Fulton and Gordon debated the issue.

MURDER AT GREEN SPRINGS

Gordon assured the court that the defense was not disputing the bullet weights already introduced into evidence, but intended to present typical weights for that caliber. Fulton argued that the book was published by a manufacturer other than U.M.C. and did not relate particularly to the ammunition in question. Furthermore, the author was not available for cross-examination. Judge Shackelford allowed the book as collateral evidence. Campbell could testify on the information in the book related to general characteristics of .38 caliber ammunition.[11]

When the jury returned, Campbell testified that nominal weights of bullets were 158 grains for .38 Special and 146 grains for .38 S&W rounds. These appeared generally accepted values in the firearms industry for those respective calibers. He reported his experience that balls of like calibers had similar weights.

Campbell described his own test firing of .38 S&W ammunition. The witness said that the odor was distinct nine hours after firing. He also shot into a two inch thick pine board. Some bullets penetrated through the board.

The witness testified that he had known Mrs. Hall for twelve years. He described her as a warm, kind-hearted, Christian woman.

On cross-examination, the prosecution reiterated the fact that the *expert* was acquainted with the accused. Campbell also admitted to Fulton that he weighed .38 caliber balls from U.M.C. and Peters. Both weighed 150 grains. Fulton asked the witness for the specific resistance of pine boards. Campbell did not know.[12]

Juror Riddell asked if a bullet would lose lead if it penetrated a hard object. Campbell could only say that he thought it would, but did not know specifically how much.[13]

Samuel H. Flannagan followed Campbell. The witness reaffirmed the testing which he and Bill Roberts performed for Gordon. Flannagan thought the barrel looked moist after firing and attributed the appearance to the lubricant. The barrel eventually looked dry in time. Responding to a juror, the witness proposed the transformation took longer under humid conditions. He further explained that they used a clean pistol in their experiments, but even had a dirty pistol had been used, the rust and old residue would have been wiped clean by the passing bullet and replaced by fresh residue. Fulton had Flannagan reveal that after their test, the pistol was placed in a holster that covered the barrel and half the cylinder potentially skewing the test.

The defense recalled Dr. Porter to the stand. He stated that he had known Mrs. Hall since she first moved to the county and was then married to Asa Dunkum. Mrs. Hall possessed an excellent reputation prior to the current matter. The witness attended Asa Dunkum when he took sick with a virulent form of pneumonia and died five or six days after starting treatment. In regards to Victor Hall's gunshot wound, it was the doctor's opinion that the bullet was fired just far enough away as to leave no powder burns.

Commonwealth's Attorney Bibb asked Dr. Porter if he thought a shot from three feet away would leave powder burns. The witness doubted so. Bibb asked him if he knew that Asa Dunkum had refused to take his medicine from the hand of Mrs. Hall. The doctor said he knew nothing of that.

Gordon objected to the line of questioning, but Bibb claimed that the defense introduced the topic. Gordon said he had done so to establish Asa Dunkum's death from natural causes to counter the pernicious rumors about his client presented earlier.

Judge Shackelford sustained the objection and banned all questions concerning Asa Dunkum. He instructed the jury to disregard all statements made relating to Mrs. Hall's first husband and charged them not to associate them with this case.

Mrs. N. W. Hall was called. The dowager's humped, old woman dressed in deepest black rose from among those seated with the defense.

The mourning mother of the murdered man took the stand, and then lifted her black veil to reveal her pleasant, care worn face.

In a quaking voice she told the story of the night of the Dunkum store fire and the shooting of her son. She frequently broke down and cried burying her face in her hands. Her testimony was heartrending as she described her son's wounds. The accused fought back tears as she listened.

The witness told how on the day of the pantry fire, Mrs. Hall moved some things to her house because she planned to stay there a while. Most everything she owned was still left at the store. Early in the day, someone at the depot told Mrs. Hall's brother Hubert Dowdy that the store would be burned that night.

Late that afternoon, Mrs. Hall, her daughters, Becky Coates, and she ate a cold supper. They kindled no fire in the stove. They left right after cleaning up. Mrs. Hall told Becky Coates to leave her clothes and come back for them the next day. About an hour after they left, they heard about the fire and went back immediately to see about it. The witness said that Mrs. Hall had always been a good and true wife to her son.

Fulton inquired about Victor Hall's health. The witness said her son had been sickly over the last year and complained of a pain in his side and frequent tonsillitis. He was not a strong man.

Ellen Hall said that on the afternoon of the fire, she went to the barn after supper and did not know where Mrs. Hall was at the time. When she returned from the barn, the rest of the family was in front of the house. That was when they left.

Bibb asked the witness about the slip on the bolster. Ellen Hall said that there was no slip on the bolster. She remembered distinctly because Mrs. Hall apologized for there not being one at the time.

Bibb had Ellen Hall identify the black kimono worn by Mrs. Hall. The witness saw Mrs. Hall in it after the shooting. She did not remember seeing blood on it. She admitted to seeing blood on Mrs. Hall's hands, but not on her face.

TRUTH OR FIDDLESTICKS

N. W. Hall was recalled to clarify that on May 14th, he returned to Green Springs in his buggy shortly after the pantry fire. He estimated that there were about fifty people standing around the store at the time.

The defense called Miss Lennie Roberts. She had known Mrs. Hall for years. They were close friends. They attended the same church and served together there in the ladies aid society. After Gordon finished his interrogation, Fulton had the witness admit that Mrs. Hall told her that she was suspected of murdering her husband in order that she might have her brother Bill Roberts.

The youthful Magistrate James E. Hester was recalled to testify to Mrs. Hall's impeccable Christian character. Hester knew the Halls well. Brother Charles had boarded at Mrs. Hall's table for twelve months.[14] James had eaten meals with his brother there occasionally.

Fulton asked Hester if he was paying court to Mrs. Hall's daughter Essie. The witness was caught off guard by the question. Hester replied reservedly, "Not so as you could notice it."[15]

The witness was obviously uncomfortable with the subject and especially so with Essie sitting there in front him. Fulton pressed the issue. Hester said that he had had several conversations with Essie after the murder, but did not admit specifically to courting her. Hester left the stand looking somewhat sheepish.

Mrs. Charles Hester, wife of a coroner's jury member and sister-in-law to the previous witness took the stand. Emma Hester testified to her friend's character and many charitable acts. However, on cross-examination, Fulton asked her if it was true that Mrs. Hall confided to her that on the day of the murder she asked people to stay for dinner because she was afraid that if she did not do so, people would talk about her. Mrs. Hester flatly denied the notion.[16]

Fulton then asked her if Mrs. Hall told her after the shooting that the first thing she did was wake Becky Coates. Mrs. Hester tried to sidestep the question, but yielded that those were Mrs. Hall's words.

Eliza and Maggie Jackson, a colored mother and daughter, were at the depot the afternoon of the pantry fire. They had come there to check their mail. Each testified as having a clear view of the area behind the kitchen and that they never saw Mrs. Hall go near the pantry. Maggie declared that regardless of what a thousand other people might say about a matter, she was bound to tell the truth.

Fulton then asked the Maggie what, if anything, Mrs. Hall carried away from the store. The witness said that Mrs. Hall had several books. It became clear that Mrs. Hall carried away the store's account ledgers.[17]

When court adjourned, Mrs. Hall sat with an expression of deep anxiety that had grown throughout the day. She had looked on helplessly while the prosecution skillfully played her own character witnesses against her.

On Wednesday, August 5th, Superintendent Jesse W. Erb took the stand on behalf of the Pinkerton National Detective Agency. Erb had been recently promoted from Assistant Superintendent of the Denver office.[18] He had arrived in Louisa the previous evening and was the first witness called. The defense hoped to clear up issues about the contract with the Hall estate. Gordon produced a letter he received from Erb, a response to an inquiry, stating that Sterling Hall requested the reports be sent directly to him at his home in Charlotte because "Mrs. Hall's mail" might be intercepted.

Under challenge by Fulton, Erb admitted that the letter mistakenly used the term "Mrs. Hall's mail" instead of "Sterling Hall's mail." The purpose for the defense calling Erb collapsed.

Despite the best efforts of the defense to prove otherwise, there was simply no evidence of impropriety on the part of the Pinkertons. The agency fulfilled the letter of the contract arranged by Sterling Hall. The reports and evidence were provided to the commonwealth's attorney per the company's national policy. It was apparent to the jury that Gordon had barked up the wrong tree.

The parade of defense character witnesses resumed for the rest of the morning. N. W. Hall's sister Jenny was followed by Mrs. Hall's daughters Essie and Mamie Dunkum. Of the two girls, only Essie was cross-examined and then only about the quantity of ink Becky spilled. It was between a pint and a half and a quart.

The defense called character witnesses from Fluvanna County: Sheriff Robert S. Campbell, Superintendent of Public Schools T. M. Sheppard and Postmaster Sinclair Omohundro. Certain Louisa County citizens followed: Sunday school teacher and elder at Wills Memorial Church Arthur G. Burnett, M. P. Anderson, and former Hall store employee Ivanhoe Seay. All these testified to Mrs. Hall's exemplary character and Christian charity.

J. Frank Bickers, a special deputy and county auctioneer testified that the value of the Hall store was $2,500. Bickers auctioned off $1,000 in store stock and $650.53 in personal furniture from the residence. Therefore, had Mrs. Hall burned her store, she would have lost at least $4,150.53, a considerable sum for that day.

After lunch recess, the defense called K. W. Cornett of Albemarle County, the store owner at Lindsay. Cornett testified that, contrary to Charles Johnston's statement under oath, Johnston did not buy anything at Cornett's store on credit on April 6th. It was the defense's final slam against Johnston's credibility.

Gordon resumed calling character witnesses. Mrs. Carrie Synan, Confederate veteran T. A. Hancock[19], Henry A. Flannagan, and Sam Melton vouched for Mrs. Hall's honesty, charity, and Christian example.

The circuit pastor of Wills Memorial Church, unable to attend, provided a statement in Mrs. Hall's behalf. Lindsay Gordon read:

"I have known Mrs. Elizabeth A. Hall for the last six or seven years, and have during this time seen her frequently, and on several occasions visited her house, and I know her general reputation in that community for truth and veracity and as being a good and virtuous woman, and it is good, indeed before the present charge against her, she stood as well in the community as any one in that neighborhood from a moral standpoint.

Given under my hand this 27th day of July 1914."

[Signed] Hugh H. Hudson[20]

The prosecution recalled N. W. Hall for cross-examination. Hall had stated that the bolster did not have a slip. Fulton expected to force Hall to admit otherwise knowing he had been at the store when Trice and Mrs. Hall examined the bolster together.

After observing days of Fulton's "slick" manners, Nicholas Hall was painfully aware how any fact might be twisted against his daughter-in-law. The exceptionally literate Hall determined not to yield any further information to Fulton about anything.

Fulton asked generalities about the pantry fire, and then turned to the subject of the bolster. Was Hall present when the bolster was displayed?

"I could not say positively," answered Hall.

Puzzled at the reply, Fulton pursued the subject of examining the clothes and the bolster, but received an array of noncommittal replies. He asked if Hall was present when Deputy Trice examined the bolster.

"I have no recollection of any examination I made," said Hall. He admitted to seeing the items but steered clear of indicating any personal participation in their scrutiny.

Fulton tried to corner Hall into admitting a misstep in his earlier testimony, but the *old man* remained evasive and repeatedly answered questions succinctly: "I do not remember. . . I cannot say that . . . Don't remember particularly . . . Not that I remember . . . I cannot say distinctly."

The game continued to Fulton's great frustration. The courtroom listened bewildered at Hall's uncharacteristic stubbornness.

The professional prosecutor carefully crafted his question, "Let me ask you – did you ever make the examination of those clothes, or see an examination made, or exhibited to you in the presence of Mrs. Victor Hall, and she was sent in to show the clothes?"

"I do not remember."

"You do not remember. You do not deny it?"

"I do not deny it, but I do not remember."

"I am going to ask you this question," said Fulton. He paused then rephrased his question again. "I am going to ask if on Friday [sic] after Victor Hall's death, if you did not go with others to look at those clothes or another, and that during the examination of those bloody clothes, including the bolster, that Mrs. Victor Hall was asked or requested to be present, and that they were shown on that morning? Now, do you remember that Mr. Hall?"

"I do not remember it distinctly."

"Do you remember it indistinctly?" asked the exasperated Fulton.

"As I said before, I remember seeing the clothes," answered Hall.[21]

N. W. Hall was so careful to deny the prosecution any additional information that the witness remained equally as guarded during re-examination by the defense.[22] Gordon tried briefly, but quit the witness.

Hall left the stand satisfied that he had held his ground. Hall later wrote, "This lawyer [Fulton] is one of the slickest of the slick, but he found his match in the witness [Hall] who was ready to split hairs with him all day long in behalf of the truth, and failed in his purpose to make him say what he wanted him to say."[23]

Though Fulton failed in his goal to substantiate the bolster slip through Hall, the general perception benefited the prosecution. One newspaper reported N. W. Hall's responses as "hostile, evasive, reticent, and refractory."[24] The general impression of *old man* Hall's behavior was not good.

In rebuttal to Hall, Fulton called Deputy Sheriff Robert Trice to testify about his examination of the bolster. Trice said that he was at the Hall store the Friday [sic] after the murder. Mrs. Hall showed him the bolster. Trice recalled a bloody case covering the pillow at the time he saw it.

Fulton asked if the bolster in the courtroom was the same one he examined.

"No," answered Trice. It did not look the same to him.

The courtroom stirred at the unexpected reply. Judge Shackelford gaveled down the commotion.

Deputy Trice asked permission to qualify his statement. The judge allowed the officer of the court to speak.

"If I had known at first," explained Trice, "that I was to be summoned as a witness in this case, I could have sworn that the bolster was in a slip and that the slip was very bloody. But since hearing others testify, I want to say that I can't positively swear that the bolster was in a slip, but I am under the impression that it was."[25]

The prosecution wanted more than just an impression, so the witness was excused. However, the impression sufficed.

By a quarter to four, most everyone was exhausted from sitting in the hot, stuffy courtroom. But even those most wearied from the daylong ordeal revived when Hill Carter called Elizabeth Ann Hall to the witness stand.

The black clothed, veiled widow rose from her chair and approached the witness stand. She placed her hand on the Bible and swore to tell the truth. After being seated, Carter asked Mrs. Hall to tell the jury what happened beginning with the evening of the Dunkum store fire. Mrs.

Hall lifted her veil and began to speak. Lindsay Gordon slid his chair closer to the prosecution's table to be able to hear more clearly. Mrs. Hall spoke with little to no nervousness detectable in her voice fanning herself all the while with a small, black fan.

Judge Shackelford politely interrupted the defendant and asked her to please speak louder for the courtroom. Mrs. Hall began her story again with the family and the teachers gathered in their bedroom before going to sleep the evening of April 14th. It was a story the accused must have repeated hundreds of times over the last four months. This time her life depended on her presentation to the twelve men who would judge her guilt or innocence.

Clearly and distinctly the courtroom heard from the accused woman's own mouth the events of the Dunkum store fire, Victor's shooting, the aftermath, hiring the detective and her falling under suspicion. Carter then had her tell what she knew about the pantry fire. Mrs. Hall delivered her testimony in fifty minutes and was then cross-examined.

Fulton questioned Mrs. Hall about the bolster and when she first realized she was suspected. The witness answered each of the prosecutor's questions in a simple, forthright manner ignoring his accusatory inflections. Mrs. Hall affirmed that Commonwealth's Attorney Bibb interviewed her the Friday following the murder and asked a good many questions. She said that Deputy Trice visited her home and examined the bolster on Saturday, the day after the Oakland fire, not Friday as Trice recalled. Mrs. Hall said that she had no idea that she was suspected until the Wednesday following the murder.

Fulton turned to a most controversial topic. He wanted to talk about whiskey.

Mrs. Hall denied telling Mrs. Alex Chewning that she gave Victor whiskey and that he drank up what they had the night he was killed. She said that she never gave Victor anything to drink. Victor kept a bottle in the washstand and had a drink whenever he wanted. Mrs. Hall said that

MURDER AT GREEN SPRINGS

she looked to give Victor whiskey only because he was shot, but it was all gone.

At five o'clock Commonwealth's Attorney Bibb announced that the prosecution estimated three more hours of cross-examination and desired to continue on the morrow. Court then adjourned until ten o'clock the next morning.

Mrs. Hall and her family filed past the press when leaving the courtroom. Contrary to previous warnings, Mrs. Hall stopped to speak with the newspapermen.

"I hope you will tell the truth now," she said.

"You made a good witness for yourself," complimented one. Others agreed.

"Well, I have nothing to fear," declared Mrs. Hall confidently and turned away.[26]

Thursday morning, the largest crowd yet filled the courthouse grounds. Many were under the mistaken impression that the trial was to have ended that day. Some had refused to leave from the day before. These camped out on the sward and planned to sleep on the few benches or in the grass. They considered it worth waiting under the stars for a chance to get inside when court opened and hear the end of Mrs. Hall's testimony. Many brought decks of cards and checkerboards. Others played mumble-the-peg or other games. Whether one left or stayed, the trial and its varied aspects ruled all conversation.

The session began promptly at ten o'clock, the prosecution and defense submitted their proposed instructions to the jury. The newspapers declared that the instructions were based on those used in the McCue and Beattie trials; however, this applied only to the prosecution's set.

Court opened and Mrs. Hall returned to the stand for the conclusion of her cross-examination. She impressed people as one who wanted the facts to be known. Her answers were frank and deliberate with every word chosen carefully. They had to be.

"When you were living with your first husband in Fluvanna County," Bibb asked, " didn't he once lock himself in his store and refused to go somewhere with you, and didn't you get mad and break out the glass to the windows?"

"I have no recollection of that," replied Mrs. Hall.[27]

"What did you tell Miss Mamie Rosson just before she went into the grand jury room?"

"I told her not to tell anything on me but the truth. I was not afraid of the truth, but I knew the grand jury was trying to find an indictment."[28]

The witness was unshakable in her positions. To the surprise of all, the prosecution finished their cross-examination in just an hour and a half. Mrs. Hall returned to her seat as confidently as she had taken the stand.

Mrs. N. W. Hall was recalled. Hill Carter asked her about the day Deputy Trice examined the bolster. Ellen Hall remembered distinctly it was Saturday, not Friday. She and Mrs. Hall showed Deputy Trice the bolster. There was no slip on it. They kept nothing in that room but rubbish and an old trunk. Becky knocked over a bottle of ink in the room one day. She knew about it because Becky told her when it happened.

Next Hill Carter put O. H. Wagner on the stand. Wagner said that when he first learned of Mrs. Hall's intentions to sell the business, he expressed interest in buying Hall's store. However, he then received an anonymous, typewritten letter strongly advising him not to buy the store. Wagner confessed that he no longer had the letter. He lost it.

The Commonwealth objected to the testimony on the grounds that the letter was not available for examination. The prosecution submitted that the anonymous letter could have actually been sent by the accused.

Carter countered that the testimony established that there was some-one interested in breaking up the mercantile business at Green Springs. The prosecution team discussed the issue among themselves and with-drew their objection. Judge Shackelford allowed the testimony.

Wagner continued. The mysterious letter cautioned Wagner that if he were to buy the store "reverses and misfortune would follow him" and that the writer "knew what was going on."[29]

The courtroom buzzed at the statements.

Shackelford gaveled order.

The prosecution then took over. Wagner reaffirmed that he lost the letter. The witness testified that he did not remember exactly when he received it. He said the cancellation on the envelope was blurred and did not know from where the letter was mailed. Consequently, as quickly as Wagner's evidence struck sensation, it suddenly became irrelevant.

In an afterthought, Gordon recalled Mrs. Hall to the stand to ask her if she had fire insurance on the property the day of the pantry fire. She said that she did not. The insurance company notified her of cancellation the day before the fire.

The prosecution called Mrs. Alex Chewning. She testified that on the day of the funeral, Mrs. Hall told her that Victor was not feeling well the day before he was killed and that he drank up all the whiskey in the house.

The prosecution then called Jesse V. Marks, Mary Dunkum's father. Marks said that he saw Mrs. Hall go in the direction of the pantry. She remained only a few seconds then returned to the rest of the family.

George Trainham was recalled to the stand and said that he spoke with Mrs. Hall after the pantry fire. Mrs. Hall told him that she had fas-tened up the house before she left.

On recall, Sterling Hall said that he was present when Common-wealth's Attorney Bibb interviewed Mrs. Hall the Friday after the murder. Afterwards he heard Mrs. Hall tell Elsie Wood that Bibb asked a lot of questions. Sterling said that he heard Mrs. Hall remind Elsie Wood about firing the pistol at the milepost.

Gordon recalled Henry Flannagan. He stated that Mrs. Hall never told him to ask Elsie Wood the change her testimony to the grand jury.

The defense then recalled Elsie Wood. She denied that Mrs. Hall ever asked her about the pistol.

"No," said the school teacher, "Mrs. Hall did not even know the pistol had been fired."[30]

The defense team requested discussion of a point of law. Judge Shackelford had the jury removed. Hill Carter stated that the evidence clearly showed the Commonwealth hostile to Mrs. Hall. The defense requested the right to introduce testimony establishing that in the days immediately after the murder, Commonwealth's Attorney Bibb was friendly to Mrs. Hall.

Fulton objected on the grounds the matter had already been disclosed in the testimony of the accused, and what the defense proposed did not constitute competent testimony. Judge Shackelford denied the request. The defense noted an exception.

When the jury returned, the defense rested its case. Judge Shackelford announced that the court would limit prosecution and defense arguments to four hours each. The judge believed the time more than ample.

Gordon protested. The court agreed to take the matter into consideration.

Early in the week, the jury had asked the court to allow them to view the crime scene. Judge Shackelford ordered a recess until two o'clock at which time the court would take the jury to Green Springs.

As soon as court dismissed, Hubert Dowdy pulled a letter from his pocket and went over to the reporters. He had something to show them. The newsmen crowded around Dowdy. The note announced the birth of

his forth child two days before: his first boy![31] Pencils frantically scribbled down every detail. The reporters so craved any morsel of information from the defense's camp that one even noted the physician's full name for publication in a front page story.[32] While Dowdy distracted the news-hounds, Mrs. Hall and her family exited the courtroom unmolested.

By two o'clock, Sheriff Wash and Deputy Trice had the necessary automobiles reserved to transport the jury to Green Springs. The drivers were told to park in front of the Louisa Hotel where the jury dinned. The streets were so congested that this was difficult. One driver had chanced upon an open space earlier in the day in front of Kent's Drug Store and dared not vacate his spot. The driver stood in front of the hotel until near time to assemble the caravan. He and his passengers then walked down the street to his car.

Jurors Nuckolls, Riddell, Bickley and Jacobs were left standing in front of Kent's Drug Store unsupervised contrary to law in the midst of spectators hostile to Mrs. Hall. J. Frank Bickers discovered the situation and caught the attention to two other people. Bickers guessed that the jurors were left unguarded ten minutes before Sheriff Wash became aware of the situation.[33]

Upon realizing the problem, Sheriff Wash ran down the middle of the street and personally took charge. Wash directed the jurors into the automobile. The driver then pulled up alongside the other vehicles in the convoy waiting in front of the Louisa Hotel. The ride to Green Springs proceeded without further recorded incident.

For about an hour, the jurors inspected the Hall Store. Judge Shack-elford oversaw the visit and called upon Mrs. Hall to answer questions about the crime scene and point out particulars. Though the scenes of the murder and pantry fire were the only features officially germane to the trip, the affecting sights of the burned store and depot were unavoidable.

Judge Shackelford and Mrs. Hall rode back to Louisa in George Trainham's automobile. A front tire punctured flat. Trainham stopped safely, but barely avoided flipping the vehicle. The car behind them stopped to assist.

John Wilmer Boston, the helpful driver. Ironies abounded. (Photo Courtesy of Edward J. Westlow)

Pinkerton Superintendent Erb and Captain Smith switched vehicles and stayed with Trainham while their driver ferried Judge Shackelford and Mrs. Hall back to Louisa. The helpful motorist had driven from Richmond to see the trial and was recruited to chauffer. The newspapers identified the driver as J. W. Boston.

MURDER AT GREEN SPRINGS

Mrs. Hall and her first husband purchased their store and property from the estate of John T. Boston, the father of J. W. Boston. Ironically, John Wilmer Boston had actually been born and reared in Hall's store![34]

On returning to Louisa, the prosecution and defense met with Judge Shackelford to finalize instructions to the jury. They debated the merits of each at length. One instruction prayed for by the defense regarded the veracity of the prosecution's witnesses. The court believed the instruction superfluous and refused it under protest by the defense. At eight thirty that evening, the attorneys reached agreement. The trial transitioned into its end game.

MURDER AT GREEN SPRINGS

CHAPTER
Ten

A MEAL TO
GAG A POSSUM

he temperature the previous two days had only approached eighty degrees. The heat returned Friday morning with a vengeance. The temperature at dawn was near the previous day's high and made a quick run up to the mid-nineties. The fifteen degree increase was uncomfortable to everyone whether inside or outside. The packed courtroom was a veritable sweat box.

Again, there were hundreds of people on the courthouse grounds with more arriving. Each faced a quandary in choosing between either a more favorable listening post in the sun and a comfortable spot in the shade.

Chairs filled every available space in the courtroom. Even the front and back halls were filled with chairs, benches and stools to accommodate listeners. An hour before court, people eager to hear the closing arguments occupied every seat. Most felt like there was hardly room to breathe, much less move.

Mrs. Hall sat at the defense table between her two daughters. They were among the few guaranteed a seat to the spectacle. The widow had her veil raised. Many saw she looked tired. Nevertheless, she bore a look of confidence consistent with her statement the previous afternoon that she expected to be "a free woman by sundown Saturday."[1]

At nine o'clock the courthouse bell rang. Seven minutes later, Sheriff Wash declared court in session.

If there was one thing upon which Virginia lawyers prided themselves, it was oratory.[2] The audience anticipated lengthy discourses. They would not be disappointed. Judge Shackelford declared that because of the seriousness of the charge, the court had reconsidered its previously announced four hour limit on arguments. Each side was now allowed as much time as needed.

The judge read the instructions to the jury. There were seventeen submitted by the prosecution and twelve for the defense; a thirteenth had been rejected by the court. The audience sat patiently listening to each statement. Some wondered how much the jury, mostly farmers, understood the legal terminology.

After the jury received the array of "if thus, then so" guidelines for evaluating the evidence, Commonwealth's Attorney Bibb stood and opened argument for the prosecution. A man checked his watch. It was nine twenty-two.

"This has been a long and tedious trial, and I have noticed your patience in the case. The time is near at hand for you to determine the duty for which you were summoned. Although you owe a high duty to the prisoner, you owe just as high a duty to the Commonwealth. The laws of the Commonwealth must be preserved. God has ordained for all generations that homicides should be punished by death. The Gospel dispensation has not abolished the death penalty. No other penalty is sufficient to prevent certain crimes."

Bibb reminded the jury that for a conviction in the first degree, they had the option to prescribe life imprisonment instead of the electric chair.

"The evidence is voluminous, and it is almost impossible for the jury to keep in mind every piece of evidence. It is, therefore, proper for me to go into the evidence and call your attention to the evidence from the standpoint of the Commonwealth."

Bibb recounted the events of April 15th placing particular emphasis on the fact that Victor Hall and his wife were alone in the lower floor of their house. The defense, he claimed, relied on a shadow to save the accused. For a burglar to enter the store illuminated as bright as day was

"absolutely ridiculous!" The family was outside, and there was no other entrance open but the store door under observation the whole time.

"The accused, according to her own statement, if we can believe her testimony on this point, explodes any burglar theory, for Mrs. Hall states that her husband told her 'Papa is at the front door; I will let him in.' What burglar? A burglar would have killed Victor at the front door, not in the back of the store at his bedroom. He would have shot Victor in the face, not the back of the head. There was nothing disturbed and nothing stolen. His father said as far as he knew, Victor did not have an enemy in the world. Furthermore, if N. W. Hall had returned, he would have gone to the house, not the store.

"Who is this myth?" demanded Bibb. "I will tell you who the myth is. It is the same that figured with the McCue case and the same that figured in the Beattie murder. There was no scream or outcry or alarm until a long time after the shooting, and then we find his head on a bolster and a quilt spread over his body.

"Gentlemen of the jury, Mrs. Hall had the chance when she was on the stand to explain all these facts, but she failed to do so, and we must take her evidence as she gave it. There was not a quiver or a tear. She was absolutely unmoved when the family came down and found Victor under a slumber robe that would last him to eternity."

Bibb called the jury's attention to inconsistencies in testimony made by the accused. "She employed a detective, and the first thing she did was to tell him an untruth," thundered Bibb. The signed statement given to the detective was "absolutely not the same" as that which she made to her physicians and on the stand under oath.

Bibb pointed to the court exhibits. "What became of this bolster and the clothes? They were put in a little room. They have been produced, but they have not been produced like they were in that room. Where is the slip that was on that bolster? Mr. Bob Trice said the slip was on the bolster, and do you think that he is the kind of man who would testify falsely against this woman? Where is that slip? I would like to know. Why is the slip not here?" demanded Bibb. "There is only one reason and that is that the accused cannot produce it."

Just what did that mean? It was clearly double talk. Bibb moved along and did not give the jury time to think.

"A strange feature of the case is that ink had been spilled on both bolster and pillow and spilled on the blood spots, and it was put on them for a purpose."

Bibb proposed no purpose, but simply left that up to the jury's imagination. In similar fashion, Bibb expounded other suspicions one by one.

"If the accused was innocent, why should she go to Miss Rosson and tell her as she entered the grand jury room not to tell anything that would put it on her? And she sends a similar message to Miss Wood. Is that the operation of a mind free from guilt, of a conscience that is clear? In every conversation this woman has had regarding this case was the operation of a guilty conscience.

"When the grand jury went to her home to see the physical conditions, she realized that the house pointed to her, and the next night she attempts to burn down the house. Every step is the operation of a guilty conscience.

"Miss Wood says she shot Victor Hall's pistol at a mile post about a month before Victor was killed. According to the testimony of Miss Rosson, it was two months prior to the murder. Victor Hall carried the pistol daily. Do you gentlemen of the jury believe that he would have failed to reload the pistol?[3]

"Heaven and earth have been moved to impeach the testimony of Charles Johnston. Mr. Wood shaking his finger in his face and demanding that the young man change his testimony, which was that he examined the revolver and found it loaded all around.

"Charles Hester testified that he found dampness in the cylinder of Victor Hall's pistol when it was examined at the coroner's inquest. W. J.

MURDER AT GREEN SPRINGS

Roberts, as expert, testified that dampness in the cylinder was an indication that it had been recently fired."

Bibb then returned to the shell game of *waking Becky*. Becky Coates said that Mrs. Hall came back to her room, woke her up, and told her that Victor had been shot in the head.

"How did she know Victor Hall was shot in the head, if she had never been in the store room to see whether or not he was shot?"

Bibb reminded the jury that Mrs. Hall told her own Pinkerton detective that the very first thing she did after her husband was shot was to go wake up the little colored girl.

"This is the most remarkable statement ever offered in a court in Virginia. She makes a statement to her own employee and then is bold enough to come and tell you that she called Rebecca after the girls got down stairs? What are we to believe in this case? I do not believe there has ever been a case in Virginia where everything points so conclusively to the guilty party."

Mr. Bibb then recalled the pantry fire evidence.

"If that house had been burned, all the incriminating evidence in this case would have been burned up," the commonwealth's attorney thundered as he hammered his clenched fist on the table in front of him.

"If anyone else had wanted to burn the house they would have waited until the darkness and stillness of the night would have protected them. When she came to the fire what did Mrs. Hall do? She went to a window and said it was open and some one had gone in and set the house afire. But, gentlemen of the jury, we had the man who pulled the screen from the window to get in and put the fire out.

"Has Mrs. Hall ever denied that she killed her husband?" shouted Bibb. "You know she has not, and her attorneys have had every opportunity to ask her the question."

Bibb revisited every dubious piece of evidence. He then crowned his presentation by effectively brushing aside the entire array of character witnesses mustered by the defense.

"Mrs. Hall's attorneys have brought many witnesses to prove her character. I tell you that your penitentiaries are filled with criminals whose reputations were once lily white."[4]

Bibb concluded, "There never was an innocent party who has as many incriminating circumstances pointing to them."[5]

Bibb's delivery was forceful and passionate.[6] After two hours and fifteen minutes, he returned to his seat wet from perspiration. He looked satisfied. Bibb knew he had done well.

At eleven forty-five, portly Hill Carter rose from his chair. Handkerchief in hand, he strolled to the jury, and began the defense's argument. He was already in his shirt sleeves and soaked with sweat. Carter declared that in his long career he had never seen a case with as much sadness as in the present. Carter spoke clearly and confidently, but his generalities betrayed his peripheral involvement.

"The woman charged in this case was once the loving and loved wife of him who fills a bloody grave, charged without motive, of a terrible crime," said Mr. Carter. "The more heinous the crime, the stricter the law and this woman must have every benefit of the law. I have been at a loss to understand this charge, how it had birth and what was its cause. The first theory was to lay this crime at the door of Buck Dunkum. Someone had asked Mrs. Hall if she did not think Victor burned Buck Dunkum's store and that Buck killed Victor, but Mrs. Hall said she knew Victor did not burn the store, and she did not believe Buck killed Victor.

"A crowd of detectives has been in the case, and they had to have a victim. They are like bloodhounds, and if they get on the wrong track they follow and nothing on earth can change them. The detectives from their very nature can only see the one object they have fixed their minds upon. I think this is the way the charge first was laid at Mrs. Hall's door.

MURDER AT GREEN SPRINGS

I don't know when it started but, like a foul fog, it came and polluted the neighborhood."

Carter believed the evidence showed that a man fired Dunkum's store from inside. The incendiary lurked in the shadows until later when he killed Victor Hall. Carter proposed that the burglar secreted himself somewhere in Hall's store. Later, footsteps awakened Victor Hall. He thought it was his father at the door and got up to let him in. Victor Hall came face to face with a man he recognized. The burglar then shot Victor Hall to save himself from prison.

Though Carter's scenario approached what happened, it was an awkward fit. The term "burglar" was inexact and presented a dubious image in view of the facts. Bibb had already convinced everyone that sneaking into and hiding in the store was "absolutely ridiculous."

Carter pointed out that there was no inconsistency in Mrs. Hall calling her little servant. Mrs. Hall found Victor shot in the head prior to summoning her the second time. The conflicting times in Mrs. Hall's statements were merely misinterpretations, not discrepancies.

"You could not convict a yellow dog on such evidence," declared Carter.

Carter emphasized that after the shot, Miss Wood heard three footfalls on the platform outside the store. It was the murderer fleeing the scene "like Cain of old."

The prosecution believed that Victor Hall was shot in bed. However, the Commonwealth provided absolutely nothing during the trial to support that theory. Carter thought that if the prosecution had a theory, they should have at least advertised it.

Attempting the dramatic, Carter turned to Fulton and Bibb and asked them what their theory was. The effect was less than desired.

Fulton replied, "We think that Mrs. Hall could have shot him in the same way anyone else might have shot him. We have no further theory than the evidence in the case."

Carter paused to mop his profusely sweating brow and neck. It was a curious delay to listeners. They expected a counter remark, but the defender offered none and moved along.

"The coroner and members of the coroner's jury and Mr. Bibb himself examined the pistol and did not think the pistol figured in the crime. But now, Mr. Bibb has become impregnated with the theory of the detectives, and we see the trail of the serpent all through the case. It is not our duty to show the pistol had not been fired, but it was the duty of the Commonwealth to show that the pistol had been fired recently."

Carter ridiculed Charles Johnston's testimony and the idea that he told Elsie Wood that the pistol was "loaded *all around.*" Carter was once a Confederate cavalryman and intimately familiar with side arms. He had often heard of a pistol being loaded or fully loaded, but never "loaded *all around.*" People did not talk like that.

"Who got Johnston to come here and make the false statement?" demanded Carter. "If they frame one witness, they would frame up others and this witness throws suspicion on all the testimony produced. I think Johnston's testimony was fixed and framed up, and has pulled the whole Commonwealth down with him.

"What have the ink spots to do with the case?" asked Carter. The stout man paused often to get his breath. The hot courtroom taxed his system. "If Mrs. Hall put the ink on the bolster what would that have to do with the case?"

Carter applied the same question of relevancy to the bolster slip and the black kimono.

Carter submitted that Victor and Mrs. Hall were devoted to one another. He wished more families were like them where peace and love were always in evidence. He pointed to Nicholas and Ellen Hall reminding the jury that the parents of the victim remained steadfast at the side of Mrs. Hall during the entire trial totally convinced of her innocence.

MURDER AT GREEN SPRINGS

Carter called the jury's attention to the fact that it was Mrs. Hall who first suggested the autopsy and that the recovery of the bullet might help identify the guilty party. He turned to Bibb sarcastically, "Do you think that act of Mrs. Hall was a bluff also?"

Carter proposed the pantry fire was set by the same man who killed Victor Hall. After all, if the fire helped convict Mrs. Hall, it would make the real murderer's freedom all the more secure. Furthermore, the pantry "was possibly set afire by some one who is assisting in this prosecution. There is no evidence to connect her with the panty fire."

Carter concluded by launching a desperate appeal for mercy. It was as if he conceded ineffectiveness in his arguments. The advocate painted a melodramatic picture of how "a conviction would take this poor woman from her children, who would be left alone and the widow would be taken to a prison cell ere the grass became green on her husband's grave."

Tears filled Carter's eyes as he outlined the fate of the daughters. The girls, having already witnessed their father's death and step-father's murder, now faced losing their mother and sole support. Carter wiped his eyes. To almost everyone, it just looked like he was blotting more sweat, but his voice carried emotion.

"Their cup of anguish is already running over," cried Carter. "It would be the heart of a Bengal tiger that would want a verdict of guilty against this poor woman."[7]

Carter had finished. The attorney waddled back to his seat, plopped down, and mopped the water streaming from his face and neck. His shirt was wringing wet.

Being one thirty, Judge Shackelford recessed for one hour. Once the judge and jury exited, discussions about the proceedings broke out immediately among the spectators. Many stood in place to stretch themselves. Almost no one left their seat.

Some women bided the time productively having brought their needlework to court. It reminded one reporter of stories told of women knitting while watching heads guillotined during the French Revolution.[8]

Those seeking to cool themselves fanned more furiously than acceptable during the session. There was no record of anyone fainting from the heat, but surely some felt like they would melt before the end of the day. The better prepared people produced lemons to suck on to slake thirst. By this time, the smell of perspiration overcame the morning's applications of lilac water. The excitement of being part of the moment made it all seem worthwhile.

As the clock approached two thirty, Lindsay Gordon returned. He entered the courtroom with his wife, attending the trial for the first time. He seated her just inside the rail behind the defense.

Sandy Gordon was absent. The press rumored him to be at the office already studying grounds for appeal.

When court reconvened, Gordon approached the jury. The informal appearance of the attorney in his white shirt sleeves and dark suspenders accentuated his cordial manner.

Gordon's passive defense strategy had relied solely on the prosecution having to prove its case. Expecting fair play from the beginning, the defense team manned a position they assumed to be as unassailable as a castle wall. However, once undermined, the defense spent much of their time frantically shoring up one collapse after another.

The fair-minded Gordon and the Victorian relic Carter were as noble as any storybook images of crusading knights and about as anachronistic. The development of Mrs. Hall's predicament should have alerted them that chivalry was dead. The widow's cause was not to be decided by a gentlemanly duel confined strictly to reason and law. Publicity, emotions and politics had chosen weapons and tactics unfamiliar to the defense.

MURDER AT GREEN SPRINGS

The wily prosecution had grasped the rules. They seized the initiative from the outset and forced the defense to counter successive calumnies and sly cross-examinations.

The defense never considered this a game. A life hung in the balance. Gordon knew his closing argument was the last chance to focus the jury's attention on the core issue; the prosecution had no proof. None!

Gordon began, "Gentlemen of the jury I expect to occupy a great deal of your time. I have no apology to offer for this. It is the most important case I was ever in. Man is a dual creation: spiritual and physical. He is dominated by one or the other and as I grow older and my body grows weaker, I have more faith in my Heavenly Father than I did when I was a boy. Man, who is dominated by the principles of God, we call a good man. When dominated by the devil, he is a bad man. The English laws try men for their life on the principles of God, not of man.

"A horrible murder has been committed in your community and I have never seen the people wrought up to such a high state of excitement. You gentlemen of the jury have sworn to give this woman a fair and impartial trial. I ask you to go with me as carefully as possible through the record, and I defy anyone to look only at the record and say this woman is guilty.

"The newspapers in Virginia have done this woman an injustice which they can never repair. They have published every fact tended against her and have suppressed every fact in her favor.

"The love of money is the root of much evil, and I think is largely responsible for the present case. Money is the mysterious thing in this case. I shall argue this case without fear of any man. I think the physical conditions in this case will clear my client.

"I want to say to this great crowd, some of whom should not be here, the newspapers publish sensational matter to sell their papers – anything that will sell their paper they will publish."

Gordon expressed wonder at Fulton for not advancing his theory of the crime. Gordon proposed that the prosecutor was afraid his own scenario could not endure objective dissection.

"The bloodhound follows his prey from instinct; the detective follows his prey for money. Remember, gentlemen of the jury, this is a detective made case." For the better part of an hour, Gordon launched an attack against the detectives and their agencies.

"When Scott testified, I felt ashamed of the state of Virginia. There was never a whisper against this woman until this man Scott came on the scene. Scott asked her if she did not know that people were saying she killed her first husband. And then he added that they were saying now that she wanted to get rid of Victor to marry Bill Roberts.

"My friend George Trainham is a very good fellow. He did not believe in this woman's guilt until he had got in touch with the detectives. We only had one detective and had for eleven days, at eight dollars a day, and he betrayed us. Mackay has come here and sworn to a deliberate falsehood and has influenced Sterling Hall."

Gordon's argument clearly strayed from objectivity when he referred to Mackay as that "little, red haired, pop-eyed individual." He challenged the reliability of Sterling Hall's testimony because of his close association with Mackay.

"Sterling Hall is here straining and stretching his evidence, like Mr. Fulton and Mr. Bibb, to try and convict this poor woman."

The frustrated Gordon claimed that Pinkerton Superintendent Erb escaped his predicament on the stand by Fulton's dexterity. Though somewhat carried away by the subject at this point, Gordon correctly predicted "Mr. Fulton will show you this same dexterity tomorrow when he comes to close this case after our mouths are closed.

"If Victor Hall's pistol did not fire the shot that took his life, then Mrs. Hall did not shoot the pistol. A man killed Victor Hall, and it was a

man known to Victor Hall," shouted Gordon with dramatic exclamation and gesture.

"Suspicion, detectives, and Fulton is all that is in this case!"

Gordon addressed Charles Johnston's testimony that the pistol was loaded *all around*.

"It was a lie! He would not have come here and made this statement, but for the detectives. It is a framed-up case all around. When Mr. Johnston came here and swore falsely, he deserved to be prosecuted for perjury. But I have wasted too much time on Mr. Johnston. But if the detective would fix up Mr. Johnston, would they not try to fix up some of the people up here in the brush? Knock Johnston's testimony in the head, and you have killed the case of the Commonwealth.

"Another shadow of falsehood is the burial of the bloody clothes. But what does it amount to? One lot was buried by the direction of the coroner and the second lot by the direction of Mrs. Ellen Hall, the mother of the dead boy.

"My idea of the commonwealth's attorney is to find out justice, justice to all alike. But has this been done? Did the Commonwealth try to show you that the bloody clothes were dug up and examined by the detectives and then buried again?"

One by one Gordon addressed the buried clothes, the black kimono, the ink spots, the bolster slip, and a host of other irrelevancies introduced as, so called, evidence. The defender declared that these were all "shadows," which when illuminated were nothing.

Gordon thanked God for the blood spattered on Mrs. Hall's face, for had Mrs. Hall shot her husband as the prosecution insinuated, she would have had no blood on her.

"When she bowed down and raised his head while he was strangling and while she was ministering to his suffering, she got that blood on her face. But that is not all, and I want to show you that this woman did not commit this foul crime. Again, I say, thank God for the blood, and she let it remain on her face and hands until dozens of people saw it. If she had shot Victor Hall, she would have eliminated those blood spots before anyone saw her."

Gordon pointed out that the prosecution never called a single member of the coroner's jury. Since the coroner's jury some mysterious work took place in the mind of Mr. Bibb. When the inquest was held, Buck Dunkum was suspected of killing Victor Hall.

"We now get to Buck Dunkum," said Mr. Gordon, "and I hate to discuss this. Was there anyone who would have had any reason to kill Victor Hall?

"The evidence shows that the partnership in the business at Green Springs had been dissolved, and the partners were competitors. The evidence shows that Buck Dunkum has shown a disposition to follow up the prosecution of Mrs. Hall and place a stain on his two nieces.

"It may have been that Buck's stock had run low. It may have become evident that the place would not support two stores. It may have been that Buck hid in Victor's store with the intention of burning it. A man who could persecute his own nieces could seek revenge for the burning of his store. A man killed Victor Hall and a man who knew the premises.

"Mrs. Hall in the kindness of her heart sent Buck word that he was suspected and not to talk too much. Buck Dunkum and his wife could see no grief, but many others saw it.

"We are in the shadows and should not judge, but Mr. Dunkum has joined the gang of bloodhounds who are seeking to show that Mrs. Hall murdered her young husband to marry poor, old Bill Roberts, with his one thumb and piece of a finger.

"I am defending this woman and not attacking Buck Dunkum. I say there is more evidence to incriminate Buck Dunkum than there is to incriminate Mrs. Hall."

Gordon declared that in all his experience at the bar he had never seen such relentless persecution and efforts to secure a wrongful conviction of a defenseless person as had been done in the present case. The attorney reviewed the character testimonies describing Mrs. Hall's Christian life filled with virtue, charity, and a host of good works.

"One of the strongest features in this case is the fact that the parents of the murdered boy are absolutely certain Mrs. Hall is not guilty of the crime. There is no stronger evidence in the woman's favor than this affection of these two old people. Had they suspected Mrs. Hall, they would have been the first to tear her to pieces."

Gordon added that he had never feared conviction, but that he did fear a hung jury and that his client could not afford another trial.

After four straight hours of address, Judge Shackelford intervened. It was then six forty-five. Most people in the courtroom had long since passed physical and mental alertness and had now reached their limit of endurance. The court adjourned until nine o'clock the following morning. After fourteen hours, Gordon resumed Saturday morning without missing stride.

Gordon declared that the pantry fire was the work of the detectives. It was a frame up and a bubble that would burst as soon as the light of truth turned upon it. The attorney proposed that Commonwealth's Attorney Bibb had become "over-balanced" through his close association with the detectives and wrongly attributed motive to the fire.

"Someone broke into the house and set the pantry afire in order to reflect upon the accused, and the act cannot be exceeded in human degradation," asserted Gordon. "The Commonwealth knew it had no case against Mrs. Hall so far as the pistol evidence was concerned, and it was necessary to get up something else; and the frame up, and the pantry fire were fixed upon. Mrs. Hall did not set fire to the pantry, and she did not kill her husband!"

Gordon declared, "The last and crowning infamy of this prosecution is the effort to fix guilt upon this poor woman through this panty fire."

Gordon's six hour oration was comprehensive and sincere. It was also exceedingly tedious and interrupted by the overnight recess which effectively separated and distanced his core murder arguments from those of the panty fire. His eloquent ramblings saturated ears. Minds wandered in the hot room and missed conclusions best approximating the truth. Gordon closed with a tender appeal for his client whom he described as the most bitterly persecuted woman in Virginia.[9] The defense rested. Their die was cast.

Shortly before eleven o'clock Fulton rose to make the closing argument for the Commonwealth. His erect posture, confidence, and precise delivery befitted a well drilled mercenary.

"Before I begin, I want to thank the court for its patience and I want to thank the jury for their close attention," he said. "I am a stranger to you all, but I am sure the Commonwealth and the accused will have a fair judgment of this: one of the most brutal murders ever committed in this county, state or country.

"The distinguished attorney for the defense tells you that if you punish this accused, you will bring disgrace upon her. I tell you punishment is not a disgrace, but the foul deed of the criminal is. Your verdict will fix the standard and ideal of society. You have a grave responsibility. Not only the life of the accused, but the protection of life, liberty, and property, and I am sure you will not abuse your authority. The great power of this country rests in its jurors more than in its armies or navies. The newspapers are not on trial; the detectives are not on trial; your county's men are not on trial. I have no defense for them, for I think they are amply

MURDER AT GREEN SPRINGS

able to take care of themselves and need no defense. We are not trying theories. We are trying this defendant on the law and evidence.

"For eleven days you have listened to this defense, listening to two of the best lawyers that money could hire, two of the most brilliant attorneys in the state.

"After eleven days of investigation by the detective, Mrs. Hall calls off the work because she says she cannot afford it, in spite of the fact that she has just received $2,000 from the life insurance policies of her husband. She calls off the work of looking for the criminal in the case, who has killed her young and loving husband.

"We took the evidence step by step and showed that no one else could have committed the crime. Mr. Carter says it was a burglar and Mr. Gordon only touches lightly on the burglar, but says a man came there and knocked Victor down and then shot him. If the counsel can't agree on theories themselves, why should their theories concern you? What inducement could a burglar have for burning Buck Dunkum's store?"

Fulton echoed Bibb's ridicule of the burglar theory. If the defense had not yet regretted using the term "burglar" to describe the assailant, it soon would.

"Why should a burglar burn the store? And what is the burglar myth? Who ever heard of a burglar burning a house and then hanging around in the shadows of the illumination and wait to rob and murder in another store? Who ever heard of a burglar desiring to commit robbery and murder going to the front door and banging loud enough to awaken Victor Hall in the back of the house? Is that the way burglars act, I ask you gentlemen of the jury? I contend that there is not one scintilla of evidence to support any burglar theory."

Fulton thundered as he played his professional trump card, "I have endeavored to get the facts in this case, not only for your satisfaction, gentlemen of the jury, but for my own satisfaction, for there is not enough money in this wide world to induce me to prosecute an innocent person."

That statement was standard for prosecutors. It was the oldest trick in the book.[10]

"I want to call your attention to the affirmative conditions of this case. Let us get out of the fog and away from the myth of the defense. All of the members of the family attended the Dunkum fire and not one of them saw any stranger about the Hall premises."

Fulton reminded the jury of testimony showing that there was no one on the first floor after the Dunkum store fire except Mr. and Mrs. Victor Hall. Mrs. Hall told Detective Mackay that the first thing she did after hearing the shot was go wake Becky and emphasized the fact that the statement was never challenged when Mrs. Hall took the stand.

"Now I tell you that abuse of the detectives does not change their physical conditions and is not argument."

Mr. Fulton quoted from the evidence of Miss Elsie Wood, whom he described as one of the few witnesses Mr. Gordon had not labeled a liar "in the Annanias club."

Victor Hall was found at the bedroom door. Victor Hall was not knocked down at the front door and then shot.

"Gentlemen, he was lying dead at her door." Fulton called Mrs. Hall's testimony "a tissue of falsehoods."

"Becky Coates stated that when Mrs. Hall woke her, she said Victor had been shot in the head. On the stand, Mrs. Hall stated that she awoke the little Negro girl and then went into the store where she found Victor lying on the floor. How could she have told Rebecca that Victor was shot in the head if she had not been in the store where Victor lay, unless she was present and saw the shooting?

"Gentlemen, I ask you, under these circumstances, after hearing a call of distress from her husband and a pistol shot, would you have gone outdoors on the back porch and called a little twelve year old colored girl? Would you have had the nerve to go into this store and view the murdered person, step over the dying body and go out into the night and call? There was no scream or call for the girls in the house. God and the defendant only know how long it was from the time of the pistol shot to the time she called the girls. I say a woman that could go about the room of the tragedy in the cool manner in which Mrs. Hall assumed had the nerve of a lion and the courage of a tiger."

Fulton exhibited the bloody bolster and reminded the jury that the slip had never been produced, although Deputy Sheriff Trice had sworn it was on the bolster days after the murder.

Judge Shackelford interrupted Fulton's argument to recess for lunch. The judge and jury retired as did the officers of the court, Mrs. Hall and her family. Again the spectators stayed put. Few associated with the defense dared eat during the break. Tensions ran high. Mrs. Hall hoped for the best, but was anxious for the matter to end either way.

Court reconvened. Mrs. Hall sat a helpless spectator as Fulton spoke to the jury for the last time.

"At two o'clock in the morning, those two people were alone in their room.

There was the time, the place and the opportunity - and the only opportunity to commit that murder.

"When Mrs. Hall sent a message to Buck Dunkum, warning him that he was suspected, and 'to be careful of what he said,' was she trying to conceal the murderer of her husband? At the same time she employed a detective and sent a warning message to Dunkum, the man who was suspected, as she said.

"Why was it that she was so anxious to make it appear that he was suspected? And did not MacKay tell her frankly that he wanted a statement from her that he would treat family and strangers alike? She knew that statement was to be used. If she told the truth, she was bound by it. If she told a lie, she was bound by it, and her counsel can take either horn of the dilemma they wish.

"If that statement is not true, why was she lying? If it is true, she is convicted out of her own mouth. You can't get rid of statements by heaping abuse on the detectives. You can't hide or suppress the truth by denunciation. She has made several statements that the first thing she did after hearing the shot which killed Victor Hall was to run and awaken Becky. And Becky tells us that Mrs. Hall told her that Victor Hall was shot in the back of the head. How did she know that? I will tell you. Because she was present when that shot was fired. If you believe what she told George Trainham, MacKay and the others, you are bound to convict her."[11]

Fulton reminded the jury of their solemn duty. He asked that they render a verdict just to society. Fulton had finished. Judge Shackelford sent the jury to deliberate.

While the jury made their decision, newspapermen spoke with citizens on the courthouse sward. The opinions seemed evenly split between guilty or hung jury and not guilty or hung jury. Some were overheard to make wagers and modify existing bets.

In a little over an hour, the jury requested clarification from Judge Shackelford on what sentences were proper according to the court's instructions. The courtroom observed the activity and wondered. Mrs. Hall guessed that she had been found guilty. She folded her fan in her lap and stared straight ahead. Three minutes later, the jury knocked and was allowed back into the courtroom. They filed in solemnly and took seats. Judge Shackelford gaveled order in the court.

Clerk Philip Porter asked, "Gentlemen of the jury have you reached a verdict?"

Foreman W. C. Massie replied, "We have."

Clerk Porter stepped to the jury box and received the paper. He handed it to Judge Shackelford who examined it and returned it for Porter to read.

"We the jury find the prisoner not guilty of murder in the first degree, but guilty of murder in the second degree and fix her punishment at ten years in the penitentiary."[12]

MURDER AT GREEN SPRINGS

"Oh! Mamma! Mamma!" cried Mamie seated beside her mother. She threw her arms around her mother's neck. Her screams were clear and audible above the commotion in the room.

"Oh! Mamma! Mamma! You didn't do it! You didn't do it!"

Mamie then ran to Nicholas Hall who wrapped his arms around the child. But Mamie would not be consoled. Crying hysterically, she broke free and paced rapidly back and forth within the rail. Her shrieks were heard outside the building. This alerted the crowd to the verdict.

As if tired and wanting sleep, Mrs. Hall turned and buried her head in Essie's lap. Essie hung her head and cried. Her tears fell profusely on Mrs. Hall's head. The courtroom buzzed with voices split evenly between agreement and disappointment. Judge Shackelford rapped for order.

As reality of the verdict replaced the initial shock, all of Mrs. Hall's family cried and sobbed. Judge Shackelford rapped harder and called for order. This proved useless.

After exceeding the court's patience, Judge Shackelford ordered the room cleared of spectators. Sheriff Wash and Deputy Trice began pushing the crowd out. People moved reluctantly and exited with heads turned back for a last glimpse at what the *Times-Dispatch* called "the saddest scene the people of Louisa County ever have witnessed."[13]

While the room emptied, Mamie rushed up and threw herself on the bench before Judge Shackelford and pleaded, "Can't you do something for my momma? She didn't do it. You know she didn't do it."

Judge Shackelford gently placed a hand on her shoulder and comforted her as if she was his own. "No, I don't know that. We have done the best we could. You must try to bear up little girl."

"But can't you do something for her? Can't you make it a little lighter?" she pleaded and wept.[14]

When the room emptied, Hill Carter stood to make the expected motion. He asked the court to set aside the verdict on the grounds that it was contrary to the law and evidence.

Judge Shackelford stated that he would hear arguments on the motion Thursday at ten o'clock. There could be no application for bail until then. The judge turned Mrs. Hall over to Sheriff Wash. Mrs. Hall stood, adjusted her veil, grabbed onto her brother Hubert's arm for support and followed Wash out of the courtroom. Mrs. Hall held tightly onto Hubert's arm as Sheriff Wash led the way out of the courthouse and down the steps. Deputies followed close behind.

The jail was just yards away to the right. A thousand spectators crowded the walkway.[15] The black veiled widow held a handkerchief up to better hide her face. Some jeered and shook their fists as the convicted *spouse slayer* passed.[16] Wash shouted at the mob to stand back and make way as he preceded Mrs. Hall and her brother.

Once Mrs. Hall was inside the jail, the door closed and bolts slammed locked. The crowd quieted as Mamie Dunkum's cries for her mother continued from the second floor window of the courthouse. The woeful shrieks moved the crowd to pity.

Back in the courtroom, Judge Shackelford commended the jurors. "This has been a sad duty. It has probably been the saddest duty you have ever performed in your lives. But you have done well and the court thanks you for your patience and for your careful consideration of this. You are dismissed."[17]

Those few still present rose while Judge Shackelford exited to his chambers. Clerk Porter declared court adjourned. Without hesitation, the expressionless jurors left for their homes.

Nicholas and Ellen Hall collected the girls to take them home. Mrs. Hall's siblings followed the Halls and the girls out of the courtroom. Reporters asked N. W. Hall if the girls would be living with them.

"No!" snapped Hall, thoroughly disgusted with the outcome, "I don't want them near Green Springs anymore. They will go somewhere else, probably with one of their aunts."[18]

MURDER AT GREEN SPRINGS

The trial was finally over. The family and friends of Mrs. Hall believed the aggressive and relentless prosecution aligned with public sentiment was as great a travesty of justice as any *kangaroo court*. But the compromise verdict was not *kangaroo court*. It was *Possum Court*!

The jury in its consideration of so many singular features begged comparison to the native Virginia marsupial. Like the scavenger sanitizing the woods, this *Possum Court* handed down a verdict scatologically consistent with the swill given it to digest.

Weird circumstances, prejudiced investigators, skewed evidence, crafted perjury, and a passive defense had all steeped in juices of local hostility, biased media, and socio-political entrenchments. Collectively, it comprised a veritable ration of factual carrion. The jury, so nourished, entered its deliberation with as many members favoring death by electrocution as those favoring acquittal.

While the prosecution team congratulated themselves on a job well done, Lindsay Gordon and Hill Carter stepped from behind the rail to leave. Eager newspapermen met them with a barrage of questions. Neither attorney had any intention of discussing the case.

Always the gentleman, Lindsay Gordon simply raised an open hand toward them in a smooth motion easily understood as both *Silence!* and *Leave be!* His eyes flashed with contempt for the press. Before turning away, Gordon allowed himself only the few words he felt compelled to deliver.

"Well, I hope you enjoyed it. – The newspapers did it."[19]

MURDER AT GREEN SPRINGS

CHAPTER
Eleven

THE NEWSPAPERS DID IT?

In the decade preceding the Hall Case, the capital murder trials of Samuel McCue and Henry Beattie excited Virginia readers. Murder was relatively rare and shocking. The McCue and Beattie crimes were especially so. These shared elements of brutality, mystery, detective investigation, cover-up, and high visibility: a sure formula for sensation and newspaper sales.

Publicity of the Hall murder began as any other report of a rural tragedy and mirrored the course of the Harrison Case the previous August. The crime occurred on a main railway involving state jurisdictions. Railroad, telegraph and telephone afforded expedient communications for investigators and reporters with their home offices. The array of detectives and big city newsmen magnified matters with the country folk and excited demands for justice.

The media displayed an ordinary interest in the Hall murder until the special grand jury convened. Ambitious reporters and competing newspapers noted unusual developments. They embellished stories with rumors and misinformation, for the most available material came from sources biased against Mrs. Hall. The burning of the C & O Depot exploded the story into a sensation.

On the heels of the nationally publicized trial of Leo Frank in Georgia, Virginia newspapers, especially those in Richmond, welcomed their own regional thriller. Newspapers accentuated similarities of the Hall Case with the infamous McCue and Beattie murders, thereby, promoting statewide interest.

THE NEWSPAPERS DID IT? 275

The first comparisons occurred as a matter of course. The Hall Case, indeed, shared some basic elements with those of McCue and Beattie; however, beyond a few, superficial facts, the Hall Case was very different. The repeated analogies made between with McCue and Beattie without any counterbalance by the stark differences established a benchmark for media bias against Mrs. Hall.

Immediately following the McCue and Beattie trials, reporters published books detailing each of those crimes. Strangely, despite all of the excitement, no one in the entire cadre of journalists covering Mrs. Hall's trial ever published a work about the case. This was truly remarkable considering the array of professional journalists covering the crime touted as "one of the most mysterious in all Virginia criminology."[1]

The very same reporters who compared Elizabeth Ann Hall with the two most notorious spouse slayers in Virginia chose later to neglect record of the Hall Case as if not wanting to call attention to their roles in the affair. Comparisons in detail of McCue and Beattie with Mrs. Hall reveal far greater disparities than similarities. These unmask the newspapers as willing accomplices in the trial's outcome and explain in part why history developed amnesia.[2]

James Samuel McCue was born to a prosperous Albemarle County family. "Sam" McCue enjoyed the advantages of private school and studied law at the University of Virginia. He practiced law in Charlottesville and quickly built a lucrative practice while earning a reputation for ruthless business dealings.

On November 4, 1885, McCue married Fannie M. Crawford from a wealthy Augusta County family. The couple had four children William, Ruby, Samuel, and Harry. Over time, their family rose to prominence in the community. Fannie immersed herself in charity work and civic activities.

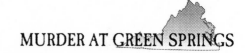
MURDER AT GREEN SPRINGS

In addition to practicing law, Sam McCue entered politics. He was elected mayor of Charlottesville in 1896 and served two consecutive two-year terms. At first, Sam declined to run for a third term, but reconsidered. He ran again and was reelected mayor in 1902.

The family attended the nearby Presbyterian Church where Sam served as deacon. The McCue family's social life centered on church as was typical for polite society of the day.

On Sunday evening September 4, 1904, Fannie McCue entered church alone after the service began. She sat in the front of the sanctuary where she and her husband normally sat. Sam McCue entered later and seated himself near his wife. At the end of service, Sam stopped to shake hands with friends. Fanny left without him. The couple usually arrived and departed together. Many people noted this unusual behavior.

Sam caught up with his wife and the two walked home. They met another couple en route and walked and talked together with these friends until parting company in front of the McCue residence at five minutes to nine.

Within half an hour, Sam telephoned his brother Dr. Frank McCue. Sam reported that an intruder had attacked them and to please hurry over to help. Dr. McCue ran grip in hand to his brother's aid.

Sam McCue and his houseboy John Perry met Dr. McCue at the door. Sam appeared dazed and clad only in a torn undershirt, dark trousers, and slippers. He claimed someone was hiding in the house when he and his wife returned from church and attacked them.

As Dr. McCue tried to tend his brother's head wound, Sam pushed him away and urged him instead to go look for Fannie. The doctor left Sam and went upstairs. Attracted by the sound of water running, Dr. McCue went into the bathroom and was struck by the gruesome site of Fannie McCue dead and partly submerged in the bathtub full of steaming, bloody water.

Dr. McCue called the police. The alarm spread. The police and others soon arrived. By ten o'clock, the house was filled with physicians, lawyers, and police conducting a murder investigation.

According to McCue, he and his wife readied themselves for bed as soon as they returned home. Sam turned the gaslights down and Fannie put on her nightdress. Sam began undressing. He pulled his shirt over his head and, while so encumbered, an assailant seized the opportunity to rush him.

"He was a kind of dirty white man with his beard out a little," claimed McCue.

According to Sam, his attacker came straight at him with a baseball bat. He parried the man's first blow then wrestled with his attacker while his wife screamed for help. The assailant tore Sam's undershirt as Sam broke free and ran for his shotgun beside the bureau. Sam said he leveled the gun, but before he could fire, the man struck him upside the head with the bat knocking him unconscious. When he came to, he did not see his wife and immediately stumbled downstairs to telephone for help.

Four physicians examined his wife's body. Her nightdress was severely torn. The lace collar was completely ripped off as in a struggle. She had been choked. She had been hit three times with a baseball bat. One blow to the right side of her head nearly tore her ear off, another landed beside her nose, and the third was to the back of the head. The shotgun blast to the left breast just below the collarbone killed her. Finally, her assailant dumped Fannie in the bathtub and turned on the hot water.

Both weapons were still at hand. The baseball bat was neatly propped up outside the bathroom door. The shotgun leaned against the wall inside the bathroom.

Police questioned Perry, the only other person in the house at the time. The houseboy said that he was asleep in the servant's quarters. He was awakened by a gunshot. After overcoming his initial fear, he made his way the most direct route available from his room in the upper rear

MURDER AT GREEN SPRINGS

of the house downstairs then to the front of the house where Perry found McCue downstairs apparently recovering from being knocked senseless.

Strangely, McCue did not seem badly hurt. While investigators tried to make sense of the situation, McCue cried and complained loudly of his injuries, yet he refused opiates and other medications. Doctors examined McCue and found the blow to his cheek little more than a bump.

None of the McCue children were at home at the time. William, their oldest, arrived shortly before his mother's body was discovered. When he asked his father what happened, McCue told him "Your mother is dead, killed by a burglar." Later McCue asked his brother if his wife was dead. Later still, he posed the same question to Dr. Venable.

With curious behavior, inconsistencies, and glaringly disproportionate injuries, McCue's story immediately fell apart. By dawn hundreds took no stock in his story.[3]

The next day, City Council reacted beyond authority and hired detectives William G. and Albert H. Baldwin to investigate the case. They offered a $500 reward for the arrest and conviction of the murderer.[4] However, investigators located no suspect matching the description given by McCue.

Friends and family had known of the McCue's turbulent home life for years. Problems began about 1894 and grew progressively worse. Sam and Fannie had frequent and violent arguments. Most confrontations concerned Sam's affairs with women.

On one particular occasion, Sam drew a pistol and told Fannie to keep her mouth out of it. She fled to son William's room and woke him up. Sam followed her in there and pointed the pistol at her until William intervened. Fannie confided to her brother Ernest Crawford that Sam threatened to kill her. After her murder Ernest stated simply, "We all anticipated this trouble."[5]

The day after the funeral, Samuel McCue was arrested and charged with the murder of his wife. Nevertheless, detectives continued their investigation. They pursued suggestions that an enemy of Sam McCue committed the crime. At one point, investigators considered his brother Edward O. McCue, the police justice; however, no evidence to this effect was found. Other than Sam McCue, the likeliest suspect was Lester Marshall, the husband of McCue's current mistress Hattie. Marshall was investigated, but had a solid alibi.

Meanwhile, the coroner's inquest proceeded cautiously. The prominent case demanded thoroughness. Local citizenry became so incensed at the murder and the perceived delay that the new mayor feared a lynch riot. The local militia was away on exercises near Manassas. Governor Montague offered state troops if required, but the release of the coroner's jury's verdict on the afternoon of September 8th defused tensions and troops were never needed.

> "The jurors sworn to enquire when and how and by what means the said Fannie M. McCue came to her death upon their oaths do say that the said Fannie M. McCue on the night of Sunday Sept. 4, 1904, between the hours of 9 and 10, from a gunshot wound in the chest, inflicted by a gun in the hands of J. Samuel McCue."[6]

McCue asserted innocence. Throughout his ordeal, McCue carried his Bible and quoted Scripture. McCue published his own announcement offering a reward for the killer. The notice appeared in the Daily Progress and distributed in handbills.

> $1,000 REWARD – A reward of $1,000 will be paid for the arrest and conviction of the person who made attempt on my life and murdered my wife at home in Charlottesville, on the night of September 4, 1904.
>
> J. Samuel M'Cue[7]

MURDER AT GREEN SPRINGS

The wealthy McCue hired four attorneys. His defense team included three top local attorneys and John L. Lee of Lynchburg, ultimately McCue's lead attorney.

Commonwealth's Attorney Frank Gilmer found himself alone against an intimidating array of legal minds. He countered by recruiting Captain Micajah Woods of Albemarle County to assist the prosecution. Woods had served as a pallbearer for Fannie McCue. He had already refused to act in behalf of the Crawford family, but Gilmer persuaded Woods to accept the challenge. The Crawford family secured additional help for the prosecution in the person of Captain R. S. Ker, the commonwealth's attorney for Augusta County.

The trial began October 18th. Judge George W. Morris presided. Because of widespread publicity, jury selection was difficult. Eventually, the court imported jurors from Petersburg, Richmond, Fredericksburg, and Warrenton.

Chief prosecutor Woods argued the case with few obstacles. Witnesses testified to McCue's long history of cruel and inhuman treatment of his wife. The house was not plundered, as with a robbery, and Fannie's wounds were beyond any outrage expected at the hands of a burglar. A piece of bloody fabric matching the tear in McCue's undershirt was found beneath the bathtub where Fannie's body was dumped. McCue's statements were inconsistent with themselves and the facts. Injuries to both victims were disproportionately severe. Three doctors testified that McCue's wound was trifling, insufficient to cause unconsciousness, and likely self-inflicted. If McCue was conscious, prosecutors argued, he killed his wife.

The defense featured the servant's testimony modified to reflect his having heard Fannie McCue calling for her husband's help. The prosecution discredited this with ease, as well as son William's denial of his father's threats. The defense submitted numerous love letters written years before hoping to prove McCue's love for his wife. The jury remained unconvinced of McCue's spotless and immaculate character.[8]

THE NEWSPAPERS DID IT?

In the end, the jury deliberated the case twenty minutes and arrived at a verdict on the first ballot. McCue was found guilty of murder in the first degree and sentenced to death by hanging.

Judge Morris refused to set aside the verdict. On appeal, the defense team filed forty-six bills of exception.[9] The Virginia Supreme Court failed to grant retrial. The U. S. Supreme Court refused to intervene. Finally, despite pleas from McCue's children, Governor Monatague denied commutation.

Shortly before execution on February 10, 1905, Samuel McCue confessed to killing his wife. He supplied no details other than "a demon in him" committed the crime and not he himself. McCue ascended the gallows and was hanged.

Readers throughout Virginia intently followed the McCue trial. The *Times-Dispatch* later commented on how "the scandal loving public" had been cheated by the prosecutions failure to call McCue's consort as a witness.[10]

Capital murder alone was not the sole cause of the sensation. It was the combination of the extremity of the crime, attempted cover-up, and the scandalous involvement of a well-known person that captivated the public. Though the murder rate increased dramatically and the Commonwealth of Virginia executed seventeen people for capital crimes in 1909, more than any year to date, the McCue murder trial remained foremost in the public's mind when Henry Beattie made headlines in 1911.

Henry Clay Beattie, Jr. was the son of a prosperous merchant. They lived in a recently annexed area referred to as *South Richmond*, which until 1910 had been the town of Manchester.[11] Much to his family's embarrassment, Henry became involved with a local beauty of dubious background named Beulah Binford. She was anything but the *marrying kind*.

MURDER AT GREEN SPRINGS

Beulah became pregnant out of wedlock. She then left the state and gave birth to Henry's son in North Carolina. Binford gave the child up for adoption, but the Beattie family maintained contact with the infant.

Two weeks before the boy's first birthday, he succumbed to cholera. The Beattie family held a funeral for the child and buried him in Shockoe Hill cemetery. Newspapers publicized the event as the first funeral in Richmond where everyone attended in motor cars, and thus, called additional attention to the family's sad situation.

A couple of months later, Henry married Louise Owens of Dover, Delaware. She was from a fine family with old Manchester ties. Her uncle Thomas Owens still lived in *South Richmond*. Benjamin Owens, another uncle, was then personal secretary to Governor Mann. The marriage pleased Henry Beattie, Sr., and so, fulfilled its primary purpose. Louise was soon in the *family way*, and the Beattie family rejoiced in the prospect of a legitimate heir.

Henry went to a baseball game in Norfolk and ran into Beulah Binford. They renewed their affair, and Henry provided her a place to live in *South Richmond*.

Upon birth of their son, Louise left Henry and moved in with her uncle Thomas Owens who lived near the Chesterfield County line. On July 18, 1911, Henry motored out to see Louise. He presented her with a bag of cheap candy and took her for "an airing" in the country without the baby.

Within the hour, Henry returned with Louise dead at his side in the front seat of the car. She had been killed by a shotgun blast at close range. According to Henry, they were driving on Midlothian Turnpike when they encountered a man in the middle of the road who refused to get out of the way. Henry said he exchanged words with the man and tried to force his way around him. As he did so, the man turned a shotgun on them and fired. Louise took a full load of No. 6 shot in her head and died instantly. Henry said he jumped out of the car and wrestled the gun away from the man.

After first calling police, Thomas Owens telephoned his influential brother Benjamin. At 1:30 A.M. Benjamin called Luther Scherer, head of the Chesapeake and Ohio Railway's police. Scherer was also a member of the State Parole Board. Scherer's clout soon effected detachment of an engine and caboose from a freight train. This expedited retrieval and delivery of bloodhounds from the state farm in Goochland County. By 5:30 A.M., Scherer, bloodhounds and local police were on the scene.

Beattie repeated his story to authorities, but the tale soon unraveled. On July 21, the day after the funeral, Henry Beattie was arrested at his home for the murder of his wife. Commonwealth's Attorney Gregory and Richmond's chief of police placed Luther Scherer in charge of the investigation. William G. Baldwin, head of the Baldwin-Felts Detective Agency and lead investigator in the McCue murder, was summoned, presumably by Scherer.

The day after the arrest, Henry's cousin Paul Beattie admitted to buying the shotgun and shells for Henry the Thursday prior to the shooting.[12] Paul Beattie and Beulah Binford were both jailed under protective custody pending the trial.

The case was an immediate media sensation. Even as the story of Louise Beattie's death made headlines, one paperboy was heard to cry "Another McCue Case!"[13]

Upon Beattie's arrest, the papers rumored employment of McCue's lead attorney, John L. Lee for the defense. Yes. People in Richmond still identified with details of the McCue trial after seven years! However, by the time the Beattie trial ended, Henry Beattie easily replaced Samuel McCue as Virginia's foremost murderer.

The wealthy Henry Beattie, Sr. hired prominent Richmond attorney Hiram M. Smith, Jr. who assembled a defense team which included the equally respected Hill Carter. Commonwealth's Attorney Gregory countered by recruiting a prosecution team headed by noted Richmond attorney Louis O. Wendenburg.

The trial at Chesterfield Court House attracted a crowd daily. Carriages shuttled Richmond spectators between Centralia depot and the courthouse. People rode bicycles fifteen miles from downtown Richmond.[14] Reporters from every Virginia paper flocked to the scene. The trial became national news, and a telegraph shed was erected outside the courthouse specifically to wire the verdict directly to the *New York Times!*

After eleven days of evidence and two days of speeches, the jury deliberated fifty-eight minutes. Beattie was found guilty of first degree murder and sentenced to death. Appeals failed. Beattie finally confessed to killing his wife shortly before being electrocuted November 24, 1911.

Newspaper sales skyrocketed. The day before the Beattie murder, circulation of the *News Leader* was 24,587 copies. The day the killing was reported this jumped to 28,697. When news of Beattie's involvement and arrest broke, two extra editions were issued and by July 23rd, circulation hit an impressive 49,114 copies, double the typical daily volume.

Circulation remained around 30,000 throughout the pre-trial period. The *News Leader* sold around 40,000 papers daily at opening of trial and neared 50,000 from mid-trial onward. The issue that included closing arguments and the verdict sold an astounding 64,019 copies. With months of elevated circulation, the Beattie trial was a windfall for newspapers and fulfilled dreams of the reporters involved.

In perspective, the *News Leader's* edition announcing the United States' entry into World War I sold 50,082 copies. The issue announcing the abdication of the Kaiser and terms of armistice barely exceeded the peak sale of the Beattie trial at 66,221 copies. Even this number was skewed upward by seven years of population growth.

In May 1914, the Hall Case suddenly loomed large to newspapers as an opportunity to profit as from the Beattie trial. Quite ironically, the timing could not have been worse for Mrs. Hall. Richmond's two largest newspapers had just become fierce, independent rivals.

Until that time, the *Times-Dispatch* and *News Leader* were sister components of the Richmond publishing empire built by Joseph Bryan. The very day Victor Hall was killed, a report rumored the sale of the *Times-Dispatch*.[15] There was no other fanfare, but the report was true. By May 1914, the *Times-Dispatch* was under new ownership and with new managing editor Colonel Charles Hasbrook, a founder of the *Associated Press*. The *Times-Dispatch* was then in direct competition with the *News Leader* and Bryan's heirs.[16]

Amidst the excitement of the grand jury investigation and the depot fire, reports surfaced that the Louisa County Board of Supervisors sought aid in prosecuting Mrs. Hall. Newspapers rumored prominent names associated with the Beattie Case. The sinister comparisons began. Others, no doubt, had similar notions, but the newspapers set the type.

The references to the McCue and Beattie trials supplied readers with a familiar, though skewed, standard by which to measure the many unique, convoluted interrelationships in the Hall Case. The public's recall of the McCue and Beattie trials was keen. Just five days before Victor Hall was killed, the *News Leader* featured an article reporting the new detective career of Paul Beattie.[17] Indeed, residuals of the Beattie trial still generated interest as the Hall story broke.

Published references to McCue and Beattie conditioned the public to associate Mrs. Hall with two notorious, confessed killers executed for their crimes. Each of the three cases involved a defendant charged with killing a spouse. Each asserted innocence. Detectives figured prominently in each case. Each defendant claimed a stranger committed the crime. Each received front-page publicity statewide, and each was prosecuted solely on circumstantial evidence.

MURDER AT GREEN SPRINGS

Sam McCue, Henry Beattie and Elizabeth Hall were each arrested at home, but the elapsed times between the murders and arrests stands out. Common to the McCue and Beattie cases, authorities pieced together sufficient facts to warrant arrests of both men within hours of their crimes. In both instances, police waited out of a sense of propriety until the day after each wife's burial to seize the suspect. Interestingly, both the McCue and Beattie arrests fit the modern axiom of the *72 Hour Rule*.[18]

Contrast the Hall Case. The killer was not obvious. Local authorities, railway detectives, a state insurance investigator, and a private detective developed their suspect in an atmosphere of escalating public hysteria. Civil unrest prompted the special grand jury investigation, not weight of evidence. Prosecution appeared doubtful when the special grand jury convened after nearly a month's preparation. The combination of the mysterious threat to Dunkum, the burning of the depot and an arson attempt on the Hall residence while the grand jury was in session secured Mrs. Hall's indictment. The second pantry fire initiated her arrest and leveraged her conviction.

The Hall, McCue and Beattie cases all developed into courtroom battles between teams of lawyers. Again, generalization greatly skewed the analogy. Both McCue and Beattie were wealthy men accused of capital crimes. These mustered the best legal defense teams in Virginia which money could buy. The commonwealth's attorneys in both cases then responded by assembling prosecution teams as best they could.

The reverse happened in the Hall Case. The Louisa County Board of Supervisors insisted on hiring additional help in prosecuting the Hall Case despite protests from Commonwealth's Attorney Bibb. The prosecution team formed first at the instigation of certain county influentials. This forced the defense to recruit additional counsel.

As if the media's general comparisons of Mrs. Hall to Beattie were not bad enough, Lindsay Gordon employed Hill Carter as assistant counsel for the defense. Thus, seated at the defense table with Mrs. Hall was an ever-present reminder of the Beattie Case. Despite Carter's experience as a defense attorney and his considerable experience in the Louisa courtroom, his involvement in the Hall Case caused the malignant comparisons with Beattie to metastasize internally.

The defense in all three cases relied heavily on establishing unimpeachable character to prove inability to commit murder. This dubious defense for any crime was the last resort for the comparably iniquitous McCue and Beattie. Hill Carter was famous for having personally delivered this very argument in defense of Beattie only three years before. Carter's repeat performance in Mrs. Hall's behalf gave everyone reason to assume a similar desperation applied. It was no wonder that the *News Leader* characterized Carter's plea as "pathetic."[19]

The Hall, McCue and Beattie cases were tried successfully on circumstantial evidence. The evidences presented in the McCue and Beattie trials were far clearer than the contradictory and confused facts of the Hall Case.

Both McCue and Beattie had turbulent marriages and ongoing adulterous relationships. In those situations, motive and opportunity were apparent. In contrast, no evidence for similar discord between Victor and Lizzie Hall was ever discovered by the prosecution. There was none. The best the prosecution could produce in this regard was to allude to one rumored disagreement between Lizzie and her first husband before the couple ever moved to Louisa County: sometime prior to 1905. The prosecution relied chiefly on demonstrating opportunity, but never once suggested motive.

Indeed, infidelity figured prominently in the sensational McCue and Beattie murders. The Hall story lacked this key element in the proven formula for a media sensation. Rather than report an incomplete analogy, reporters drew upon rumors and innuendo to supplement the deficiency. Readers craved a sordid love interest, so the newspapers manufactured one.[20]

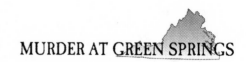

MURDER AT GREEN SPRINGS

Throughout developments of the drama, the media was quick to emphasize Bill Roberts' unusual attentiveness to Mrs. Hall. However, sticking to facts was not enough. Days after Mrs. Hall's arrest, the *News Leader* published the blatant, unfounded "opinion" that if Mrs. Hall was acquitted, ". . . she and Roberts will be married immediately following the trial."[21]

Furthermore, after presenting the alleged marriage plans, the article detailed Roberts' multiple amputations. No mention of Roberts' unique physical condition ever appeared prior to this. Printed alongside the article about Robert's was the full-front photograph of the one armed, two fingered man.[22] The *Daily Progress* copied the story.[23]

Thus, the *News Leader*, the newspaper with the largest circulation in the state, sought to generate even greater readership with an attention grabbing, freakish-love contrivance. Considering a woman's life was at stake, this qualifies as one of the finest pieces of yellow journalism ever produced in Virginia, perhaps anywhere.

Both McCue and Beattie killed their wives with shotguns. The murder weapons were never in doubt. In the Hall Case, the murder weapon was always in doubt. The spent cartridge in Victor Hall's .38 S&W pistol became a compelling factor only by the words of a perjured witness.[24] The prosecution's evidence regarding the murder weapon was soundly refutable.

Unfortunately, the defense's firearms evidence was largely overlooked having been presented by the most implausible group of firearms *experts* imaginable. All of them were friends of the accused. Each did more harm than good, especially Bill Roberts, whose physical condition and familiarity with the accused made the defense look extremely desperate, if not, utterly ridiculous.

McCue and Beattie each attempted to hide his crime by a poorly fashioned tale blaming a fictitious stranger. The prosecution accused Mrs. Hall directly of attempting to conceal her crime like McCue and Beattie. The comparison fixed the notion that the widow's burglar story must have been similarly contrived. The prosecution promoted the idea in the courtroom; the newspapers conveyed it to the public.

The series of six mysterious fires on the Dunkum-Hall properties was newsworthy material. Collectively, these focused attention on the families living at Green Springs Depot and diverted it from suspects with motives. Even though the pantry fires occurred in an outbuilding detached from the store, the prosecution argued that the purpose of the second occurrence was to destroy the murder scene. Prosecutors only hinted at evidence targeted for destruction, but the court admitted the second pantry fire into consideration anyway. The testimonies regarding the pantry fire became vital to the prosecution's success. From the newspapers' perspective, the alleged cover-up was the final element needed to complete the McCue and Beattie analogies.

In fairness to reporters, the defense completely shunned the press. During the investigation, the *Times-Dispatch* approached Gordon twice and Mrs. Hall once offering to publish any statements they cared to make but were refused.[25] This left the media only with gossip and sources favoring the prosecution. Nevertheless, even when the prosecution introduced blatant obfuscations involving the black kimono, missing bolster slip, buried clothes, ink stains, coffee smell and whiskey, the newspapers never challenged any of this *evidence*, but enthusiastically huckstered these sideshows.

In both the McCue and Beattie trials, the question of guilt was clear. Each jury readily returned first-degree murder verdicts, and each of the condemned men confessed his guilt before execution. In the Hall Case, the decision of the jury was extremely subjective. Fortunately, the uncertainty generated sufficient dissention amongst the jurors to produce the compromise verdict.

The newspapers never once called attention to any of the stark contrasts between Mrs. Hall and the two notorious, philandering, confessed wife slayers to which they compared her. The newspapers steered a predetermined course around these facts knowing that the truth was less interesting; readers paid money for thrills. They left their intent glaringly in print. For example, Newspapers commented that the instructions to the jury were modeled after those from the McCue and Beattie trials. Left unsaid was that this was true only of instructions from the prosecution. No newspaper ever mentioned any of the thirteen instructions prayed for by the accused.

The *News Leader* published their "list in part" of the Commonwealth's instructions. The *News Leader* selected eight of the seventeen. The definitions of first-degree murder and reasonable doubt were accompanied by conditions to infer premeditation and malice; proof of motive was unnecessary for conviction; and actions show intent. All were faithfully copied and corresponded verbatim to the instructions to the McCue and Beattie juries.

However, the legal balance contributed by the unpublished instructions was lost: the definitions of second degree murder and various manslaughters; that the law presumes second degree murder unless proved otherwise; the weight of doubts; proof of criminal intent; reliability and credibility of witnesses; and consideration of the evidence and instructions as a whole. These were omitted and left the reader no means to discern to what extent the list had been skewed.

The last week of the Beattie trial earned front page treatment in the *New York Times* every day. The commercial success of the Beattie story was neither repeated nor approached by the Hall Case, but not due to any lack of sensational coverage. By the time the trial started, Elizabeth Hall's great influence on newspaper sales vaporized because of a certain Serbian anarchist.

THE NEWSPAPERS DID IT?

In June 1914, the assassination of Arch Duke Francis Ferdinand started a chain reaction in Europe. The tremendous newspaper sales of July, August, and beyond were due primarily to the European crisis, not the Hall Case.

The Hall trial, indeed, achieved prominence on the front pages of Virginia newspapers, but elevated circulation remained high well after Mrs. Hall disappeared from view. Rather than generating sales like those during the Beattie trial, the Hall Case simply became a high visibility feature in editions already sold. Newspapers still made substantial money, but the gravy train expected from Louisa had been derailed by the outbreak of the First World War.[26] Profits specifically from the Hall Case were arguably nil.

Newspapers kept residuals from the Beattie trial alive until the very day Victor Hall was murdered. The same newspapers printed their last mention of Mrs. Hall when she entered prison. Interest evaporated, and no effort was ever made to remind the public about her.

All things considered, Gordon's condemnation of the newspapers[27] and reporters was justified. Evidence suggests that truth was intentionally distorted, withheld, substituted or otherwise skewed to sell papers. Charmed by the sirens of money and ambition, newspapers and their hirelings became willing accomplices in sacrificing a woman and her family on the altar of public opinion. Ultimately, they sold their integrity for naught.

Even so, the powerful influence of newspapers on the Hall Case comprised the least of the three major evils to curse the hapless widow. Secondary was Louisa County's unfathomably complex social politics. Above all else, the general outrage in Louisa County against Mrs. Hall sprang from facts familiar only to county residents. Mrs. Hall's infamy logically consummated the extraordinary history of *that store* at Green Springs Depot.

MURDER AT GREEN SPRINGS

THE NEWSPAPERS DID IT?

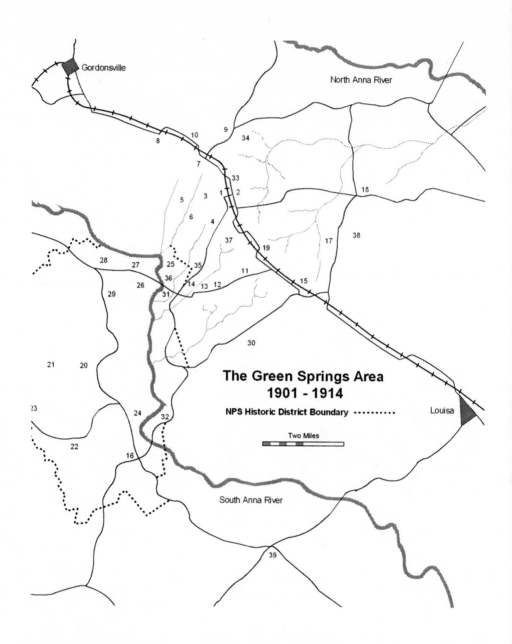

Gordonsville

North Anna River

9
10
8
34
7
33
2
18
5
3
1
6
4
37
38
17
19
28
27
25
35
11
36
14
15
26
13
12
29
31
30
21
20
23
24
32
Louisa
22
16

The Green Springs Area
1901 - 1914

NPS Historic District Boundary ···········

Two Miles

South Anna River

39

Map by J. K. Brandau

MURDER AT GREEN SPRINGS

GREEN SPRINGS AREA MAP KEY

Number	Location / Individuals
1	Green Springs Depot & Hall's Store / Victor K. Hall & David Asa Dunkum Families
2	Dunkum's Store / William Richard "Buck" Dunkum & Family
3	Nicholas W. Hall & Family
4	John Sims Johnson, Sr. & Family
5	George L. & Grover N. Kennon
6	Littleton "Lit" Napper & Family
7	Forest Hill Baptist Church & Forest Hill School
8	Melton's Store / Lewis F. Yancey & wife Elsie
9	Dr. Phillip Pendleton May
10	James B. Madison
11	Lennie, Eddie & William J. "Bill Roberts
12	Henry A. Flannagan
13	Alphonse J. Chewning, wife Kate, and daughter Ruby Chewning
14	Valentines Mill / Henry R. Pollard, Jr.
15	Trevilians Depot
16	Poindexters Post Office / W. O. "Ollie" Wood & daughter Elsie Wood
17	James E. Hester & wife "Emma"
18	Oakland Academy / Rev. Isaac Newton May
19	Danne's Store / Charles Danne, Jr.
20	Bracketts (Plantation) / Carl H. Nolting
21	Sylvania (Plantation) / Frank C. Morris
22	Green Springs (Plantation) / George W. Morris
23	Harkwood (Plantation) / George H. Browne
24	Ionia (Plantation)
25	Corduroy (Plantation) / Charles B. Vest
26	Westlands (Plantation) / Fritz T. West
27	Millard Filmore "M.F." Peers
28	Belle Monte (Plantation) / Quarels Family
29	Belle Meade (Plantation) / Arthur G. Burnette
30	Lasley Methodist Episcopal Church
31	Wills Memorial Church (Presbyterian)
32	Berea Baptist Church
33	Mount Olive Church (African American)
34	Isaac Newton Poindexter
35	Knighton's Store (1903) / Joseph H. Knighton, wife Sarah, sons Josey, and Roy
36	The Elms (Plantation) / George McDuffie Blake, later Prof. John F. Blackwell's School
37	George W. Chewning, Jr.
38	Joseph Grady
39	Bells Cross Roads

THE NEWSPAPERS DID IT?   *295*

CHAPTER
Twelve

NEXT STOP:
GREEN SPRINGS DEPOT!

MURDER AT GREEN SPRINGS

ontemporary with establishment of the first large Green Springs plantations in the early 1700's, Gilbert Gibson received a substantial land grant along watershed between the North Anna and South Anna rivers. Gibson settled just north of the South Anna River and established a gristmill on what is now called Mill Creek.

Shallow, poor soil covered the ridge. The many steep, irregular gullies and creek beds cutting into this high ground made the topography suitable only for small, subsistence farms. These conditions encouraged settlement by people unable to afford better land and contrasted markedly with the expansive, rolling, fertile land of the neighboring *Green Springs Valley* where men of means established large, prosperous plantations.[1]

A few freeholders along with, poor whites, antebellum freedmen, indigenous remnants, and mulattos of various derivatives populated the ridge. By the late eighteen hundreds, the geographic and economic isolation fostered nearly a century of interdependency and intermarriage. The Gibsons, Branhams, Chewnings, Johnsons, Kennons, Nappers, Halls and others became more than neighbors; they were kinfolk. The development of the railroad brought the poor Green Springs Depot community increased contact with an outside world comprised mainly of Louisa County's upper castes who generally viewed the depot "clans" with predictable condescension.[2]

The Louisa Railroad Company was chartered by the Commonwealth of Virginia in February 1836 and opened its first section of track on December 20, 1837.[3] The stretch ran twenty-three miles from Hanover Junction (Doswell) to Fredericks Hall. The railroad expanded as funds

NEXT STOP: GREEN SPRINGS DEPOT!

were raised. The following year, twelve more miles of track opened to Louisa Courthouse. On January 1, 1840, new rails stretched through Trevilians and over the watershed ridge to Gordonsville.[4] The railroad not only provided a convenient way to ship the county's crops to ready markets, but reduced the isolation of the smaller farms along its stretch as merchants built stores near depots.

The Louisa Railroad grew to become the Virginia Central Railroad, which served as a lifeline for transporting supplies and troops between Richmond and the Shenandoah Valley during the Civil War. After the war, the newly formed Chesapeake and Ohio Railway assimilated the company. At some point, the C & O constructed the Green Springs Turnout to facilitate produce shipments from the Green Springs plantations.[5]

Local entrepreneur John Terrill Boston owned a number of interests in Louisa County.[6] He and his brother-in-law already owned a general store at Frederick Hall when he began purchasing property surrounding the turnout in October, 1873.[7] The C & O Railway built a supporting depot about the same time that John Boston built his store there [eventually Hall's store].[8] By September 1874, *Green Springs Depot* had a post office.[9]

John Terrill Boston – The Louisa County entrepreneur was the original owner of Hall's store at Green Springs Depot. (Photo Courtesy of Edward J. Westlow)

MURDER AT GREEN SPRINGS

John Boston's first child Channing Moore Boston was born at Green Springs Depot on June 17, 1874.[10] John Boston raised his growing family at his Green Springs store and managed the depot. Boston dealt primarily in general merchandise, but also purveyed wines and liquors.[11]

Sales and consumption of alcohol were growing concerns. These were already abhorrent to many people, who became ever more emotional over the issues. In 1874, the National Women's Christian Temperance Union began campaigning for legislation against alcohol. Year by year, Prohibitionists gathered political support in Virginia.

In the meantime, John Boston stocked his store as he saw fit. The entrepreneur also established a broom factory across the tracks from the depot. Son Channing assisted him in his endeavors and became the depot telegrapher.[12] However, the family's prosperity at Green Springs was not guaranteed and ended abruptly before the younger children assumed roles in their father's enterprises.

John Boston died in 1890 from a chronic condition which had plagued him since his discharge from the Confederate Army.[13] The successful business man died intestate resulting in decades of legal complications for the family. His wife moved to Richmond with the younger children. However, sixteen year old Channing Boston remained in the area as evidenced by his involvement as secretary in the organization of Wills Memorial Church later that same year.[14] Closely associated with Channing Boston was the church's librarian Roy Knighton.[15]

Channing Boston kept busy overseeing the store and commuting between Green Springs and his family in Richmond. In 1893, the church appointed elder J. Reid Wills "to see Channing Boston and tell him of the talk that is going on in the community about him."[16] There was neither mention of specifics nor whether or not Wills' being the Louisa County Sheriff had any bearing on the errand. The record simply bore witness to the gossipy nature of the neighborhood.

In 1896, young merchant George McDuffie Blake sensed opportunity. Blake leased Boston's store, sold his holdings in Richmond, and moved his family to Green Springs Depot.[17] Liquor sales had always been a significant portion of Blake's Richmond business; he likely sold spirits at his store in Green Springs as had Boston.[18]

The Anti-Saloon League of America had been founded the previous year. By this time, the temperance movement already had gained support of church denominations throughout Virginia, even in its smallest rural communities like Green Springs.

In 1897, the Prohibition Party in Virginia ran its own gubernatorial candidate Rev. Landon A. Cutler, pastor of the Louisa Christian Church.[19] Louisa's activist preacher lost the election, but his campaign demonstrated the considerable and growing support for the temperance movement in Virginia.[20]

That same year, church elders of Wills Memorial Church raised other concerns about Green Spring's character as "the session learned with anxiety and regret the establishment of a race course in our community and feels constrained to warn the church against the evil tendencies of horse racing which often leads to gambling and dissipation, accordingly we affectionately urge our members not to participate in the races nor even to encourage them by their presence."[21] Indeed, the church was largely responsible for eliminating at least one race course at *Belle Meade*: a horse track innocently established by Arthur G. Burnett, the church's own Sunday School Superintendent.[22]

In 1900, Louisa born author Rosa Pendleton Chiles published *Down Among The Crackers*, a novel about an ignorant caste in the hills of Georgia. Chiles, a first cousin to W. E. Bibb, stated in the preface to her book that some incidents were true. These stories had been "gathered from a broad area" and presented using composite characters "of the class delineated." Chiles knew her subject well; the ignorance, poverty, mistreatment of women, blind stills, groceries selling moonshine and shootings were all consistent with happenings within her native county, particularly around Green Springs Depot.

By 1900, the neighborhood's character became sufficiently alarming that Blake decided against renewing his lease on Boston's store. Blake then expended time, energy, and resources to reestablish his grocery business in Richmond and returned his wife and daughter there to live. The mood set by local roughs and bootleggers likely encouraged this decision, but in any event, Blake quit *that store* on social rather than economic grounds as evidenced by his continued pursuit of business ventures in the area while preferring to raise his family somewhere other than Green Springs Depot.[23]

In 1901, *that store* was briefly operated by thirty-two year old Roy Knighton. Many general stores in Louisa County were common sites for gathering and drinking local *white lightning*.[24] However, Knighton, a member of Wills Memorial Church, eschewed alcohol, refused liquor sales and forbade use of spirits on his premises.

Nevertheless, on March 8th that year a group of bored young men congregated in the store. Some had been drinking. Roy's eldest brother Josey[25] was drunk and exceedingly boisterous. When a disagreement ensued, Roy tried to throw his brother out of the store. Josey, being the stronger of the two, resisted Roy and stayed.

As a result, the humiliated Roy exchanged words with another of the group Luther Napper. Roy held Luther responsible for supplying his brother liquor. Either during, or shortly before this discussion, Luther's youngest brother Littleton arrived at the store with his shotgun, allegedly on his way home from hunting. The disagreement between Luther and Roy escalated.

Roy demanded that Luther leave. Luther refused. Roy then threatened to shoot Luther if he did not get out of his store. Luther scornfully dismissed the threat and countered with his own. That was the last straw. Roy jumped behind the counter and pulled out his revolver. On seeing the weapon, everyone scrambled for the exit.

Once outside, Josey stopped and drew his pistol. As "Lit" Napper exited, he encountered the drunken man standing with his gun drawn. Josey either stumbled into or struck Lit. Lit Napper raised his shotgun and fired point blank into Josey Knighton killing him instantly.[26]

On April 10, 1901, the court in Louisa arraigned Littleton Napper on a murder charge. The special grand jury delivered an indictment the next day.[27] On April 15th, Littleton Napper was convicted of second degree murder and received the maximum sentence of eighteen years.[28]

On January 2, 1903, Virginia Governor Montague received a petition to commute Napper's sentence.[29] Signatures included R. L. Gordon, Jr., the commonwealth's attorney who prosecuted the case. Other signatures of local significance on this petition included: Dr. H. W. Porter, F. V. Winston, W. T. Meade, C. B. Madison[30], Jno. K. Deane, J. J. Porter, W. R. Goodwin, W. E. Bibb, W. C. Bibb, V. K. Hall, W. S. Hall, [Victor and Sterling Hall signed. N. W. Hall did not.], J. H. Hester, James Hester, Jr., and L. F. Yancey: most of these names were later connected with the Hall Case. Judge Frederick W. Sims, who judged the case, added a note in favor of clemency.

Another undated petition followed asking Governor Montague to deny the request for commutation. Among the signers are six jurors in the case and several people who signed the first petition. Judge Sims attached the following note withdrawing his support; this included like reconsiderations by two other officials:

> "I declined to sign the petition for the present pardon of Lit Napper, but did append a statement thereto based on the evidence introduced before me at the trial, that I thought it was a case for executive clemency after the expiration of five years of Napper's sentence. I am now informed that there was testimony derogatory to Napper which was not gotten before the court at the trial, and that his pardon would greatly and generally outrage the best sentiment of the community in which the crime was committed.

MURDER AT GREEN SPRINGS

Hence I append this statement to this petition as in part qualifying my statement appended to said petition for pardon, to the extent that I desire to make it known that if the information I now receive be correct and had been received by me prior to my appending said statement to said petition for pardon, I would not have appended said statement thereto.

Respectfully, F. W. SIMS, Judge of Louisa County Court.

If the statement by Judge Sims is true, I would not have signed Mr. Napper's petition.

Jesse J. Porter, Clerk Louisa County Court.

W. R. Goodwin, Clerk Louisa Circuit Court."[31]

A letter dated October 28, 1903 to the governor from the victim's mother Mrs. S. F. Knighton stated that her son Josey caught Napper at their home earlier that day and ordered him to get off their property. Later Napper killed him [at the store].[32] Mrs. Knighton further advised that "The Nappers are bad people. Littleton Napper used to beat his mother. . . . People talk of driving them out of the neighborhood. . . ."[33] "I pray that his pardon may be refused and he die where he is," wrote Mrs. Knighton. "Our friends was [sic] anxious to send a mob to kill him, but we opposed it, we thought he would stay at the penitentiary."[34]

On June 23, 1904, the governor denied Littleton Napper's request for commutation.[35] There is no further record of application for parole, but Napper eventually received a conditional pardon on September 25, 1911.[36]

As a result of the murder, Channing Boston terminated Roy Knighton's lease on the store. Roy's mother mentioned his going to work for R. L. Gordon "after the murder."[37] Roy Knighton soon established another dry goods business in his home two miles south of Green Springs Depot.[38]

Knighton found the competition with the depot store overwhelming and moved his business to Madison in neighboring Orange County.

At Yancey's Store in Fluvanna County, John and Kate Yancey ran the general merchandise business supported by the Page Mine and other local gold mining activities on Long Island Creek. Two of their sons Lewis F. and Silas M. Yancey seized the opportunity to branch out on their own and leased the store at Green Springs Depot from Channing Boston. The Yancey Bros. general merchandise business promised a bright future and provided employment for a number of people including a young clerk named Sterling Hall.[39]

In early December 1902, Silas boarded the train to Richmond to buy goods to sell for Christmas. Silas arrived at Main Street Station and marveled at the dazzling new facility, which had just been open two weeks.[40] The young merchant secured modest accommodations across the street at the Davis Hotel. The lodgings were within easy walking distance to many wholesalers. The quarters featured gas lighting fuelled by *artificial gas*. This was a dangerous departure from the oil lamps familiar to Silas.[41]

When Silas went to bed on the evening of December 11th, he dimmed or extinguished the lights. Whether due to error or faulty equipment, the gas leaked into the room. That Friday morning, hotel employees discovered Silas unconscious from gas asphyxiation. He was taken to City Hospital, the *Almshouse*, for treatment.

When Lewis Yancey received word of the accident, he rushed to his brother's bedside. There he found Silas unconscious and in a room with two other men named Toler and Stone. Lewis attended his brother until his death that Sunday. The hospital staff was much affected by Lewis'

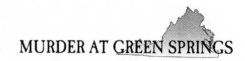

display of dedication and tearful grief. Lewis arranged for local members of their fraternal order to escort his brother's body home. The train took them to Green Springs. From there the remains traveled by wagon to their family's home at Yancey's Store in Fluvanna County. Silas was buried there in the family plot.

That Christmas proved especially difficult for the Yanceys. Silas' tragic death preceded the holiday business at the store. Lewis' eldest brother forty-three year old Alexander Campbell Yancey, known as "Cammie," and their sister Ella came to help Lewis.[42] By Christmas Day, Lewis was very ill. By the 28th it was apparent from the eruptions that Lewis' fever was more serious than any common affliction. Cammie also became sick. The family summoned Dr. Philip P. May. The good doctor immediately recognized the symptoms. Smallpox!

The dreaded killer appeared sporadically in Virginia. There had been recent cases in nearby Culpepper and Fredericksburg, but those had been diagnosed early and contained. When May contacted Superintendent Davis at the City Hospital in Richmond, he received shocking news that a few days after Silas Yancey's roommate Toler was discharged, he returned sick with smallpox and died. The hospital maid who cleaned their room also contracted smallpox.

Davis explained that he had admitted the indigent, third roommate Stone, at request of the Salvation Army. Stone was then sick with an unrelated ailment; however, neither Stone nor the Salvation Army disclosed that he had recently been released from the smallpox hospital in Charlotte, North Carolina. Stone exposed everyone in the room to smallpox. Upon discovering the source of Toler's exposure, Davis feared Lewis Yancey might develop smallpox. Indeed, he did.

On December 30th, Dr. May conferred with Dr. H. W. Porter and Dr. Scott of Gordonsville. Others exposed at the Yancey Bros. store became sick. Dr. May met with the Louisa County Board of Supervisors the next day. The Board under Chairman Weir R. Goodwin gave Dr. May charge of all cases in the district and hired him to supervise vaccinations for the next ninety days.[43] Unless the smallpox was contained, the county faced epidemic.

Green Springs Depot was quarantined! A yellow flag flew over the depot. All railroad passenger and freight service there ceased. The county used the depot shed for detention of asymptomatic individuals exposed to smallpox. The store and residence became the smallpox hospital for those sick with the disease. Dr. May hired David Woolfolk and an "old colored nurse" to prepare provisions and procure necessities.[44]

While detained in the station, Joe Turner became sick. He was immediately transferred to the store.[45] Those confined in the store included Lewis and Cammie Yancey, their sister Ella, Charles Jennings, Joe Turner, a Mrs. Turner, a Mr. Gibson, and the young store clerk Sterling Hall.[46]

Five cases of smallpox were reported during the outbreak at Green Springs. Two cases remained unnamed. Lewis, Cammie and Joe all suffered smallpox in its worst form. Though many despaired of Lewis, he miraculously recovered. Cammie and Joe succumbed to toxemia and died on January 16th and 18th, 1903 respectively. A. C. Yancey and Joseph S. Turner were buried in separate plots on the store property. The graves were later fenced and marked with headstones.[47] These were the first on site burials of many sad ends.

Lewis Yancey survived smallpox only to face financial ruin. In addition to loosing two brothers, his store had been used as a smallpox hospital for over three months. Those quarantined lived largely off the stock of the store. Much of the remaining goods were ordered destroyed. Lewis sued the Louisa County Board of Supervisors for compensation.[48]

Lewis F. Yancey: smallpox survivor and resilient businessman. (Photo Courtesy of Alice S. Murphey)

The Louisa Circuit Court awarded Yancey $2,777.78 in damages.[49] However, the Louisa County Board of Supervisors appealed the case. Litigation dragged on for years. Meanwhile, Lewis Yancey lost his lease on his store and was reduced from store proprietor to clerk for the new owners. In May 1906, the appellant court sided with Yancey and upheld the original award except for $115 for a box of shoes under the ban.[50] The Louisa County Board of Supervisors refused to accept the ruling and appealed to the Virginia State Supreme Court.

Young attorney William C. Bibb represented Yancey and filed a motion to dismiss the appeal. Bibb argued fair accounting of the original award. Clerk Sterling Hall had kept accurate account of supplies consumed during operation of the temporary hospital. However, since there was no differentiation between consumption of goods by family and non-family patients, the Board of Supervisors claimed it owed Yancey only

$270.66, a figure arrived at by mere guess.[51] Furthermore, Bibb was adamant that the Board of Supervisor's action in establishing the temporary hospital was contrary to state statute and constituted illegal seizure of private property.

The matter was finally settled in January 1909. The Virginia Supreme Court decided in favor of the Louisa County Board of Supervisors represented by Louisa County's Commonwealth's Attorney R. Lindsay Gordon, Jr.

Between the ravages of disease and resulting litigation, those six years devastated Lewis Yancey and his family. Lewis eventually recovered, but it was a slow process.

Months prior to the court's decision, Yancey quit work at the store at Green Springs Depot [Dunkum Bros.] to manage the store at Meltons. Yancey then began several businesses of his own including The Virginia Stock and Poulty Food Company and The Gordonsville Bargain House.[52] But throughout the drama of Lewis Yancey's legal battles, tragedies continued to plague *that store* at Green Springs Depot.

David Asa Dunkum and his brother William Richard Dunkum were born and reared at Arcanum in Buckingham County. They first worked in the mercantile business at Dillwyn. On June 28, 1894, D. A. Dunkum married Elizabeth Ann Dowdy [Mrs. Hall] at nearby Salem Church. "Acey", "Lizzie" and "Buck" Dunkum soon moved to Wilmington in neighboring Fluvanna County. The Dunkum brothers leased a general merchandise store and post office. Acey and Lizzie's daughters Essie and Mamie were born there. The Dunkums lived about three miles from Yancey's Store on the opposite bank of Long Island Creek.

When smallpox broke out at the "Yancey" store at Green Springs Depot, the Yancey family's store in Fluvanna County was also quarantined.

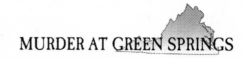

MURDER AT GREEN SPRINGS

Thankfully, no outbreak occurred there. The Dunkums were familiar with the Yancey family and the tragic deaths at Green Springs.

The store at Green Springs Depot was both Channing Boston's birthplace and his father's legacy. Nevertheless, circumstances made it his family's most problematic asset. Boston offered the store and property for sale.

Tragedies aside, the store at Green Springs Depot had great selling points. It was on the railroad. There was a depot with a turnout for shipping, receiving, and ice delivery. The large acreage enveloped nearly a mile of the railway and the main county road. It boasted a little broom factory. There was telegraph, telephone, and the depot bore the prestigious name *Green Springs*.

The Dunkums viewed the property as particularly attractive. It was an opportunity to own their own store rather than continue leasing. More over, gold mining, the chief industry at Wilmington, was marginally profitable. The local mercantile business slowed with each mine curtailment. It was time to move.

Title to the "Boston" property conveyed to D. A. Dunkum on January 24, 1905 by attorney R. Lindsay Gordon, Jr.[53] The plat drawing was completed by county surveyor James B. Madison who, at time of sale, served as both Green Springs Depot manager and local magistrate. The four hundred and thirty-four acre purchase placed the Dunkum family in the upper seven percent of all land owners in Louisa County.[54]

Acey Dunkum moved his wife Lizzie and their two daughters into the store. His brother and partner Buck Dunkum lived with them too. Among their first acquaintances at the depot was Victor K. Hall, who was just turning eighteen and operated the telegraph at the depot.

The family's first months at Green Springs Depot were filled with the excitement of their new home, new surroundings, new endeavors, and the expectation of a new baby. The joyous birth of Mattie Cathron Dunkum on March 6, 1905, however, was dashed by her death two days later. She became the first Dunkum and third burial at *that store*.

Isaac Newton Poindexter farmed in the vicinity of Green Springs Depot. The Poindexter name had been a familiar one in the county since it first appeared as *Poigdester* in the 1700's.[55] Members of this particular Poindexter family were descendants of antebellum freed slaves. In fact, I. N. Poindexter's father had moved the family to Illinois during the Civil War to avoid threats of being returned to slavery by Virginia law.[56]

I. N. Poindexter married in Illinois. His wife bore their first three children there. He moved back to Louisa County after 1880 and settled near Green Springs Depot. Poindexter, like others previously consigned to black status prior to the Civil War by the infamous *one drop rule*, were now accepted locally as white. He fathered and raised more children in Green Springs including his youngest son Robert C. Poindexter.

On Saturday October 7th, 1905, a real estate agent named T. W. Ross[57] from Gordonsville visited I. N. Poindexter on business. Their discussion turned ugly, and Poindexter threatened to kill Ross.

Poindexter was a little man with a temper and had recently shot a man in Richmond.[58] Ross was convinced that Poindexter meant business and went immediately to Magistrate James B. Madison, at Green Springs Depot to demand protection.

Madison did not have a regular constable handy, but Ross pressed for action. Madison haled the first man available forty-eight year old George W. Chewning, Jr. Madison's desperation was evident. Chewning was another feisty little man, but also a loiterer of foulest repute who hated Poindexter intensely.

Madison asked Chewning to go arrest Poindexter and bring him in for appearance. Chewning replied, in pretense, that he was scared of the man. He offered to go if he could take along his sidekick Joseph Grady.

MURDER AT GREEN SPRINGS

The exasperated Madison reluctantly agreed and swore in both Chewning and Grady as temporary constables.

Chewning seized the opportunity to settle an old score. When Chewning and Grady went to arrest Poindexter, Chewning posted Grady in the woods beside the road and instructed his easily led accomplice to shoot Poindexter when he passed. Chewning asserted that if Grady did not do it, then he would.

Chewning arrested Poindexter at his farm and ordered him to go back with Chewning to Green Springs Depot. Poindexter's son Robert, perhaps suspecting something amiss, hitched up their buggy and accompanied his father. Robert's unexpected presence took Grady by surprise. He did not shoot Poindexter as planned, but simply joined his frustrated partner in delivering their prisoner alive.

Upon arrival at Green Springs Depot, Poindexter appeared before the magistrate. After a brief trial, Madison required that the defendant post a one hundred dollar peace bond for twelve months or go to jail. Poindexter agreed to the bond, but explained that he did not have that kind of money handy and begged Madison to allow him to go to Louisa to raise the cash. The magistrate approved the request, but only under the escort of the *constables*.

Chewning and Grady exited the depot with their charge at about four thirty in the afternoon. Poindexter stomped over to his buggy, climbed up and seated himself beside son Robert. Meanwhile, Chewning stopped Grady at the hitching post to talk and delayed mounting their horses. Chewning had a new plan.

The Poindexters drove away expecting their escort to catch up. As soon as the buggy crossed the railroad tracks, Chewning drew his pistol and ran after Poindexter. Grady copied Chewning's actions. For the moment, it appeared to bystanders as if Poindexter was trying to escape.

Chewning and Grady ran a straight line from the depot across the railroad tracks and through the wood lot to intercept Poindexter turning onto the courthouse road.[59] They stopped just beyond the stacks of new railroad ties. Having closed the distance and afforded a clear shot, Chewning raised his pistol and ordered Poindexter to stop. The command was not intended for the driver to actually hear and obey, for he was given no time to react.

Shots rang out. Both Chewing and Grady fired. Chewning emptied his gun. A lifeless body tumbled off the buggy onto the road.

After a fumbling delay, the buggy's reigns pulled tight, and the horse reared to a stop. Satisfied at the result, Chewing started toward his victim.

Isaac Poindexter jumped down and hurried to his son. A bullet had slammed into the back of young Robert's head killing him instantly.

Chewning realized he had shot the wrong man. He turned and ran for his horse. Onlookers rushed to the boy's aid. Grady stood dumbfounded, but soon decided that it was best to follow his partner. The two *constables* mounted up and galloped away.

The neighborhood became enraged. As tragic as the killing of young Poindexter was, anger rose in proportion to Madison's poor judgment. Chewning had a well earned reputation in the neighborhood as a depraved character. Circuit court records documented Chewning's behavior as early as 1887 when a special grand jury indicted Chewning for carrying a concealed weapon, unlawful shooting, and disrupting a religious service; he was found guilty of the latter two offenses and given a $100 fine and six months in jail. But most damning of all was the fact that everyone knew that this was the Chewning's second killing within a year!

"Chewning stole a heifer from Andrew Easton, a Negro living some four miles from him and sold it to a Mr. Harris who kept it about twelve months when the heifer got out and returned to the home of Easton, there was a trial of the matter before a Justice [likely Madison] and the heifer was returned to Eason. It was said Chewning tried to make this half-witted Negro "Alec Elis" swear that he knew the heifer and had seen it as a calf-sucking its mother

MURDER AT GREEN SPRINGS

at Chewning's home and because Elis refused to act so Chewning got very angry with him and took this opportunity when there was no one to witness it to kill him. The Negroes in the neighborhood were so much afraid of Chewning they would not appear against him and he was left to go free. Chewning claimed that the Negro com [sic] to his house and tried to break in and he shot him in self defense, but no one in this community believed any such story for though Elis was crazy at times, he was considered perfectly harmless and besides the two men were very intimate and visited each other frequently."[60]

Newspaper reports touted rumors of Poindexter having vengefully beat Justice Madison and posses bent on lynching Chewning. Though the former was deserved and the latter generally desired, neither the assault nor lynching took place. However, the fomenting hostility convinced Chewning that chances of his being lynched grew by the hour. He went to Louisa early the next day and surrendered himself to Sheriff J. Reid Wills. Later that same morning, Deputy Sheriff J. Frank Bickers found Grady at home and arrested him. The two men appeared before Magistrate G. D. M. Hunter who charged both men with murder. The court placed Chewning and Grady under $1,000 and $500 bonds respectively.

Again, as in the Napper trial, Commonwealth's Attorney R. Lindsay Gordon, Jr. prosecuted the case. On October 27th, both Chewning and Grady were indicted for killing young Poindexter. D. A. Dunkum, L. F. Yancey, Isaac N. Poindexter, Zac Butler, and G. W. Sherwood appeared as witnesses for the prosecution against Chewning. James B. Madison and Lee Rosson appeared as witnesses for Chewning's defense. The court continued Chewning's trial until December 6th and placed all witnesses on $50 bonds to appear.[61] Grady was not scheduled for trial but remanded to jail while attention focused on Chewning.

Chewning's trial lasted three days. The defense centered on whether or not a constable was permitted to shoot someone guilty of a misdemeanor. Grady's testimony swayed jurors that the shooting was an unjustified, hateful act. The jury found Chewning guilty of second-degree murder and sentenced him to the maximum eighteen years in the state penitentiary.

Other notable witnesses summoned were Mrs. D. A. Dunkum [Mrs. Hall], G. W. Trainham, Dr. H. W. Porter, and W. C. Woody [all associated later with the Hall Case].[62] Attorneys W. E. and W. C. Bibb argued that their client Grady was an ignorant man duped into action by Chewning. The court dismissed the charge against Grady.

The embarrassment of Magistrate Madison's bad judgment in deputizing Chewning likely drove Madison into retirement by early 1906. He did not live long afterwards as evidenced by the settlement of his estate in July 1909.[63] Young telegraph operator Victor K. Hall assumed the positions of station master and express agent vacated by Madison.[64]

George W. Chewning, Jr. served seven years before applying for parole. His letter to Governor Mann on January 6, 1913 provided insight into the man. The letter contained as many grandiose words spelled correctly as it did simple words misspelled. His penmanship being unsightly, Chewning added a postscript to "Excuse orthography." The communication reeked with superficiality and contributed to the flat denial of pardon. But even if Chewning had been as eloquent and persuasive as he had intended, the letter from W. C. Bibb eliminated any consideration of release:

1-20-13

His Excellency,

    Wm. Hodgers [sic] Mann

        Governor of Virginia,

            Richmond, Va.

MURDER AT GREEN SPRINGS

Dear Sir;

I have before me your letter of the 18th., inst- enclosed letter from Geo. W. Chewning asking for clemency, which letter I herewith return as requested.

Mr. R. L. Gordon was Commonwealth's Attorney of this county at the time of this trial, but my Father, the late W. E. Bibb and myself represented a party named Grady who was a principal in the second degree in the murder. The evidence disclosed the fact that Grady, who was not mentally what he should have been, was merely a tool used by Chewning and he was released, the commonwealth entering a nol. pros. in this case.

I see no reason why executive clemency should be extended to Chewning. The murder was a brutal one and premeditated, although Chewning killed Poindexter's little son instead of the Father at whom he was shooting. I understood from the jury after the trial that Chewning only escaped the electric chair by a small margin, as nine of the jury were for murder in the first degree and three for murder in the second degree and 18 years. In the circumstances as I know them I cannot recommend clemency in this case.

Yours very truly,

(signed) W. C. Bibb[65]

Governor Mann denied Chewning's pardon on January 21st, 1913.[66] He wrote Chewning a personal note stating that pardon was out of the question because Chewning so narrowly avoided the electric chair.[67]

Another petition was submitted to Governor Mann soon afterwards, but arrived during the transition in administrations. Mann's successor Governor Henry Stuart reviewed the request in 1915. The petition asked for mercy and stated the sad facts that Chewning's wife and three daughters depend on neighborhood charity and that Chewning's only son died about a year before. Among those who signed the document were N. W. Hall and [by then, the late] V. K. Hall. The petition appeared on R. L. Gordon, Jr.'s letterhead with a note stating his belief that the punishment fit the crime.[68] A separate letter from C. B. Vest protesting Chewning's release assured another denial.[69]

> "Before Chewning was imprisoned, our milk houses and mills were constantly being robbed and while the community was satisfied that Chewning was responsible for it all, we could get no proof, since his imprisonment our neighborhood has been entirely free from such robbings and we can lie down and sleep without fear of being molested.
>
> Chewning is known for miles around to be a very bad man . . . . . ."[70]

Two years later, Governor Stuart contacted Charles B. Vest for his opinion of a third request for parole under the condition that Chewning not be allowed in Louisa or any neighboring county.[71] C. B. Vest reluctantly agreed to these terms, but predicted Chewning would return to Green Springs regardless of any stipulation.

George W. Chewning, Jr. received a conditional pardon on December 10, 1917. C. B. Vest was correct. Not long after George Chewing's release, he was back in Green Springs despite the imposed restrictions.

There is no accounting for other despicable acts likely and never documented, but George W. Chewning, Jr.'s recorded exploits at Green Springs Depot contributed greatly to the depot's soiled image in the region. Chewning provided the Dunkum family a violent welcome to life at Green Springs Depot. The Richmond newspapers covered Poindexter's death and Chewning's trial on their front pages as they had the smallpox outbreak at Green Springs. The two events were spaced sufficiently far

MURDER AT GREEN SPRINGS

enough apart that few readers outside the county attached significance to the location. However, area residents had repeatedly focused their attention on deadly violence and tragedies at *that store* at Green Springs Depot for years. Drunkenness! Pestilence! Murders! The place had a sordid reputation throughout Louisa County.

The Dunkum Bros. mercantile business prospered. The brothers divided the land. Acey claimed all the "Boston" property west of the railroad, Buck everything east. Their success allowed Buck Dunkum to build his own house and marry his childhood sweetheart Mary Lou Marks from Curdsville. They wed on November 20, 1907, and by February 1908, Buck and Mary were expecting their first child.

George McDuffie Blake, an earlier proprietor of the store, purchased *The Elms* just two miles down the road. He moved his family back to the area (this time, to the *real* Green Springs) and assumed the role of a country squire.[72] Blake commuted by train to his business in Richmond and occasionally visited his former enterprise at the depot.

Like the preceding store managers, the Dunkum brothers brokered sales of railroad ties and pulp wood. In March 1908, David Asa Dunkum contracted with Miletus Poindexter to cut, season, and deliver wood.[73] Poindexter's land bordered that owned by Dr. Philip P. May. Poindexter was paid in stages: first for his pine on the stump, next for wood cut and stacked in situ, and then for the seasoned wood delivered to the depot.

The Dunkum's entrepreneurial spirit extended to maintaining the broom factory. Broom manufacture required minimal skills, a clamping vise, sewing awls and a manually operated wire wrapping machine. The Dunkums committed a modest acreage to broom corn. The cord and wire was always available from store stock. Locals made various tool handles for sale in the store; the same produced broomsticks. Employees Abram and Mary Garnett, a middle aged, black couple, made the brooms.[74] The Dunkums sold finished products in their store and shipped them to market by rail.

Once again, deep sorrow overshadowed the Dunkums' successes. Lizzie gave birth to their only son David Asa Dunkum, Jr. on April 20, 1908. The child only lived twelve days.[75]

Early that summer, Lewis Yancey left his job at Dunkum Bros. to manage the store at Meltons.[76] Ambitious, young Victor Hall replaced Yancey. He clerked for the Dunkums while managing his various depot offices.

About this same time, little Mamie played near the railroad and wedged her foot in the tracks. Acey worked frantically to free his daughter without success. Mamie remained trapped as the next train approached. Miraculously, the depot hands flagged the train to stop just before it reached the desperate girl.[77] The men then pried the tracks enough to set her free and secured them again for the train to proceed.

The Hall Store Residence circa 1910 – Essie, Mamie and Lizzie Dunkum [Mrs. Hall] posed for a traveling photographer while Acey and Buck minded the adjoining store. (Photo from author's collection)

MURDER AT GREEN SPRINGS

Mary Dunkum gave birth to their first child Ruby Florence Dunkum on November 13, 1908. With so much going on that fall, Lizzie and Mary still made time to join the ladies aid society at their church.[78] The family's charity was evident to many. Hobos marked the Dunkum store with their cryptic symbols to indicate an easy hand out.[79] The family prospered and life proceeded uneventfully for the next two and a quarter years.

On February 5, 1911, Essie Dunkum turned thirteen. Her father gave her a gold locket upon this attainment of young ladyhood.[80] The family also anticipated new additions. Buck and Mary expected a baby in a couple of months and Lizzie was pregnant again.

Consistent with the Dunkums' experiences at Green Springs Depot, this was a memorable time, but not in a happy sense. About a month after Essie's birthday, Acey Dunkum became sick. Dr. Porter attended him throughout this illness. Nevertheless, he developed a virulent case of pneumonia and died in less than nine days.[81]

On March 21st, the day of his death, D. A. Dunkum's estate purchased a casket from A. B. Woodward.[82] David Asa Dunkum was buried in the cemetery behind the store next to his two babies and near one of the smallpox victims.

Lizzie recorded the date of her husband's death in her Bible just as she had her marriage and the births and deaths of her children.[83] Lizzie never considered another event significant enough to add to that record. Never!

Lizzie entered a period of deep mourning as was then customary. The situation bred even deeper despair when she miscarried.[84] Lizzie took her daughters to visit family in Richmond, Cumberland County, and Buckingham County. Buck Dunkum ran their business while she was gone. Victor Hall and Lewis Yancey inventoried the store for settlement of Acey Dunkum's estate.[85]

Buck's grief over his brother was eased considerably by the birth of his second daughter Blanche Elizabeth Dunkum on May 1, 1911. But the family's cloud of gloom returned when little Blanche died on January 25, 1912.

While on a visit to Richmond, Lizzie received a letter from Victor Hall. She had already received several notes of a consoling and friendly nature, but this letter expressed admiration bordering on affection. One year after Acey Dunkum's death, the accepted minimum for deep mourning, Victor's letters crossed the romantic threshold and spoke of love. At first, Lizzie though he was joking, but when she realized Victor was serious, she began to love him "with all her heart."[86]

By November 1912, Elizabeth Ann Dunkum, nee Dowdy, had become Mrs. Victor Kelso Hall. The couple began their lives together happy enough. They lived at the store and ran it with partner Buck Dunkum very much as they had always done. Soon after their marriage, Lizzie Hall became vice-president of the Lasley Ladies Aid Society at that Methodist Church.[87]

Within their circle of family and friends, the only difference in their lives was that twenty-five year old Victor Hall and thirty-eight year old Lizzie were now man and wife; however, among certain base and ignorant elements, the age difference was scandalous. Essie Dunkum was almost fifteen; there was less difference in age between Victor Hall and his stepdaughter than between he and his wife. This peculiar remarriage occurred in a poor, rural area where the normal course of life was for the wife, usually the younger of the two, to die before her husband.[88] Rumors and innuendo spread about the couple.

Jesse Mae Dunkum was born on November 20, 1912, Buck and Mary's fifth wedding anniversary. While Jesse's birth and Lizzie's remarriage punctuated life at the depot with some degree of joy, business ownership issues became increasingly troublesome. The respected name "Dunkum Bros." no longer described the business. Equity allocations between Buck Dunkum; his brother's widow; his nieces; and Victor Hall, his employee and brother's widow's husband confused everyone.

In spring 1913, Buck Dunkum's broom factory mysteriously burned. Investigators suspected arson, but no one could prove it. The very next week while Dunkum and his family were at church, his house likewise burned to the ground. The family returned home to find smoldering ruins. The weather was fair. Neither hearth nor cook stove had been in use. It was broad daylight; no lamps were lit. There was no explanation for the loss other than arson. But again, no one could prove it.

The Broom Factory circa 1905 – Last remnants of sign for "JOHN BOSTON'S BROOMS" appears above political placards for "CORKER". The first arson attack against Dunkum burned this building. (Photo Courtesy of Edward J. Westlow)

Until the house could be rebuilt, Buck and his family moved into the store with Victor and Lizzie's family. There was plenty of room. Essie and Mamie helped Lizzie and Mary with household chores and caring for little Ruby and Jesse. The family hired hands to do heavy work like laundry and tending livestock. Victor ran the depot while Buck and Lizzie minded the store. Life with two families under one roof was manageable, but hardly friction free.

The fires provided a solution to the store's ownership dilemmas. Buck Dunkum decided to build his own general store and dissolve the partnership. By late summer, Buck and his family moved into their newly rebuilt home, and upon completion of his house, Buck constructed his own store within yards of where the broom factory once stood. It opened for business in early autumn 1913 with nearly double the floor space of the old store.

With Buck and Lizzie's partnership ended, Victor arranged to buy out Lizzie's interests and make the old store officially his own. Thus, the Hall store and Dunkum store became separate entities competing for the same business at the little depot. Ownership problems disappeared, but these were only replaced by gossip and rumors of bad blood between the families.

Up to this point, the Dunkum kin had been plagued with tragedy. But as 1914 began, the Dunkum and Hall families were the most prosperous in the neighborhood. Their position and generosity in the community earned them many friends. Essie and Mamie, who had been privately tutored in their home, now attended Professor Blackwell's private school at *The Elms*.[89]

The Dunkums and Halls interacted with families like the A. J. Chewnings, the Flannagans, the Wests and the Peers. Said families resided either on one of the Green Springs plantations or properties bordering such, and they were socially connected to the best circles of county society.

At last! Life was very good!

Most poor folk around the Green Springs Depot admired, even envied, the Dunkum and Hall families. A jealous few despised them. The latter fact manifested itself in the wee hours of April 15th, 1914.

On May 2nd, 1914, Charlottesville's *Daily Progress* published an article stating "Green Springs Depot is the *Five Points* of Louisa. Three murders have been committed there: two in the front yard [of Hall's store]."[90]

Five Points referred to the infamous New York City slum, an unrivaled concentration of poverty, squalor, and misery. "Five Points was the most notorious neighborhood in nineteenth-century America."[91]

The average reader in 1914 understood the metaphor, and thereby, associated Green Springs Depot and its residents with degeneracy and depravity. Though the comparison was clearly overstatement, events at Green Springs Depot in the years leading up to Victor Hall's murder arguably justified this license. A more accurate term might have been the *Wild West of Louisa County*, but certainly, many contemporaries considered the Green Springs station a veritable *Depot of the Damned!*

When Mrs. Hall first moved to Green Springs Depot with her family in 1905, the depot already possessed an unhappy reputation throughout Louisa County. Not only did this reputation deteriorate dramatically, but the brief and tragic history of Green Springs Depot centered on the very building that was Mrs. Hall's store. Unfortunately for Elizabeth Ann Hall, the dark stigma associated with the depot in general and her residence specifically marked her for general disdain throughout Louisa County simply by living there.

CHAPTER
Thirteen

ONLY TEN YEARS

MURDER AT GREEN SPRINGS

*M*rs. Hall spent the first five days after her conviction in the Louisa County jail, a small, two-story, brick building on the southeast side of the courthouse. The jail looked contemporary with the new courthouse (ca. 1905) even though it had been built in 1868 from bricks salvaged from the previous lockup. The internal wood structure was damaged by fire during an escape in 1881 and repaired.[1] The Sheriff's office occupied half of the ground floor. The two eight-by-eighteen foot jail cells on the second floor were adequate for county needs.[2]

In anticipation of receiving Mrs. Hall, the county employed James Hackney to repair and clean the cells. These were normally dirty cages regarded suitable for men deserving confinement. Preparations in deference to the woman prisoner also fronted a favorable impression to outsiders eyeing the county during the trial.

Once Mrs. Hall was inside, jailor J. C. Trice bolted the door as a precaution. Trice registered the prisoner as "E. A. Hall, 5 ft. 4 in., yellow hair, blue eyes, no scars, forty years old, merchant."[3] The logbook never noted sex. Trice led the party upstairs where he locked Mrs. Hall in her cell. Sheriff Wash extended Hubert Dowdy an offer to stay. Hugh accepted and kept his sister company that first, difficult night.

Lindsay Gordon and Essie Dunkum visited early Sunday morning. Essie brought her mother's Bible, a change of clothes and other personal items. Lizzie then said goodbye to her brother. Hugh needed to return to his family in Cumberland County and greet his new son. Besides, there was little more he could do for his sister now. This became especially true when news of Hubert's stay at the jail reached a certain party, who immediately secured an order from Judge Shackelford to put a stop to overnight and prolonged family visits.[4]

The prisoner's breakfast arrived from the Louisa Hotel. Mrs. Hall ate while Gordon discussed her situation. Meanwhile, sundry, unchurched busybodies positioned themselves in shady vantages around the grounds to view activity at the jail.

Gordon excused himself and went downstairs leaving Mrs. Hall and Essie alone briefly. After Essie said goodbye, she and Gordon left together. Observers seeing this assumed Essie spent the night with her mother, and so, the late arriving *Times-Dispatch* reporter recorded the event thusly.

It was Sunday, the *Lord's Day*. Church bells rang calls to worship. Mrs. Hall sat alone. Gordon had encouraged her that the compromise verdict itself indicated the jury had doubts. Coupled with the conduct of the trial, Gordon was confident in being able to successfully contest the decision.

Mrs. Hall's battle was slated to resume Thursday, but for the moment, she and her family were exhausted. Lizzie welcomed the opportunity just to sit and have a quiet *Sabbath*. Circumstances, as it happened, denied her this luxury.

James Hackney soon delivered another inmate named Suzie Courtney. That morning the young black woman had gone violently insane. She was so beyond the control of her family and physician that they called the sheriff to restrain her in a straightjacket. Records indelicately credited Hackney with having "dressed the lunatic" and carried her to jail.[5]

Suzie would stay in jail until authorities placed her in a more appropriate facility. Meanwhile, the "maniacal cries" of the straitjacketed woman could be heard throughout much of Louisa.[6] Every moment of this co-confinement became a battle for Mrs. Hall to retain her own sanity.

Church services ended at noon. Virtually everyone dismissed from the Baptist and Methodist churches across the street were repelled by the

MURDER AT GREEN SPRINGS

situation and went directly home. A few dared not miss this rare show even on the *Lord's Day*. These ate their Sunday dinners and returned to spend the afternoon with fellow connoisseurs of misfortune. They hoped to catch a glimpse of the *murderess*, but to their disappointment, Mrs. Hall stayed away from her little window despite the sweltering heat and stagnation of her upper floor cell.

On Monday, family visits resumed with the utmost care not to push their welcome.[7] They supplied physical necessities and much needed encouragement.

Early that week, Dr. Harry W. Porter caught the train to Richmond. A reporter recognized the good doctor and questioned him. The physician stated that the general feeling in Louisa was that Mrs. Hall received a light sentence. Dr. Porter revealed that three jurors voted for first degree murder and electrocution. Six favored second degree murder with the maximum eighteen years in prison. Three strongly believed the evidence did not support conviction, but fearing that Mrs. Hall might fair worse at retrial agreed to the compromise verdict.

On August 13th, Judge Shackelford heard arguments for setting aside the verdict. Hill Carter asserted that the evidence was insufficient to justify the decision of the jury.

Judge Shackelford disagreed. The motion was refused.

Lindsay Gordon requested bail while the defense filed appeal. Judge Shackelford granted it in the amount of $10,000.[8] Mrs. Hall was freed and spent most of her time between Martha Gordon's and N. W. Hall's.

Lindsay Gordon was a very busy man. He served other clients and had legislative duties as a member of the Virginia General Assembly. Political demands interfered with assembling Mrs. Hall's appeal. After the trial, Lindsay Gordon directed much energy into promoting passage of the state's Prohibition Act. Sandy Gordon drafted the appeal while his brother focused on the referendum.

Lindsay Gordon hired Essie Dunkum to work in his Richmond office. He also enrolled her in stenography school. Essie moved to Richmond and stayed with her Aunt Carrie's family. The opportunity provided modest income and security for the girls in the event fortunes remained contrary to their mother.

On September 22nd, voters approved the measure for statewide ban on the manufacture, sale, and distribution of alcoholic beverages in Virginia to become effective November 1, 1916. Virginians voted two to one in favor of the law. The results mirrored sentiments in Louisa County.

In Richmond, Attorney General John Garland Pollard announced the victory in front of the headquarters of the Anti-Saloon League. In reaction to his speech, many hailed him as "the next Governor of Virginia."[9] Indeed, the measure's success fulfilled the main campaign promise of recently installed Governor Stuart and provided Pollard a significant stepping stone for succession. Another benefit was that strong support in Louisa reflected positively on its delegate and provided Lindsay Gordon leverage for reciprocal support: the favor of a pardon for instance.

At the end of September, Lindsay and Sandy Gordon completed the petition for a writ of error comprised of seven bills of exception. The first bill regarded the inspection of the crime scene by the grand jury contrary to law. The second bill addressed the failure to quash the *venire facias*. This request was routine if the jury pool was believed biased. Gordon considered the particular array the workings of Louisa's *courthouse clique*. Also Gordon's only previous murder defense won the successful acquittal of a Negro charged with killing Sheriff Wash's uncle. Perhaps, this had factored into play.

Bill three concerned the pantry fire, for which no evidence existed to support a formal charge. Bill four related to rejected testimony that all members of the coroner's jury and Commonwealth's Attorney Bibb concluded at the inquest that the pistol had not been fired recently. Contentions continued. Bibb penciled a note to Judge Shackelford on the back, "This is about as close as Mr. Gordon & I will ever get together on this bill & I have agreed to it."[10]

Bill five addressed rejection of the defense's jury instruction weighting the veracity of the prosecution's witnesses. The sixth bill contested the court's admission of Detective Scott's statements regarding rumors that Mrs. Hall poisoned her first husband and killed Victor Hall in order to be with Bill Roberts. The seventh and last bill regarded the separation of the jury immediately prior to the trip to the crime scene.

Despite the submission of sworn affidavits from J. Frank Bickers, Bibb's own uncle, and Robert C. Hart testifying to the jury's separation amidst a hostile crowd, Commonwealth's Attorney Bibb contested the evidence. Ultimately, Judge Shackelford certified all but this last bill. Gordon was unable to pursue the bill beyond Judge Shackelford on account of either statutory restriction or, most likely, the deadline for filling appeal was at hand.

Surely, Gordon would have sought further hearing on the jury separation issue if able; this was no small matter. In an earlier, emotion driven murder trial in the state, this very point had spared two innocent women from death and a third a lengthy prison term.[11]

On September 30th, the very deadline, R. Lindsay Gordon, Jr. filed the petition on behalf of Elizabeth Ann Hall asking the Virginia Supreme Court of Appeals for a new trial. The petition numbered about fifty pages comprised mostly of supporting excerpts from the thirteen hundred page trial transcript. Gordon argued that the verdict was contrary to the law and the evidence; the evidence was plainly insufficient to convict the defendant; the court misdirected the jury and refused to instruct them as prayed for by defendant; and the court permitted illegal testimony to go to the jury and be considered by them over the objection of the defendant.

Gordon renewed Mrs. Hall's bail bond. This allowed her to remain free while the high court considered her case. The appellant court considered the evidence conflicting and confusing. As common in such instances, the seasoned jurists deferred to the wisdom of the jury which had actually heard the case. On November 12th, Judge Richard H. Cardwell announced the denial of the writ of error. Mrs. Hall would not receive a new trial. Since there was no constitutional issue deemed sufficient to recommend the case to the United States Supreme Court, executive clemency remained her last hope.

The next morning, Friday the thirteenth, Lindsay Gordon and Mrs. Hall took the train to Richmond to meet with Governor Stuart only to be informed upon their arrival that the governor was out of town. Suddenly, that day felt unlucky indeed. Gordon learned that the governor would return on the morrow. There was nothing else to do but secure a tentative appointment for then.

Lindsay Gordon retired to his office with the disappointed and anxious Mrs. Hall at his side. Gordon, Mrs. Hall, and Essie collected themselves and returned to Louisa that evening on the train. Gordon trusted that the governor would intervene, but the situation now demanded that Mrs. Hall surrender herself to Sheriff Wash.

November 14th was gray and overcast throughout Virginia.[12] Things had again assumed a routine at Green Springs Depot. It was Saturday, the busiest day of the week at Buck Dunkum's new store and post office. The store was again the center for community activity with about as many there to *lollygag* as to actually buy something or pick up mail.[13]

The Chesapeake and Ohio Railway had built their new depot next to Dunkum's store rather than on its original site. The new arrangement was more convenient for Dunkum, its new station master.

Across the tracks, the oak trees around the Hall store were bare. The leaves which budded and greened in April now lay brown and dead covering the yard and littering the porches.

The vacant, old, gray weatherboard store and residence; its empty outbuildings and barn; its pasture of tall, tan, dormant grass; and just beyond the kitchen, its dried up, untended vegetable garden overtaken with dead weeds were a picture of desolation. At the back of the property in the little cemetery, now cared for by his parents, Victor Hall's grave stood out from the others, being only partially covered with grass.[14]

In Louisa, the dreary sky intensified the oppressive gloom experienced by the Hall family. The day was cool and overcast, disturbingly reminiscent of the day Victor was taken from them. Lindsay Gordon caught the 6:11 A.M. train to Richmond to meet with Governor Stuart. Mrs. Hall arrived at the courthouse midmorning with her bondsmen to surrender herself.

After formalities, the court turned Mrs. Hall over to Sheriff Wash who again locked her upstairs in the jail. Mrs. Hall kept her cloak on because of the chill. She sat on the bunk and waited. Sheriff Wash notified the state penitentiary that their prisoner was in custody. He then allowed her family inside to visit until time of transfer.

In the early afternoon, Gordon telegraphed news of his audience. The governor refused to intervene. Mrs. Hall had to go to the penitentiary.

Prison official John Moore arrived in Louisa at 4:03 P.M. to take custody of Mrs. Hall and escort her to Richmond on the return train. The sheriff politely ejected the family and sent them to the train station where deputies secured a corner of the waiting room.

ONLY TEN YEARS

Wash and Moore shackled the black clad widow and transported her by surrey to the terminal. Word of Mrs. Hall's departure spread through Louisa and a crowd gathered. Mrs. Hall's guard led her inside and seated her beside him. Daughters Essie and Mamie waited with her as did Nicholas and Ellen Hall.

When the train arrived, the few incidental passengers detrained and boarded as normal. The deputies cleared the way for the prisoner. Moore and Wash led the veiled widow outside onto the crowded platform with her family close behind. Essie and Mamie cried, as did Ellen Hall. Animated gawkers craned their necks to fill their eyes with the pitiful scene. Mrs. Hall, in her widow's weeds and shackles, remained composed just as she had throughout her ordeal. She received her daughters' last hugs and kisses unable to return their embraces. In the twilight, a photographer captured their last moment together.[15]

Moore and Wash helped Mrs. Hall up into the cadmium yellow railcar where she took a window seat in view of her daughters. The train whistle blew. Sheriff Wash returned to the platform. The conductor shouted, "All 'board!" The train's bell rang as the steam engine thrust off from the station on schedule at 5:22 P.M. Mrs. Hall waved goodbye to her family. Essie, Mamie and the parents of Victor Hall waved back. The girls watched through tears and sobbed as the train rolled away and carried their mother to prison.

The crowd had seen the *black widow* of Green Springs for the last time. Mrs. Hall's departure was the finale to the greatest public event ever in Louisa County. The excitement was over. Twilight turned to darkness.

At 7:20 P.M. the train pulled into Main Street Station. A crowd had gathered to see the celebrated *murderess*. Officer Moore and his prisoner

MURDER AT GREEN SPRINGS

remained seated until joined by a second officer sent to meet the train. Moore helped the shackled woman adjust her heavy, black veil.

Most of the other passengers had already filed through the gate when the two guards helped Mrs. Hall to the platform. They walked slowly out the gate, up the steps and through the station. Onlookers were disappointed in not being able to see her face. Still, they savored being part of the moment when the notorious woman passed.

The guards led Mrs. Hall down the front steps to the waiting prison hack. They helped Mrs. Hall up and between them in the rear seat. The horse then clopped off up Main Street to the state penitentiary a mile and a half away.

By eight o'clock, the guards turned Elizabeth Ann Hall over to the matron at the Virginia State Penitentiary. Her few personal effects were taken; she had already left her wedding ring and other jewelry with Essie.[16] She was given a heavy, prison striped, cotton shirtwaist, and then photographed.[17] Now designated prison inmate No. 12696, she was locked alone in a six-by-ten foot cell. The space was about one third that of her cell in the Louisa jail.[18]

Lizzie arrived too late for food. That did not matter. She was not hungry under the circumstances even though she had only picked at breakfast and had not eaten since. The place was dark, dank and smelled bad enough to take away one's appetite anyway.

Heavy rain fell that black, moonless night as if the aftermath of a great battle: two inches in some places.[19] Lizzie wept. She slept a fitful first night shivering beneath her single wool blanket. One needed to acclimate to the conditions. Indeed, there was much to get used to.

Sunday was a rest day. Even so, Lizzie awoke to the unaccustomed racket. Sounds reverberated off the walls. Things clanged. Guards shouted. Breakfast was grits, she thought, and coffee. In prison, cornbread or potatoes were also typical breakfast fare. Sometimes there was salted fish.

Dinner, the main meal at midday, was stewed meat and vegetables. There was little variation. Sundays were special. Women received a bath and clean clothes. And visitation? Family once a month? Every night inmates ate the same supper: a tin mug of coffee and about a four inch block of bread made of Indian meal or some other coarse flour.

Monday was Lizzie's first real exposure to prison routine. Monday through Saturday inmates worked ten hour days. Most worked in the shoe factory.[20] Of the eighty-eight women in the penitentiary, the overwhelming majority were poor, young and black.[21] Lizzie held property and was *old* and white.

The system matched prisoners to the hardest work suitable to their sex and fitness.[22] By midweek Lizzie was in a shop making overalls.[23] The contrast of her present condition to her former life at Green Springs was surreal. Nevertheless, Lizzie did not despair. She was innocent. Lizzie knew she did not belong there. She knew Lindsay Gordon was working hard to free her. She expected to be home again soon with Essie and Mamie. That thought kept her going.

Attorney Lindsay Gordon invested every hour not demanded by his many other legal and legislative duties working to persuade Governor Stuart to release Mrs. Hall. Letters began arriving at the governor's office. In addition to those expected from family and friends, a significant number came from some of Louisa's most solid citizens. Every letter encouraged Mrs. Hall's release. By this time, publicity about Mrs. Hall had ceased completely, and the public was never privileged to this aspect.

On November 19th, G. H. Johnson, former Mayor of Louisa, wrote Governor Stuart in support of Mrs. Hall. Attorney John G. May of Lou-

MURDER AT GREEN SPRINGS

isa, a spectator at the trial, wrote the governor pointing out that the instructions to the jury were such that unless the prosecution had proved that Hall's pistol had been the murder weapon, a not guilty verdict was indicated. The attorney asserted that the jury ignored the fact that the prosecution never presented the proof demanded.[24]

That same day, Dr. Thomas M. Taylor, identifying himself as the son of George Keith Taylor, former clerk of the Virginia State Court of Appeals, wrote that the evidence against Mrs. Hall was "utterly insufficient to warrant her conviction." The attending physician and signer of Victor Hall's death certificate declared, "In my judgment, she would never have been convicted by the jury but for the brutal murder and the intense desire of the public to find someone to punish for the tragedy."[25]

These letters were soon followed by more requests for clemency from R. B. Winston, Commissioner of Revenue for Louisa; Arthur G. Burnett, Presbyterian elder; Dr. Harry W. Porter; and Marshall J. Campbell, Mayor of Louisa.[26] Burnett wrote, "I know her to be a good woman, big hearted, charitable, kind to the poor and any one in trouble. I heard all the evidence at the trial and know much of it was perjury, and I believe her absolutely innocent."

The following month, Rev. C. T. Thrift, wrote that the pantry fire was set to "fasten the murder conviction on her." Even so, "Every material fact had been examined and could be put as evidence if the house was destroyed. There was no evidence at that time that the fire could destroy. Again the fire was started so far from the part of the building where the murder occurred that there is practically no probability that it could, under the circumstances reach that part of the building where the murder occurred. . ."[27]

N. W. and Ellen Hall wrote the governor identifying themselves as the parents of the murdered man. They blamed the result of the trial on "*poisoned public sentiment*" [emphasis Hall] and adamantly asserted "that not one thing has been proved against her."[28]

Among the most powerful letters in support of Mrs. Hall was one written by Commonwealth Attorney Bibb's own uncle Special Deputy J. Frank Bickers, a man of unquestionable integrity.

J. Frank Bickers, Licensed Auctioneer, Louisa, Va.

December 30, 1914

His Excellency, H. C. Stuart, Governor of Virginia, Richmond, Va.

Dear Sir:

Permit me to write you in behalf of Mrs. Elizabeth A. Hall, whose application for a pardon is pending before you. I was born and raised in Louisa county, and was Deputy Sheriff of the county for many years, and have been doing all the auctioneering business, practically, of the county for the last fifteen or twenty years, and I am therefore well acquainted with the people of this County. I was present when the Coroner's Jury met to investigate the murder of Mr. Victor K. Hall, and went for the purpose of aiding the Commonwealth's Attorney in investigating the crime, and locating the guilty party. I have had a great deal of experience in such matters, and have usually been called upon to investigate almost every important case in the County, and I went to Green Springs in entire sympathy with the Commonwealth, and was really seeking the guilty party, but my investigation fully satisfied me, that Mrs. Hall had nothing to do with the murder. At that time the general impression was that Mr. W. R. Dunkum had committed the murder. From that time on I was intimately acquainted with the proceedings of the case, and talked freely, both to the

MURDER AT GREEN SPRINGS

Commonwealth's Attorney, and the counsel of Mrs. Hall, and I know that after the Coroner's Inquest, and the examination of the pistol, the Commonwealth's Attorney had reached the conclusion that there was nothing in the case, reflecting upon Mrs. Hall, and it was only after a definite movement on the part of some of the citizens of the community, and the employment of detectives, and various false and misleading publications, in the public press, that the Commonwealth Attorney changed his position, and determined to prosecute her. I am fairly well acquainted with all of the evidence in the case, and I am satisfied that it is utterly insufficient to convict her. Indeed, from my knowledge of Mrs. Hall, and all of the circumstances surrounding her case, her previous life, and her relations with her husband (with whom I was well acquainted), I am entirely satisfied of her innocence, and feel assured that no jury would ever have convicted her, but for the temporary excitement in the county.

Since her conviction, however, I think there has been a remarkable change in the sentiment against her, and I believe that if you could extend to her executive clemency, it would meet the approval of a very large majority of the honest, fair-minded men of the county.

Very respectfully yours,

[Signed] J. Frank Bickers[29]

Bickers' reference to "a definite movement on the part of some of the citizens of the community" was further evidence of a cabal. Coupled with his observed decrease in hostile sentiment and assured approval of most "honest, fair-minded men" in Louisa County, Bickers communicated the remarkable situation stopping short of actually naming conspirators.[30]

By New Years Day 1915, Mrs. Hall had spent nearly seven weeks in prison. Both Essie and Mamie now lived with Aunt Carrie. This helped make the best of a bad situation. The residence was in a nice neighborhood, gave the girls the security of family, and kept them within a couple of miles of their mother. They could take the street car as far as Pine Street, just two blocks from the prison. The daughters visited their mother as often as rules allowed.

The governor's office continued to receive letters urging pardon. Mrs. Hall's seventy-one year old mother Kate Dowdy wrote Governor Stuart on January 6th. The crude grammar did not detract from her astute analysis of the compromise verdict:

> "While she in prison serving a ten yr. Sentence for the most brutal murder ever committed, only think of that. If true it ought to be life imprisonment if untrue it is wrong to punish and persecute her."[31]

Just five days later, Judge George Shackelford surprised everyone by tendering his resignation. Four years before, Shackelford filled the unexpired judgeship vacated by the death of Judge Grimsley.[32] The General Assembly had just approved Shackelford's appointment for his first, full, eight year term in January 1914.[33] Shackelford's resignation letter to Governor Stuart less than a year after his effective date stated that "costs of living and education" forced him to leave for more lucrative private practice.[34] Inflation was then very low, and surely the judge was astute enough to count the cost of service before accepting an eight year term.

A necrology later stated that Shackelford's reason for leaving office was that he was not suited to "the retirement of the bench."[35] Indeed,

MURDER AT GREEN SPRINGS

Shackelford's last year as judge was viewed as anything but a retirement. The timing and indefinite grounds surrounding Shackelford's resignation suggested that his involvement in the Hall Case created an intolerable distaste for the judgeship. Decorum required polite excuses.

N. W. Hall sent Governor Stuart a six page letter addressing the fact that the second pantry fire occurred "while the place was said to have been under guard, which doubtless means that same were on hand watching for a chance to start the fire and lay it on Mrs. Hall."[36] A letter from juror Julian J. Jacobs stated that he "thought at the time the evidence was entirely insufficient to convict her, and I only consented to the verdict, because there was [sic] some men on the jury, who wanted to inflict the death penalty and the verdict was a compromise."[37]

In a letter to the executive declaring support for Mrs. Hall, Iona May Cutler stated that she had once lived with Mrs. Hall while employed as tutor for her daughters. Miss Cutler carefully pointed out that her father Rev. L. A. Cutler had been the Prohibition Party's candidate for governor.[38] Since Stuart had won office largely through Prohibition politics, the Cutler name carried weight, but not enough.

Securing Mrs. Hall's release had become more daunting and lengthy than Lindsay Gordon anticipated. After nearly six months, his client remained behind bars, and more mundane matters required attention. In May 1915, Gordon had the Louisa court appoint W. J. Roberts administrator of the David Asa Dunkum estate [property from Mrs. Hall's first marriage], for which privilege Roberts posted $1,000 bond.[39] The court declared Sheriff Andrew M. Wash administrator of Victor K. Hall's estate.[40] The court awarded R. Lindsay Gordon, Jr. legal guardianship of Essie and Mamie Dunkum.[41] These steps effectively delegated authority to act in behalf of Mrs. Hall and her daughters until her situation changed.

Despite the many sincere and credible entreaties in Mrs. Hall's behalf, Governor Stuart refused to act. Henry Carter Stuart was a politically astute vestige of the antebellum South. Born in 1855, he grew up during the Civil War. His father sold salt to the Confederacy, and his uncle was the legendary cavalry leader General J. E. B. Stuart. Henry Stuart was a successful farmer and businessman. His holdings spread throughout a four county area in southwestern Virginia, and his cattle operation was the largest east of the Mississippi River.[42] Stuart issued employees his own script for use in his company stores.[43] The governor was accustomed to living life, essentially, as a feudal lord.

Stuart charted his political course more on expediency than principle. Stuart, a firm believer in local option, forsook his personal stance on the issue and committed his gubernatorial influence to Prohibitionists for their reciprocal support. Prohibitionist backing assured Stuart the Democratic Party nomination unopposed, which in Virginia was "tantamount to election."[44] It must have become painfully obvious to Lindsay Gordon that unless a life was at stake, Stuart would never chance a political misstep.[45]

Efforts to release Mrs. Hall were further complicated by the fact that it was just too small of a world. Virginia's Attorney General John Garland Pollard, in addition to providing legal guidance to Governor Stuart, afforded unique insight into the situation politically with respect not only to the state generally, but to Louisa specifically. Pollard's perspective stemmed from the fact that his cousin, the son of his uncle and law partner Henry Robinson Pollard,[46] was a neighbor of Mrs. Hall. Indeed, H. R. Pollard, Jr. lived just two miles from Green Springs Depot at Valentine's Mill within the confines of the prestigious Green Springs neighborhood: the *real* Green Springs.

Furthermore, John Garland Pollard had just announced his candidacy for governor that February.[47] Being so closely associated with the current administration, any resulting backlash from freeing Mrs. Hall would diminish Pollard's chances of election. Therefore, Attorney General Pollard had as much reason as Governor Stuart to actively avoid any political threat posed by facilitating a pardon for the headlined *murderess*.

MURDER AT GREEN SPRINGS

But despite even these formidable obstacles encountered and in fairness to Governor Stuart, other circumstances developed which made it politically impossible to pardon Mrs. Hall. The Georgia state judicial system had created an adverse climate of such nationwide sensitivity that no governor of any state dared commute the sentence in a high profile case short of surrender and confession by the actual killer.

In 1913, Leo Frank was wrongly convicted of a brutal murder in Georgia and sentenced to hang. In the later part of 1914, his publicized court appeals drew national attention. In 1915, legal issues surrounding Frank generated increasing turmoil. Ironically, like Mrs. Hall, Frank was innocent and convicted through the combination of dubious investigation; a contrary Pinkerton detective hired by the accused; misinterpreted circumstantial evidence; perjured prosecution witnesses; introduction of alleged, uncharged crimes; and public opinion polarized by hostile newspaper publicity.[48] The parallels were uncanny.

By June 1915, all of Frank's avenues of appeal were exhausted. Georgia Governor Staton commuted Frank's sentence to life imprisonment. In response, rioters cried out for the lynching of Governor Staton. The militia mustered; shots were fired and arrests made. Governor Staton fled Georgia for his own safety.

Thus, any intervention by the Governor of Virginia in behalf of Mrs. Hall during the Leo Frank controversy maximized every political risk. A similar response by citizenry in the Commonwealth of Virginia like that having occurred in Georgia, though unlikely, was not unthinkable; the memories of the Roanoke Riot of 1893 still haunted Virginia.[49]

Had Mrs. Hall's trial resulted in a death sentence, the situation would have, hopefully, been different. But the fact remained that Mrs. Hall's sentence was universally perceived as a light. It was *only* ten years. Any governor could gracefully extend a pardon after serving half her sentence with good behavior. Mrs. Hall had to wait.

Furthermore, as a reactionary precaution, Governor Stuart moved to eliminate the provision in the Code of Virginia giving the State Parole Board authority to parole prisoners independent of the executive.[50] Stuart succeeded and restricted the power to parole as the sole prerogative of the governor. Thus, he prevented any possible circumvention. Stuart's concerns were justified by the action of his predecessor's opponents to usurp that governor's decision to deny pardons to Floyd and Claude Allen.[51]

It was, therefore, no coincidence that efforts to free Mrs. Hall ceased as the drama surrounding Leo Frank intensified and climaxed. In August, Frank was abducted from prison and lynched. A cooling off period of four full months elapsed before anyone dared renew attempts to persuade Governor Stuart to pardon Mrs. Hall.

In December 1915, Gordon acquired the endorsement of no less a figure than *retired* Judge George S. Shackelford who tried the case. Gordon first contacted the governor informally to test the waters; but unfortunately, the political issue was still too sensitive. Stuart reacted by imposing the most difficult of all stipulations: Bibb's endorsement.

Stuart must have known of the strained relations between Gordon and Bibb. The mutual animosity generated over the Hall Case and the Yancey Trustee battle before the Virginia Supreme Court had created an unbridgeable chasm between the two men. If Stuart sought to shield himself completely from the political threat represented by the Hall Case, this condition did it.

Gordon pressed ahead and wrote to Stuart formally announcing Shackelford's intent. Gordon stated that "If, therefore you [Stuart] make it a condition that I secure the recommendation of the commonwealth's attorney [Bibb], it is useless to carry the matter any further."[52] Nevertheless, a week later, Gordon forwarded Shackelford's letter to the governor. There was nothing to lose and everything to gain.

MURDER AT GREEN SPRINGS

Judge Shackelford explained that he "did not set aside the verdict because the law gives the jury the province of judging the weight of evidence. At the same time, I would not have been surprised if the jury had acquitted Mrs. Hall."[53] Shackelford added,

> "She [Mrs. Hall] established a character by witnesses who had known her from childhood which any woman might have been proud, as a kind, religious, hospitable and charitable woman. If she committed the crime of which she was convicted, it was her first offense, the truth about which is locked in her own breast. I should think her suffering had expiated her offense against society if guilty, and if innocent reparation could never be made to her and her two innocent daughters."[54]

"I add my voice," Shackelford concluded, "to those who invoke your favorable consideration of Mrs. Hall's petition."[55]

Gordon encouraged the governor to reconsider his prerequisite:

> "I have not asked the Commonwealth's Attorney to endorse Mrs. Hall's application for a pardon, because the political and personal relationships between us are such that I could not do so without a sacrifice of a certain manly pride, which all honest men should cherish and preserve and I trust that the lack of his endorsation [sic] will not prevent your favorable action."[56]

Governor Stuart never faltered. As a last resort, Gordon followed Shackelford's letter by a petition from the Virginia legislature:

> We, the undersigned, members of the General Assembly of Virginia, respectfully request that you grant executive clemency in the case of Elizabeth A. Hall, of the county of Louisa, now in the penitentiary, serving a sentence for felony:[57]

The document was signed by fifty-four of the one hundred members of the Virginia House of Delegates.

There was nothing else Gordon could do. Stuart was immovable. Clearly there would be no pardon for Mrs. Hall during Stuart's term in office.

The frustrated N. W. Hall could not ignore such obdurate resistance without comment and wrote Governor Stuart again.

"I regret exceedingly that Com. Attorney Bibb refuses to ask her pardon, knowing as I do that it is without just cause. His course toward Mrs. Hall ever since her counsel refused to let her go before the grand jury has been hard and unfeeling. I am truly sorry to see as young a lawyer as he is so overbalanced with bitterness as a prosecutor. In my humble judgment Judge Shackelford's recommendation ought to outweigh Mr. Bibb's refusal."[58]

At this point, the family resigned themselves to the situation. Mrs. Hall's siblings looked after the girls. Essie continued secretarial training and employment by the kindhearted Lindsay Gordon in his Richmond office. To best provide for her daughters, Mrs. Hall had Gordon sell the store and half its acreage in May 1916. Real estate agent L. W. Harris purchased the property in exchange for two hundred dollars cash and a house and lot on Fairfield Avenue in Richmond. The transferred deed reserved the cemetery for future burials of descendants of D. A. Dunkum. To specifically protect Buck Dunkum's business, the deed also prohibited all mercantile operations on the property for a period of ten years.[59]

Collateral Victims: Essie and Mamie Dunkum circa 1917 – Their "cup of anguish" overflowed. (Photo from author's collection)

The unrelenting N. W. Hall compiled one last list of arguments for Mrs. Hall's release and sent them to Governor Stuart.

Green Springs Depot

June 13, 1916

To His Excellency Henry C. Stuart, Gov. of Va.:

Dear Governor – I beg your kind indulgence to read one more letter from me.

In view of the fact that we can never rest satisfied while the murderer of our poor boy is at large and his innocent wife punished instead;

In view of the fact that Judge Shackelford has written you asking the pardon of Mrs. Victor K. Hall;

In view of the fact that three fourths of the members of the last Legislature have signed a petition requesting her pardon;

In view of the strange and unfeeling and unreasonable course of Co. Atty. Bibb, who is said to have given as a reason for refusing to ask pardon for Mrs. Hall, that Mr. Gordon voted against Judge Sims;[60]

In view of the fact that Mrs. Hall could have had no motive, and that her character, her reputation, and disposition, as well as her material welfare, were against the thought of her doing such a deed;

In view of the fact that she has done nothing to be pardoned for, and not one thing was proved against her;

In view of all the dirty things which were done to secure her prosecution and conviction;

In view of the way this woman was treated by the meddlers, the busybodies, the detectives and the newspaper reporters, while the chief meddler of all was never put on the witness stand, although the Co. Atty. told me with his own lips that his man had done more talking than anybody else;

In view of the fact that Mrs. Hall was really proved innocent by the evidence showing that the pistol had not been recently fired, by the reputation of Charlie Johnston's false testimony and Bob Trice's "bloody bolster: lies, and the false so-called "evidence" to show that she started the "pantry fire," which was fully refuted by reliable evidence – when- even if the false testimony had been true it would not have connected her with the fire, - there was no connecting line;

In view of the fact that the "burglar" theory which the commonwealth undertook to fight was not the most plausible one (though not impossible itself), and that it is most likely that Victor Hall actually went to the front store door and was struck a severe blow on the forehead, and then followed by his assailant and shot in the back of the head right where he was found lying on the floor;

In view of the fact that all the mysterious fires were started at the very time and for the very purpose of confirming suspicion on Mrs. Hall, and that it could have been proved that she had nothing whatever to do with them;

In view of the fact that Mrs. Hall, in the very time of her sore bereavement and distress, suffered months of suspense and anxiety, was driven away from her home, her business ruined, her children made homeless, her household goods sold at a sacrifice, her future livelihood uncertain;

In view of the fact that she has already suffered more that 18 months of unjust imprisonment;

In view of all this and much more, I most earnestly implore you, after this long delay, to exercise your clemency toward her.

It is not simply because Mrs. Hall is my daughter-in-law, that I make this appeal. My sense of justice has been shocked and outraged. If the treatment and punishment of this woman is to be called justice, I am ashamed of my own country and state, and shall be forced to conclude that it is possible for public sentiment to force a miscarriage of justice as to cause an innocent person to be indicted, convicted, sentenced, and to pass before all the powers of resort without redress – the only appeal left being to the Great Judge of all, the God of the poor man Lazarus, the God of the widow and the fatherless, the poor and the wronged and down-trodden and oppressed of the earth.

And now, dear Governor, in closing, if you turn Mrs. Hall down again, please do not give it to the newspapers. They have done enough already in turning public sentiment against her. And I have one special request to make. It is this: If you do not pardon Mrs. Hall that you will kindly write and tell me what it is that stands in the way – what is your one great reason for not doing so.

Humbly and Sincerely Yours,

[Signed] N. W. Hall[61]

If Governor Stuart responded, no record survived. No further requests for Mrs. Hall's release were sent to this governor. Mrs. Hall and her supporters bided their time until Stuart left office.

In 1917, Attorney General John Garland Pollard ran for Governor of Virginia. Fortunately for imprisoned widow, the politically progressive Westmoreland Davis outmaneuvered Pollard for the Democratic Party's nomination, won election and, thereby, eliminated any threat Pollard represented to Mrs. Hall's release.

Soon after Davis' inauguration in 1918, the campaign to free Mrs. Hall resumed. As in the past, letters from family and friends were bolstered by support from noteworthy individuals. An appeal by J. Reid Wills, Treasurer of Louisa County [formerly sheriff],[62] was followed by a second request for clemency by Judge George Shackelford.[63] W. C. B. Winston, a juror at the Hall trial;[64] Charles E. Hester, a coroner's juror;[65] Mrs. L. F. Yancey, a witness for the prosecution;[66] and a second letter from juror Julian J. Jacobs[67] asked the new governor to pardon Mrs. Hall. The

letters from witnesses for the defense Mrs. S. B. Henson [formerly Elsie Wood][68] and her father A. O. Wood[69] testified again in her behalf.

If there was any man likely to sail contrary to political winds, it was Westmoreland Davis. Davis reviewed all the letters including those received during Stuart's administration. All were favorable. However, even for the fair minded Davis, it was just too late in the game to oppose the one man adamantly opposed to the woman's release.

October 31, 1918.

Mr. A. G. Taylor,

Mattoax, Va.

Dear Mr. Taylor:-

I have taken up the matter of pardon for Mrs. Elizabeth Hall, and find your letter of July 10th on file. After Mrs. Hall has served half of her time I shall take her case up again, but do not feel that, in view of the opposition offered by the Commonwealth's Attorney, I can do anything more at present.

Yours very truly,

Governor[70]

On the fifth anniversary of Victor Hall's death, Mrs. Hall appealed to Governor Davis personally. Though apparently coached on what to say, the spelling, grammar, and scrawl were clearly her own as were the poignant emphases.

April 14th, 1919

State Prison

To his excellency-

Westmoreland Davis, Governor of Va.

From petitonner Elizabth Hall – now an imate of Va. Penitentiary – respectfully represents, unto your excellency, the follering
facts – that I was tried in Louisa Co 1914 and was convicted for
the murderer of my husband – of which I am not *Guilty*. I think if
you read the record of my trial - you will find the evidence *circum-
stancial* and *contradictry* – I umbly beg, you to have mercy on me. I
have been in trouble 5 – yrs 15th day of April – I was Sentensese
to Prison for 10 years on Nov. 14, 1914 – My age is 45 – to your
honor wont you grant me a pardon. Hoping I may be granted the
fore going request

I am your most Obediant Servant

[Signed] Elizabeth Hall[71]

Governor Davis proved true to his word. Extending mid-sentence
pardons to well behaved prisoners was established custom. Commonwealth's Attorney Bibb offered no further resistance. *Justice* had been
served. On November 6th, 1919, the governor granted Mrs. Hall a conditional pardon. Lizzie Hall was free at last. She had served half of her
pronounced sentence, the one so frequently referred to by her detractors
as "*only* ten years."

CHAPTER
Fourteen

POST MORTEMS
ON A COUNTER TOP

MURDER AT GREEN SPRINGS

A RETURN TO NORMALCY

*I*n November 1919, Warren G. Harding began campaigning for President under the slogan "Return to Normalcy." Few desired "normalcy" more than Mrs. Hall and, remarkably, little stood in her way. She was freed and reunited with her daughters at last. They stayed in Richmond. The city directory listed "Elizabeth A. Hall, widow of V. K. Hall." The family allowed themselves to recall only good from their past as if nothing bad had ever happened. Newspapers took no notice of Mrs. Hall's release.

The three women supported themselves. Lizzie made dresses. Essie worked as a stenographer at C. P. Lathrop & Co. Mamie was likewise employed as a stenographer for the Fourth U.S. Circuit Court of Appeals.

Essie became engaged to Edward McAuley, an accountant where she worked. They married in 1920. That autumn, Mamie entered the evening division of the T. C. Williams Law School at the University of Richmond as a special student. Her application listed R. Lindsay Gordon, Jr. as guardian.[1]

Lizzie and Mamie changed addresses a number of times. They shared apartments together through 1929. Lizzie secured work as linen matron at Grace Hospital. By April 1930, she was head of the linen room and lived with Mamie on East Grace Street.[2]

Mamie married Richard M. F. Williams, Jr., a man with whom she had worked for years. "Dick" Williams served as assistant clerk for the Fourth U.S. Circuit Court of Appeals and was raising two sons from his previous marriage. He prepared the boys for "stories" they might hear about his bride's mother and emphasized that the matter was never to be discussed again.[3] The taboo subject was never revisited despite the incredible irony that Dick's brother Tom, by then a local attorney, had been one of the courtroom stenographers at Mrs. Hall's trial.

Following Mamie's marriage, Mrs. Hall moved to 918 West Grace Street and resided there several years.[4] About 1935, Mrs. Hall purchased a house at 1811 Hanover Avenue.[5] She then boarded young women pursuing nursing and secretarial careers. Some came from Louisa County.[6] Mrs. Hall continued to host boarders after her retirement from the hospital in 1939.

In the 1940's Mrs. Hall developed diabetes. Her condition deteriorated. She died from related complications at Richmond's Retreat for the Sick on November 22, 1946.

The *News Leader* and *Times-Dispatch* carried only the obituaries submitted by the grieving family for "Elizabeth Ann Hall, widow of Victor K. Hall." The newspapers themselves paid no attention to the passing of their former headliner.

Essie and Mamie shunned the vacant plot in the family cemetery at Green Springs Depot reserved for their mother between their father and stepfather. Ed and Essie McAuley purchased a new plot in Richmond's Forest Lawn cemetery. They buried Mrs. Hall there and marked her grave with a simple bronze plaque: "Elizabeth A. Hall, 1874 – 1946, Rest In Peace."

After prison, Lizzie enjoyed twenty-seven years with her daughters and their families. Photographs taken in the 1940's captured Elizabeth Ann Hall smiling as if she had always lived a happy life of unassailable security. Her face showed no trace of the losses, calumnies, and hardships endured. Her countenance reflected a heart grateful to her Lord and Savior who gave her Grace to endure, ability to forgive, and blessed her latter days.

MURDER AT GREEN SPRINGS

Elizabeth Ann Hall poses in her own back yard in Richmond, circa 1943. (Photo from author's collection)

Mrs. Hall had four grandchildren. These grew up knowing that David Asa Dunkum and his brother Buck ran a store at Green Springs. The succeeding generation knew that after Asa Dunkum died, grandma married a man named Hall who also died, but none of them knew of the murder, trial, or imprisonment. Essie and Mamie shared stories of their childhood at Green Springs, but accounts strangely omitted their teenage years. No one knew why; they just did not talk about that time.

Essie occasionally visited "Uncle Buck" in Green Springs and carried her daughter Evelyn with her. Evelyn must have seen the old Hall's store and knew what it was from family photographs. However, she never learned what happened there until over a decade after Essie died. Even then, Evelyn died before researching the matter in depth.

After Mrs. Hall sold her store, neighbors Billy and Jimmy Johnson bought it in 1919.[7] They lived and based a lumber business there until August 1922 when they sold the property to Buck Dunkum.[8] Tenants rented the property from time to time, but no other businesses operated out of the old store. The associated barn and outbuildings disappeared by the 1930's.

Buck Dunkum established two other businesses on plots of his land bordering the county road. Dunkum built a forge shop across the road from and due east of his store. The blacksmith was George E. "Chick" Chewning, nephew of the notorious George W. Chewning, Jr.[9] On the southeast side of this shop, Dunkum built an engine driven gristmill run by George L. Kennon.

The railroad eventually improved the track bed and increased its elevation with additional ballast. The double switched turnout was converted to a single switch siding. The state purchased right of way to straighten the crooked county road that crossed the tracks nine times between Louisa and Gordonsville.[10] The Hall store was demolished in 1939 and the new section of Virginia Route 33 paved over the sites of the Hall Store and the original depot shed. Also on June 1st that same year, the house that once belonged to Nicholas and Ellen Hall burned to the ground.[11]

Between the Depression and the end of World War Two, the village economy of Green Springs Depot waned. Many locals moved to cities for employment.[12] The blacksmith shop passed away with Chick Chewning as did the gristmill with George Kennon. Most of the log homes near the depot vanished. Mary Dunkum succeeded her husband Buck as postmaster in 1945. The C & O railway demolished the *new* depot when passenger service ceased about that time. Five years later, the name of the post office changed officially from "Green Springs Depot" to simply "Green Springs." Buck Dunkum died in 1952. The post office closed in 1956 when mail delivery consolidated in Gordonsville.[13] Mary Dunkum died in 1965.[14] The railroad removed the disused rail siding about 1967.

At this writing, CSX Corporation maintains the single set of railroad tracks through Green Springs. The Dunkum store, rebuilt in 1914, stands vacant at the rail crossing at Dunkum Store Road. The Dunkum house, rebuilt after the 1913 fire, remains occupied just a stone's throw away. Three hundred yards beyond the other side of the tracks, in a hay field that once was the Hall store property, is the fenced cemetery where Victor Hall lies buried with his parents and aunt. They rest there with Acey Dunkum, his and Lizzie's babies born at Green Springs, and the two smallpox victims. The headstones, some toppled, obscured by weeds, and a few archived records testify to their brief existences; otherwise, they are all now very much as if they never were.

Buck Dunkum's store and home as they appeared in December 2003 as viewed from the Hall's store site. Both buildings are those rebuilt after fires upon the original foundations. The broom factory stood just beyond and to the right of Dunkum's store. (Photo from by author's collection)

POST MORTEMS ON A COUNTER TOP

HOW THE WEST WAS WON

In 1914, professional law enforcement was relatively new. Even in large American cities, organized police forces were only about a century old. Traditionally, county sheriffs and local magistrates represented the law and organized posses as needed to handle threats. Other than this, the long arm of the law had little presence at Green Springs Depot.

Green Springs Depot was a close community of interrelated families struggling to scratch livings out of some of the poorest land in the county. The majority made the best of their lots in life, working hard, helping one another, and generally minding their own business. Crandall A. Shifflett noted their noble character.[15] Life was fairly peaceable for residents who behaved themselves and *voted right*. Nevertheless, Green Springs Depot earned its reputation as one of the roughest areas in the county.

Like most rural folk, the residents of Green Springs Depot were independent spirits. They lived together by general application of the *Golden Rule* and its American corollary: *If you don't want trouble, then don't make trouble*. The neighborhood generally settled problems among themselves either man to man or by groups appointing themselves to the task.[16] On account of the railroad, idlers and drifters accounted for some problems. An occasional rogue threatened order, but such were exceptions.

Railroads, telegraphs, highways, and telephones broadened concepts of community. Availability of effective law enforcement and acceptance of legal processes replaced old habits of taking the law into one's own hands. However, change occurred slowly, and vestiges of the old ways surfaced from time to time.

The incorrigible George W. Chewning, Jr. returned to Green Springs in defiance of the terms of his 1917 pardon.[17] Amazingly, his pardon remained in force after his arrest in 1922. Chewning was convicted of a misdemeanor, sentenced to thirty days in jail, and fined fifty dollars and

MURDER AT GREEN SPRINGS

court costs.[18]   Three years later, Chewning was arrested again, this time charged with "felonious possession of still and mash capable of being manufactured into ardent sprits."[19] Chewning was convicted and sentenced to five years in the state penitentiary. He remained there at least into 1930.[20] Chewning died at home in Green Springs Depot July 30, 1931.[21]

Bootlegging was common around Green Springs Depot, especially during Prohibition. Louisa County Prohibition Agent J. B. Vaughn routinely confiscated moonshine stills.[22] A number of men in Green Springs were arrested and fined for manufacturing or possessing illegal liquor.[23] One infers from the low number of convictions and modest judgments related to similar arrests and seizures that the penalty enforced in Chewning's case represented a favorable opportunity for the community to finally rid themselves of a particularly persistent nuisance.

Sixteen years after the Hall Case, Mrs. Hall's neighbor John S. Johnson, Sr. [65] was charged with the murder of one William Harry Snow [42]. Johnson then worked at *Corduroy*, formerly the estate of C. B. Vest, but at that time, the farm of State Senator William Worth Smith, Jr. On the evening of November 2, 1929 while Johnson and other farm hands celebrated the completion of harvest, Johnson allegedly gave his foreman W. H. Snow moonshine laced with strychnine. Snow was found later that evening dead in his car.[24]

Old Sheriff Wash[25] sent the jar of suspicious liquor away for analysis. The container passed through many hands between the sheriff, his runner, the pharmacy in Gordonsville, and the laboratory in Richmond.

Johnson was arrested and released on $10,000 bail with W. R. Dunkum among those who signed the bond.[26] The case was continued a number of times but finally tried on April 9, 1930. Arguments by John Q. Rhodes, Jr., attorney for the defense, challenged the validity of the evidence.[27] The court ruled the chemical analysis inadmissible. The jury found Johnson not guilty.[28]

Over a decade later, Johnson admitted that he poisoned Snow. The justification was something along the lines that the man had been "a thorn under my saddle for a long time."[29]

Arguments as to whether or not Snow *needed killing* pursuant to any *Code of the West* are beyond the scope of this work, but clearly, a vestige of the *old ways* of Green Springs had manifested itself.[30] In contrast to the 1914 circus that was the Hall Case, the legal process in Louisa appeared to have advanced somewhat by 1930.

SHORT COLT VS. SMITH & WESSON

The prosecution's case against Mrs. Hall hinged on Victor Hall's pistol with the spent cartridge.[31] The spent cartridge was bogus in light of two facts. First, everyone agreed on the day of the murder that the pistol had not been fired recently. Second, common, best practice was to keep an empty chamber beneath the firing pin to prevent accidental discharge if dropped.[32] The defense overlooked the latter point.

Gordon's hasty, homespun ballistics failed to generate acceptable results. The well intentioned experiments were poorly planned, poorly executed, and void of scientific controls necessary to withstand critique. Gordon submitted the unsubstantiated, though not unfounded, argument that the murder weapon must have been another pistol of inferior manufacture because the bullet did not pass completely through the victim's head.[33] Even had this evidence been well received, Gordon's reliance

only upon Mrs. Hall's friends for firearms *expertise* undermined credibility, and without a doubt, the utilization of Bill Roberts in this capacity achieved total absurdity.

In Gordon's defense, the science of ballistics did not gain general acceptance in courtrooms until the Sacco – Vanzetti Case in 1920, and the invention of the comparison microscope for precise bullet/weapon correlation did not occur until 1923. One can only speculate that the recruitment of a credible firearms expert, a Smith & Wesson factory representative for instance, would have eliminated Victor Hall's pistol as the murder weapon and collapsed the prosecution's case. All things considered, Gordon had the right idea, but was working ahead of his time and with limited resources. The unrealized potential of Gordon's efforts was, essentially, a stillbirth of modern forensics.

None of the *expert* testimony introduced by either the prosecution or defense involved trained technicians, established procedures, or calibrated equipment. *Experts* on both sides consistently reported 150 grain measurements for nominal 146 grain ammunition.[34] Records bear witness that there was never consideration given to precision, accuracy, calibration or technical competence. This was understandable; attorneys were men of letters, not scientists.

The prosecution introduced evidence that the fatal bullet weighed 138 grains and the bullets in Victor Hall's pistol weighed 150 grains. One astute juror asked how much weight a bullet might lose when fired. Some loss was assumed. No one knew exactly. The discrepancy in mass between the lethal bullet and the unfired rounds in the victim's pistol remained unresolved.[35] This uncertainty favored the prosecution's implications since they held momentum in the courtroom. But given the disparity between the prosecution's measurements and nominal values, published data for the various .38 caliber pistol cartridges, and other details, an initial fatal bullet weight of 130 grains was not only reasonable, but likely.[36]

Testimony indicated that the bullet taken from Victor Hall's head was deformed and intact. The most important fact was that this bullet was *externally grooved and externally lubricated*. Taken as a whole, the fatal bullet's caliber, weight, and external lubrication were consistent *ONLY* with .38 Short Colt ammunition.[37] The lighter bullet responsible for killing Victor Hall differed materially from heavier, *internally grooved and internally lubricated* .38 S&W ammunition taken from the victim's pistol.[38] Therefore, the fatal bullet could not have come from the spent .38 S&W U.M.C. cartridge in Victor Hall's revolver; Victor Hall was not shot with his own pistol; and the case against Mrs. Hall had no validity whatsoever.

THE SECOND PANTRY FIRE

Lindsay Gordon, Nicholas Hall and a host of others suspected the detectives of setting the second pantry fire to incriminate Mrs. Hall. Immediately after the destruction of the C & O depot and first pantry fire, Judge Shackelford ordered the Hall store guarded to prevent another arson attempt. Consequently, the store remained under constant surveillance of at least one official representative of the Louisa County Sheriff's Department, the Virginia State Bureau of Insurance, Pinkerton's National Detective Agency, or Special Agents of the Chesapeake and Ohio Railway. Records infer several guards present much of the time. Again, each man was specifically assigned to prevent another arson attempt on the Hall store.

Yet, the very first person to discover the fire was nine year old Johnny Graves who saw black smoke rolling from beneath the eaves of the pantry as he stood on the road in front of the store. Either one or more detectives were involved in setting the fire or the blaze was a miracle worthy of Elijah the Prophet.

MURDER AT GREEN SPRINGS

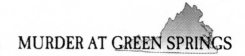

Whether acting alone or in cahoots with others, circumstances mark the *Railroad Dick* Monte Angle as particularly suspicious. Angle's performance in the Harrison murder investigation just months prior to the Hall shooting established his propensity for presumptive, if not, Machiavellian methods. Angle again revealed his deceitful approach to police work in advancing a distorted version of Ruby Chewning's statement as called into evidence against Mrs. Hall before the grand jury. Angle also displayed a particularly confrontational attitude toward Mrs. Hall after the depot burned and the first attempt to fire her home. No other investigator behaved thusly.

Angle grew up in pre-1900 Richmond where every neighborhood had its own boy gang. These groups were exclusive, fiercely loyal, territorial bands which gathered for fun and sport among themselves and rock battles against opposing gangs. Known by names like the *Shockoe Hill Cats* and the *Fourth Street Horribles*, these gangs operated unsupervised under their own moral codes.[39] The gangs essentially mirrored patterns set by adults during Reconstruction through Prohibition eras when Odd Fellows, Freemasons, Knights Templars and numerous other fraternal orders and mutual aid societies flourished.

The boy gangs of old Richmond were essentially tribal orders. Memoirs record that gang values of loyalty and leadership served many later in successful careers, but extant nostalgia was inevitably written by leaders rather than followers. Angle's nearly consumptive appearance suggests lifelong frailty, a definite disadvantage growing up in tough surroundings and, perhaps, foundation for a pathological craving for affirmation as an adult.

Monte Angel was the product of Richmond's working class, the grandson of immigrants who were part of the city's sizeable German community.[40] His father Myer S. Angle, Sr. was a mere youth during the Civil War, but his position as corporal in a second class militia unit gave him venerable status as a soldier of the South.[41] The senior Angle worked a number of jobs as mail carrier, clerk and pipe fitter. In 1905, he worked a year as a barkeep then became a magistrate for Henrico County, an office held until his death in 1908. As magistrate, political leverage may have helped his son secure his railroad detective position by 1907. Despite all the proprieties demanded by social veneer, the bromide "It is not what you know, but who you know." was never more applicable than in 1914 Virginia.

Until the end of the First World War, late Victorian mores demanded public conformity to established order and etiquette. Appearances were everything, and the interests of the individual always ranked below those perceived beneficial to the common good. Proper manners and protocols masked a multitude of hypocrisies and selfish ends, especially when supported by one's official title, church affiliation or the subculture of a fraternal order. Powerful employers frequently overlooked questionable conduct if it facilitated business or repaid a favor. Despite the proclaimed high moral standards of society in general, pretentious, unethical and corrupt behavior was commonplace. The network of fraternal ties rescued many as in the case of Detective Angle's uncle.

Captain of Richmond Police James B. Angle was forced to resign to avoid prosecution in a gambling and prostitution scandal in 1902.[42] But rather than face social ruin on account of the scandal, as one might expect, Captain Angle's connections soon secured him a job with the prestigious Virginia Fire and Marine Insurance Company.[43] Obviously, moral turpitude was not necessarily a sure path to condemnation. Consequences of questionable conduct greatly depended on one's circle of friends and the social strata affected. As long as one operated without upset to one's own class and higher, the concept that an end justified the means was often acceptable. It was simply the way of the world, a way familiar to Special Agent Monte Angle.

 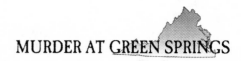

MURDER AT GREEN SPRINGS

The second pantry fire was staged to incriminate Mrs. Hall. Though other *civic minded* individuals may have contemplated the same course, evidence suggests that Special Agent Angle acted as the clandestine expediter of justice. Rationalization was easy. *Everyone in the county knew she did it.*[44] Therefore, conviction of Mrs. Hall was good for the community, the newspapers, and potentially Angle's career.

Angle spent the day of the pantry fire at Green Springs and had time to study the situation and plan his moves. Detective Mallory arrived late in the day to relieve Angle. However, Angle ordered Mallory back to Louisa within minutes to warn officials that another arson attempt was imminent. How did Angle know this? Why did Angle not accept his relief and go himself?

When Mrs. Hall left the store preceded by her family walking away to the tune of Becky Coates' noisy wheel barrow and rattling ham boiler, the diversion provided ample opportunity to set the fire. Having full police authority and a justified presence guarding the premises, Angle could move at will.

The firebug, whoever it was, grabbed the first tinder at hand: the towels hanging on the porch outside the kitchen. Even though the kitchen door was locked and testimony declared that Essie had the key, the crude, warded lock required only a detective's skeleton key for access. Once inside, Becky Coates' clothes and kerosene were readily available. A cigarette in a matchbook, a piece of candle, or improvised wick would have made a convenient delay fuse consistent with the timing of the blaze.[45]

The pantry fire effectively sealed Mrs. Hall's fate. However, Angle reaped little benefit from the incident. Curiously, Special Agent Angle had been actively involved in the murder investigation from the day of the shooting. Yet, the prosecution called him to the stand only once, and this was simply to identify Becky Coates' clothes involved in the pantry fire.

Obtuse Angle recalled the charred items in vague generalities, as if not wanting to appear too familiar with the items. In contrast, Captain A. G. Smith of the Pinkertons, who also examined the same rags after the fire, vividly remembered details down to an unfastened safety pin in a missing, *blood stained* shirtwaist.

In 1914, the title of detective had broader meaning than simply investigator. Depending on the circumstances, a detective was also an armed guard, a gunman, a spy, and an *agent provocateur*. Clients expected results. In language of the time, employers encouraged detectives to *cultivate suspects* and *work up evidence*.[46] Angle's work on the Harrison and Hall cases was contemporary with actions of the Baldwin-Felts detectives in the Colorado coal miners' strike which culminated in the Ludlow Massacre on April 20, 1914.[47] If guilty, Angle's tactics were as criminal as they were despicable, but such behavior was then common to his profession.

Angle's boss Luther Scherer, the famous detective and head of railway police, attended the trial on the day of Angle's testimony. Perhaps, Scherer had misgivings about his employee. Newspapers made a point to note Scherer's presence; he was, after all, a celebrity. In contrast, public mentions of Angle were always incidental or in exchange for information, never in recognition of achievement.

The pantry fire aside, records indicate that while the prosecution prepared for trial, Special Agent Angle personally recruited fellow C & O employee Charles F. Johnston to testify that a week before the murder, Victor Hall's pistol was loaded *all around*. In doing so, if by no other act, Special Agent Angle defined his role by promoting the key perjurer against Mrs. Hall.

Lindsay Gordon suggested that the second pantry fire was a deliberate act against his client "not exceeded in human degradation." But Gordon's rhetorical assessment overlooked both Angle's recruitment of the perjurer Johnston and Angle's earnest attempt just months before to have an innocent man executed for the Harrison murder. A man with Angle's record would have thought nothing of staging the second pantry fire.

SIDETRACKED INVESTIGATIONS

Buck Dunkum was suspected of shooting Victor Hall immediately after the sheriff cleared the escaped convict. It was only natural to associate the burning of his store with the murder of his business rival. Circumstances incriminated the innocent man. Dunkum then faced the very real threat of eventual execution by electric chair!

Fortunately for Dunkum, narrow, simplistic reasoning was the hallmark of detectives. As soon as the array of weird circumstances within the Hall household came to light, investigators looked no farther than Mrs. Hall. Presumption and fixation supplanted thorough investigation. The resulting injustice allowed the real killer to escape and devastated the victim's widow and family. On the bright side, this outcome likely spared Dunkum's life.

Buck Dunkum was just one example. There were actually a number of men upon whom free-ranging suspicion and its lethal jeopardy might have fallen. The fact that others feared accusation helps explain why some elements passively resigned Mrs. Hall to her fate. Even mutual friends of Buck Dunkum and Lizzie Hall, when forced to choose, rallied to Dunkum's defense.

A woman made the best scapegoat. Amidst public cries for vengeance, everyone knew that no white woman had ever been executed in Virginia. The number of letters written after Mrs. Hall's conviction by prominent people urging the governor's pardon supports this view, for few expressed favorable opinions openly until after the trial.

Lindsay Gordon and the Halls suspected that Victor Hall was killed on account of business jealousy. This was true in part, but downplayed the three arson attacks directed specifically against Dunkum. Notwithstanding the fact that Buck Dunkum was most likely the ultimate target of a frame up, Gordon declared publicly that there was more evidence against Buck Dunkum than Mrs. Hall. This may have also been true, but records documented as much, if not more, evidence against others who were never investigated. Over a dozen had motive. All of them were men.

Take Lewis Yancey, for instance. While managing the store at Green Springs Depot, Lewis Yancey lost two brothers and survived smallpox only to face financial ruin. Heaped on top of this was the humiliation of clerking for the Dunkums, the recipients of the very success denied Yancey.

For years, Lewis Yancey fought expensive legal battles with the county and creditors. He was still on the road to recovery when Victor Hall was killed. Yancey had managed the store at Meltons since mid 1908, but Meltons was no Green Springs and had no depot.

By October 1913, Yancey sold his holdings at Meltons.[48] The competition from the stores at Green Springs Depot must have been a factor in his decision, but to what extent is not known. Yancey established the Gordonsville Bargain House and by April 1914 had applied for a post office franchise.[49] But as late as 1915, Lewis Yancey was still harassed by creditors seeking reimbursement from his 1903 business losses at Green Springs.[50]

Lewis Yancey had had a hard life filled with personal tragedies and indebtedness, but he was neither a bitter nor violent man. Yancey and his family maintained warm relationships with the Dunkums and Halls at least until the trial. Lewis was summoned by the prosecution, but was never called to the witness stand. Lewis' wife Elsie and her mother Mrs. Alex Chewning testified for the prosecution, but only to the extent of repeating statements Mrs. Hall made to them personally.

The detectives were intimidating men and placed the Yanceys in a difficult position. The family intended their friend Mrs. Hall no harm, but neither dared they risk fighting in her corner. For had suspicion been diverted from Mrs. Hall, any investigator seeking a suspect with reason for jealousy against Buck Dunkum and Victor Hall might well have fingered Lewis Yancey.

The possibility of Yancey's involvement in the crime was extremely remote. Yancey's standing in the community was further attested by his past associations with the commonwealth's attorney and his service as a special deputy for Louisa County.[51] Nevertheless, an accusation based on resentment over losses and retaliation against *exploiters* would have been compelling in the emotionally charged environment. Even so, others had grounds upon which to base jealousies and resentments against the Dunkums and Halls.

Green Springs Depot boasted two known killers Littleton Napper and George W. Chewning, Jr. Chewning was still in prison in 1914. Though he had served almost half of his eighteen year sentence, his prospects of parole remained doubtful largely due to W. C. Bibb's correspondence with the governor. Chewning may have mistakenly blamed Buck Dunkum.

Both Nicholas and Victor Hall signed a petition for Chewning's release. Dunkum, on the other hand, refused to put his name to the document. After all, Dunkum testified against Chewning at trial. Chewning had no way of knowing about all oppositions to his release, but may have learned of Dunkum's refusal.

Chewning's only son had recently died. His wife and daughters suffered want. Chewning had behaved himself behind bars, yet someone actively opposed his release. Who might Chewning have suspected?

Among the most respected men living at the crime scene, only Dunkum resisted. Did Chewning direct his anger against Dunkum from inside prison?

Chewning recruited Grady to kill Poindexter. Did Chewning solicit a clan member to burn out and frame Dunkum?

Conceivably, Chewning could have made such arrangements with another poor, disgruntled resident of Green Springs Depot. Ironically, Chewning's wife Florence was Littleton Napper's sister. Yes, Chewning and Napper were brothers-in-law! Furthermore, they served time together in the state penitentiary; their sentences coincided five full years. Napper had been out of prison since 1911 and assumed back in Green Springs.[52]

The arson fires on Dunkum's property began following the death of Chewning's son and shortly after denial of his parole. Since the fires alone proved ineffective against Dunkum, framing him with murder was a logical escalation. Strangely, Dunkum's store was burned and Victor Hall shot on the thirteenth anniversary of Napper's conviction. The details are intriguing.

While these and other suspicious men and motives surface in records, the arson/murder at Green Springs occurred in the midst of one particularly volatile situation next door to the Hall store involving two sisters of Littleton Napper. Suzie Mallory [42] and Lucy Gibson [35] lived on twenty acres of land inherited from their father Lewis Napper. The land adjoined the properties of Mrs. Hall[53], John S. Johnson, Sr. and George Mack Kennon.

Kennon's twenty-eight year old son Grover C. Kennon lived on his father's place and sought to acquire the land owned by the Napper sis-

ters. The two sisters lived by themselves without benefit of male protection. Mallory's husband had deserted her; Gibson was widowed; and their brothers lived elsewhere. Their land and log house were all they had. Understandably, they refused to sell.

By 1913, Grover Kennon began intimidating the poor women. He verbally threatened "to tear down their house and destroy it." That winter Kennon actually knocked out large portions of "pointing" [chinking] from between the logs of the house and exposed the helpless women to "intense cold." Thus bullied, the sisters agreed to sell to their tormentor.

Grover Kennon offered a mere thirteen dollars for land and improvements easily worth five hundred. Financially ignorant and too afraid of Kennon to resist, the women agreed to the terms. The deed transferred into Kennon's name on February 28, 1914. The new owner then demanded that the sisters leave their home. The women were destitute. They had nowhere to go. Notwithstanding, Grover Kennon filed a legal complaint to have the women evicted from the premises.

Incensed at this outrage, some concerned person(s) secured legal counsel for the women. The attorney filed a "cross bill" petitioning the court to annul Kennon's deed. In the meantime, Grover's nineteen year old brother George L. Kennon threatened the women a number of times and twice drew "a lethal weapon" to frighten them.

The court ruled in favor of the women on September 14, 1914. The women's ownership of the land was restored upon the return of Kennon's thirteen dollars.[54] Oddly, Grover and George Kennon calmly accepted this defeat contrary to all past behaviors without any further record of violence or threats against these women. Why? What had changed?

Grover Kennon must have intensely resented the *meddler(s)* involvement. If Kennon grew wroth against the champion(s) of the poor women's cause, the timing of his rage would have coincided nicely with the arson/murder.

Be it remembered that near neighbor Grover Kennon was at the Hall Store the day of the murder as evidenced by his presence on the coroner's jury over the body of Victor Hall. The Kennons had opportunity. Since the Dunkums and Halls were most likely the ones who secured aid for the women, both motive and past behavior justified suspicion against the Kennons.

Opportunity! Motive! Pattern of behavior! Did the detectives know any of this? What if the "lethal weapon" brandished by young bully George Kennon was a *.38 Short Colt* revolver? In any event, the number of suspicious men identifiable from existing records establishes the fact that the 1914 investigations at Green Springs Depot were unjustifiably narrow.

WHO KILLED VICTOR HALL?

The burning of Dunkum's store and the shooting of Victor Hall occurred mysteriously on a dark and stormy night during an unusually heavy rain. Historical weather data for Louisa County does not exist prior to May 1916. However, 1914 climatology records do exist for Charlottesville, Gordonsville, and Columbia.[55] This information allows one to approximate weather for Louisa County situated within this triangle.

The inclusive dates January 1st to April 15th, 1914 contained seventeen days of measurable rainfall. Only five days had rains in excess of one half inch in a twenty-four hour period common to all three stations. Heavy rains bearing one inch or more in a twenty-four hour period occurred only on January 3rd and the evening of April 14/15th. Only the latter occurred at temperatures above freezing without risks of ice and snow.

The storm was reasonably predictable by rural folk. The day's prevailing wind recorded at Columbia was from the northeast, a common indication that an approaching storm bears significant rain.

Louisa County maintained two bloodhounds. The county jailor Deputy Sheriff J. C. Trice trained and kenneled these dogs.[56] Heavy rain is desirable to evade tracking dogs; heavy rain washes away scent.[57] Sheriff Wash stated specifically that the reason the tracking dogs were not used the day of the shooting was on account of the heavy rain.[58] Data shows the weather conditions were most favorable for a premeditated attack on midnight April 14th/15th. Investigators ignored this as a factor, but the arson/murder at Green Springs Depot occurred on a "dark and stormy night" by design.

A person or persons who hunted regularly would, naturally, consider scent and weather factors in planning such an assault. There were many such individuals among the subsistence farmers in the depot area who supplemented their diets with wild game. In addition to a hunter's stealth, the number of mysterious fires was also characteristic behavior of the social strata living near the depot. A resident of the Green Springs Depot with a grudge against Buck Dunkum would have been expected to set fires. "Barn burning" was a common expression of frustrated, "poor whites."[59]

The author submits that there was a man in Green Springs who disliked Buck Dunkum. Dislike grew into hatred. Hatred inspired action to burn out Dunkum. The man torched Dunkum's broom factory. A week later, he burned Dunkum's home to the ground while the family was at church. This failed to drive Dunkum away. Instead, the fires inflicted blessing rather than injury. Buck rebuilt his house on its foundation, and then built his own store near the site of the broom factory.

Hatred grew into rage. Dunkum's enemy formulated a more sinister plot to frame Dunkum for murder. He must have also disliked the Halls to include them as collateral targets. The man planned his attack and waited for a dark and stormy night. The northeaster on April 14th provided ample cloud cover to avoid being seen by moonlight and sufficient rain to wash away his scent.

The man fired Dunkum's store. He then either went back home to wait or concealed himself across the tracks in the outbuildings at Hall's store. Either course was easy. Victor and Lizzie had several cats to control vermin, but no dog. The man knew that there would be no barking to alarm folks. He may have hidden to watch the excitement. Nicholas Hall checked the barn for fire. If the culprit hid there, he easily went undetected, for Hall sought only glowing embers, not people.

The man later knocked at the front door of the Hall store until Victor Hall responded. Predictably, Hall entered lamp in hand from his bedroom at the back of the store, made his way to the front and stopped to place the lamp on the counter. Hall unlocked the door and opened it.

It was four o'clock in the morning. Victor was surprised to see someone other than his father. Some words were spoken. The man had a pistol. His intent was clear. In order to save himself, Victor bolted for the bedroom to get his own gun. The man followed after him. Victor was ill and lacked his usual agility. The man grabbed a handful of Victor's nightshirt and reined him back. Jolted by his sudden capture Victor screamed, "Oh, Lord! Have Mercy!" all the while straining desperately for the door knob just inches beyond his grasp.

Upon seizing his victim, the man raised his pistol in line with Victor's head and pulled the trigger. Bang! The range was not point blank, but so close to as to be sure of the mark and no need for multiple shots. Victor collapsed instantly falling in the direction pulled by his captor. Victor's cheek struck the counter or the floor as he "crumpled up" *with his head away from the bedroom door!* The man ran out of the store, across the porch, and into the night confident that he had killed Victor Hall.

Thus, a profile emerges. Mrs. Hall's intuition was correct; Victor knew who shot him. The man was a native of Green Springs Depot, and likely, lived close enough to strike on foot. The killer hated Buck Dunkum. He resented the Hall's and all their *high and mighty* ways. Typical of rural barn burners, he was a poor, angry, white man, no church goer, probably a drinker and, perhaps, a bootlegger. Agility suggests the assailant was relatively young.

The killer used a .38 Short Colt revolver. He was too young to be the original owner of that pistol and ammunition. The obsolete model may have been purchased by a relative or neighbor decades before; but by 1914, this was a gun a poor man could afford and few others would want.

The man was ruthless, but may not have been totally depraved if, upon seeing his "frame-up" go awry and Dunkum back in business, he set the depot fire to strike Dunkum again and then threw fire into the remotest part of Mrs. Hall's house to draw suspicion away from the widow. Yet, that too was miscalculated.

Predictably, the murderer allowed the widow to go to prison rather than deliver himself to a death sentence. Whether or not he would have kept silent and allowed Mrs. Hall to die in the electric chair, had the jury so decided, will forever be for speculation. Other than these generalizations at this writing, Victor Hall's killer remains a man known only to God.

A VICTIM OF CIRCUMSTANCES

1914 was a momentous year. The Great War started and changed the world forever. Sir Arthur Conan Doyle intended his last Sherlock Holmes story. Albert Einstein began publishing his theories on general relativity explaining that dimensions of time and space vary with one's frame of reference.

Indeed, perceptions of Mrs. Hall varied relative to an observer's position. Green Springs Depot served as a portal between natives and the outside world. Those on the inside looking out had different frames of reference from those outside looking in. Mrs. Hall lived at this center, an object in every line of sight and scrutinized from many angles. Insiders considered her an outsider and *vise versa*.

The flood of detectives was an unusual intrusion of authority that was both exciting and threatening. Natives of Green Springs Depot were clannish, a law unto themselves and justifiably suspicious of outsiders. After all, outsiders had no vested interest in the neighborhood unless pursuing some self-serving social, economic, or political goal just as business opportunities first drew the Boston, Blake, Yancey, and Dunkum families to the community.

Elizabeth Ann Hall was from outside Louisa County. She was, nevertheless, a product of rural Virginia, a woman of simple speech and country ways. She was a wife, a mother, a helpmate, a sister, and a friend. She was a neighbor, a Christian, a church member, a charity worker, twice widowed and in mourning.

However, Mrs. Hall was also a woman living beyond accepted norms. In 1914, few of the *fairer sex* were independent, financially secure, owned property, and managed a business. She was also the wife of a man young enough to have been her son. To some she was permanently branded a

MURDER AT GREEN SPRINGS

come here, a *cradle robber*, and worst of all, she lived in *that store* at Green Springs Depot.

Extraordinary situations grabbed attentions. Excitement advanced monstrous notions. The detectives agreed on Mrs. Hall. They got *their man* and rode away on their iron horse like so many paladins taking with them the black cloud of lethal vulnerability their dreaded accusation brought. A number of innocent men sighed relief and accepted their deliverance without any overt admission that if any one person must be wrongfully convicted, it was best Mrs. Hall.

The Hall Case was a synergy of complex circumstances, convoluted relationships, local sociology and corporate mindsets: each an identifiable, yet enigmatic component. Some aspects of the case were universal while others were unique to time and place. Since 1914, legal processes evolved to provide witness and evidence discoveries as well as pretrial depositions eliminating many of the legal snares which trapped Mrs. Hall. Currently, forensic science and professional certifications enable detection and verity beyond anything imaginable at the time. Most regrettably, the capricious factors of public sentiment, political climate, and media bias endure.

The principal and ancilliary personalities were very human with hearts and brains of various sizes and bents. Collective behaviors were carnal, mob mentality. Individuals, no doubt, acted upon what seemed to them good ideas at the time, but no one boasted afterwards of having had a role in the Hall Case. That generation never wanted the matter revisited and allowed time to pave over the memory, much like the state paved over the depot site. Nevertheless, the story bursts forth nearly a century later to fulfill a prediction:

"The Hall mystery was the most sensational case ever heard in Louisa County and will be regarded as one of the most famous criminal cases in Virginia."

The Virginian Pilot - Norfolk Landmark

Front Page - August 9, 1914

END NOTES

END NOTES FOR CHAPTER ONE – SOMEONE SHOT VICTOR!

[1] In court testimony, Nicholas Hall described the night of son Victor's murder as "a dark and stormy night." *The News Leader,* July 29, 1914, p. 5.

[2] *Hall Trial Transcript,* p. 1093.

The Code of Virginia § 17.1-213 allows disposal of criminal court records after twenty years at the discretion of the local clerk of court. However, the statute specifies permanent retention of all criminal cases involving felony convictions after January 1, 1913 deemed by the local clerk of court to have historical, genealogical or sensational value. Nevertheless, the 1,300 page Hall trial transcript was discarded even though subject record met all three retention criteria.

It is unclear exactly when the transcript was thrown away. Phillip Pendleton Porter was the local clerk of court during the Hall trial. Twenty years after the Hall trial, P. P. Porter was still the local clerk of court and served until 1935.

A. G. "Sambo" Johnson stated that he received part of the transcript from his aunt Grace Sherwood. She received it from her brother William T. Johnson who saw the document discarded and rescued a portion because of his family's close association with the event. History owes the Johnson family a debt of gratitude for preserving day eight of the trial. Author

[3] Accounts overlooked husband Eddie Harris. Harris, a carpenter, was either already there among the neighbors or home sick. Author

[4] Train schedule information for Green Springs Depot was determined from a copy of the 1914 Richmond - Gordonsville timetable courtesy of the Chesapeake and Ohio Historical Society.

[5] *Hall Trial Transcript,* p. 1011.

[6] *The News Leader,* July 31, 1914, p. 11.

[7] The 1914 telephone directory listed 106 telephone numbers for all of Louisa County. Telephone numbers within the town of Louisa were

two digits. Other areas of the county had four digits with the first two designating the locality. Dr. Porter's phone number was 32. The number for Green Springs Depot [The Hall Store] was 2313. Pattie Cooke, 1914 *Louisa County Telephone Directory,* "Walking Tour of Louisa County," *Louisa County Historical Society Magazine (Hence: LCHSM),* Fall 1998, Vol. 29, No. 2, p. 93.

There were so few phones that people generally cranked for the operator and asked for the desired party. Author

[8]   *Hall Trial Transcript,* p. 999.

[9]   *The News Leader,* July, 30, 1914, p. 2.

[10]   Slumber Robe: a contemporary, regional name for an afghan comprised of knitted or crocheted squares sewn together. Author

[11]   *The Times Dispatch,* July 31, 1914, p. 9.

[12]   *The Central Virginian,* April 29, 1993, p. 8.

[13]   Dr. Phillip Pendleton May was a pillar of the Green Springs Depot community. He served as local physician for many years. May was a founding member of the Forest Hills Union Church. He served Louisa County as Treasurer and as Chairman of the Board of Supervisors. *Louisa County Law Order Book 1904-1911,* p. 603. Crandall A. Shifflet, *Patronage and Poverty in the Tobacco South, Louisa County, Virginia 1860 – 1900* (Knoxville, TN: 1982), p. 80.

For photographs of Dr. P. P. May, see Pattie Gordon Pavlansky Cooke, Louisa and Louisa County (Dover, NH: 1997), pp. 22, 127.

[14]   Jimmy Johnson later recalled the situation as "the most frightening night of his life." The Central Virginian, April 29, 1993, p. 8.

[15]   *The Times Dispatch,* August 2, 1914, p. 7.

[16]   *The News Leader,* July 29, 1914, p. 5.

[17]   Census record shows son-in-law Charles Danne [III] resided with Dr. P. P. May. Danne's father, also Charles, owned Danne's store in 1914. Same had ridden with Mosby's Rangers in the Civil War and appears on the roster of Co. F, 43rd Battalion Virginia Cavalry as Charles Danne, Jr. Author

[18]   A. G. "Sambo" Johnson recalled his father Jimmy Johnson saying that he "rode to Melton's" to get a doctor. However, in 1914, Melton's Store had neither telephone nor telegraph and the closest known practicing physicians were in Gordonsville and Louisa.

The well known Green Springs physician Dr. Philip P. May lived in the direction of Melton's Store and had a telephone. The 1910 Census lists son-in-law Charles Danne [III] living with Dr. May. Danne was a railroad locomotive engineer and son of local store owner Charles Danne, Jr.

Jimmy Johnson likely rode to Dr. May's house for help. Charles Danne [III] then telephoned the Louisa operator who, in turn, facilitated contact with Dr. Taylor. This peripheral involvement explains why Charles Danne [III] was later summoned as a witness at the Hall trial but never called to testify. The scenario also accounts for Dr. Taylor being the first physician on the scene.

Though not listed in the telephone directory at the time, Dr. Taylor may have recently acquired a telephone. Although the 1915 directory was unlocatable, Dr. Taylor's name and number appeared in the 1916 telephone directory. Author

[19]   Charles Chisholm's father, also named Charles, pastored the Mount Olive Church. The black congregation built their church on a small parcel donated by John T. Boston in the 1880's. Boston's estate eventually sold the large parent plantation which was subdivided by 1914 between Mrs. Hall and Buck Dunkum. Mount Olive Church bordered Dunkum's property.

Charles Chisholm [Jr.] began working as hired hand for Mrs. Hall and her first husband about 1910. By summer 1914 he worked for Buck Dunkum. A. G. "Sambo" Johnson remembered Charles Chisholm working as butler for Henry R. Pollard, Jr. at Valentine's Mill in the 1930's. Author

[20] General interest in the *Titanic* extended to Louisa County as evidenced by the special lecture presented by Rev. C. W. Leftwich of the Louisa Methodist Church [1909-1912] held in the Fall of 1912. *The Central Virginian*, November 7, 1912, p. 1.

END NOTES   *385*

[21] Particulars on Bill Robert's injuries appeared only in one article and presented here in the order stated. *The News Leader*, May 22, 1914, p. 13.

The author questions the sequence of Robert's injuries. Though possibly the results of farm accidents, these particular injuries were consistent with those particularly common to railway brakemen. The author supposes that Bill Roberts first lost the fingers on his right hand in a railcar coupling mishap, and then later lost his left arm in similar manner. The latter injury then prevented his return to railroad work and resulted in difficulty supporting his family.

Railroad employment was common to the area and within families. Bill's brother Walton Roberts worked for the Chesapeake and Ohio Railway. Newspapers reported at least one of Bill's accidents occurred in Pennsylvania. The tabloid spirit that huckstered unfounded rumors about Mrs. Hall further justifies skepticism in the stated order of injuries. Author

[22] *Patty W. Roberts vs. W. J. Roberts*. Divorce filed January 8, 1912 on grounds of desertion for three years. *Louisa County Chancery Book*, Vol. 11, p. 229.

[23] Pattie Roberts, nee Wale, contracted tuberculosis and died February 14, 1913. Born March 18, 1878, she was the daughter of H. J. Wale and Sallie A. Bibb. Her death certificate lists her marital status as divorced. The document was signed by Dr. P. P. May. Deaths, Louisa County, File No. 3906, Virginia Bureau of Vital Statistics.

[24] William J. Roberts was the son of Richard and Louise Roberts of Green Springs and the oldest of five children. "Bill" married and moved from home before 1900. That year the Roberts family consisted of Robert [62], Louise C. [54], Lizzie E. [26], Lennie C. [24], Walton [15], and Edward L. [13]. *1900 United States Census*.

[25] For photographs of Dr. Harry Wilson Porter, see Cooke, *Louisa and Louisa County*, pp. 75, 93. For photograph of Dr. Porter in his automobile, see *The News Leader*, May 22, 1914, p. 13.

[26] For photograph of N. W. and Ellen Hall, see *The News Leader*, July 31, 1914, p. 11.

END NOTES FOR CHAPTER TWO – FAMILY MATTERS

[1]   For photographs of Charles Ellis Hester and America Gooch Hester, see Cooke, *Louisa and Louisa County*, pp. 82, 106.
America Gooch Hester was known to friends as "Emma." Author

[2]   The Dunkum and Hall families belonged to Lasley Methodist Church. Rev. C. T. Thrift preached the Louisa circuit of the Methodist Episcopal Church South from 1913 to 1916. Author

[3]   On April 13, 1914 in Culpeper, Virginia, the gas stove in Bell's Bakery exploded setting fire to that establishment. The flames spread rapidly and grew into a major conflagration. The Culpeper Harness Co., the Yancey Building, the Eclipse Theater, and the Goodyear Co. were destroyed. The New Theater, a garage, and the Masonic Temple were badly damaged. Nineteen year old Carter Parr was killed by a falling wall. Twenty year old Robert Rosson was taken to the hospital in Charlottesville for treatment and assumed fatally burned. Louis L. Whitestone was seriously burned. Jersey Hansbraugh was injured and hospitalized in Washington, D.C. *The Daily Progress*, April 16, 1914, p. 5.

[4]   *The Richmond Virginian*, April 16, 1914, p. 2.

[5]   Grover Kennon appears in court documents as Grover N. and Grover C. Kennon. He could not write and made his mark on documents where indicated. Author

[6]   The same Charles B. Vest rode with Mosby's Rangers during the Civil War: Co. C, 43rd Battalion Virginia Cavalry. Author

[7]   For photograph of Fritz Wills and Charles B. Vest, see Cooke, *Louisa and Louisa County*, p. 47.

[8]   "Coroner's Report Over Body of Victor Hall," Louisa County Circuit Court Judgments, November Term 1914.

[9]   Ibid.

[10]   Ibid.

[11]   Ibid.

¹² According to Frances Atkins, her grandfather Ollie Wood owned and operated the general merchandise store and post office at Poindexter. This was later purchased by Morris J. Maddox. Thence known as Maddox's Store, the local landmark still stands on the west corner of the intersection of Rt. 613 and Rt. 640. Author

A current photograph of Maddox's Store appears in "Green Springs," brochure, U. S. National Park Service, Department of the Interior.

¹³ Rural Virginia folk commonly buried people on the day following death. The custom changed with the growing acceptance of embalming. For Louisa County deaths in April 1914, two of every three burials were on the day following death [a 2:1 ratio]. A. B. Woodward, employed by the Hall family, was one of at least four undertakers serving families of Green Springs Depot. Woodward handled ten burials that April: nine buried the day after death and one on the second day afterwards.

Contrasting burials for the same month in the City of Richmond where embalming practices were better established, the ratio of burials one day or less after death to those exceeding one day was 62:99 [a 2:3 ratio]. Sixteen occurred on the third day and at least three burials took place as late as the fourth day following death. Virginia Bureau of Vital Statistics, microfilmed death certificates at The Library of Virginia.

¹⁴ *The News Leader*, April 15, 1914, p. 1.

¹⁵ A. B. Woodwards Funeral Home was located on Main Street. For photograph of A. B. Woodward's storefront, see Cooke, *Louisa and Louisa County*, p. 84.

¹⁶ William Owens documents the local gossip at the depot on the evening of April 15 as the origin of suspicions against Mrs. Hall. "This theory was debated and discussed several days and finally developed into a well defined rumor that Mrs. Hall was the perpetrator of the crimes." *The News Leader*, May 15, 1914, p. 2.

¹⁷ 1914 fell within transitional years for American funerary customs. Final preparation of the body traditionally performed by family members became increasingly the task of professional undertakers.

Regardless of who actually prepared Victor Hall's body, investigators assumed sinister intent on the part of Mrs. Hall. For this reason, A. B. Woodward later appeared before the special grand jury and was summoned as a witness at the Hall trial. Author

[18] *The Central Virginian* was founded by owner and managing editor George McDuffie Blake. The same managed the "Hall" store in the 1890's.

[19] Description of the depot is based on a photograph in *The Richmond Virginian*, May 14, 1914, p. 1.

[20] Excerpt from Hymn No. 242 for the burial of the dead taken from Essie Dunkum's personal copy of *The Hymnal: Revised and Enlarged* (New York: 1893), p. 223.

END NOTES FOR CHAPTER THREE – DETECTIVES PUT ON THE CASE

[1] Luther Scherer was formerly employed by the Baldwin Detective Agency and supervised their Richmond office. Ronald W. Hall, *The Carroll County Courthouse Tragedy: A True Story of the 1912 Gun Battle That Shocked the Nation: Its Causes and Aftermath* (Lynchburg, VA: 1998), p. 227.

The Chesapeake and Ohio Railway contracted their security with the Baldwin Detective Agency until 1907. The C & O then established its own department of Special Agents, and Scherer resigned his position with the Baldwin Detective Agency to become Chief Claims Agent for the C & O.

Originally named Baldwin's Railroad Detectives, the Baldwin Detective Agency became the Baldwin-Felts Detective Agency in 1910. John A. Velke, III, *The True Story of the Baldwin-Felts Detective Agency* (n.l.: 2004), pp. 5, 44, 156, 168.

[2] Angle's first name appears as both Myer and Meyer in historical records. Angle was first listed in Hill's Richmond City Directory as a detec-

tive in 1907, the same year in which the C & O Railway first hired their own Special Agents. Author

3   Starting in 1904, Virginia allowed railroad presidents and certain other executive officers to appoint detectives vested with full police authority upon approbation of circuit court of any county or corporation court of any city. H. S. Dewhurst, *The Railroad Police* (Springfield, IL: 1955), p. 19.

4   *The Daily Progress*, September 18, 1913, p. 1.

5   Harrison was a member of the Order of Railway Telegraphers, Junior Order United American Mechanics, and Scottsville Masonic Lodge No. 45 A.F. & A.M. People clamored for an arrest. *The News Leader*, August 25, 1913, p. 5.

6   The 1913 trial of Leo M. Frank for the murder of Mary Phagan was a contemporary sensation through 1915. For details, similarities to and influences on the Hall Case, see note 48, chapter 13.

7   *The Daily Progress*, September 19, 1913, p. 2.
     Jackson claimed that "local authorities" had given him the gun. He likely received the pistol from officials when the town hired him as their detective. Author

8   Special Agent "Monte" Angle escorted Jackson to Scottsville for a preliminary hearing before Mayor Jackson Beal, Commonwealth's Attorney R. T. W. Duke, Jr., and Magistrate Frank M. Dawson. *The News Leader*, September 19, 1913, p. 2.

9   Climatology records confirm 0.16 inches of rainfall at Columbia on the morning of August 24, 1913. Virginia State Climatology Office.

10   *The News Leader*, September 19, 1913, p. 2.

11   *Albermarle County Law Order Book No. 37, Jan. 1912 to Jan. 1915*, p. 275.

12   Ibid., p. 304.

13   The judge ordered Mrs. J. D. Staples summoned on the 4th day of February, 1914 and to show cause why she should not be fined. Other

witnesses for the Commonwealth M. Sutherland, Dr. R. L. Stinsen [sic], E L. Manberry, D. L. Manberry, Bill Harris, Ed Harris, and Lou Mack were recognized in the sum of $25 to appear on that same date as were the two witnesses for the defense Miss Bell C. Shaw and Herbert Faulconer. In addition, the witnesses for the defense were ordered not to leave the area. Ibid.

[14] The jury included W. B. Bibb, W. B. Carr, Eugene Cox, Oscar C. Deane, Geo. D. Crickenberger, H. D. Dunn, Wm. Flowers, James Garland, L. E. Pritchett, D. E. Waddell, H. G. White, and Thomas E. White. Ibid., p. 323.

[15] Death certificate for Richard Wheat Harrison states that he was last seen alive at 6 P.M. August 23, 1913. He was born February 9, 1988 to Cassius A. Harrison and Bettie Harrison, nee Butler. Information was supplied by Charles B. Harris, Jr. Date of death was August 24, 1913. He was buried August 26, 1914. Report was filed by Dr. B. L. Dillard on August 29, 1913. File No. 18929 Albemarle County, Virginia Bureau of Vital Statistics.

[16] United States Census 1910, Enumeration District #11, Scottsville, Albermarle County, Virginia.

[17] *The News Leader*, August 25, 1913, p. 5.

Census records confirm the witness' name as "Herbert Faulconer." The newspaper misspelled last name as "Faulcover." Author

[18] *Albermarle County Law Order Book No. 37, Jan. 1912 to Jan. 1915*, p. 323.

[19] Between October 1913 and January 1914, Jailor C. M. Thomas accounted for ten prisoners held in the Albemarle county jail. L. L. Jackson was the only white man. Ibid., pp. 275-327.

[20] The killer of Richard Harrison has never been identified. Author

[21] *The News Leader*, April 15, 1914, p. 1.

[22] *The Richmond Virginian*, April 16, 1914, p. .

[23] *The Daily Progress*, April 16, 1914, p. 1.

END NOTES

24 $2 per day was the published rate at the Louisa Hotel on April 1, 1913. Pattie Gordon Pavlansky Cooke, *Louisa and Louisa County* (Dover, NH: 1997), p. 58.

25 *The Hall Trial Transcript*, p. 1083.

26 Description of Scott was based on snapshot published in *The News Leader*, May 15, 1914.

27 Case No. 188 involving the burning of store and contents of W. R. Dunkum was cited in *Ninth Report of the Commissioner of Insurance of Virginia For the Fiscal Year Ending April 30, 1915 Covering Business of 1914 Fire, Marine, Life, and Miscellaneous Companies and Fraternal Associations*, Richmond: David Bottom, Superintendent Public Printing, 1915, p. 14.

28 This description of Angle was based on the published photograph in *The News Leader*, July 29, 1914, p. 5. Note also the description of contemporary Atlanta Police Detective John Black who was "Rarely seen without a porkpie hat he wore pushed far back on his head, he more closely resembled a railroad dick that a celebrated detective, . . ." Steve Oney, *And The Dead Shall Rise: The Murder of Mary Phagan and the Lynching of Leo Frank* (New York: 2003), p. 24.

29 *The News Leader*, August 1, 1914, p. 2.

30 Dialogue between Mrs. Hall, Essie Dunkum, and Sheriff Wash is verbatim per actual handwritten notes: likely George Trainham's. Punctuation edited by author. Penciled notebook sheets, "Elizabeth A. Hall," Louisa County Circuit Court Judgments, November Term 1914.

31 The little structure is currently maintained by the Louisa County Historical Society and known today as the "Crank" building. Author

32 *The Richmond Times*, October 3, 1902, p. 1.

33 Ibid.

34 Death certificate for Pattie W. Roberts, age 34. Died February 14, 1913 of tuberculosis. Daughter of H. J. Wale and Sallie A. Bibb. Dr. P. P. May, attending physician. File No. 3906, Louisa County, Virginia Bureau of Vital Statistics.

[35] W. J. Roberts Against R. L. Gordon, Jr., *Louisa Law Order Book 1912-1916*, p. 167.

[36] Lindsay Gordon described Victor Hall's pistol as "a .38 caliber Smith & Wesson pearl handle pistol, which was loaded in four cylinders with the remaining cylinder containing an empty shell, the plunger resting upon the empty shell, this pistol is known as a Smith & Wesson squeezer and is hammerless, that it is fired by pressure of the hand on the squeezer which is on the top of the pistol while pulling the trigger, . . ." Bill of Exception #4, "Elizabeth A. Hall," Louisa County Circuit Court Judgments, November Term 1914.

[37] The milepost between the depot and school is currently milepost number 155 on the track of the CSX Piedmont Subdivision. The mileposts in 1914 were unpainted, brown concrete posts about six feet tall and ten inches square capped by a four inch pyramid. The mileposts still appeared thus when first examined in 2001; however, by 2003 the mileposts were painted white with black numerals.

There was both a milepost and a whistle stop along the tracks between Green Springs and Forest Hills School. Lindsay Gordon stated that Miss Wood "fired this pistol once at a whistle post missing the post . . ." Bill of Exception #4, "Elizabeth A. Hall," Louisa County Circuit Court Judgments, November Term 1914.

Lindsay Gordon's statement contradicts a surviving notion of some that Miss Wood hit the target at which she fired. Author's range work reinforces the great unlikelihood of anyone striking such a target at fifty feet with an untried pocket revolver. If Miss Wood fired from the road, the actual distance was much greater.

Whether or not the target was actually the whistle stop or milepost, all other references refer to the act as shooting at a milepost. Both milepost and whistle stop still exists at this writing. Author

[38] *The Times-Dispatch*, August 4, 1914, p. 1.

END NOTES

393

END NOTES FOR CHAPTER FOUR –
HER VERY OWN PINKERTON MAN

[1]   The Oakland Male Academy was established in the early 1880's by Rev. Isaac Newton May, brother of Dr. Phillip P. May. The boarding school became coeducational in the 1890's and changed its name to Oakland Academy. Rev. May died February 17, 1913. The school finished the current term, but never reopened. Attorney John G. May inherited the property.

In order to establish the date of Robert Trice's visit to her house on April 18th, Mrs. Hall testified that "the fire at Oakland" occurred on Friday night April 17th, 1914 and that Wash returned to the scene the next day. Hall Trial Transcript, p. 1114.

This fire is not to be confused with the devastating fire at Oakland almost exactly one year later. Author

On April 19, 1915, a spark from a locomotive started a fire near Trevilians. For days, wind swept the blaze along a ten mile path. The fire eventually destroyed the multi-building Oakland Academy save one stable. Porter C. Wright, "Oakland Academy," LCHSM, December 1970, Vol. 2, No. 2. p. 22.

Estimated total damage was $10,000. *The News Leader*, April 20, 1915, p. 13.

The destruction of the vacant school in Louisa attracted minimal attention beyond the county because a number of other large fires in the state occurred at the same time. A worse fire in Chesterfield County burned concurrently along 20 miles of the Southern Railway and destroyed 4,000 acres and did $20,000 in damage. *The Times-Dispatch*, April 20, 1915, p. 12.

Also at the same time, another large fire burned along yet another stretch of Southern Railway in Faber, Virginia. This fire swept across Appleberry and Butler mountains and destroyed a sawmill. *The Daily Progress*, April 23, 1915, p. 4.

2   *Hall Trial Transcript*, p. 1080.

3   *The News Leader*, August 6, 1914, p. 5.

4   The fifty mile trip was reasonable, but taxed the limit of a day's buggy ride. Author

5   At the time of the shooting, Essie and Mamie Dunkum attended Mr. Blackwell's school. Hall Trial Transcript, p. 996.

    Professor John F. Blackwell of Norfolk purchased *The Elms* in 1911 and opened an upscale private school in his basement. Chisholm, p. 186. The educator eventually became principal of Mineral High School. Free, "George McDuffie Blake," *LCHSM*, Spring 1996, Vol. 27, No. 1, p. 7.

    Prior to attending Blackwell's school, Essie and Mamie Dunkum were privately tutored at home. Author

    Iona May Cutler stated that she had, at one time, lived with the family and tutored the girls. Iona May Cutler, letter dated March 28, 1915, "Elizabeth A. Hall," Box 530, Secretary of the Commonwealth of Virginia Executive Papers, November 6, 1919.

6   *Hall Trial Transcript*, p. 1113.

7   *The Times-Dispatch*, August 5, 1914, p. 1.

8   *The Times-Dispatch*, August 4, 1914, p. 4.

9   Newspaper clipping from Mrs. Hall's personal effects. Assumed: *The Central Virginian*, April 23, 1914. Author's Collection.

10   *The Times-Dispatch*, August 1, 1914, p. 3.

11   *The Times-Dispatch*, August 1, 1914, p. 1.

12   *Louisa County Deed Book No. 32*, p. 581.

13   Elizabeth Ann Hall, undated letter, "Elizabeth A. Hall," Louisa County Circuit Court Judgments, November Term 1914.

14   *The Times-Dispatch*, August 1, 1914, p. 3.

END NOTES

END NOTES FOR CHAPTER FIVE – BUT I'M INNOCENT!

[1]   William Emmett Bibb served as Virginia state senator from 1885 to 1888. *The Central Virginian*, September 10, 1992, p. 17.

[2]   William E. Bibb won election as commonwealth's attorney November 5, 1907 when R. Lindsay Gordon declined to run for the office in order to pursue a Congressional seat. *Louisa County Law Order Book 1904-1911*, p. 295.

[3]   After serving his father's unexpired term of office, William C. Bibb won election as commonwealth's attorney November 7, 1911. Ibid., p. 608.

[4]   Per Wayne Dunn, his mother Jesse told him that the family stayed in the chicken house while their home was rebuilt after the 1913 fire. Jesse, Buck Dunkum's youngest at the time was then only a toddler. Records report the Dunkums moved in with the Hall family during the rebuilding. Whether or not they first lived in the chicken house before accepting the Hall's hospitality or ended up there due to resulting tensions is subject to speculation. Author

[5]   The detectives based their conclusion on the coroner's report which stated that the entrance wound was "one and a half inches above the bony promince [sic] at the back of the head." The ambiguous wording allowed misinterpretation.

Physicians on record later described the wound with the correct anatomical label: *bony protuberance*. The bullet's path traced from its entrance point one and a half inches above the bony protuberance to a point above the left eye socket was consistent with a person shot from behind.

Those unschooled in skeletal anatomy, likely placed the wound one and a half inches above a point at *the extreme back of the head* rather than the base of the skull: thus, the error defined a trajectory at least seventeen degrees higher than actually described. This mistake demanded alternate explanations that Victor Hall was either shot from above or while lying in bed. Author

6   *The Daily Progress*, August 6, 1914, p. 4.

7   For treatment of the popular disregard for legal system in Virginia at the time, see Fitzhugh W. Brundage, *Lynching in the New South: Georgia and Virginia, 1830-1930* (Urbanna, IL: 1993), pp. 140-160.

8   *Louisa County Law Order Book 1912-1916*, p. 317.

9   *The Daily Progress*, May 2, 1914, p. 3.

10   *The News Leader*, July 31, 1914, p. 11.

11   Mrs. V. K. Hall, undated letter, "Elizabeth A. Hall," Louisa County Circuit Court Judgments, November Term 1914.

12   Reenactments of Mrs. Hall's actions by the author demonstrated three minutes as a reasonable time. Elsie Wood testified before the coroner's jury that she came downstairs in "about half a minute after the shot." Wood's highly subjective "half a minute" was clearly too short of a time. On the other hand, ten minutes was far too long. The time factor was problematic. A jury would have difficulties with either extreme. Even if Elsie Wood restated the time reasonably, any revision conflicted with a previously sworn statement. Author

13   Charles K. Walton was Sheriff Andrew M. Wash's uncle. William Thomas Baker, *The Baker Family of England and of Central Virginia* ([s.l.]: Baker, c1974), pp. 223-224.

Walton was a Confederate veteran. He was conscripted late in the war, joined the Albemarle Light Artillery Regiment, served in Sturdivant's Battery, and surrendered at Appomattox. W. Cullen Sherwood and Richard L. Nichols, *Amherst Artillery, Albemarle Artillery and Sturdivant's Battery* (Lynchburg, VA: 1996), p. 226.

14   Tried separately, Albert Mitchell was convicted of first degree murder September 26, 1889 and sentenced to hang. William Talley was acquitted the following day. Codefendant Ann Eliza Jackson's trial ended in a hung jury September 29, 1879. Her case was scheduled to be retried next term, but no record of same was entered. After exhausting the appeals process, Albert Mitchell was hanged by the county sheriff [Thomas

END NOTES   *397*

McGehee] November 5, 1880. *Louisa County Law Order Book 1870 -
1880*, pp. 541 - 615.

[15] Regarding the death of R. Lindsay Gordon, Jr., "The poor of Louisa
County lost one of their best friends. Many, many times has he served
them without money and without price." *The Central Virginian*, August 1,
1940, pp. 1-2.

[16] Per newspaper report, R. Lindsay Gordon, Jr. received nomination for
the convention on March 8, 1901. Same newspaper noted that Louisa
entrepreneur George McDuffie Blake refused to enter his name in the
Democratic primary. *Richmond Dispatch*, March 8, 1901, p. 1.

Among other things, the Virginia Constitutional Convention
of 1901-1902 established the Virginia Corporation Commission
and the Virginia State Bureau of Insurance. However, characteristic to the time and place, the disenfranchisement of black voters was the achievement in which many delegates took particular
pride. Author

[17] For photograph of the Gates building, see Cooke, *Louisa and Louisa
County*, p. 70.

[18] John Gwathmey, *Legends of Virginia Courthouses* (Richmond, VA:
1934), p. 111.

[19] Ibid.

[20] *The News Leader*, May 11, 1914, p. 1.

[21] The grand jury consisted of and John K. Deane, foreman, mechanic;
Harry C. Morris, farmer; R. A. Hubbard, farmer; W. L. Bumpass, merchant; A. F. Estes, farmer; I. F. Nunn, farmer; and R. S. Hopkins, farmer.
The Daily Progress, May 12, 1914, p. 1, and *The Times-Dispatch*, May 14,
1914, p. 2.

[22] *The News Leader*, May 11, 1914, p. 11.

[23] *The News Leader*, May 14, 1914, p. 2.

[24] Ibid.

[25] Independent sources as late as 2003 told tales that the mysterious, late
night visitor at Dunkum's was Mrs. Hall dressed like a man. Even more

elaborate lore survives that Mrs. Hall allegedly disguised herself as a man to commit all the various and related arsons at Green Springs. Author

26   *The News Leader*, May 13, 1914, p. 11.

27   *The Times-Dispatch*, July 31, 1914, p. 1.

28   *The News Leader*, May 12, 1914, p. 2.

29   M. J. Maddox received brief mention only in *The News Leader*. He was listed as a witness summoned before the grand jury and to Mrs. Hall's trial as a witness for the prosecution. He testified before the grand jury on May 12th. *The News Leader*, May 6, 13, and July 29, 1914. There is no record that he testified at Mrs. Hall's trial.

At the time, Morris J. Maddox was a county merchant in business with his brother John R. Maddox. The brothers eventually had separate stores. M. J. Morris later bought Ollie Wood's store in Poindexter.

In a letter to Gov. Stuart, N. W. Hall referred to an unnamed man as the "chief meddler" who was never put on the witness stand at the trial. Hall wrote, "the Com. Atty. told me with his own lips that this man had done more talking than anybody else; . . . " Letter dated June 13, 1916, "Elizabeth A. Hall," Box 530, *Secretary of the Commonwealth of Virginia Executive Papers*, November 6, 1919.

Three merchants were called as witnesses to the Hall trial and never put on the witness stand: Morris J. Maddox, Lewis F. Yancey, and Lee Rosson. Of these, the most likely to have spoken most to the commonwealth's attorney was Lee Rosson, a county supervisor and father of Mamie Rosson. Author

30   *The News Leader*, May 12, 1914, p. 1.

31   *The Pen*, No. 193, 1915.

32   Jennie Hall, Hall Trial Transcript, p. 985.

33   *The News Leader*, May 14, 1914, p. 1.

34   *The News Leader*, May 16, 1914, p. 2.

The article names "Trent Drug Company." In 1914, there were two drug stores in Louisa: Kent's Drug Store and the Louisa Drug Co. Kent's Drug is assumed the correct intent. Author

[35]   The detective is not identified specifically in sources; however, the presumptive and imaginative motive attached to the camphor bottle by the unnamed Richmond operative suggests Myer S. Angle, Special Agent for the Chesapeake & Ohio Railway, the only detective know to have pursued leads in that city. Author

[36]   *The Times-Dispatch*, May 16, 1914, p. 2.

[37]   Miss Ruby Chewning was never summoned as a witness to Mrs. Hall's trial. After her appearance before the grand jury, Miss Chewning's testimony was no longer valued by the prosecution, thereby establishing its total irrelevance. Author

[38]   *The Times-Dispatch*, May 15, 1914, p. 10.

[39]   *The News Leader*, May 13, 1914, p. 11.

[40]   William G. Owens, the only known reporter on the scene that day, was the sole record of the sightings of the two strange men. *The News Leader*, May 14, p. 2.

[41]   *The News Leader*, May 15, 1914, p. 1.

[42]   *The Virginian Pilot-Norfolk Landmark*, August 5, 1914, p. 10.

[43]   *The Times-Dispatch*, August 1, 1914, p. 3.

[44]   *The Times-Dispatch*, May 15, 1914, p. 10.

[45]   The photograph of the pantry window taken the morning of the first pantry fire shows the pantry window without a screen and missing the left shutter. *The News Leader*, May 15, 1914, p. 1.

[46]   *The News Leader*, May 15, 1914, p. 2. Trainham is misidentified as "Mr. Trevillian" in the newspaper's report. Author.

[47]   *The Times-Dispatch*, May 15, 1914, p. 10.

[48]   Ibid.

[49]   Ibid.

[50]   *The Times-Dispatch*, May 15, 1914, p. 1.

[51]   Ibid.

END NOTES FOR CHAPTER SIX – EXILE AND CABAL

1   *The Times-Dispatch*, May 16, 1914, p. 2.

2   Bibb was, no doubt, sincere in his preference for the Richmond facility over the Louisa County jail, but he likely never viewed the conditions in Richmond first hand. In September 1911, Bibb used the Richmond city jail to temporarily hold Thorton "Punch" Barker convicted in Louisa of second degree murder and sentenced to five years in the state penitentiary. *Louisa County Law Order Book 1904-1911*, p. 602.

3   The Richmond city jail was a deplorable collection of run-down structures situated next to the city stables and city dump. Typical of southern cities, the jail population was mostly black men with few white men and even fewer women: two on average at any given time. Suzanne Lebsock, *A Murder In Virginia: Southern Justice On Trial* (New York: 2003), pp. 109, 112, and 372.

The "other things" Gordon referred to included filth, vermin, physical abuse, moral turpitude and disease. Even as poorly maintained as the Louisa County jail must have been, it was empty, easily monitored and far safer than a crowded urban facility.

For example, just two weeks later the Virginia State Penitentiary in Richmond was quarantined because of a smallpox outbreak. *The News Leader*, May 25, 1914, p. 1. Prior to that in March 1913, the Virginia State Penitentiary had 1,300 cases of measles. Ronald W. Hall, *The Carroll County Courthouse Tragedy: A True Account of the 1912 Gun Battle That Shocked the Nation; Its Causes and Aftermath* (Lynchburg, VA: 1998), p. 229.

4   Dr. Walton O. Smith was the dentist in Louisa. Smith [63] and his wife Maggie [49] were good friends of Mrs. Hall. Author

5   *The News Leader*, May 15, 1914, p. 1.

6   *The Times-Dispatch*, May 16, 1914, p. 1.

7   "Green Springs," National Park Service, U.S. Department of the Interior (Philadelphia, PA: n.d.).

[8] Crandall Avis Shifflet, "Shadowed Thresholds; Rural Poverty In Louisa County, Virginia, 1860 – 1900" (University of Virginia: 1975), p. 73.

[9] Fitzhugh W. Brundage, *Lynching in the New South: Georgia and Virginia 1830-1930* (Urbana, IL: 1993), p. 151.

[10] Virginia inventor Cyrus McCormick demonstrated the successful operation of his reaper at *Sylvania*. The grain harvester was of little interest to slave owners but received wide acceptance by wheat growers in the Midwest. Author

[11] *Harkwood* was styled as an Italian villa by architect Alexander Jackson Davis. Davis also designed the main buildings for Virginia Military Institute *Harkwood* was later the boyhood home of Virginia Lt. Governor J. Sergeant Reynolds. Emmie Ferguson Farrar and Emilee Hines, *Old Virginia Houses: the Heart of Virginia* ([n.p.] Hale publishing: 1974), p. 57.

[12] Ervin L. Jordan, Jr. *Black Confederates and Afro-Yankees In Civil War Virginia* (Charlottesville, VA: 1995), p. 261.

[13] *The Dispatch*, April 18, 1893, p. 6.

E. O. Nolting emigrated to Richmond from Prussia and went to work for his uncle A. W. Nolting, an established tobacco exporter. After 1850, E. O. Nolting started his own business and eventually became head of Nolting & Kohler tobacco merchants and a very wealthy man. In his long career E. O. Nolting also served as President of the Bank of the Commonwealth, the National Bank of Virginia, and the Tobacco Exchange He was head of the Board of Trade and the Chamber of Commerce. In 1852 he was appointed Belgian Consul and officiated in this office until his death in 1893. He served as director for a number of companies including, the Virginia Steamboat Company, the Mutual Assurance Society of Virginia, Marshall Mills Cotton Manufacturing, and last, but not least, director of the Virginia Fire and Marine Insurance Company.

[14] In 1914, Carl H. Nolting was a member of the Louisa County Board of Review of Land Assessments. He served on the Virginia Agricultural

Commission of Safety from 1917 to 1919. In 1925, he received appointment to the Virginia Commission of Fisheries. From 1928 to 1933, he was chairman of the Louisa County Democratic Committee. In 1933, he became Virginia Commissioner of Game and Inland Fisheries. In 1953 he was Chairman of the Louisa County Board of Supervisors. He died at Bracketts April 9, 1958.

[15] *The Times-Dispatch*, May 17, 1914, p. 2.

[16] *The News Leader*, May 22, 1914, p. 13.

[17] The distinction between the two Green Springs is as evident at this writing as in 1914. The area referred to by newspapers as "the Green Spring [sic] valley section" was designated as the *Green Springs Historic Landmark District* in 1973 by the United States Department of the Interior and is currently administered cooperatively by the National Park Service. The brochure "Green Springs," published by the National Park Service lists thirty-nine significant historic plantations, homes and features.

The northernmost boundary of the *Green Springs Historic Landmark District* terminates just one and one half miles from the site of Green Springs Depot. This officially separates the two localities contained within Louisa County's Green Springs District. "Green Springs," National Park Service, U.S. Department of the Interior.

[18] The clarification was too little and too late to affect the general public. Stigma from the Hall case linked itself to the name "Green Springs" so much that many residents chose rather to associate themselves with "Trevilians" instead as evidenced by changes in the next local directory. Doris Perkins Meredith, "1915 Louisa County Directory," *LCHSM*, Vol. 31, No. 1, pp. 8-28.

[19] "Yet, even a minimal control over county offices would have made little difference for political power has never been exercised in disregard of those with economic power. There is no evidence that Louisa County was any different, while much evidence exists that political decisions were made which supported their exalted economic position." Shiflett, p. 105.

END NOTES

[20] The extent of influence exerted by the economically powerful residents of Green Springs in the Hall Case is subject to conjecture. Their peripheral involvement appears primarily directed at defending neighborhood prestige. Under the circumstances, it is difficult to imagine their efforts limited only to the reporter's entertainment that one particular afternoon.

There is no known record documenting whether or not Carl H. Nolting ever discussed the events at Green Springs Depot with members of the Louisa County Board of Supervisors or Commonwealth's Attorney Bibb. Carl Nolting was socially and politically positioned to freely converse with any of them, especially "Willie" Bibb.

Nolting and Bibb shared University of Virginia backgrounds, both men were active Masons and members of St. James Episcopal Church in Louisa where both served as vestrymen. Both served at times as directors of the Bank of Louisa, and both men were prominent in local Democratic Party activities.

Whatever concerns Nolting had about the Hall Case, it is highly probable that he communicated them with some or all of the board. This said, County Supervisor Lee Rosson, also being in a position to interact with Nolting, surfaces as a wildcard in the drama since he fits the description of N. W. Hall's "chief meddler" [Chapter 5, Note 28.]. This raises the possibility that the reactions of the Green Springs residents might have been incited by Rosson, which, if true, presents Rosson as "chief meddler" indeed.

Coincidence suggests that the fires at Green Springs Depot indirectly impacted the Nolting family financially. Carl's brother Frederick E. Nolting, President of Frederick E. Nolting & Company investment brokers was a wealthy and politically minded individual in the family tradition. Though Frederick E. Nolting does not appear to have held public office, his influence certainly paved the way for son Frederick E. "Fritz" Nolting, Jr. to eventually become U.S. Ambassador to Viet Nam under President John F. Kennedy.

Carl Nolting likely held interest in The Virginia Fire and Marine Insurance Company since his father was once a director and his brother Frederick Nolting was a director in 1914. The Virginia Fire and Marine Insurance Company was underwriter for William R. "Buck" Dunkum's property. What roll, if any, this relationship played in the story remains undetermined. The actual sums of money involved were pittances to the Noltings, but the business connection to Dunkum and Green Springs Depot, however convoluted and incidental, existed nevertheless. Author

[21] Report dated May 15, 1914, *The Times-Dispatch*, May 16, 1914, p. 1.

[22] Edward Grimsley was the son of the late Judge Daniel Grimsley. Judge George Shackelford was appointed to the bench to fill the unexpired term of Judge Daniel Grimsley. Author

[23] *The Times-Dispatch*, May 17, 1914, p. 2.

[24] *The Central Virginian*, April 29, 1993, p. 9.

[25] *The Richmond Virginian*, May 17, 1914, p. 1.

[26] *The Daily Progress*, May 25, 1914, p. 2.

[27] *Louisa County Supervisors Journal*, Book 4, pp. 98-99.

[28] *The Daily Progress*, August 7, 1914, p. 2.

[29] Ronald W. Hall, *The Carroll County Courthouse Tragedy: A True Account of the 1912 Gun Battle That Shocked the Nation; Its Causes and Aftermath* (Lynchburg, VA: 1998), p. 225.

[30] *Louisa County Supervisors Journal*, Book 4, p. 102.

[31] *The Central Virginian*, November 7, 1912, p. 1.

[32] The Louisa County Board of Supervisors appropriated $550.00 to hire M. J. Fulton for about a month. In perspective, William C. Bibb's salary as commonwealth's attorney was $175.00 per quarter. *Louisa County Law Order Book 1912 – 1916*, p. 387.

The considerable sum spent by a poor county to secure prime talent to prosecute Mrs. Hall was further evidence of cabal. Author

[33] Judge George S. Shackelford, letter, July 5, 1914, "Elizabeth A. Hall," Louisa County Circuit Court Judgments, November Term 1914.

[34] *Sulphur Mines Co. vs Thompson Heirs, 93 Va. 293, June 25, 1896.* Carter secured retrial in the appeal argued in Richmond and decided in Wytheville.

[35] John H. Gwathmey, *Legends of Virginia Lawyers* (Richmond, VA: 1934), pp. 81-82.

[36] The coroner's jury examined Victor Hall's pistol less than eight hours after the shooting. Others at the scene examined the pistol earlier. All declared that the pistol had not been fired recently.

Personally conducted tests using a .38 caliber Smith & Wesson Safety Hammerless (S/N 258033) confirm the fact that had Victor Hall's pistol been recently fired, residual odor would have been discernable ten hours after firing Tests demonstrated detection reasonable even after twenty-four hours.

Each test consisted of one round fired from a clean pistol under controlled conditions approximating the environment of the Hall store on the morning in question. After firing, the pistol was placed in a bureau drawer for fifteen minutes, next pocketed in a cloth coat outdoors for one hour, and then placed on a wooden counter in a still room for the remainder of the test. The pistol was examined periodically with notation made at ten hours and twenty-four hours. Tests evaluated both black powder and smokeless powder cartridges with same results.

Test pistol was identical to Victor Hall's with immaterial exceptions The exact barrel length of Hall's pistol was undocumented. Barrel length of test pistol measured three a quarter inches Test pistol's finish was nickel plated rather than blued Black powder cartridges for test were special ordered to 1914 U.M.C. .38 S&W specifications. A sample cartridge was selected, disassembled and verified to contain 11 grains propellant by a calibrated, analytical balance and verified genuine black powder by negative methylene blue test for perchlorates. Smokeless powder cartridge was current Remington .38 S&W. Author

[37] The plea cited contravention to common law per Section 8 of the Declaration of Rights, Sections 3989 and 3990 of the Code of Virginia 1887, and rights violated under the Fourteenth Ammendment of the Constitution of the United States. Commonwealth vs. Elizabeth Ann Hall, Plea dated July 14, 1914, "Elizabeth A. Hall," Louisa County Circuit Court Judgments, November Term 1914.

[38] Bill Roberts testified to conducting residue detection testing on July 8th and 9th. These dates are exclusively per *The News Leader*, August 4, 1914, p. 10.

Sam Flannagan testified that he and Bill Roberts conducted the bullet penetration experiments at the direction of R. Lindsay Gordon, Jr. on July 17th, 1914. Bill of Exception #4, "Elizabeth A. Hall," Louisa County Circuit Court, November Term 1914.

END NOTES FOR CHAPTER SEVEN – VORTEX OF VISCERAL VIRTUE

[1] The Confederate monument was dedicated August 17, 1905. Judge Daniel A. Grimsley addressed the crowd. R. Lindsay Gordon, Jr. accepted the monument on behalf of the citizens of Louisa County. *The Central Virginian*, Online, June 16, 2005.

[2] *The News Leader*, July 28, 1914, p. 2.

[3] *The Daily Progress*, July 29, 1914, p. 5.

[4] Ibid.

[5] *Journal of the House of Delegates of Virginia: Session Which Commenced at the State Capitol Wednesday, January 14, 1914* (Richmond, VA: 1914), p. 419.

Under the old law, a first degree murder conviction automatically imposed a death sentence. Virginia changed its method of execution from hanging to electrocution in 1908.

The new law passed during Lindsay Gordon's first session as legislator gave juries the option of imposing either death by electrocution or life imprisonment for first degree murder. Because Victor Hall was killed between the time the new law was passed and the time it took effect July 1, 1914, the accused had the choice under which law to be tried. Author

[6] See Chapter 13, Note 48.

[7] *The Daily Progress*, July 29, 1914, p. 5.

[8] The prosecution used these measurements to draw unscaled floor plans of the Hall store. It was from the original data and sketches that the author produced his scale drawings. Hall Store Drawings, "Elizabeth A. Hall," Louisa County Circuit Court Judgments, November Term 1914.

[9] A. L. Woolfolk, David Swift, R. A. Crawford, and A. J. Pleasants were stricken from the list of sixteen impaneled jurors. The remaining twelve names comprising the regulation jury were W. J. Hiter, S. C. Woodson, Julian Jacobs, C. W. Isbell, M. E. Nuckolls, O. C. Kean, C. B. Winston, R. E. Riddell, W. C. Massie, C. V. Jackson, J. L. Proffit, and W. M. Bickley. *The Times-Dispatch*, July 30, 1914, p. 1.

[10] *The Times-Dispatch*, July 30, 1914, p. 1.

[11] Ibid., p. 3.

[12] Ibid.

[13] *The News Leader*, July 29, 1914, p. 5.

[14] *The Times-Dispatch*, July 30, 1914, p. 3.

[15] Ibid.

[16] Bill of Exception No. 4, "Elizabeth A. Hall," Louisa County Circuit Court Judgments, November Term 1914.

[17] *The Daily Progress*, July 30, 1914, p. 1.

[18] *The News Leader*, July 30, 1914, p. 2.

[19] *The Times-Dispatch*, July 31, 1914, p. 1.

[20] *The Times-Dispatch*, August, 8, 1914, p. 8.

[21] *The Times-Dispatch*, July 31, 1914, p. 1.

[22] *The News Leader*, July 30, 1914, p. 2.

[23] *The Times-Dispatch*, July 31, 1914, p. 9. Other newspapers covering the trial quoted Mamie Rosson thus: "Don't say anything that will give me away."

[24] *The News Leader*, July 31, 1914, p. 11.

[25] Dialogue, Ibid.

[26] Ibid.

[27] *The News Leader*, August 1, 1914, p. 11.

[28] *The Times-Dispatch*, August 1, 1914, p. 1.

[29] *The News Leader*, July 31, 1914, p. 11.

[30] Ibid.

[31] Author notes that referenced letter was not found among other extant papers exhibited at trial and preserved in a folder together. "Elizabeth A. Hall," Louisa County Circuit Court Judgments, November Term 1914.

[32] *The Daily Progress*, August 1, 1914, p. 4.

[33] *The News Leader*, August 1, 1914, p. 2.

[34] Ibid.

[35] Loose pages torn from a pocket spiral notebook consistent with Trainham's testimony are preserved at the Louisa courthouse. "Elizabeth A. Hall," Louisa County Circuit Court Judgments, November Term 1914.

[36] *The Times-Dispatch*, August 1, 1914, p. 1.

END NOTES FOR CHAPTER EIGHT – TRIAL BY FIRE

[1] The victory medals authorized by the Allies at the end of the First World War referred to the conflict as "The Great War for Civilization." The victory medal issued by the United States bore same inscription on

its reverse side. In addition, the Commonwealth of Virginia and the City of Richmond each issued their own victory medals to their veterans of "The Great War for Civilization." Author

[2] A large number of white families with property kept black children as live-in servants. The practice extended at least through the 1930's. Poor blacks sent children to live with white families in informal foster child type arrangements. The host family provided support and education in exchange for chores.

A. G. Johnson remembered that while growing up in the 1930's most white families he knew had a little black child. Interview, March 15, 2003.

Frances Atkins recalled a black boy living with her family in said capacity when she was little. Interview, June 28, 2004.

In Louisa County, about sixty percent of white families were poor as compared to ninety-nine percent of black families. "Within the client class, racial differences separated the poor from the desperate." "Whole families worked to make a living and perhaps in this way many black families were able to acquire enough to purchase small plots of land." Crandall A. Shifflett, *Patronage and Poverty in the Tobacco South, Louisa County, Virginia 1860-1900* (Knoxville, TN:1982), pp. 39, xv.

[3] *The Times-Dispatch*, August 2, 1914, p. 1.

[4] *The News Leader*, August 1, 1914, p. 1. Dialogue appears as published. Other newspapers retained vernacular speech when quoting Becky Coates and others. The author chose to use each quote as published respective to source.

[5] Ibid., p. 2.

[6] *The Times-Dispatch*, August 2, 1914, p. 7.

[7] Ibid.

[8] *The News Leader*, August 1, 1914, p. 2.

[9] Ibid.

[10] Mrs. S. B. Henson (Elsie Wood), Letter to Governor Westmoreland Davis dated July 17, 1918. "Elizabeth Ann Hall," Box 530, *Secretary of the Commonwealth Executive Papers*, November 6, 1919.

[11] Photograph of Johnny Graves. The News Leader, July 31, 1914, p. 11.

The snapshot of a young boy captioned "C. H. Gates" was most likely that of ten year old Johnny Graves. The only C. H. Gates in Louisa County at the time was a middle aged real estate agent who lived at Trevilians. Author

[12] *The Times-Dispatch*, August 2, 1914, p. 7.

[13] Racial diversity in Green Springs Depot was evident. King Bibb, Robert Woody, Buck Dunkum, Johnny Johnson, and Otto Sherwood were white. Charles Chisholm, Lansey (Lanzy, Lanzey) Riley, Isaac Gilmore, and Burnley Harris were black. All were neighbors. Author

[14] The photograph captioned "The last photo of Victor Hall" eventually appeared on page 5 of *The News Leader*, August 6, 1914.

[15] Dialogue, *The Times-Dispatch*, August 2, 1914, p. 7.

[16] Sheriff Wash was a Baptist. Since the Baptist and Methodist churches across the street from the courthouse were next door to each other, one infers that most of the jurymen were Methodists. Author

[17] Reverend John Q. Rhodes, Sr. lived locally and served as pastor for the Louisa circuit from 1898 to 1901. He had since retired for health reasons. W. D. Keene, Jr., "*Memoirs – 200 Years!*" *1745 – 1987* (Decorah, Iowa: 1988), p. 432.

[18] *The Times-Dispatch*, August 3, 1914, p. 5.

[19] John H. Gwathmey, *Legends of Virginia Lawyers* (Richmond: 1934), pp. 15-16.

[20] Frederick Wilmer Sims was born July 23, 1862, attended the University of Virginia, and was admitted to the Louisa bar in 1885. He was elected Louisa County Court Judge in 1891 and served until 1904 when the new Virginia Constitution abolished county courts.

In 1901, Judge Sims prosecuted Littleton Napper for a shotgun slaying actually committed at Hall's store! [See Chapter

END NOTES

10] Sims was intimately familiar with the reputation of Green Springs Depot.

Sims was elected to the Virginia State Senate in November 1905 and served as Mayor of Louisa from March 1906 to May 1908. In 1914, Sims was in private practice, a prominent citizen of the state and an active Freemason.

Frederick Sims was later elected to the Virginia Supreme Court of Appeals in March 1917 and became President of that body in February 1924. Sims died February 8, 1925 at which time the Virginia Bar Association asked William C. Bibb to write his necrology. W. C. Bibb, "Hon. Frederick W. Sims," *Virginia Bar Association* (Richmond: 1925), pp. 188-195. Pattie Cooke, "The Town of Louisa: Mayors and Town Officials," *LCHSM*, Spring, 1998. Vol. 29. No.1. p. 20.

[21] In Hillsville, Virginia on March 14, 1912, Floyd Allen stood in the Carroll County courtroom convicted of interfering with a law officer in the performance of his duty. Judge Thornton L. Massie pronounced one year in the state penitentiary.

Floyd declared, "Gentlemen, I ain't a going!" Allen, his family, and officers of the court all drew pistols and fired on each other. Panic ensued. The blazing gun battle moved outside. The Allens escaped in the smoke and confusion, except for Floyd left for dead.

Judge Massie, Commonwealth's Attorney Foster, and Sheriff Webb, were killed. Floyd Allen, his brother Sidna, Clerk of Court Dexter Goad, and four others were wounded: a juror and a witness mortally.

Governor Mann sent 100 militiamen and 30 Baldwin-Felts detectives after the *Allen Gang*. Luther L. Scherer coordinated efforts. William G. Baldwin and Thomas L. Felts personally led investigations. Felts was both a close friend of Goad and the largest taxpayer in Carroll County.

Metropolitan newspapers headlined the story and portrayed the Allens as wild, bootlegging, gun slinging hillbillies. However, the situation proved the culmination of a long political rivalry between the wealthy, Democratic Allen family and the Republican *courthouse clique*.

Floyd Allen was a special policeman for Carroll County who had intervened in the illegal extradition of two nephews who had fled to North Carolina to avoid arrest on trumped up charges. Goad had had issues with Floyd for years and seized the opportunity to prosecute. Members of both factions entered the courtroom armed.

Floyd Allen and son Claude were tried, convicted and executed. Four other family members served lengthy prison terms.

Luther Scherer supported commutation as did his brother the Rev. J. J. Scherer, spiritual advisor to the condemned men.

For thorough treatments see: Elmer Jackson Cooley, *The Inside Story of the World Famous Courtroom Tragedy as Told by a Native Countryman Familiar with the Facts and Conditions Surrounding the Event that Shocked the Civilized World* (Charlottesville, VA: 1961); Rufus L. Garner, *The Courthouse Tragedy: Hillsville, VA* (Mount Airy, NC: 1967); Ronald W. Hall, *The Carroll County Courthouse Tragedy: A True Account of the 1912 Gun Battle That Shocked the Nation; Its Causes and Aftermath* (Lynchburg, VA: 1998).

[22] The published account of this meeting appears in *The Richmond Virginian*, August 4, 1914, p. 4.

[23] White ribbon temperance badges symbolized personal support for Prohibition. The fervor over manufacture, distribution, sale and use of alcoholic beverages gradually became strictly a *Wet or Dry* issue. By 1914, temperance badges had become exclusively a visible sign of *Dry* voters.

"Up to the present campaign, the man who believed in local option had the right to wear a white ribbon and call himself a temperance man." *The News Leader*, September 21, 1914, p. 1.

[24] Mrs. W. M. Bickers was elected chapter president on September 5, 1911 and served five years. Headquartered at Broad and Third Streets in Richmond, the Richmond-Henrico County Chapter was composed of fourteen Unions working diligently for statewide Prohibition. Their efforts extended into public schools, Sunday schools and other educational institutions. Elizabeth Ironmonger, *History of the Woman's Christian Temperance Union of Virginia and a Glimpse of Seventy-Five Years, 1883-1958* (Richmond, VA: 1958), p. 248.

[25] Elsie Chewning Yancey, her mother Mrs. Alex Chewning, Mrs. Richard Dunkum [Mrs. W. R. "Buck" Dunkum], Mrs. Edward Synan [Carrie Synan] and Mrs. Acy Dunkum [later Mrs. Hall] were close friends and members of the Lasley Aid Society. Cooke, "Lasley Ladies Aid Society Ledger," *LCHSM*, Fall 2005, Vol. 36, pp. 34, 40.

[26] Dialogue. *The Times-Dispatch*, August 4, 1914, p. 4.

[27] *The News Leader*, August 3, 1914, p. 8.

[28] *The Times-Dispatch*, August 4, 1914, p. 4.

[29] To evaluate the effects of a shell "boiled in a coffee pot" and stored in a matchbox, author processed four sets of four .38 S&W shells to create a matrix of four conditions. Each set was boiled in an enamelware coffee pot with fresh coffee w/grounds for one minute. Shells were removed and placed on a wood surface to air dry. Once cool and dry, these were stored a matchbox. The process was repeated to evaluate sets representing smokeless and black powder shells and matchboxes containing wooden strike-anywhere matches and wooden safety matches.

After storing at ambient room conditions for twenty-four hours, sets were examined independently by each of three analytical chemists: a frequent pistol shooter, an occasional shooter, and a non-shooter.

Results: Each analyst regarded each shell as odorless.

After one year, a subsequent test was conducted using same analysts: each on separate occasions and without prior warning.

Author transferred one tablespoon of commercial, ground coffee by thumb, index, and middle fingers to a second container. Within minutes of transfer, the author approached an analyst and removed a clean, odorless .38 S&W shell from a matchbox with the same fingers used to transfer the coffee. The shell was given to the analyst, who was then asked, "What does that smell like?" Analyst smelled the shell and commented.

Results: One said, "It's a familiar smell." Another said, "Something like old coffee grounds." Another said, "Coffee. It smells like coffee."

Conclusions:

1) No coffee odor is expected on shells after actually *boiling in a coffee pot.*

2) Aromatic oils can be transferred by contact after handling coffee.

Roasting, grinding, and brewing coffee were routine in Mrs. Hall's household. The shell Mrs. Hall handed to Mackay may have smelled like coffee, but if so, it was most likely attributable to direct transfer of aromatic oils while handling, not boiling in coffee. Author

[30] Dialogue. *The News Leader*, August 3, 1914, p. 8.

[31] *The Richmond Virginian*, August 4, p. 2. *The Virginian Pilot-Norfolk Landmark*, August 4, 1914, p. 7.

END NOTES FOR CHAPTER NINE – TRUTH OR FIDDLESTICKS

[1] Dialogue with Charles Johnston was extracted from two sources. *The News Leader*, August 3, 1914, p. 8 and *The Times-Dispatch*, August 4, 1914, p. 4. Author's emphasis.

[2] The reference is to John Williams Flannagan, called later to testify. See note 5.

[3]   Originally from Missouri, A. O. Wood's full name was Alderman Ollie Wood. Author

[4]   *The News Leader*, August 4, 1914, p. 10.

[5]   John Williams Flannagan was a well respected man of social connection in the county. His son John W. Flannagan, Jr. served as Ninth District Congressman from 1931 to 1949. Author

[6]   Ibid.

[7]   Elsie Wood. Dialogue. Ibid. Author's emphasis.

[8]   Bill of Exception #4, "Elizabeth A. Hall," Louisa County Circuit Court Judgments, November Term 1914.

[9]   Roberts testimony concerning the lubricant and the position of the grease groove on the fatal bullet as recorded in the Hall Trial Transcript pp. 768-769 is preserved in Bill of Exception #4, pages 6 through 7, Elizabeth Hall folder, November Term 1914, Louisa Circuit Court.

[10]   The incident reported by the article may have actually involved the more powerful Smith & Wesson .38 Special cartridge. Author

[11]   An obsolete round like the .38 Short Colt would not likely have appeared in a current ammunition catalogue and, therefore, overlooked as a possibility. Author

[12]   The *Ordnance Manual of 1874* assumed a one inch penetration into white pine at a given range equated to a "dangerous wound." David F. Butler, *United States Firearms: The First Century 1776 – 1875* (New York: 1971), p. 212.

This established the fact that, circa 1914, penetration into pine board was a recognized measurement of ballistic power. However, such ballistic data was often inconsistent. Another source listed expected pine penetrations at a range of fifteen feet for both .38 S&W and the significantly more powerful .38 Special bullets as the same 0.75 inches. Henry M. Stebbins, *Pistols; A Modern Encyclopedia* (Harrisburg, PA: 1961), pp. 218, 221.

To test and evaluate bullet penetration, five rounds of each: Remington .38 S&W 146 grain, lead, round nose (LRN); specially ordered U.M.C. replica 146 grain, LRN, with 11 grains black powder; and Winchester .38 Special 158 grain, LRN were fired at range of six feet into commercial, pressure treated, 2 x 12 inch pine stock. No bullet passed completely through. Average penetrations: Remington, 0.75 inch; U.M.C. (replica black powder cartridge), 0.70 inches; .38 Special, 1.05 inches.

Of the ten .38 S&W type rounds fired in the test, three failed to strike hard enough to embed themselves completely into the target. The test suggests that Lindsay Gordon's argument was not justified that a .38 caliber ball from Victor Hall's, *high quality*, Smith & Wesson pistol would have passed completely through the victim's head. Perhaps the jury knew this.

Test pistols: Smith & Wesson Safety Hammerless [S/N 258033], .38 S&W and Taurus, .38 Special [S/N TD27003]. Author

[13] The prosecution presented data generated by Pinkerton Detective Mackay that the U.M.C. brand .38 S&W bullets from Victor Hall's pistol measured 150 grains and the fatal bullet recovered from Victor Hall's head measured 138 grains: an apparent weight loss of 12 grains. The discrepancy was neither explained nor unaccounted for in court, but the presentation inferred that the weight loss was consistent with expectations.

T. Arthur Campbell stated for the defense that .38 S&W bullets normally were 146 grains. However, Campbell then testified to having personally weighed bullets from U.M.C. and Peters cartridges and both measured 150 grains, bullets specifically manufactured and sold as 146 grains. This 150 grain value was the same number arrived at by the prosecution. There was obviously a problem with precision and accuracy of the measurements.

Of all the companies manufacturing .38 S&W ammunition circa 1914, only United States Cartridge Co. used a 150 grain bullet. Remington, Peters, and U.M.C. all used 146 grains. Winchester and Western both used 145 grains. *The Remington Society*, response to inquiry August 8, 2002.

END NOTES

U.M.C. ammunition was manufactured by The Union Metallic Cartridge Company. The U.M.C. .38 S&W round featured a 146 grain, lead, round nose bullet. Remington and U.M.C. merged in 1912. Remington still manufactures U.M.C. brand cartridges at this writing; however, their .38 S&W round is marketed only under the Remington brand and remains a 146 grain, lead, round nose bullet.

To test and evaluate ballistic weight loss, bullets were pulled from five randomly selected rounds from a recent box of Remington .38 S&W. All bullets weighed 145+ grains. When rounded to the nearest whole grain per ASTM E-29, data confirmed each ball as the stated 146 grains.

Another five rounds randomly selected from same box were fired from a Smith & Wesson Safety Hammerless revolver [S/N 258033 mechanically identical to Victor Hall's pistol] at a range of six feet into commercial, pressure treated, 2 x 12 inch pine stock. The projectiles were removed and weighed. The median and minimum values measured 144.07 and 142.03 grains respectively.

This represents a median weight loss of 2% and in the worst case 4%. The prosecution's evidence inferred an 8% weight loss. All measurements were conducted on an analytical balance calibrated traceable to NIST standards and accurate to +/- .003 grains. Author

[14] Charles Hester, letter dated July 1, 1918, "Elizabeth A. Hall," Box 530, *Secretary of the Commonwealth of Virginia Executive Papers*, November 6. 1919.

[15] *The Times-Dispatch*, August 5, 1914, p. 1.

[16] *The Virginian Pilot-Norfolk Landmark*, August 5, 1914, p. 10.

[17] Ibid.

[18] Originally a contract painter, Jesse Ward Erb was employed as a Secret Operative by the Denver Office of the Pinkerton National Detec-

tive Agency in November 1904. In March 1912 while on assignment in Pueblo, CO, Assistant Superintendent Erb entered a hotel bar late at night and happened upon a robbery in progress. The thug held the hotel manager and two others at gunpoint.

Erb mistook the scene for a prank staged in his behalf. He boldly confronted the masked man ignoring demands to halt. Barely six feet from the man, Erb realized the situation was real and drew his revolver. The robber shot barely missing Erb's right cheek. Another shot went wild. Erb shot twice striking his target in the left ear and right arm causing him to drop his gun. The police rushed in after hearing the gunfire and arrested the robber.

The Denver Post declared Erb a hero. He refused a $100 reward collected by the grateful people of Pueblo for apprehending the locally notorious criminal. A glowing account of the event with newspaper clippings was placed in his personnel file. The notoriety and favorable publicity were largely responsible for Erb's appointment at age 33 to Superintendent of the Pinkerton's Richmond, VA office in 1914 just prior to the Hall Case.

Eventually, Erb proved unsuited to the position. In 1917, his superiors asked Erb to sign a statement stating that he was aware that it was a criminal offense to impersonate a federal agent. In 1919, Erb was in trouble for poor job performance. General Manager George D. Bangs summoned Erb to his New York office to discuss his deficiencies. "He has not made an altogether satisfactory Supt.," wrote Bangs that February. Alan and William Pinkerton discussed giving Erb another chance. This they did. But, after more problems, including two incidents of intoxication and a threat to seek other employment, Bangs demanded Erbs resignation in May 1922. Erb returned to "interior decorating."

Records of The Pinkerton National Detective Agency, Box 28, Folder 8, Manuscript Division, Library of Congress.

[19]   T. A. Hancock served as a musician in the 46th Virginia Infantry under Colonel R. T. W. Duke, Sr. See note thirty-five, chapter thirteen. Author

[20]   Statement by Hugh H. Hudson, "Elizabeth A. Hall," Louisa County Circuit Court Judgments, November Term 1914.

[21]   Hall Trial Transcript, p. 1057.

[22]   *The Daily Progress*, August 5, 1914.

[23]   N. W. Hall, *The Pen*, Vol. XII-No.21, 1915. "Elizabeth A. Hall," SCVEP, November 6, 1914.

[24]   *The Daily Progress*, August 6, 1914, p. 4.

[25]   *The Times-Dispatch*, August 6, 1914, p. 4.

[26]   Dialogue, *The Times-Dispatch*, August 6, 1914, p. 4.

[27]   Dialogue, *The Daily Progress*, August 7, 1914, p. 2.

[28]   Dialogue, *The News Leader*, August 6, 1914, p 5.

[29]   *The Times-Dispatch*, August 7, 1914, p 9.

[30]   Ibid.

[31]   Hugh Coleman Dowdy was born August 4, 1914. Per sister Lucy Kathryn Bubb, nee Dowdy.

[32]   Dr. Ernest B. Bichols. *The Times-Dispatch*, August 7, 1914, p. 1.

[33]   J. F. Bickers, Affidavit, "Elizabeth Ann Hall," November Term 1914 Judgments, Louisa Circuit Court.

[34]   Thirty-seven year old John Wilmer Boston was born and raised in the store at Green Springs Depot built by his father. This later became Hall's store. Boston attended the Oakland Male Academy and moved with his mother and his younger siblings to Richmond after his father's death in 1890. In 1914, J. W. Boston worked for the American Lace Leather Company in Richmond. The business was located on the corner of Main and Belvedere in Richmond, the present site of Virginia Commonwealth University's Engineering Building. Boston later retired from that firm as executive vice-president and part owner. Per Edward J. Westlow, great-grand nephew, email July 18, 2002.

END NOTES FOR CHAPTER TEN – A MEAL TO GAG A POSSUM

[1]   *The Richmond Virginian*, August 7, 1914, p. 1.

[2]   Suzanne Lebsock, *A Murder In Virginia: Southern Justice On Trial* (New York: 2003), p. 81.

[3]   The point was lame. Sadly, there is no record that the defense ever challenged this.

> Ever since revolvers first appeared, safety dictated that the hammer rest on an empty chamber to prevent accidental discharge. In 1914, many people still applied this rationale even to "hammerless" models like Victor Hall's pistol. This common practice was noted in the 1912 courtroom shootout in Hillsville, VA.

> "Most witnesses agreed that Floyd never pulled his gun until after the first two or three shots had been fired. When he did pull it, it came from his left side from underneath his sweater. It was a five shot, 38 Special hammerless revolver loaded with just 4 shells as a safety precaution in the event that the gun might be dropped. Like most people, Floyd later said he kept an empty chamber under the firing pin." Ronald W. Hall, *The Carrol County Courthouse Tragedy: A True Account of the 1912 Gun Battle That Shocked the Nation; Its Causes and the Aftermath* (Lynchburg, VA: 1998), pp. 83-85.

[4]   The jury was well aware at the time that personal character had been the desperate, ineffective, and only defense for both spouse slayers McCue and Beattie.

> As commentary on a 1907 trial pointed out, "Evidence of good character in a capital charge counts for nothing." John Mortimer, *Famous Trials* (New York: 1984), p. 212.

[5]   In fact, there was never a more Freudian summation of the whole problem, but the psychological term was then unknown. Author

[6]   Bibb's closing arguments were based on coverage in *The News Leader*, August 7, 1914, pp. 1, 5, 12.

[7]   Carter's closing arguments were based on coverage in *The News Leader*, August 7, 1914, p. 12.

[8]   *The Daily Progress*, August 8, 1914, p. 6.

[9]   Gordon's closing arguments were based on coverage in *The News Leader*, August 8, 1914, p. 10 and *The Times-Dispatch*, August 8, 1914, p. 8.

[10] Lebsock, pp. 90-91.

[11] Fulton closing arguments were based on reports in *The News Leader*, August 8, 1914, p. 10 and *The Times-Dispatch* August 9, 1914, p. 5.

[12] *Louisa County Law Order Book 1912-1916*, p. 367.

[13] *The Times-Dispatch*, August 9, 1914, p. 1.

[14] Dialogue, *The Times-Dispatch*, August 9, 1914, p. 1.

[15] *The Central Virginian* stated the size of the crowd present at the Hall verdict in its 250th anniversary salute to Louisa County. The article referenced an August 1914 issue. *The Central Virginian*, September 10, 1992, p. 10.

[16] The description of the walk to the jail before a jeering mob was based on a photograph last known in the possession of the late Helen Waltman, daughter-in-law to Mamie Crank nee Rosson and staff writer at *The Central Virginian*.

   Waltman displayed said picture and other related materials to Evelyn Harris [Essie's daughter] and Mary Ann Haske [one of Mamie's daughters] on their visit to that newspaper's office in 1989. Harris described what she had seen several times before her death in 1992. Haske related the same details in January 2003. Author

[17] Ibid.

[18] *The Times-Dispatch*, August 9, 1914, p. 5.

[19] Ibid.

END NOTES FOR CHAPTER ELEVEN –
THE NEWSPAPERS DID IT?

[1] *The Daily Progress*, May 15, 1914, p. 2.

[2] Similarly, despite a newspaper sensation, the memory of the unjust conviction of three black women for the 1895 axe murder of white woman Lucy Pollard in Lunenburg County succumbed to racial repression at the end of that century. Suzanne Lebsock, *A Murder In Virginia: Southern Justice On Trial* (New York: 2003), p. 334.

[3] James H. Lindsay, *The McCue Murder: Complete Story of the Crime and the Famous Trial of the Ex-Mayor of Charlottesville, Virginia* (Charlottesville, VA: 1904), p. 11.

[4] Ibid, p. 9.

[5] Evan Ragland Chesterman and Joe F. Geisinger, *History of the McCue Case: Full Particulars of the Crime, Inquest, Trial and Conviction* (Richmond, VA: 1904), p. 22.

[6] Ibid, p. 24.

[7] Lindsay, p. 9.

   Note that $1,000 in 1907 corresponds to about $50,000 at this writing. Author

[8] *The Times-Dispatch*, July 22, 1911, p. 1.

[9] Lindsay, p. 146.

[10] *The Times Dispatch*, July 22, 1911, p. 1.

[11] Henry Clay Beattie, Sr. was also a former city councilman and postmaster for Manchester. Benjamin B. Weisiger, III, *Old Mancester & Its Environs, 1769 – 1910* (Richmond, VA: 1993), pp. 27, 139. Sketch of the Beattie department store, p. 51.

[12] Paul Beattie purchased the shotgun shells at a hardware store at corner of Harrison and Main Streets from business owner W. B. Kidd. *The News Leader*, August 28, 1911, p 1.

   William Benjamin Kidd was second great-uncle to author.

[13]   Ibid.

[14]   James Everett Mann, author's maternal grandfather, often spoke of having borrowed a bicycle to ride from his Oregon Hill neighborhood in Richmond to Chesterfield Courthouse to attend the Henry Beattie trial. Mann was twenty at the time. Author

[15]   *The Daily Progress*, April 16, 1914, p. 2.

[16]   The independent rivalry between the *Times-Dispatch* and *News Leader* was short lived. Joseph Bryan's heirs repurchased the newspaper in 1929. Earle Dunford, *Richmond Times-Dispatch, The Story of a Newspaper* (Richmond, VA: 1995), pp. 38-39.

[17]   "Paul Beattie Now On Duty As Sleuth: Former Elevator Dispatcher's First Prison is Sent to Jail Today" The article summarized the arrest of a trespasser on C & O Railway property by Paul Beattie. Beattie received the job from "his old friend, Luther L. Scherer, Chief Claims Agent for the Chesapeake and Ohio. . ." *The News Leader*, April 9, 1914, p. 2.

[18]   The 72 Hour Rule: If an arrest is not made within seventy-two hours, the crime is likely to be categorized a cold case. Frank Morn, *Foundations of Criminal Investigations* (Durham, NC: 2000), pp. 173-174.

[19]   *The News Leader*, August 7, 1914, p. 12.

[20]   Manufactured news was common whenever newspapers saw a need. Note that in the weeks following the 1912 courtroom massacre in Hillsville, Virginia, newspapers printed two particularly sensational stories. A desperate gun battle allegedly occurred between detectives and the "Allen Gang" surrounded at the home of Sidna Allen which reportedly resulted in the death of Sidna Allen's wife. Another story told of the heroic action of Jezebel Goad, the eighteen year old daughter of Clerk of Court Dexter Goad, who allegedly remained by her father's side throughout the courtroom shoot-out to reload her father's pistol.

In fact, neither story was true. Sidna Allen was later captured in Iowa and returned to Virginia where his wife was very much alive and visited him in jail. And even though Dexter Goad admitted in court that the story about his daughter Jezebel was totally false, Miss Goad was, nevertheless, awarded a medal for her heroism and received a congratulatory note from Governor Mann.

"When news got scarce, the reporters were not above inventing some as evidenced by the fictitious shoot-out at Sidna Allen's home and the heroine role assigned to Jezebel Goad." Ronald W. Hall, *The Carrol County Courthouse Tragedy* (Lynchburg, VA: 1998), p. 137.

[21]   *The News Leader*, May 22, 1914, p. 13.

[22]   Ibid.

[23]   *The Daily Progress*, May 25, 1914, p. 2.

[24]   Keeping a spent cartridge beneath the firing pin of a revolver was a common safety practice. See note 3, Chapter 10.

[25]   *The Times-Dispatch*, August 8, 1914, p. 8.

[26]   The Hall trial was not the first time that a sensational regional story had been upstaged by an overriding event. The famed courtroom massacre in Hillsville, Virginia occurred on March 14, 1912. Newspapers intently covered the aftermath including the subsequent manhunt and capture of the *Allen Gang*. The related sensational newspaper coverage continued until eclipsed by the sinking of the *Titantic* on April 15, 1912. Author

[27]   *The Central Virginian*, owned and edited by George Mc Duffie Blake, maintained objectivity throughout the Hall controversy. Blake was the same who managed the "Hall" store in the 1890's.

END NOTES FOR CHAPTER TWELVE – NEXT STOP: GREEN SPRINGS DEPOT!

[1]   The following anecdote illustrates both the character of the ridge land and the county's peculiar social order:

"Jesse Porter, for many years Clerk of Louisa County, was a gallant soldier and a lieutenant in the Louisa company in the War Between the States. He was wounded in the Wilderness and thereby incapacitated for many months. He was captured at Winchester and remained in a Federal prison until June, 1865.

Long after the war Mr. Porter, at one period of his life, took an interest in dabbling in real estate and sold numerous tracts of the poor land between Louisa Courthouse and Trevilians to Northern buyers.

These Northern farmers, attracted by the low prices of the land, proved for the most part shiftless and were unable to make a living on the land they had purchased. So they would go back North, forfeiting their first payments. The land would come back to Mr. Porter and he would re-sell it to other Northern buyers. There was nothing questionable in these transactions. The buyers, in the first place, might have known from the ridiculously low prices asked for the land that it was not river bottom.

One day Mr. Porter was sitting in the Clerk's office talking with Judge Daniel Grimsley, then presiding Judge of that circuit. The conversation reverted to the war.

Bill Trice, quite a character at Louisa, leader in the fish fries, drinking bouts, coon hunts and other pastimes, and quite a wag, laughed and inserted a paragraph of his own in the conversation: 'I'll tell you, Mr. Porter, you didn't do the Yankees much harm during the war, but your have certainly been giving them hell ever since.'"

John H. Gwathmey, *Legends of Virginia Lawyers* (Richmond, VA: 1934), pp. 67-68.

Many examples of nepotism characterized Louisa County's government. In dynastic fashion, Jesse Porter's son James succeeded him as clerk of court. James Porter was then succeeded in same office by his brother Philip [See note 85]. Note also that Philip Porter and Deputy Sheriff Robert Trice held the similar county offices in 1914 respective to Jesse Porter and Bill Trice years earlier. Robert Trice eventually became Sheriff and then Commissioner of Revenue for Louisa. Author

    Jesse Porter was a member of the *courthouse clique* and the county social class that dispensed economic favors. Jesse Porter was named specifically by Shifflett to illustrate the hierarchy of socio-economic control in Louisa County. Crandall A. Shifflett, *Patronage and Poverty in the Tobacco South, Louisa County, Virginia 1860-1900* (Knoxville, TN:1982), pp. 36-38.

[2]   Remnants of this attitude survive at this writing. In reference to the 1975 shotgun slaying of Judge Stuart A. Cunningham in the Louisa courtroom, a long-time resident of the area noted the killer as being from "one of *the clans*." Author

[3]   Patrick Dorin, *The Chesapeake and Ohio Railway* (Seattle, WA: 1981), p. 11.

[4]   Charles W. Turner, *Chessie's Road* (Richmond, Virginia: 1956), p. 25.

[5]   Harris mentioned Green Springs Depot as the site near which Wade Hampton's troops retired during the Battle of Trevillians in 1864. Malcolm H. Harris M.D., *History of Louisa County, Virginia* (Richmond, VA: 1936), p. 100.

    The station does not appear on Gilmer's official 1863 map of the area, but is clearly indicated on maps later than the mid-1870's. Harris likely used the depot merely as a reference point familiar to his readers rather than a geographic feature contemporary to the event. Author

[6]   Chisholm, Claudia A., "The Village of Fredericks Hall: The Poindexters and Other Merchants of Fredericks Hall," *LCHSM*, Vol. 25, No. 1, p. 35.

[7]   *Louisa County Deed Book*, Vol. 1, p. 674.

[8]   Most of the 434 acres of land comprising the "Boston" property purchased by D. A. Dunkum was the result of multiple purchases made by J. T. Boston in late 1873 and early 1874. *Louisa County Deed Book*, Vol. 1, p. 674 and Vol. 2, pp. 117, 133.

Boston actively acquired other holdings in the area through 1885. *Grantee Index to Deeds, Louisa County, VA.*, No. 3, A-K, p. 27.

9   Papers of Porter Clay Wright, "Post Offices of Louisa County," *Louisa County, Virginia 1742-1992 Sestercentenial 250th Anniversary* (Louisa?, VA: 1992), p. 21.

10   *The Times-Dispatch*, March 19, 1936, p. 2. Also photograph of Channing M. Boston.

John Terrill Boston was an Episcopalian and named all three of his sons after prominent Anglican clergy: thus, Channing Moore Boston, John Wilmer Boston, and John Seymore Boston. E-mail, Edward J. Westlow, grandson of C. M. Boston, July 18, 2002.

11   Chattaigne, Henry J., *The Chesapeake and Ohio Directory* (Richmond, VA.: 1881), p. 220.

12   *The Times-Dispatch*, March 19, 1936, p. 2.

13   Riggs, David F., *13th Virginia Infantry* (Lynchburg, VA.: 1988), p. 102.

14   *Session Minutes Wills Memorial Church*, April 27, 1890.

15   Ibid.

16   Ibid. July 23, 1893.

17   Ann Cottrell Free, "George McDuffie Blake, 1859-1944," *LCHSM*, Spring 1996, Vol. 27, No. 1, p. 6.

18   A 1915 advertisement published in Louisa for Blake's Richmond business read: "Pure Wines and Liquors For Family Use. . . . .All Kinds of Wines, Malt Whiskey, Rum and Gin. . . . .Geo. McD. Blake & Co." Doris Perkins Meredith, "1915 Directory of Louisa County," *LCHSM*, Spring 2000, Vol. 31, No. 1, p. 28.

19   The Reverend Landon A. Cutler was ordained by the Disciples of Christ and served as pastor of Louisa Christian Church in Louisa. He had previously been pastor of Marshall Street Christian Church in Staunton, Virginia and then First Christian Church in Charlottesville, Virginia.

Reverend Cutler was born February 9, 1837 and died November 25, 1903. He was first buried at Louisa Christian Church. His body was later re-interred in Hillcrest Cemetery in Louisa.

Porter Clay Wright, Footnote, "Marriage Register of Rev. L. A. Cutler," *LCHSM*, Fall 1974, Vol. 5, No. 2, p. 31.

[20] In Richmond, the resulting number of votes for the Virginia gubernatorial candidates reflected the unassailable position of the Democratic Party at the time.

J. Hoge Tyler (Democrat) 3,829, Patrick H. McCaull (Republican) 504, L. A. Cutler (Prohibitionist) 40, John J. Quanto (Social Democrat) 35, James S. Cowdon (Independent) 3.

Even in the Louisa Courthouse precinct in the candidate's home county, Cutter received just 27 votes. *The Richmond Dispatch*, November 3, 1897, p. 1.

Prohibitionist support was sufficient to field a candidate in 1897. In 1906, the Mann Law closed rural saloons in the state. The temperance movement grew sufficiently strong by 1913 that promises made to secure Prohibitionist support assured the election for Henry Stuart as Governor of Virginia. In September 1914, the state passed the referendum to go completely *dry* effective November 1, 1916, three years before the Volstead Act for national Prohibition. Author

[21] *Session Minutes Wills Memorial Church*, September 26, 1897.

[22] Jill Ramsey, "Grandma Jo Remembers Her Childhood," *LCHSM*, Fall 2002, Vol. 33. No. 2, p. 79.

[23] Four years later, George McDuffie Blake bought property in the *real* Green Springs taking title to the "Valentines Mill" property on November 5, 1904. *Louisa County Deed Book*, Vol. 24, p. 322.

A 1906 map identifies "Valentine's Mill" as "Blake's Mill." Hugh H. Bennett and W. E.McLendon, *Soil Survey of Louisa County* (Washington, D.C.: 1906), Survey Map.

Blake retained this property briefly until swapping it with Henry R. Robinson, Jr. for *The Elms* and 37.5 acres across the road and next to *Corduroy* on October 19, 1906. Robinson, in turn, assumed the Valentine's Mill property. The Blake family moved to *The Elms* and lived there in the real Green Springs until selling the property February 2, 1911. *Louisa County Deed Book*, Vol. 29, p. 49.

[24] Ibid, Chisholm.

[25] Joseph H. Knighton, Jr. His nickname is spelled both as Josey and Josie in records. Author

[26] Petition for Clemency, *Secretary of the Commonwealth of Virginia Executive Papers [Hence: SCVEP]*, June 23, 1904.

[27] *Louisa County Order Book 1896–1901*, p. 541.

[28] Ibid, p. 548.

[29] Petition for Clemency, SCVEP, June 23, 1904.

[30] C. B. Madison is likely a typographic error intending J. B. Madison, the county surveyor, local magistrate and depot master at Green Springs Depot. Author

[31] Ibid.

[32] Ibid. Letter dated 10/28/03, Mrs. S. F. Knighton, SCVEP, June 23, 1904.

[33] Ibid. Undated, unsigned letter, same as Mrs. S. F. Knighton's hand, SCVEP, June 23, 1904.

[34] Ibid. Letter dated 10/28/03, Mrs. S. F. Knighton, SCVEP, June 23, 1904.

[35] Ibid.

[36] Accession No. 35177, Vol. 1902 – 1921, The Library of Virginia.

[37] Letter dated 11/25/03, Mrs. S. F. Knighton, SCVEP, June 23, 1904.

[38] Letter dated November 25, 1903, Roy Knighton, SCVEP, June 23, 1904.

Knighton wrote governor Montague opposing Napper's pardon on paper bearing the letterhead "Roy Knighton, General Merchandise, Two Miles South of Green Springs Depot." The location coincides with the Knighton homeplace on the north side of "Valentine's Mill Road" on property bordering *The Elms*. Author

[39] Sterling Hall clerked and kept records for Yancey Bros. *Bibb, W. C., County of Louisa Appellant, v. Yancey's Trustees et als, Appellee, Record No. 91. In the Supreme Court of Appeals of Virginia at Richmond* (Richmond, VA.: 190?). [Motion to dismiss appeal].

[40] Main Street Station opened November 27, 1901. Author

[41] The local gas works manufactured *artificial gas*, also known as *coal gas*, by thermal decomposition of coal. Composed of mainly hydrogen and carbon monoxide, the gas was highly toxic. Asphyxiation was common in hotels then equipped with gas lighting. Author

[42] *The Midland Virginian*, undated clipping, courtesy Alice S. Murphey.

[43] *Minutes of the Louisa County Board of Supervisors*, Book 2, p. 278. Dec. 31, 1902.

[44] *The Richmond Dispatch*, January 1, 1903, p. 1.

[45] *Bibb, W. C., County of Louisa Appellant, v. Yancey's Trustees et als, Appellee, Record No. 91. In the Supreme Court of Appeals of Virginia at Richmond* (Richmond, VA.: 190?). [Motion to dismiss appeal].

[46] Sterling Hall was listed specifically among those quarantined in the store. *The Richmond Dispatch*, January 1, 1903, p. 1.

[47] Curiously the two graves are about 150 feet apart and individually fenced. The reason for the separation is unknown. The Dunkum burials began adjacent to A. C. Yancey's plot, possibly because of friendship with the Yanceys. The multi-burial Dunkum-Hall family cemetery was later fenced. All known burials are marked and face east in Christian tradition. Author

[48] L. F. Yancey filed suit for compensation against Louisa County on October 20, 1903. Louisa County Law Order Book 1902-1904, p. 146.

[49] L. F. Yancey was awarded damages on November 10, 1903. *Louisa County Law Order Book 1902-1904*, p. 155.

[50] "The County of Louisa Appellant vs. L. F. Yancey, May 17, 1906." *Louisa County Law Order Book 1904-1911*, p. 162.

[51] *Bibb, W. C., County of Louisa Appellant, v. Yancey's Trustees et als, Appellee, Record No. 91. In the Supreme Court of Appeals of Virginia at Richmond* (Richmond, VA.: 190?). [Motion to dismiss appeal].

END NOTES

[52] "W. Worth Smith, Jr. – L. F. Yancey," Box 33, *Papers of W. E. Bibb and Other Louisa County, Va. Families, 1830 – 1940.* Accession No. 4171, Special Collections, Alderman Library, University of Virginia.

[53] *Louisa County Deed Book*, Vol. 24, p. 198.

[54] In 1900, seven percent of Louisa County landowners held more that 300 acres. Twenty-three percent owned between 101 and 300 acres. Seventy percent owned 100 acres or less. Crandall A. Shiflett, *Patronage and Poverty in the Tobacco South: Louisa County, Virginia 1860 – 1900* (Knoxville, TN: 1982), p. 20.

[55] Free, p. 3.

[56] Ervin L. Jordan, *Black Confederates and Afro-Yankees in Civil War Virginia* (Charlottesville, VA: 1995), Confederate response to the Emancipation Proclamation returning free blacks to slave status, p. 320. "Threats to enslave Virginia free blacks were never put into effect, ..." p. 256.

[57] T. W. Ross also appears in records circa 1914 as a Justice of the Peace for Orange County. *Louisa County Deed Book* No. 33. p. 364.

Ross and Madison were likely counterparts in their respective counties. Author

[58] The article refers to I. N. Poindexter shooting a man named Curtis in Richmond with no other details of the incident. *The Times-Dispatch,* December 9, 1905, p. 10.

[59] Chewnings path was traced on a crime scene sketch used at trial. Louisa Circuit Court, Judgments, Special Term December 1905.

[60] Letter C. B. Vest to Alexander Forward, Secretary to Governor H. C. Stuart. February 23, 1915. SCVEP, May 4, 1915.

[61] *Louisa County Order Book 1904 – 1911*, pp. 124 – 125.

[62] Louisa Circuit Court, Judgments, Special Term December 1905.

[63] James B. Madison, July 15, 1909, *Louisa County Fiduciary Settlements 1907 – 1916*, p. 76.

[64] In 1914, Charles Cannon testified that he remembered Victor Hall purchasing his pistol from the Sears & Roebuck Catalogue eight years before. *Hall Trial Transcript*, p. 1077-1078.

Inferring that Victor Hall had reason to arm himself at that time, he became depot master and express agent in 1906. Author

[65] W. C. Bibb, letter dated January 20, 1913, SCVEP, January 21, 1913.

[66] *Secretary of the Commonwealth of Virginia Executive Journal February 1910 – February 1914*, p. 332.

[67] Letter from Governor Mann to George W. Chewning, Jr., SCVEP, January 21, 1913.

[68] Undated Petition for Parole, SCVEP, May 4, 1915.

[69] C. B. Vest, letter dated December 18, 1914, SCVEP, May 4, 1915.

[70] Ibid., C. B. Vest, letter dated February 23, 1915.

[71] Letter from Governor Stuart to C. B. Vest, SCVEP, December 10, 1917.

[72] Free, p. 7.

[73] *Louisa County Deed Book*, Vol. 26, pp. 133-134.

[74] U.S.Census 1910, Green Springs District.

[75] As late as 2003 a rumor repeated to the author stated that Becky Coates worked for the Acey Dunkums when subject baby was born. The rumor suggested that when Becky left the home the evening before, the baby was fine. When she returned the next day, the baby was dead. Considering the fact that Becky Coates was six years old in 1908, the tale lacks substance. Author

[76] George W. Cooke established the store at Meltons about 1872. Cooke served as postmaster there from 1872 to 1908. Cooke, *Louisa and Louisa County*, p. 42.

Financial records of Lewis F. Yancey at the store at Meltons begin July 25, 1908. "Smith, William Worth Jr. Legal Cases: L. F. Yancey," Box 33, *Papers of W. E. Bibb and Other Louisa County, Va. Families, 1830 – 1940*. Accession No. 4171, Special Collections, Alderman Library, University of Virginia.

One concludes that Lewis Yancey took over management of the store at Meltons when George Cooke retired. Author

[77] Notes prepared for the 1983 Dunkum family reunion by Mary Ann Haske. Details last clarified by e-mail, Mary Ann Haske, April 28, 2005.

[78] Mrs. Richard Dunkum and Mrs. Acy Dunkum appear in list of new members in 1908. Pattie Cooke, "Lasley Ladies Aid Society Ledger," *LCHSM*. Fall, 2005. Vol. 36., p. 40.

[79] Mary Ann Haske related her mother Mamie's memory of the hobo signs in a paper prepared for 1983 Dunkum family reunion. Author's collection.

[80] The solid gold locket, still in the family's possession, measures 1.125 inches diameter and 0.125 inches thick. The obverse side was embellished with stylized initials E.I.D. for Essie Irene Dunkum. The year 1911 on the reverse side is similarly engraved. Author

[81] Dr. Harry W. Porter, Letter dated November 25, 1914, *SCVEP*, November 6, 1919.

[82] Ambercrombie, Janice L., *Louisa County Death Records 1853-1896* with Addendum from *Records of Woodward Funeral Home 1907-1911* (Athens, GA.: 1997), p. 324.

[83] Elizabeth Ann Hall's Personal *Bible*, Record Pages, Author's collection.

[84] *The Daily Progress*, August 7, 1914, p. 2.

[85] D. A. Dunkum Estate was appraised at $2370.255 [sic] by L. F. Yancey, V. K. Hall, and James E. Porter, the son of Clerk of Court Jesse J. Porter. *Louisa County Will Book*, Vol. 21, p. 48.

James E. Porter briefly became Clerk of Court after father Jesse's death in 1912. Phillip P. Porter succeeded his brother James as Clerk of Court in April 1913. Dr. Harry W. Porter was yet another brother. Author

[86] *The Times-Dispatch*, August 1, 1914, p. 3.

[87] Mrs. Lizzie Hall was elected vice-president of the ladies aid society in 1912. Information extracted from "Lasley Ladies Aid Society Ledger" by Pattie Cooke, email November 1, 2005.

[88] Hard work causing early deaths in women was just one consequence of indigence typical of the Green Springs Depot neighborhood as discussed

under the heading "The Demography of Poverty." Crandall A. Shifflet, *Patronage and Poverty in the Tobacco South, Louisa County, Virginia 1860-1900* (Knoxville, TN: 1982), p. 98.

[89] Essie Dunkum acknowledged attending "Mr. Blackwell's" school. *Hall Trial Transcript* p. 996.

John F. Blackwell purchased The Elms from George McDuffie Blake on February 2, 1911. *Louisa County Deed Book*, Vol. 29, p. 49.

[90] "Sensation in Louisa Tragedy", *The Daily Progress*, May 2, 1914, p. 3.

[91] "FIVE POINTS! . . . The very letters of the two words, which mean so much, as they are written, to redden with bloodstains of unavenged crimes. There is Murder in every syllable, and Want, Misery and Pestilence take startling form and crowd upon the imagination as the pen traces the words. What a world of wretchedness has been concentrated in this narrow district.

Frank Leslie's Illustrated Newspaper, August 16, 1873."

Tyler Anbinder, *Five Points: The 19th-Century New York Neighborhood That Invented Tap Dance, Stole Elections and Became the World's Most Notorious Slum* (New York: 2001), p. 1.

END NOTES FOR CHAPTER THIRTEEN – ONLY TEN YEARS

[1] The jail was renovated in 1937 under the WPA program at which time the wooden jail floor was replaced with reinforced concrete and the two cells were divided into four. The jail remained in active use until 1967, at which time it was considered the worst county jail in the state. At this writing, the jail building houses the Louisa County Historical Society. Porter C. Wright, "From a Jail to a Museum," *LCHSM*, Fall 1972, Vol. 4, pp 69-74.

[2] Jail cell dimensions provided from plat drawing. Pattie Cooke, e-mail September 30, 2004.

[3] *Louisa County List of Felons 1871 – 1948.* Louisa County microfilm Reel 89, The Library of Virginia. Last viewed August, 2001. Banned from public access by 2002.

[4] *The Times-Dispatch,* August 10, 1914, p. 8.

[5] As separate line items, the Louisa County authorized payments to Hackney on August 21, 1914: $5 for fixing and cleaning the jail and $1 for "dressing the lunatic & carrying her to jail." *Louisa County Board of Supervisors Journal,* Vol. 4, p. 111.

> Since one newspaper reported Courtney as having been "straightjacketed," one infers the term "dressing the lunatic" included employment of said restraint. Author

[6] *The Times-Dispatch,* August 10, 1914, p. 8.

[7] Records bear no further witness of Suzie Courtney. Author assumes that she was either removed or quieted down by the next day.

[8] Signers of the bail bond include: R. L. Gordon, Jr., Ellen F. Hall, N. W. Hall, J. F. Bickers, James E. Hester, W. J. Roberts, E. C. Dowdy, H. H. Dowdy, S. P. Dowdy, and Jennie Leistra. *The News Leader,* August 14, 1914, p. 7.

> Guilelmus "Elmus" C. Dowdy; Hubert Henry Dowdy; Shirley Preston Dowdy; and Virginia "Jennie" H. Dowdy, Mrs. Jacob Leistra were three brothers and a sister of Mrs. Hall. Author

[9] *The News Leader,* September 23, 1914, p. 1.

[10] *Bill of Exception #4,* "Elizabeth A. Hall," Louisa County Circuit Court Judgments, November Term 1914.

[11] Two innocent black women condemned to die for an 1895 murder in Lunenburg County received new trials and acquittals because the court record of their first trial failed to show proper jury custody. Consequently, "the judgement of the trial court must be reversed, the verdict set aside, and a new trial awarded." Suzanne Lebsock, *A Murder In Virginia: Southern Justice On Trial* (New York: 2003), p. 195.

[12] Data provided per the Virginia State Climatology Office.

[13] William R. Dunkum was officially appointed postmaster of Green Springs Depot on July 21, 1914. "Postmasters of in use and discontinued stations, Louisa Co., Va., 1909-1958," Postmasters and Rural Appointments Division, Bureau of Operations, Post Office Department, United States, Special Collections, University of Virginia, p. 3.

[14] Nicholas W. Hall, Ellen F. Kennon [Ellen Hall, wife of Nicholas W. Hall], and Louisa Jane Hall ["Jennie" Hall, sister to Nicholas W. Hall] were later buried in the cemetery with Victor K. Hall. Author

[15] The description of Mrs. Hall and her daughters at Louisa Station was based on a photograph described by Evelyn Harris and Mary Ann Haske. These women were shown the photograph at the office of The Central Virginian by the late Helen Waltman, then staff writer. Current location of said photograph is unknown. Author

[16] The platinum, combination diamond engagement-wedding ring bearing initials E.A.H. remains in the family. Author

[17] The collection of glass plate negatives preserved by the Library of Virginia ends at inmate number 12199 taken in early 1914. It is assumed that the Virginia Department of Corrections transitioned thereafter from glass plate to degradable celluloid negatives, and the institutional image of Elizabeth A. Hall, inmate number 12696 perished. Author

[18] Nineteen years earlier, Mary Barnes, another innocent woman in her forties convicted of a similar crime, was sentenced to ten years in the same facility.

As the major prison reforms instituted in the 1920's by Governor Westmoreland Davis were well in the future, the author draws on conditions compiled by Lebsock and applied to Mary Barnes in 1885 since they were largely the same as shared by Mrs. Hall in 1914. See Lebsock, pp. 115-116.

[19] Data provided per the Virginia State Climatology Office.

[20] Note that Littleton Napper was also employed in the shoe factory during part of his sentence. U.S. Federal Census, 1910.

END NOTES

[21] In May 1914, the Virginia State Penitentiary held 754 men and eighty-eight women. The Virginia penal system also hosted another 1,500 men on road gangs. The article omits mention of the State Farm in Goochland County. *The News Leader*, May 25, 1914.

In 1885, there were eighty-five women. Only five were white, and fewer than ten in their forties. Lebsock, p. 115.

[22] Section 4125 of the Virginia State Penal Code amended in 1904 stated "The convicts shall be kept to the hardest labor suitable to their sex and fitness. . ." James Marvin Good, "A Brief History of the Virginia State Penitentiary" (s.l.: 1973), The Library of Virginia, p. 10.

[23] *The Daily Progress*, November 17, 1914, p. 1.

The overalls were manufactured for a private company. Goods manufactured in the Virginia State Penitentiary were contracted for private concerns until reforms in the 1920's restricted prison labor to manufacture of goods consumed only by state agencies. Author.

[24] Letter, John G. May, dated November 19, 1914. "Elizabeth A. Hall," Box 530, *Secretary of the Commonwealth of Virginia Executive Papers*, November 6, 1919 [Hence: SCVEP, November 6, 1919.].

[25] Letter, Dr. Thomas M. Taylor, dated November 19, 1914. SCVEP, November 6, 1919.

[26] Letters R. B. Winston, dated November 22; A. G. Burnett, dated November 23; Dr. H. W. Porter, dated November 25; and Marshall J. Campbell, dated November 26, 1914. SCVEP, November 6, 1919.

[27] Letter, Rev. C. T. Thrift, dated December 11, 1914 SCVEP, November 6, 1919.

[28] Letter, N. W. and Ellen Hall, dated December 18, 1914. SCVEP, November 6, 1919.

[29] Letter, J. F. Bickers, dated December 30, 1914. SCVEP, November 6, 1919.

[30] Being the Commonwealth's Attorney's uncle, J. F. Bickers observed firsthand the change in Bibb's attitude toward Mrs. Hall and the factors

affecting it. His affidavit about witnessing the separation of the jury and his willingness to sign Mrs. Hall's bail bond after the trial exhibited exceptional courage considering risks to his standing with those influential of the county. Author

[31] Letter, Kate Dowdy, dated January 6, 1915. *SCVEP*, November 6, 1919.

[32] C. C. Taliaferro of Orange nominated George S. Shackelford to fill the 9th Circuit Court judgeship vacated by death of Daniel A. Grimsley. *Journal of the House of Delegates 1910*, pp. 357-358.

[33] George L. Browning of Orange nominated George S. Shackelford for judge of 9th Circuit Court for eight year term beginning February 1, 1914. *Journal of the House of Delegates 1914*, p. 176.

[34] Judge George S. Shackelford, letter of resignation dated January 11, 1915. "Resignations", Box 52, *Governor Henry C. Stuart Papers*.

[35] R. T. W. Duke, Jr. "Judge George S. Shackelford," Necrology, *Report of the Thirtieth Annual Meeting of the Virginia State Bar Association*, Volume XXXI [1919], pp. 125-126.

Note that R. T. W. Duke, Jr. and W. E. Bibb both grew up at the same time in Albermarle County where R. T. W. Duke, Sr. was commonwealth's attorney 1858-1870. During the Civil War, the senior Duke was lieutenant colonel of the First Battalion Virginia State Reserves. W. E. Bibb served in this unit. Duke, Sr. became colonel of the 46th Virginia Infantry and state senator 1880-1881.

R. T. W. Duke, Jr. and W. E. Bibb both became attorneys and both admitted to the Albermarle County bar in 1870. Both became commonwealth attorneys for Albermarle and Louisa Counties respectively. Be it remembered that Duke, Jr. was commonwealth's attorney for Albermarle County in 1914 and prosecuted L. L. Jackson for the Harrison murder. See chapter three.

When Judge Shackelford died from a heart attack at his home in Orange County on December 30, 1918, local members of the

Virginia Bar Association called upon R. T. W. Duke, Jr. to write Shackelford's necrology. These complex and convoluted relationships further illustrate that the region in 1914 was just too small of a world. Author

[36] Letter, N. W. Hall, dated January 12, 1915. *SCVEP*, November 6, 1919.

[37] Letter, Julian J. Jacobs, dated March 18, 1915. *SCVEP*, November 6, 1919.

[38] Letter from Iona May Cutler to Governor Stuart, dated March 28, 1915. *SCVEP*, November 6, 1919

[39] *Louisa County Order Book 1912-1914*, p. 458.

[40] Ibid.

[41] Ibid. p. 461.

[42] Roslyn and Edwin C. Luther, III, *Governors of Virginia 1776 – 1974* (Accomac, VA: 1974), p. 195.

[43] Ibid.

[44] Jack Temple Kirby, *Westmoreland Davis: Virginia Planter – Politician, 1859 – 1942* (Charlottesville, VA: 1968), p. 62.

[45] Later as Governor Stuart energetically led Virginia in support of the nation's war effort, he passively allowed "superpatriot" excesses against Virginians of German extraction. Ibid. p. 203.

[46] Henry Robinson "Speaker" Pollard (1845 – 1923) was born in King & Queen County, Virginia. After serving in the Confederate cavalry during the Civil War, Pollard attended prestigious Columbia College (George Washington University). He joined his father in law practice and was elected a Delegate from his native county to the Virginia General Assembly. He presided over the Virginia Democratic conventions of 1885 and 1901. He was elected Richmond City Attorney in 1898 and held that office until 1921 when he assumed the specially created office of Richmond Advisory Counsel. H. M. Smith, Jr., "Henry Robinson Pollard," *Report of the Thirty-Fifth Annual Meeting of the Virginia State Bar Association*, Volume XXVI. (Richmond, VA, 1924), pp. 111-117.

Interestingly, in 1885 through 1887, Pollard served as defense counsel for the notorious murderer Thomas J. Cluverius. Pollard's ties to Green Springs completes a trinity of indirect influences on Mrs. Hall by all three of Virginia's most infamous murders of the era: Cluverius (1885), McCue (1904), and Beattie (1911).

"In that same neglected period, the Richmond press made hay of three other sensational murder stories, all with a young white man suspected of killing his (white) wife or lover. All three earned permanent places in local lore, popping up in memoirs, steaming up the pages of local histories, and reprised for periodic rehashing in the press." Lebsock, p. 334.

Note also Henry R. Robinson's necrology was written by Hiram M. Smith, Jr., the lead defense attorney for Henry Beattie. Author

[47] On February 3, 1915, John Garland Pollard "threw his hat in the ring" to run for governor in the 1917 election. Kirby, p. 63.

[48] For thorough treatment of the Leo Frank case see Steve Oney's *And The Dead Shall Rise: The Murder of Mary Phagan and the Lynching of Leo Frank* (New York, 2003).

The Leo Frank Case offered many similarities to the Hall Case including the timeline the year before. April 26 – Thirteen year old employee Mary Phagan was murdered at the National Pencil Company. May 8 – Company manager Leo M. Frank was ordered held for the murder. May 23 – Leo Frank was indicted for murder. July 28 – Trial begins. August 25 – Frank found guilty and sentenced to death.

The case featured intense nationwide publicity, strong anti-Semitism, political aspirations of the prosecutor [who eventually became governor], inflamed public sentiment, and false testimony. Greater tragedy unfolded when, after reviewing the facts of the trial, Georgia Governor Slaton commuted Frank's sentence to life imprisonment on June 21, 1915. On August 17, 1915, Leo Frank was kidnapped from prison by conspirators and lynched.

On March 4, 1982, Alonzo Mann admitted he saw another factory employee acting alone carrying the body of Mary Phagan. Georgia posthumously pardoned Leo M. Frank of the crime on March 11, 1986.

Originally scheduled to hang April 18, 1914, Leo Frank's stay of execution was on the front page of the *Times-Dispatch* April 16, 1914. The newspaper's first report of the Hall story appeared on page 9 of the same issue. Author

[49] In Roanoke, Virginia on September 20, 1893, what the *Roanoke Daily Record* described as an "unprecedented harvest of death" began when a white woman received a head wound while delivering fruit to a basement under escort by a Negro Thomas Smith. Whether or not she was intentionally harmed, Smith ran scared. The fleeing Negro caught the attention of people on the street. These happened to hail no less a figure than Detective William G. Baldwin passing on horseback. After failing to hop a train, Smith was nabbed by Baldwin and taken to jail.

When the woman's injury was discovered, intentional assault was assumed. A ridiculous tale about the woman wrestling a razor away from the attacker only to be struck senseless by a handy brickbat wielded by the Negro circulated rapidly. Early in the afternoon the customary lynch mob formed in defense of Southern womanhood. Thousands of angry citizens gathered to demand Smith's life.

Mayor Trout and the Commonwealth's Attorney tried to reason with the mob to no avail. The Mayor mustered a company of militia to guard the prisoner and placed another on standby. When the crowd learned that Smith might be moved to Wytheville for safe keeping, they stormed the jail twice. The mob was first repulse by bayonets, then by volleys killing ten men outright and seriously wounding over thirty. The mob overcame the guard only to find the prisoner had been removed from the jail. Mayor Trout fled the city fearing for his life.

MURDER AT GREEN SPRINGS

When attempting to return the prisoner to jail the next day, a group of citizens ambushed the guard detail and seized Smith. The man was dragged to a nearby hickory tree and hanged. The site was across the street from where another hapless Negro had been similarly lynched just seventeen month's before [William Lavender, Attempted Rape. Bundage p. 282]. A sign on the back of the dangling body declared Smith "Mayor Trout's Friend." Angry citizenry first intended to bury to the corpse in the Mayor's front yard, but eventually burned the remains beside the railroad tracks. *Roanoke Daily Record*, September 21, 1893.

50 Luther, p. 202.

51 On March 27, 1913, the day before the scheduled execution of Floyd and Claude Allen, attorneys schemed to have Lieutenant Governor Ellyson commute the men's sentences after Governor Mann left that morning for Philadelphia. Ellyson, a political opponent of Mann, had the authority to act while the Governor was out of state. Mann was informed of the plot at 2 A.M. the next morning and caught the first return train. Upon reaching Alexandria, Mann stopped to fire a telegram to Ellyson that he was back in Virginia. Arriving in Richmond late morning, Mann issued orders to proceed with the executions. The Allens were electrocuted as scheduled. Ronald W. Hall, *The Carroll County Courthouse Tragedy: A True Story of the 1912 Gun Battle That Shocked the Nation: Its Causes and Aftermath* (Lynchburg, VA: 1998), p. 233.

52 Letter R. Lindsay Gordon, Jr., dated December 11, 1915, SCVEP, November 6, 1919.

53 Letter, George S. Shackelford, dated December 15, 1915. SCVEP, November 6, 1919.

54 Ibid.

55 Ibid.

56 Letter R. Lindsay Gordon, Jr. dated December 18, 1915. SCVEP, November 6, 1919.

[57] The undated petition is consistent with the 1916 membership roster. *Journal of the House of Delegates. General Assembly of Virginia.* In any event, N. W. Hall refers to the governor's consideration of the petition as a past act in his letter dated June 12, 1916.

[58] Letter, N. W. Hall, dated January 13, 1916. SCVEP, November 6, 1919.

[59] *Louisa County Deed Book*, Volume 35, p. 342.

[60] Judge Frederick Wilmer Sims was finally elected to the Supreme Court of Appeals of Virginia on March 6, 1917. Lindsay Gordon must have opposed Sims or preferred another individual in an earlier nomination. Author.

[61] Letter N. W. Hall, dated June 13, 1916. SCVEP, November 6, 1919.

[62] Letter J. Reid Wills, dated January 15, 1918. SCVEP, November 6, 1919.

[63] Letter George S. Shackelford, dated April 4, 1918. SCVEP, November 6, 1919.

[64] Letter W. C. B. Winston, dated June 19, 1918. SCVEP, November 6, 1919.

[65] Letter C. E. Hester, dated July 1, 1918. SCVEP, November 6, 1919.

[66] Letter Mrs. L. F. Yancey, dated July 1, 1918. SCVEP, November 6, 1919.

[67] Letter Julian J. Jacobs, dated July 1, 1918. SCVEP, November 6, 1919.

[68] Letter Mrs. S. B. Henson, dated July 17, 1918, SCVEP, November 6, 1919.

[69] Letter A. O. Wood, dated July 1918. SCVEP, November 6, 1919.

[70] Carbon copy, letter Governor Westmoreland Davis, dated October 31, 1918. SCVEP, November 6, 1919.

[71] Letter, Elizabeth Hall, dated April 14, 1919. SCVEP, November 6, 1919.

MURDER AT GREEN SPRINGS

END NOTES FOR CHAPTER FOURTEEN –
POST MORTEMS ON A COUNTER TOP

[1] Information per Mary Ann Haske, daughter of Mamie Williams, nee Dunkum.

[2] 1930 U.S. Census.

[3] Information per Mary Ann Haske.

[4] By strange coincidence, Albert W. Pollard remembered visiting his grandfather Henry Robinson Pollard, Sr. [died August 3, 1923] living at "918 West Grace Street." Virginia D. Cox, *Old Houses of King & Queen County* (Richmond, VA: 1973), p. 102.

[5] Richmond city tax assessment records describe the property as a two story, single family dwelling, 2280 square feet, eleven rooms, and built 1912 on a 0.058 acre lot. Author

[6] *The Central Virginian*, April 29, 1993, pp. 8-9.

[7] *Louisa County Deed Book*, Vol. 40, p. 179.

William T. Johnson and James S. Johnson were the middle and youngest sons of John S. Johnson, Sr. Author

[8] *Louisa County Deed Book*, Vol. 44, p. 127. W. R. Dunkum purchased the store and land on August 3, 1922. His heirs retained possession of the property until sold to Robert Johnson, son of Johnny Johnson, February 25, 1988. *Louisa County Deed Book*, Vol. 335, p. 767.

[9] George Edward Chewning was clearly the son of Charles Chewning, a brother of George W. Chewning, Jr. Yet, court records document George E. Chewning possessing 25 acres from his "father George W. Chewning" in consideration of money paid to siblings. *Louisa County Deed Book*, Vol. 61, p. 56.

One native of Green Springs in 2003 remembered Chick Chewning as the son of the infamous George W. Chewning. The conflicting data remains unexplained at this writing. Author

[10] Mrs. Hall deeded the Commonwealth of Virginia 2.96 acres of her remaining land for the new road on May 23, 1938. *Louisa County Deed Book*, Vol. 56, p. 130.

On January 6, 1939, Mrs. Hall sold the remaining 99.14 acre balance of her land from the J. T. Boston estate for $900 cash to none other than Wilford Sterling Hall. *Louisa County Deed Book*, Vol. 56, p. 541.

[11] Jimmy Johnson and his family were residents at the Hall house when it burned. Interview with A. G. "Sambo" Johnson, March 15, 2003.

[12] Between 1940 and 1945, the population of Louisa County decreased twenty percent. The wartime economy offered particularly attractive opportunities to poor farmers and laborers.

In 1940, ninety-two percent of residents in the Green Springs District farmed. One third of these were tenant farmers. Only seven percent of Louisa County residents had a shower or a bath in their homes. Only three percent had central heat. Ninety-seven percent cooked with wood. Twenty-six percent of white men and sixty-nine percent of black men had less than a fifth grade education.

By 1945, only twenty-four percent of county residents had electricity; only twenty-two percent had running water; and only thirteen percent had telephones. In these respects, Louisa County lagged behind ninety percent of Virginia counties.

W. E. Garnett, *Housing of Louisa Farm Folk* (Blacksburg, VA: 1948), n.p.

[13] Mr. William R. Dunkum was appointed postmaster at Green Springs Depot July 21, 1914. Mrs. Mary L. Dunkum succeeded him April 1, 1945. "Green Springs Depot" was shortened to "Green Springs" on April 1, 1950. Green Springs post office was discontinued in lieu of Gordonsville on January 31, 1956. "Postmasters of In Use and Discontinued Stations, Louisa Co., Va., 1909-1958," Postmasters and Rural Appointments Divi-

sion, Bureau of Operations, Post Office Department, United States, Special Collections, University of Virginia, p. 3.

[14] William Richard "Buck" Dunkum died May 29, 1952. Wife Mary Lou Dunkum nee Marks died April 28, 1965. Both are buried in Hillcrest Cemetery, Louisa, VA. Author

[15] "High infant mortality, delayed marriages, definite spacing of children, early deaths of working women, shifting household composition, and the caretaking role of family, all underscore the personal meaning of indigence. Decisions about marriage, family size, arrival of children, even about where to call home, were not merely normative issues but hard economic questions. And they were scarcely decisions at all, in the sense that the word implies a real choice. For the poor, life was simple. Most things had already been decided by the same fate that had marked out some for poverty, others wealth. Life was a matter of *keeping on, keeping on*. They understood its hopelessness and kept on. There lies their heroism." Crandall A. Shifflett, *Patronage and Poverty in the Tobacco South: Louisa County, Virginia, 1860 - 1900* (Knoxville, TN: 1982), p. 98.

[16] After the shooting of Josey Knighton, neighbors offered to organize a lynch mob to kill Lit Napper. Letter dated 10/28/03, Mrs. S. F. Knighton, SCVEP, June 23, 1904.

[17] The 1920 U.S. Census lists George W. Chewning living in Green Springs.

[18] Chewning was convicted of the misdemeanor November 13th, 1922 after withdrawing a not guilty plea on September 11th. *Louisa County Law Order Book 1921-1925*, p. 114.

Perhaps Chewning's withdrawal of his not guilty plea was leveraged by a threat to revoke his conditional pardon. Author

[19] *Louisa County Law Order Book 1925-1930*, p. 523.

[20] George Chewning was listed April 7, 1930 in the Virginia State Penitentiary as a 74 year old laborer. 1930 U.S. Census.

[21] Death Certificate 17205, George W. Chewning, Louisa County, 1931, Virginia Bureau of Vital Statistics.

[22] For example, on September 18, 1925, Prohibition Agent J. B. Vaughn received forty dollars for capturing stills. *Louisa County Law Order Book 1921-1925*, p. 634.

[23] For example, on December 5, 1929, O. H. Wagner of Green Springs Depot, a witness for the defense at the Hall trial, was charged with "misdemeanor & felony possession of ardent spirits." *Louisa County Law Order Book 1925 – 1930*, p. 549.

[24] Death Certificate 27017, William Harry Snow, Louisa County, 1929, Virginia Bureau of Vital Statistics.

[25] After serving as Sheriff since November 7, 1911, Sheriff Wash died April 3, 1930. Deputy Robert E. Trice officially replaced Wash as Sheriff on April 10, 1930. *Louisa County Law Order Book 1925 – 1930*, p. 585.

On November 3, 1931, Trice was elected Commissioner of Revenue and J. F. Bickers, Jr. elected Sheriff. *Louisa County Law Order Book, 1930 – 1935*, pp. 148, 150.

[26] *Louisa County Law Order Book 1925-1930*, p. 547.

[27] As a young student, John Q. Rhodes, Jr. served as courier for Commonwealth's Attorney W. C. Bibb during the Hall Case. Rhodes received $25 for 30 days related work. W. C. Bibb received $4.45 reimbursement for John Q. Rhodes' travel expenses. *Louisa County Board of Supervisors Journal*, Book 4, p. 111.

His father the Rev. John Q. Rhodes, Sr. believed Mrs. Hall innocent. John Q. Rhodes, Jr. became a prominent attorney in Louisa County and law partner of W. C. Bibb. Like Lindsay Gordon in the Hall Case, Rhodes had just been elected to the Virginia House of Delegates November 5, 1929 and had completed his first session in the legislature when called upon to defend Johnson.

Rhodes was soon appointed head of the Virginia Division of Motor Vehicles by Governor John Garland Pollard and served in this capacity until 1938, at which time Rhodes was expected to become governor of Virginia. However, James H. Price with strong Masonic ties outmaneuvered Rhodes politically and won the Democratic Party nomination and the governorship. After his election, Governor Price removed John Q. Rhodes, Jr. as head of DMV and as well as Rhodes' supporter Carl H. Nolting as Commissioner of Game and Inland Fisheries.

For photographs of John Q. Rhodes, Jr., see Pattie Cooke, *Louisa and Louisa County* (Dover, NH: 1997), pp. 39, 82.

[28] In the matter of John S. Johnson, Sr. charged with the murder of W. H. Snow: "We the jury find the accused not guilty as charged in the Indictment," Geo. E. Diggs, Foreman. *Louisa County Law Order Book 1925-1930*, p. 584.

[29] Quote was related by grandson from grandfather. Interview A. G. "Sambo" Johnson, February 22, 2004.

[30] A late manifestation of the *old ways* occurred on February 13, 1975. Stuart A. Cunningham began his legal career reading the law under R. Lindsay Gordon, Jr. He was admitted to the bar, practiced law in Louisa and was eventually appointed judge of Louisa General Court. Inside Louisa courthouse on said date during the afternoon court session, young Curtis Darnell Poindexter entered the courtroom, approached the bench, produced a sawed off shotgun from under his raincoat and killed Judge Cunningham. Poindexter fled through the clerk's office and fired again wounding Sheriff Henry A. Kennon and a deputy. The reasons for the assault were unclear. Author

[31] Taken at face value, the inference of the spent cartridge was inescapable. Note the similar circumstance used as an illustration in a later textbook. "For example, an ordinary residence with a spent gun cartridge is inconsistent." Frank Morn, *Foundations of Criminal Investigations* (Durham, NC: 1996), p. 12.

[32] See Chapter 10, Note 3.

[33] Gordon's arguments on pistol quality had some validity. Tolerances of cheap firearms were not as tight as more expensive makes. Cheap revolv-

ers with loose tolerances were poorly bored, poorly chambered and poorly fitted with excessive gap between the barrel and cylinder. Imprecise timing caused misalignment of the cylinder and bore. These problems were exacerbated with improper care. "A revolver so made, or in such condition, simply cannot give either the accuracy or power built into its ammunition." Henry M. Strebbins, *Pistols: A Modern Encyclopedia* (Harrisburg, PA: 1961), p. 209.

[34]   The author randomly selected five .38 S&W cartridges manufactured by Remington with lead bullets of nominal 146 grains. The unseated bullets consistently measured 146 grains on a calibrated analytical balance accurate to +/- 0.003 grains. Author

[35]   Experiments by the author under controlled conditions using Remington .38 S&W ammunition, 146 grain lead bullets in a Smith & Wesson Safety Hammerless, 3.5 inch barrel [S/N: 258033] predict mass loss <1% due to firing the bullet into water tank. Final mass loss of individual bullets after retrieval from firing into pine board generally measured <2% and always <3%. Test pistol is presumed functionally identical to Victor Hall's pistol. Author

[36]   Given the facts that the "138 grain" fatal bullet was deformed, not fragmented; still possessed visible lubricant; other stated measurements established inaccuracies; Mackay possessed dubious technical qualifications and bias; draft free, controlled laboratory conditions were unlikely; and inherent non-linearity of a dubiously maintained balance with uncalibrated weights; an initial projectile mass of 130 grains must be considered equally as reasonable an initial bullet weight as the "150 grains" insinuated by the prosecution's witness.

For if nominal 146 grain balls appeared 150 grains, a nominal 130 grain ball would have likely measured 134 grains. All things considered, the standard .38 caliber pistol ball closest to the stated 138 grains was actually the 130 grain bullet in .38 Short Colt ammunition. Author

[37] The 1897 Sears Roebuck Catalogue offered pistols chambered for .38 Short Colt and .38 Short Colt ammunition. The 1902 Sears, Roebuck Catalogue offered .38 Short Colt ammunition on page 323 with an illustration showing the pronounced, external grease groove. Pistols chambered for this obsolete round were no longer advertised. The 1908 edition of the catalogue no longer featured .38 Short Colt ammunition. By 1914, .38 Short Colt ammunition had been discontinued and disfavored for so long that it was unfamiliar to most and unrecognizable as a possibility, except by a genuine expert. Author

[38] Furthermore, the diameter of .38 Short Colt cartridge brass is less than that of corresponding .38 S&W brass and, therefore, not considered interchangeable between weapons chambered for those respective rounds. Author

[39] Charles M. Wallace, *Boy Gangs of Old Richmond* (Richmond, VA: 1938), p. 9.

[40] Richmond's only daily and Sunday newspaper in 1860 was the *Taglicher Anzeiger* serving the city's German speaking community. Samuel J. T. Moore, Jr., *Moore's Complete Civil War Guide To Richmond* (Richmond, VA.: 1978), p. 85.

[41] During the Civil War, Myer S. Angle, Sr. was a member of Company D, Virginia State Reserves.

[42] *The Dispatch*, October 2, 1902, p. 1.

[43] In the Richmond city directory, James B. Angle is listed as an insurance agent in 1903 and specifically as a solicitor for the Virginia Fire and Marine Insurance Company in 1904. *Hill's Richmond Virginia, City Directory.*

The Virginia Fire and Marine Insurance Company insured W. R. Dunkum's property. Author

[44] "Most of the county believed she was guilty." *The Central Virginian*, September 10, 1992, p. 10. Article references *The Central Virginian*, August 1914 (no day, no page).

[45] The fire kinetics are noteworthy, especially the minimum oxygen concentrations necessary to support flaming combustion. A 6-by-8-by-8

foot space the size of the pantry affords 10,867 liters of air. Assuming a modest ten kilowatt fire consuming 0.76 grams of oxygen per second, the limiting oxygen index of wood [20%] is reached in about three minutes and that of the kerosene accelerant [17%] in about ten.

Understandably, the first pantry fire of burning excelsior and kerosene in the middle of the floor was starved to a smolder before being discovered. The second fire of kerosene rags in the corner of the same room burned oxygen lean and produced black smoke. It then flared dangerously short of flashover when Johnson opened the window.

The pantry was the most remote location in a separate building beside the residence/murder scene. All things considered, both pantry fires were primarily intended more for diversion than destruction. Author

[46] Superintendent Jesse W. Erb of the Richmond office of the Pinkerton National Detective Agency wrote concerning an attempted burning of the Accomack County courthouse ". . . , and we now have an *operative there cultivating the German suspects, . . .*" Excerpt letter to Governor Stuart dated August 28, 1917. "Detectives," Box 11, *Governor Henry Stuart Papers.*

Insurance Solicitor, L. Everett Mosby wrote "In regard to sending detectives here [Columbia, VA] *to work up evidence against* those liquor fellows, ..." Excerpt letter to Governor Stuart dated March 11, 1916. "Detectives," Box 11, *Governor Henry Stuart Papers.* Author's emphases.

[47] In October 1913, the Colorado Fuel and Iron Company controlled by John D. Rockerfeller hired the Baldwin-Felts Detective Agency to evict striking miners and protect company property. Baldwin-Felts sent their *detectives* who improvised an armored car with a machinegun against the strikers camped nearby. The detectives' contraption was dubbed *The Death Special.* The detectives drove by and machine-gunned the tent camp housing miners and their families. The miners refused to leave.

MURDER AT GREEN SPRINGS

Ultimately, the Colorado militia was summoned. On April 20, 1914, the combined force of militia and detectives attacked and burned the tent city killing twenty inhabitants. The event became know as the Ludlow Massacre. Author.

[48] J. W. Yancey, letter dated October 31, 1913. Merchant John Yancey of Wilmington, Virginia mentions brother Lewis having recently sold his holdings in Meltons. Letter from collection of Alice S. Murphey.

[49] Letter dated April 4, 1914 Lewis Yancey to attorney W. W. Smith, Jr. "Smith, William Worth Jr. Legal Cases: L. F. Yancey," Box 33, *Papers of W. E. Bibb and Other Louisa County, Va. Families, 1830 – 1940*. Accession No. 4171, Special Collections, Alderman Library, University of Virginia.

[50] H. O. Lyne, surviving partner of Bouton Lyne sought payment due from the bankrupt Yancey Brothers. The Louisa Circuit Court revived and executed an order issued May 13, 1905 against Lewis Yancey, the surviving partner in the amount of $449.39 plus $7.89 costs. *Louisa County Order Book 1912-1916*, p. 418.

[51] L. F. Yancey was appointed special deputy by Sheriff J. Reid Wills on September 12, 1911. *Louisa County Law Order Book 1904-1911*, p. 593.

[52] Littleton "Lit" Napper's whereabouts in 1914 cannot be documented. He never seemed to ever have had a permanent residence. People remembering the 1930's recalled Lit Napper in Green Springs. He died June 21, 1948 in Charlotte County, Virginia.

Concerning the 1914 whereabouts of other siblings, the locations of brothers Jesse and James Napper in 1914 are not known. Brother Luther Napper tenant farmed in Mineral. Sisters Suzie Mallory and Lucy Gibson lived on property adjoining that of the Hall Store. Sister Bertie Napper's residence in 1914 is not known having sold her property to Asa Dunkum in 1910. Author.

[53] Technically in 1914 a third party owned a narrow strip of land between the properties of Mrs. Hall and Mallory/Gibson. David Asa Dunkum purchased those 17.75 acres of adjacent Napper land in 1908. Essie

Dunkum inherited this parcel upon her father's death in 1911. Victor K. Hall purchased the land in June 1912, and then resold it that September to John W. Templeton. *Louisa County Deed Book*, Vol. 29, p. 40 and Vol. 31, pp. 9-10.

The narrow strip between lands actually belonging to Mrs. Hall and the Napper sisters remained unimproved and still gave the impression of adjacent properties. Author

[54] *G. C. Kennon v. Lewis m. Nappier, Suzie Mallory, and Lucy Gibson*, September 14, 1914. *Louisa County Chancery Book*, Vol. 11, p. 421. Details of counter suit: *http://freepages.genealogy.rootsweb.com/~rosadove/DeeDovey'sPage/susiemallorylucygibsonansbillgckennon.htm* last accessed April 20, 2005.

[55] 1914 Virginia State Climatology Office Records

[56] At meeting August 21, 1914, the board approved payment of $4 to J. C. Trice for training county dogs. *Louisa County Board of Supervisors Journal*, Book 4, p. 111.

[57] "Appendix F, Tracking and Countertracking, Evasion, Escape and Survival," *FM 7-93 Long Range Surveillance Unit Operations* (Washington D.C.: 1995), p. F-7.

[58] *The Daily Progress*, April 16, 1914, p. 1.

[59] Crandall A. Shifflett, "Shadowed Thresholds: Rural Poverty In Louisa County, Virginia 1860 – 1900" (PhD. diss. University of Virginia: 1975), p. 41.

BIBLIOGRAPHY

ARCHIVAL SOURCES

Fluvanna County Courthouse, Palmyra, Virginia
    Deed Books for Fluvanna County

Captain John Smith Library, Christopher Newport University
    The New York Times

Chesapeake and Ohio Historical Society
    Train Timetable Richmond-Gordonsville, 1914.

Library of Congress: Manuscript Division.
Administrative Files of the Pinkerton National Detective Agency

Library of Virginia, Richmond, Virginia
    Governor Henry C. Stuart Papers
    Journal of the Virginia House of Delegates
    Louisa County Fiduciary Settlements
    Louisa County List of Felons [Last accessed July 2001. Now Restricted]
    Louisa County Medical Register
    Richmond City Directories
    Roanoke Daily Record
    Secretary of the Commonwealth of Virginia: Executive Journal
    Secretary of the Commonwealth of Virginia: Executive Papers
    Sulphur Mines Co. vs. Thompson heirs, 93 VA. 293.
    The Central Virginian
    The Daily Progress
    The Richmond News Leader
    The Richmond Dispatch
    The Richmond Times
    The Richmond Times-Dispatch
    The Virginia Pilot-Norfolk Landmark
    Virginia Bureau of Insurance Reports

Louisa County Courthouse, Louisa, Virginia
   Minutes of the Board of Supervisors for Louisa County
   Order Books for Louisa County Circuit Court
   Term Records for Louisa County Circuit Court
   Deed Books for Louisa County

Louisa County Historical Society
   The Central Virginian [July 14, 1914]

Newport News Public Library, Newport News, Virginia
   The Daily Press

University of Virginia – Alderman Library
   The Central Virginian [Nov. 7, 1912]
   United States, Post Office Department, Bureau Of Operations, Post-
   masters and Rural Operations Division, *Postmasters of In Use and
   Discontinued Stations in Louisa*, Co., Va., 1909-1958, Accession
   #437-e, Special Collections.
   *Papers of W. E. Bibb and Other Louisa County, Va. Families, 1830 –
   1940*. Accession No. 4171, Special Collections.

University of Virginia – Virginia State Climatology Office
   1914 Meteorological Data for Charlottesville, Culpepper, and Columbia Stations

William Smith Morton Library, Union Theological Seminary &
   Presbyterian School of Christian Education, Richmond, Virginia.
   *Session Minutes and Register 1890-1921, Wills Memorial Chapel, Louisa
   County, VA*

UNPUBLISHED RESOURCES

Atkins, Frances A. Interview June 28, 2004.

Bubb, Kathryn D. Notes on Dowdy family.

Bumpass, Eugenia T. Interview June 8, 2003.

Dunkum, Charles C. Interview October 25, 2001.

Dunn, Wayne G. Notes on Dunkum and Marks families.

Gordon, R. Lindsay, III. Interview March 21, 2002.

Haske, Mary Ann. Notes on Dunkum family.

Johnson, Albert G. Interviews December 8, 2002; February 12, 2003; March 15, 2003; May 20, 2003; February 22, 2004 and *Hall Trial Transcript: August 5, 1914.*

Murphey, Alice S. Yancey obituaries from *The Midland Virginian*, J. W. Yancey letter dated October 31, 1913 and photographs.

Randall, Dee Dovey. "G. C. Kennon Answer & Bill of Susie Mallory & Lucy Gibson" Transcript.

Waldrep, Dr. G. C., III. Notes from Louisa County Chancery Records

Westlow, Edward J. Notes on Boston family and photographs.

PUBLISHED SOURCES AND DISSERTATIONS

Abercrombie, Janice L. *Louisa County Death Records 1853 – 1896: With Addendum from Records of Woodward Funeral Home 1907 – 1911*. Athens, GA: Iberian Publishing Co., 1997.

Amory, Cleveland. *The 1902 Edition of the Sears Roebuck Catalogue*. New York: Bounty Books – Crown Publishers, 1969.

Anbinder, Tyler. *Five Points: The 19th-Century New York Neighborhood That Invented Tap Dance, Stole Elections and Became the World's Most Notorious Slum*. New York: The Free Press., 2001.

Baker, William Thomson. *The Baker Family of England and of Central Virginia: Their Many Related Families and Kin: An Easy to Read, Easy to Understand Genealogy and Historical Narrative of the Bakers and Their Related Families of England and of Virginia, As Taken From Public Records, Documents, And Other Historical and Genealogical Sources*. [s.l.]: Baker, c1974.

Bennett, Hugh H. and McLendon, W. E. *Soil Survey of Louisa County*. Washington, D.C.: Government Printing Office, 1906.

Bibb, W. C. "Hon. Frederick Wilmer Sims." *Report of the Thirty-Sixth Annual Meeting of the Virginia State Bar Association*. Volume XXXVII. Richmond: Richmond Press, Inc., 1925. 188-195.

Bibb, W. C. *County of Louisa, Appellant, v. Yancey's Trustee et als, Appellee, Record No. 91. In the Supreme Court of Appeals of Virginia at Richmond*. Richmond: Richmond Press, 190?.

Bibb, W. C. *Modern Baal and Other Poems*. William Chew Bibb, Louisa, Virginia: 1940.

Bruce, Philip Alexander. *Virginia: Rebirth of the Old Dominion*. Chicago: The Lewis Publishing Company, 1929.

Brundage, W. Fitzhugh. *Lynching in the New South: Georgia and Virginia, 1880 – 1930*. Urbana: University of Illinois Press, 1993.

Butler, David F. *United States Firearms The First Century 1776 – 1875*. New York: Winchester Press, 1971.

Cappon, Lester Jesse. *Virginia Newspapers 1821-1935; A Bibliography with Historical Introduction and Notes*. New York: Appleton-Century, The University of Virginia Institute for the Social Sciences. 1936.

Carter, John B. *Soil Survey of Louisa County, Virginia*. Washington, D.C.: United States Department of Agriculture, 1976.

Chataigne, J. Henry. *The Chesapeake and Ohio Railway Directory*. Richmond, VA: [s.n.], c. 1881.

Chesterman, Evan Ragland and Geisinger, Joe F. *History of the McCue Case; Full Particulars of the Crime, Inquest, Trial and Conviction*. Richmond: The Williams Printing Co., 1904.

Chiles, Rosa Pendleton. *Down Among the Crackers*. Cincinnati, OH: The Editor Publishing Co., 1900.

Chisholm, Claudia Anderson, and Lillie, Ellen Gray. *Old Home Places of Louisa County*. Orange, VA: Green Publishers, Inc., 1979.

Chisholm, Claudia A. "The Village of Fredericks Hall: The Poindexters and Other Merchants of Fredericks Hall." *Louisa County Historical Society Magazine [LCHSM]*. Vol. 25. No. 1. Spring 1994. 31-43.

Cocke, William Ronald, *Hanover County Chancery and Will Notes*. Baltimore, MD: Geneological Publishing Co., 1978.

Cooke, Pattie Gordon Pavlansky. *Louisa and Louisa County*. Dover, NH: Arcadia Publishing., 1997.

Cooke, Pattie: "Lasley Ladies Aid Society Ledger," *LCHSM*. Vol. 36., Fall 2005. 34-41.

Cooke, Pattie. "Walking Tour of Louisa County." *LCHSM*. Vol. 29. No. 2. Fall 1998. 67-100.

Cooke, Pattie. "Worshipful Masters of Day Lodge No. 58." *LCHSM*. Vol. 20. No. 2. Fall 1989. 79-81.

Cooley, Elmer Jackson, ed. *The Inside Story of the World Famous Courtoom Tragedy as Told by a Native Countryman Familiar with the Facts and Conditions Surrounding the Event That Shocked the Civilized World*. Charlottesville, VA: Michie Co., Printers, 1961.

Cox, Virginia D., and Weathers, Willie T. *Old Houses of King & Queen County Virginia*. Richmond: Whittet & Shepperson, Inc. for The King & Queen Historical Society, 1973.

Crank, W. Earle. "William Chew Bibb." *Report of the Fifty-Third Annual Meeting of the Virginia State Bar Association*. Volume LIV. Richmond: Richmond Press, Inc., 1942. 107-108.

MURDER AT GREEN SPRINGS

Dewhurst, Henry Stephen. *The Railroad Police.* Police Science Series. Springfield, IL: Charles C. Thomas Publisher. 1955.

Dorin, Patrick. *The Chesapeake and Ohio Railway.* Seattle: Superior publishing Company., 1981.

Duke, R. T. W. Jr. "George Scott Shackelford." *Report of the Thirtieth Annual Meeting of the Virginia State Bar Association.* Volume XXXI. Richmond: Richmond Press, Inc., 1919. 125-126.

Dunford, Earle. *Richmond Times-Dispatch, The Story of a Newspaper.* Richmond, VA: Cadmus Publishing. 1995.

Family Cemeteries in Fluvanna County, Virginia. Sponsored by The Fluvanna County Historical Society and the Point of Fork Chapter, Daughters of the American Revolution. Palmyra, VA: Seven Islands Co., 1996.

Farrar, Emmie Ferguson, and Hines, Emilee. *Old Houses: The Heart of Virginia.* [n.p.]: Hale Publishing., 1974.

Fleshman, Harvey J. "Masonry in Virginia and Louisa County." *LCHSM.* Vol. 20. No. 2. Fall 1989. 77-79.

FM 7-93 Long Range Surveillance Unit Operations. Washington D.C.: Headquarters, U. S. Department of the Army, 1995.

Free, Ann Cottrell. "George McDuffie Blake." *LCHSM.* Vol. 27. No. 1. Spring 1996. 3-17.

Gardner, Rufus L. *The Courthouse Tragedy: Hillsville, VA.* 4th ed. Mount Airy, NC: Reliable Print Co., 1967.

Garnett, W. E. (William Edward) *Housing of Louisa County Farm Folk.* Report No. 48. Blacksburg, VA: Virginia Polytechnic Institute. Virginia Agricultural Experiment Station and Agricultural Extension Service Cooperating., February 1948.

Gilmer, Jeremy Francis. Map Collection. "Louisa County 1863." Restored in 1942 by the Sons of the American Revolution in Virginia. Richmond, VA: The Virginia Historical Society, 1998.

Glass, Robert Camillus. *Virginia Democracy, a History of the Achievements of the Party and its Leaders in the Mother of Commonwealths: the Old Dominion.* Springfield, IL: Democratic Historical Association, Inc., 1937.

Good, James Marvin. "A Brief History of the Virginia State Penitentiary." [s.l.: s.n.], 1973.

Grant, Robert, and Katz, Joseph. *The Great Trials of the Twenties: The Watershed Decade in America's Courtrooms.* New York: Sarepedon., 1998.

"Green Springs." Philadelphia, PA: National Park Service, U.S. Department of the Interior, (no date).

Gwathmey, John H. *Legends of Virginia Courthouses.* Richmond, VA: Press of the Dietz Printing Company Publishers., 1934.

Gwathmey, John H. *Legends of Virginia Lawyers.* Richmond, VA: Press of the Dietz Printing Company Publishers., 1934.

Hall, Ronald W. *The Carroll County Courthouse Tragedy: A True Account of the 1912 Gun Battle That Shocked the Nation; Its Causes and the Aftermath.* Lynchburg, VA: The Carroll County Historical Society, 1998.

Harris, Malcolm H. M.D. *History of Louisa County*. Richmond: The Dietz Press Publishers., 1936.

Horan, James D. *The Pinkertons: The Detective Dynasty That Made History*. New York: Crown Publishers, Inc., 1967.

Horn, John D. "The Golden Paradox of Fluvanna: XIII, The Page Mine." *The Bulletin of the Fluvanna County Historical Society*. No. 20. May 1975. 28-29.

Ironmonger, Elizabeth. *History of the Women's Christian Temperance Union of Virginia and a Glimpse of Seventy-Five Years, 1883 – 1958*. Richmond, VA: Cavalier Press, 1958.

Israel, Fred L. (ed.). *1897 Sears, Roebuck Catalogue*. New York: Chelsea House Publishers, 1993.

Jordan, Ervin L. *Black Confederates and Afro-Yankees In Civil War Virginia*. Charlottesville, VA: University of Virginia Press., 1995.

Keene, W. D. Jr. (ed.). *"Memoirs – 200 Years!" 1745 – 1987*. Decorah, Iowa: Amundsen, 1988.

Kirby, Jack Temple. *Westmoreland Davis: Virginia Planter – Politician, 1859 – 1942*. Charlottesville, VA: University Press of Virginia, 1968.

Lavine, Sigmund A. *Alan Pinkerton, America's First Private Eye*. New York: Dodd, Mead & Company, 1963.

Lebsock, Suzanne. *A Murder In Virginia: Southern Justice On Trial*. New York: W. W. Norton & Company, 2003.

Lindsay, James H. *The McCue Murder: Complete Story of the Crime and the Famous Trial of the Ex-Mayor of Charlottesville, Virginia.* Charlottesville, VA: The Progress Publishing Company, 1904.

"Louisa County v. Yancey's Trustee et al." (Supreme Court of Appeals of Virginia. Jan. 21, 1909.) *The Southeastern Reporter.* Vol. 63. St. Paul, MN: West Publishing Co. 1887-1939. 452-455.

Luther, Roslyn and Edwin C. III. *Governors of Virginia 1776 – 1974.* Accomac, VA: The Eastern Shore News, Inc., 1974.

Mackay, James. *Alan Pinkerton: The First Private Eye.* New York: John Wiley & Sons., 1996.

McKenney, Carlton Norris. *Rails in Richmond.* Glendale, CA: Interurban Press, 1986.

"Marriage Register of Rev. L. A. Cutler." *LCHSM.* Vol. 5. No. 2. Winter 1973-1974. 31.

Massie, J. Quintus and Cooke, Pattie. "John Poindexter Addendum." *LCHSM.* Vol. 22. No. 2. Winter 1991. 93-95.

Meredith, Doris Perkins, (contributor). "1915 Directory of Louisa County." *LCHSM.* Vol. 31. No. 1. Spring 2000. 8-28.

Montague, Winston and Gwathmey, John H. *Virginia Sportsman Directory for 1940-41.* Richmond: Virginia Sportsman's Directory., 1940.

Monte, George C., Jr. *Firearms Encyclopedia.* New York: Outdoor Life, Harper & Row, 1973.

Moore, Samuel J. T. Jr. *Moore's Complete Civil War Guide To Richmond.* Richmond, VA: Moore, 1978. Rev. ed.

Morn, Frank. *Foundations of Criminal Investigations.* Durham: Carolina Academic Press, 2000.

Morn, Frank. "The Eye That Never Sleeps:" *A History of the Pinkerton National Detective Agency.* Bloomington: Indiana University Press, 1982.

Mortimer, John. *Famous Trials.* New York: Penguin Books., 1984.

Ninth Report of the Commissioner of Insurance of Virginia For the Fiscal Year Ending April 30, 1915 Covering Business of 1914 Fire, Marine, Life and Miscellaneous Companies and Faraternal Associations. Richmond: Davis Bottom, Superintendent Public Printing, 1915.

Oney, Steve. *And The Dead Shall Rise: The Murder of Mary Phagan and the Lynching of Leo Frank.* New York: Pantheon Books, 2003.

Page, Roswell. "William E. Bibb." *Report of the Twenty-Third Annual Meeting of the Virginia State Bar Association.* Volume XXIV. Richmond: Richmond Press, Inc., 1911. 77-78.

Porter, Duval. *Official Virginia: A Composition of Sketches of the Public Men of Virginia at Present Time.* Whittet & Shepperson, 1920.

Portraits in the Historic Hanover County Courthouse. Hanover, Va.: Hanover County Historical Society, c1985.

Ramsey, Jill. "Grandma Jo Remembers Her Childhood." *LCHSM.* Vol. 33. No. 2. Fall 2002. 73-87.

Register of Prisoners Pardoned or Paroled, Discharged, Died or Escaped, 1902 – 1971. Accession No. 35177. State government records collection. The Library of Virginia.

Riggs, David F. *13th Virginia Infantry.* Lynchburg, VA: H. E. Howard, Inc., 1988.

Schroeder, Joseph J., Jr. *1908 Sears, Roebuck Catalogue: A Treasured Replica from the Archives of History.* Northfield, IL: Digest Books, Inc., 1971.

Schwing, Ned and Houze, Herbert. *Standard Catalogue of Firearms* 3rd Edition. Iola, Wisconsin: Krause Publications, Inc., 1993.

Scott, Glen Allen. "Springs of Controversy." *The Commonwealth: the Magazine of Virginia.* Vol. 38. No. 12. 23-27.

Scott, Mary Wingfield. *Houses of Old Richmond.* Richmond, VA: The Valentine Museum, 1941.

Sherwood, W. Cullen and Nichols, Richard L. *Amherst Artillery, Albemarle Artillery, and Sturdivant's Battery.* Lynchburg, VA: H. E. Howard, Inc., 1996.

Shifflett, Crandall. *Victorian America, 1876 to 1913.* New York: Facts On File, Inc., 1996.

Shifflett, Crandall A. *Patronage and Poverty in the Tobacco South: Louisa County, Virginia 1860 – 1900.* Knoxville: The University of Tennessee Press., 1982.

Shifflett, Crandall A. "Shadowed Thresholds: Rural Poverty In Louisa County, Virginia 1860 – 1900" Ph.D. diss. University of Virginia. 1975.

Siringo, Charles A. *Two Evil Isms: Pinkertonism and Anarchism.* Austin, TX: Steck-Vaughn Company, 1967. [Facsimile Reproduction of 1914 edition. Introduction by Charles D. Peavy.]

Smith, H. M. Jr. "Henry Robinson Pollard." *Report of the Thirty-Fifth Annual Meeting of the Virginia State Bar Association.* Volume XXVI. Richmond, VA: Richmond Press, Inc., 1924. 111-117.

Stebbins, Henry M. *Pistols: A Modern Encyclopedia.* Harrisburg, PA: The Stackpole Company, 1961.

Tate, Suzanne. *Logs & Moonshine: Tales of Buffalo City, N.C.* Nags Head, NC: Nags Head Art, Inc., 2000.

Telephone Directory: February 16, 1916: Richmond, Ashland, Fredericksburg, Gordonsville, Louisa, Waverly, West Point, and Williamsburg, VA. Richmond: The Chesapeake & Potomac Telephone Co., 1916.

The Hymnal: Revised and Enlarged, Protestant Episcopal Church in the United States of America, New York: James Potts & Co., 1893.

The Great Beattie Murder Case: Life, Crime and Full Confession of Henry C. Beattie, Jr.: Sensational Story of Beulah Binford, "The Woman In The Case". Baltimore: The Phoenix Publishing Co., 1911.

Towler, Sam. "The Chewnings of Green Springs, Louisa County". *LCHSM.* Vol. 28. No. 1. Spring 1997. 13-22.

"Tracking and Countertracking, Evasion, Escape, and Survival." *FM-7 Long Range Surveillance Unit Operations, Appendix F.* Washington, D.C.: Headquarters of the Army, 3 Oct. 1995.

Turner, Charles W. *Chessie's Road*. Richmond: Garrett & Massie, Inc., 1956.

Velke, John A., III. *The True Story of the Baldwin-Felts Detective Agency*. [s.l.]: Velke, c2004.

Waldrep, G. C., III. *Southern Workers and the Search for Community: Spartanburg County, South Carolina*. Urbana, IL: University of Chicago Press, 2000.

Wallace, Charles. *Boy Gangs of Old Richmond In the Dear Old Days: A Page of the City's Lesser History*. Richmond: Richmond Press, Inc., 1938.

Weisiger, Benjamin B., III. *Old Manchester & Its Environs, 1769 – 1910*. Richmond, VA: William Byrd Press, Fine Books Division, 1993.

White, Bertha Rothe. *Crimes and Punishment Primer*. Legal Almanac Series No. 32. Dobbs Ferry, NY: Oceana Publications, Inc., 1986.

Wickham, Henry T. "Hon. Hill Carter." *Report of the Twenty-Ninth Annual Meeting of the Virginia State Bar Association*. Volume XXX. Richmond: Richmond Press, Inc., 1918. 95-98.

Williams, Perdita Farson Musser. *Glimpses of Ruaral Retreat: A Study of Social Change in the Area of Rural Retreat, Virginia*. Radford, VA: Commonwealth Press, Inc., 1979.

Wright, James Walton, Jr. "Yancey Bros. vs. The County of Louisa." *LCHSM*. Spring 1996. Volume 27. No. 1. 27-28.

Wright, Porter C. "From a Jail to a Museum." *LCHSM*. Vol. 4. No. 2. December 1972. 69-74.

Wright, Porter C. "Oakland Academy." *LCHSM.* Vol. 2. No. 2. December 1970. 19-22.

Wright, Porter Clay. "Post Offices of Louisa County," *Louisa County, Virginia 1742 – 1992 Sestercentenial, 250th Anniversary.* Louisa, VA: The 250th Anniversary Committee, 1992.

Young, Edward (ed.). *The Governors of Virginia 1860 – 1978.* Charlottesville, VA: University of Virginia Press, 1982.

INDEX

MURDER AT GREEN SPRINGS

MURDER AT GREEN SPRINGS

MURDER AT GREEN SPRINGS

MURDER AT GREEN SPRINGS

INDEX

MURDER AT GREEN SPRINGS

Printed in the United States
95805LV00002B/130-144/A